SCATTERED
Hegemonies

SCATTERED
Hegemonies

Postmodernity and Transnational Feminist Practices

Inderpal Grewal and Caren Kaplan, editors

 University of Minnesota Press
Minneapolis
London

Tani Barlow, "Theorizing Woman: *Funü, Guojia, Jiating* (Chinese Women, Chinese State, Chinese Family)" was originally published in *Genders* 10 (Spring 1991): 132–60. Reprinted by permission of the author and the University of Texas Press.

Norma Alarcón, "Traddutora, Traditora: A Paradigmatic Figure of Chicana Feminism," was originally published in *Cultural Critique* 13 (Fall 1989): 57–87. Reprinted by permission of Oxford University Press.

Published by the University of Minnesota Press
111 Third Avenue South, Suite 290, Minneapolis, MN 55401-2520
Printed in the United States of America on acid-free paper

Fourth printing, 2002

Library of Congress Cataloging-in-Publication Data

Scattered hegemonies : posmodernity and transnational feminist practices / Inderpal Grewal and
    Caren Kaplen, editors
        p.   cm.
    Includes bibliographical references and index.
    ISBN 0-8166-2137-3 (hc: : alk. paper).-ISBN 0-8166-2138-1 (pbk. : alk paper);
    1. Feminist theory. I. Grewal, Inderpal. II. Kaplan, Caren, 1955–
    HQ1190.S3   1994
    305.42-dc20   93-14232

YBP $16.86 5-5-05 (5)

Contents

PART TWO
Global-Colonial Limits

Acknowledgments

We would like to acknowledge the varied feminist communities that have inspired our lives and our scholarship. In particular, for discussing and reading our work, we would like to thank Norma Alarcón, Denise Albanese, Tani Barlow, Chinosole, Pamela Fox, Akhil Gupta, Kim Hall, E. Ann Kaplan, Lydia Liu, Donald Lowe, Michael Ragussis, Ella Shohat, Eric Smoodin, and Kamala Visweswaran. The activists from the Asian Women's Shelter, the Cultural Defense Group, and NARIKA in the Bay Area continue to shape our feminist politics. The contributors to this volume powerfully influenced our ideas and we would like to thank them for forming a scholarly community with us. At the University of Minnesota Press, Janaki Bakhle and Robert Mosimann have provided us with expert advice and aid. We are grateful to the following friends and coworkers for help with producing the manuscript: Al Jessel, Aarti Kohli, and Eric Smoodin. Inderpal Grewal received an Affirmative Action award from San Francisco State University to help with production costs. Thanks also to Professor Chinosole, chair, Women Studies and the School of Humanities, SFSU, for course release time. Caren Kaplan would like to acknowledge Georgetown University's Department of English for a two-year reduced teaching load as well as the Humanities Institute at SUNY Stony Brook for a postdoctoral fellowship. Thanks also to Carla Atkins, Althea Grannum-Cummings, and the Women's Studies Department at the University of California at Berkeley.

Al Jessel and Eric Smoodin gave us encouragement, food, child care, and dog care and got off the phone when we needed it.

ONE

Introduction: Transnational Feminist Practices and Questions of Postmodernity

Inderpal Grewal and Caren Kaplan

When we began formulating our ideas for this collection, we were looking for ways to broaden and deepen the analysis of gender in relation to a multiplicity of issues that affect women's lives. The most path-breaking and exciting articulations of feminism seemed to us to be emerging from work done by our peers in ethnic, regional, cultural, and women's studies as well as by activists in First and Third World locations. Because some forms of feminism appeared to us to be unable to account for contemporary global conditions, we envisaged a collection of essays that would raise as many questions as possible about how and why such denials and erasures have occurred as well as how to practice feminism differently.

This project stems from our work on theories of travel and the intersections of feminism, colonial and postcolonial discourses, modernism, and postmodern hybridity. Our proposal for a collection of essays that attempted to bridge constituencies, disciplines, and academic hierarchical divisions received a variety of responses. There were those who welcomed our approach as necessary and important. Others agreed cautiously and gave us valuable critiques. We also incurred outright hostility from our attempt to use the term "postmodern" in conjunction with the feminist left. We began this project as junior faculty, without "star" currency in academia, intending this collection to include the work of as many lesser-known as better-known writers. As we complete this phase of our work, we acknowledge that there are many more areas of research to pursue than we have been able to cover. We hope that readers of this volume will be able to use our work as a springboard to launch other transnational, feminist, collaborative projects.

We believe that we must work collaboratively in order to formulate transnational feminist alliances. This book does not result from our own collaborative planning, writing, and editing (conducted over 3,000 miles of phone, fax, and postal lines of communication) alone. The ideas and methods found in this volume also can be seen as the work of all those who welcomed our proposal and formed a writing community with us. Many of our close allies are not necessarily represented by essays in the collection but their work with us in study and writing groups is reflected in these pages. In particular, our understanding of the issues of gender and geopolitics has been transformed by our work over the years with a study group on feminism and nationalism, the Asian Women's Shelter, the Cultural Defense Working group, the Bay Area representatives of the journal *Positions*, the Group for the Critical Study of Colonial Discourses as well as individual friends and colleagues. In attempting to work across differences in culture, discipline, and profession, we have found that the transnational links we advocate in this collection are a crucial part of the condition of feminist thinking, working, and writing.

In this collection of essays, we are interested in problematizing theory; more specifically, feminist theory. In many locations in the United States and Europe, theory often tends to be a homogenizing move by many First World women and men. That is, theory seems unable to deal with alterity at all or falls into a kind of relativism. Refusing either of those two moves, we would like to explore how we come to do feminist work across cultural divides. For we are committed to feminism and to seeing possibilities for political work within postmodern cultures that encompass, though very differently, contemporary global relations.

To begin, we want to explore how crucial key terms and concepts circulate. Given that we are not looking for terms that remain pure, authentic, or unmediated, we argue that the way terms get co-opted constitutes a form of practice, just as the way that they contain possibilities for critical use is also an oppositional practice. In particular, we critique the way that specific terms lose their political usefulness when they are disciplined by academia or liberal/conservative agendas.

In raising questions about the historical specificity of some of the primary terms in use in cultural criticism today, we are inquiring into the system of effects that structure postmodernity. Asking how postmodernisms and postcolonialisms are variously deployed by feminists and others in different locations provides us with an opportunity to trace the direction of flows of information and "theory" in transnational cultural production and reception. We see postmodernism as a critique of modernist agendas as they are manifested in various forms and locations around the world.[1] Our critiques of certain forms of feminism emerge from their willing participation in modernity with all its colonial discourses and hegemonic First World formations that wittingly or unwittingly lead to the oppression and exploitation of many women. In supporting the agendas of modernity, therefore, feminists misrecognize and fail to resist Western hegemonies. Thus we pursue two lines of questioning: (1) What kinds of feminist practices engender theories that resist or question modernity? (2) How do we understand the production and reception of diverse feminisms within a framework of transnational social/cultural/economic movements?

In response to these kinds of questions, the essays in this collection insert alternative, counterhegemonic feminist reading and writing practices from around the world. The essays also interrogate the discourse of postmodernism, which has been expressed in the West primarily as an aesthetic or cultural debate rather than a political one. Such debates ignore the radical changes in global economic structures that have occurred since the middle of this century. If the world is currently structured by transnational economic links and cultural asymmetries, locating feminist practices within these structures becomes imperative. Drawing on the languages and methods of contemporary cultural criticism, the essays in this collection develop a multinational and multilocational approach to questions of gender.

Debates about postmodernism and the construction of culture have raised many possibilities for just such an approach, specifically in regard to the analysis of power relations between different cultures. Yet most of the recent collections on postmodernism do not consider the role of colonial and postcolonial modes of representation in the construction of modernity and postmodernity.[2] On the other hand, the recent publication of texts that address nationalism and colonialism in the context of theories of culture and modernity do not rigorously address feminist participation in these discourses.[3] Other anthologies on politics and postmodernism include scattered pieces on race or Third World cultural production or geopolitics but they rarely include a critical approach that combines all these issues with gender.

Although many advances and contributions to the study of gender and colonial discourse have been made, we strongly feel the need for viewpoints of feminists from various locations around the globe.[4] Very often, feminist poststructuralist or psychoanalytic theorists do not utilize a transnational frame or consider colonial discourse or discourses of race.[5] Development studies offers the feminist colonial discourse critic some materials to work with, yet its history of connections to discourses of modernization makes for a troubled relationship.[6] Feminist critiques of ethnographic authority within the discipline of anthroplogy or scientific enterprises have contributed to the possibility of transnational projects.[7] On the other hand, some feminist practices continue to use colonial discourse critiques in order to equate the "colonized" with "woman," creating essentialist and monolithic categories that suppress issues of diversity, conflict, and multiplicity within categories. Despite an unprecedented volume of theorization and innovations in methodologies, there remains a great need for *feminist* critiques of the Western model of sisterhood in the global context.[8]

Mapping Postmodern Moves: The Terrain of Postmodernism/Postmodernity

The term postmodernism elicits strong reactions. Too often postmodernism is construed as an aesthetic movement in opposition to modernism or in direct conflict with the aims and methods of modernism. Although postmodernism can be practiced as an oppositional critique of modernism, it remains on a continuum with modernism; it does not exist without the latter term. There is no position outside modernity. Even Samir Amin's notion of "delinking," while liberating local economies from global multinationals, relies on a discourse of modernity in order to construct its politics; for example, it depends on Marxism and class struggle for its opposition to economic domination and exploitation.[9] Yet postmodernism provides one of the most effective critiques of modernism and modernity. The concept exists precisely because of anticolonial critiques, opposition to Western hegemony, and a consideration of sociopolitical formations in diverse locations.

Thus the most compelling definitions or analyses of postmodernism make a clear distinction between the aesthetic effects of postmodernism in contemporary culture and the historical situation of postmodernity. Therein lies the difference between the *ism* and *ity* of the postmodern. That is, social theorists who analyze modernity locate a temporal, historically specific social formation that can be termed "postmodernity." For example, David Harvey characterizes this formation as a set of relationships between the "rise of postmodernist cultural forms, the emergence of more flexible modes of capital accumulation, and a new round of 'time-space compression' in the organization of capitalism."[10] Lyotard's "postmodern condition of knowledge" has been extended, then, to include most of the aspects of contemporary life that Jameson has identified as the hallmarks of the logic of late capitalism.[11] Thus, while some feminist critics reject postmodernisms, it is a study of postmodernity that offers feminists a complex, dynamic model of social, economic, and political relations.

The possibilities for social change can be found in analyses and expressions of postmodernity that locate and link diverse social theories and political practices. In terms of the conventional Marxist debate about cultural imperialism and critiques of mass culture, therefore, we resist following either Habermas's or Jameson's lines of argument even as we remain alert to issues of cultural hegemony and historical specificity.[12] On the other hand, we have difficulty embracing Lyotard's ludic view of the play beyond modernism. Our discomfort with these theories of postmodernity lies either in their complete dismissal of any postcolonial cultural productions (including theory) or their lack of interest in gender or their overreliance on a center-periphery model of world culture that inaccurately reflects the circulation of ideas and social practices in contemporary life on a global scale.

As Chilean critic Nelly Richard argues, there are postmodern practices occurring at political margins that challenge cultural centers. For example, colonial discourse critiques have destabilized the humanist subject and brought into critical consideration categories such as gender, race, and nationality. Thus it can be asserted that postmodernism has enabled the inclusion of hitherto marginalized voices. Nevertheless, cultural critics often argue that by questioning the very assumptions of history and subjectivity upon which political practices are based, postmodernism contradicts the legitimation of "marginal" voices. Kobena Mercer suggests that

> the contradictoriness of the postmodern requires a *relational* emphasis because what is experienced as a loss of identity and authority in some quarters is also an empowering experience which affirms the identities and experiences of others *for precisely the same reasons*.[13]

Our discussion of postmodernity does not seek to justify or defend a pure postmodern practice as a utopian theoretical methodology. We argue that postmodernity is an immensely powerful and useful conception that gives us an opportunity to analyze the way that a culture of modernity is produced in diverse locations and how these cultural productions are circulated, distributed, received, and even commodified. For example, bell hooks identifies the possibility of resistance to modernity in what she calls a "radical postmodernism" that alerts us to "those shared sensibilities which cross the boundaries of class, gender, race, etc." to establish "fertile ground for the construction of empathy — ties that would promote recognition of common commitments, and serve as a base for solidarity and coalition."[14] In working to construct such a terrain of coalition and cooperation, however, we have to rearticulate the histories of how people in different locations and circumstances are linked by the spread of and resistance to modern capitalist social formations even as their experiences of these phenomena are not at all the same or equal.

If Western theorists of postmodernism cannot allow for unequal, uneven, and nonsynchronous expressions of modernity in reading and interpreting the cultural productions of the so-called Third World, for example, any possibility for solidarity between feminists and others who work within differences is obstructed. Is it racism that leaves the issue of race out of most considerations of postmodern theory? Is it modern colonial discourse or a new neocolonial variant that leaves the locations of the non-West out of the pages of most Western publications on "postmodern theory?" Why is it that, apart from a few "stars," the works of scholars in regional or ethnic studies do not appear in Western theory collections? Is it ethnocentrism that collapses specific historical differences between countries such as India and Great Britain in order to read Salman Rushdie as a purely "postmodern" writer? These few examples of pitfalls in recent theorizing on postmodernity and postmodernism indicate the danger of a supposedly antibourgeois, subversive attack on master narratives becoming its own unifying discourse, its own master narrative with its own exclusive, elitist rhetorics and academic gatekeeping. Without attention to the so-called Third World, these bad habits will assert themselves, leading to an impoverished theory that cannot help us address the most pressing contemporary issues.

Some African-American critics have been problematizing the debates about postmodernism in terms that are useful for our inquiry here.[15] In "The Race for Theory," Barbara Christian's powerful salvo against the totalizing and alienating qualities of academic poststructuralist high theory, particularly the variant "French feminism," she asks a vitally important question: "for whom are we doing what we are doing when we do literary criticism?"[16] Bell hooks addresses such exclusionary practices in "Postmodern Blackness," writing that she has been disturbed not so much by the "sense" of postmodernism as by its "conventional language," a language that often leaves her "on the outside of the discourse looking in."[17] Exploring the responses of black communities to "theory," and to "postmodernism" in particular, hooks constructs a multiply positioned strategy. She asks African-American critics and readers to critique identity politics that leave the category of "race" unexamined, unhistoricized, and essentialized even as she insists that white, bourgeois academic theorists not displace "race" as a specific category of analysis with "difference":

> Postmodern theory that is not seeking to simply appropriate the experience of "Otherness" to enhance the discourse or to be radically chic should not separate the "politics of difference" from the politics of racism. To take racism seriously one must consider the plight of under-class people of color, a vast majority of whom are black.[18]

Hooks imagines links between the diverse readers of her essay, a "yearning" for "critical voice" that suggests a critical practice that cuts across "boundaries of race, class, gender, and sexual preference."[19] Here hooks identifies the powerful possibilities of postmodern critiques that provide a map of the structural links that divide and bridge differences.

Following hooks, postmodernism cannot be dismissed simply as the apolitical celebration of Western popular culture. Rather, it can be read as part of the operations of transnational culture; as the cultural expression of what Inderpal Grewal describes as "scattered hegemonies," which are the effects of mobile capital as well as the multiple subjectivities that replace the European unitary subject.[20] Such a conception of postmodernity both gives rise to formations such as syncretism and hybridity in contemporary mass culture and makes possible a critique of cultural relativism. For postmodern articulations of difference and global connections can be used to reify dominant social relations, or they can be used to oppose the hegemony of Western imperial culture. That is, articulations of hybridity can be read to argue that Western culture is not pure, is not the origin or the destination of everything. Yet, what seems to get *theorized* in the West as "hybridity" remains enmeshed in the gaze of the West; Westerners see themselves alone as the ones that sort, differentiate, travel among, and become attached or attracted to the communities constituted by diasporas of human beings and the trade of commodities. Western culture continues to acknowledge difference primarily by differentiating the "exotic" from the "domestic." Syncretism in this neo-imperialist mode is signaled by the anomalous spread of things Western in supposedly non-Western locations (i.e., the bottle of Coca-Cola that lands on the African tribesman's head in *The Gods Must be Crazy*); that is, the supposedly amusing or anomalous juxtapositions of the "primitive" or the "traditional" with the "modern."[21] Rather than acknowledging the contradictory positions that allow some of us to live in the "West" without being "Western" or that structurally inhibit unitary identities, the postmodern celebration of hybridity often retains the "us" and "them" paradigm that stems from modernist modes of description and representation.[22]

Our reading of postmodernity displaces Western mystification of non-Western cultures. For example, when music from Senegal is inserted into the work of U.S. white musicians and celebrated as syncretism, postmodern critique as oppositional practice would require a recognition of the politics of reception as part of the reproduction of "world beat" as a cultural commodity.[23] Postmodernism used as a critique of its own approval of relativism would investigate the terms of travel and interpretation in a text such as Pico Iyer's *Video Night in Kathmandu*.[24] This travel memoir is representative of an emerging genre that celebrates the pastiche effect of aestheticized postmodernism while emulating both modernist primitivism and the jump-cut impressions of the First World tourist in the era of MTV. This text's reference to the circuits of transnational capital through a celebration of hybridity constructs an apolitical collage of locations and people, linked not through their historicized social relations but through their mystified experiences as players in a field of global travel. What does not get recognized in this form of neocolonial discourse is that Western culture is itself, as is every cultural formation, a hybrid of something. Yet the dominant Western attitude toward hybridity is that it is always elsewhere or it is infiltrating an identity or location that is assumed to be, to always have been, pure and unchanging.[25]

Nelly Richard describes this process of assimilating and articulating differences as a stage in Western appropriation:

> Postmodernism defends itself against the destabilizing threat of the "other" by integrating it back into a framework which absorbs all differences and contradictions. The center, though claiming to be in disintegration, still operates as a center: filing away any divergences into a system of codes whose meanings, both semantically and territorially, it continues to administer by exclusive right.[26]

Critiques of postmodernity can map the distinction between "hybrid" and "non-hybrid" as related instances in a Western hegemonic discourse of culture that constructs centers and margins in an ongoing effort to create the diversified markets that limit discourses of multiplicity. While some Western cultural critics deny the subversive aspects of decentering, there are theorists in the "Third World" who continue to do so as well, attacking postmodernism as a purely Western "import." Richard argues, however, that such a view on postmodernism's "origin" ignores the multidirectional flow of culture that provides both hegemonic and counterhegemonic possibilities. Insisting on exploring counterhegemonic aspects of modernity, Richard focuses on decentering and plurality as "Third World" postmodern strategies:

> By creating the possibility of a critical re-reading of modernity, postmodernism offers us the chance to reconsider all that was "left unsaid" and to inject its areas of opacity and resistance with the potential for new, as yet undiscovered, meanings.[27]

Kumkum Sangari has explored this terrain of postmodern possibilities, linking the histories of modernity and colonialism. Thus, although modernity's tendency to universalize works against any destabilization of colonial legacies, Sangari argues that postmodern relativity is "precisely the recognition that the world is open to change: it is necessary to prevent a foreclosure by a single meaning so that different meanings may become possible."[28] Despite this positive assessment, Sangari is troubled by the collapsing of space-time in postmodernism as a rejection of the "politically charged time of transition" that defers and deflates social contradiction, hindering and fragmenting the "ground of praxis."[29] It is just this rejection of the historical conditions of praxis that makes purely aesthetic versions of postmodern practice untenable in certain locations. Sangari's rigorous critique of the possibilities and limits of postmodernism acknowledges the transnational effects of postmodernity, supporting Kwame Anthony Appiah's statement that "postmodern culture is global — though that emphatically does not mean that it is the culture of every person in the world."[30]

Models predicated upon binary oppositions cannot move us out of the paradigms of colonial discourse, nor can they provide us with accurate maps of social relations in postmodernity. Examining the key terms "postcolonial" and "transnational" provides a framework for moving beyond center-periphery models in the postmodern critique of modernity.

Transnational Structures of Cultural Exchange

Most social theorists and cultural critics agree that advanced capitalist societies are in a period of transition. There is also significant consensus over the transnationalization of accumulation, shifts that challenge the older, conventional boundaries of national economies, identities, and cultures. Yet interpretations of this growing "global ecumene" vary. As we have seen in discussions of postmodernism, some theorists celebrate the cosmopolitan possibilities of new articulations of spatial relations and the technologies that express and shape the new "communities." Other theorists identify new forms of Western economic hegemony and warn against increasing cultural homogenization. Does the new global matrix engender liberatory spaces that deconstruct the old regimes of the nation-state or does this phenomenon continue the process of uneven development that marked earlier colonial and neocolonial social formations? Just as we have argued that it is impossible to analyze postmodernity without an understanding of geopolitics, it is difficult to make sense of the theories of culture emanating from economics and political theory without a clear connection to theories of the postmodern. Without a densely delineated map of the debates around cultural production and reception, we cannot theorize the production and reception of diverse feminisms around the globe.

Wallerstein's influential notion of a world-system argues that the world is divided into center and periphery (with a semiperiphery zone that mediates the two).[31] As a response to both structural functionalism and modernization theory, world-system theory revised Marxist sociology. Rejecting the view that societies are relatively stable, holistic units, the theory that has come to be associated with Wallerstein acknowledges the role of conflict and history in social change and seeks to map the dynamics of asymmetries in capitalist culture. The center-periphery model has been expanded, challenged, reworked, and reasserted over the last two decades but it remains deeply embedded in the interdisciplinary discourses of global relations in late capitalism.

In classic world-system theory, groups are represented as monolithic rather than multiply constituted. For example, gender is often left out or oversimplified not only in Wallerstein's analysis but in the work of political economists in general.[32] The terms generally used by the left (such as dominant-dominated, colonizer-colonized) to mark the interplay of power in the era of imperialism often overlook complex, multiply constituted identities that cannot be accounted for by binary oppositions. David Washbrook has charged that world-system theory is Eurocentric in that it suggests that the "West," as the "center," is the predominant mover and shaker in world social relations.[33] Many binary terms such as dominator-dominated, center-periphery, and colonizer-colonized are open to the same charge.

Armand Mattelart has argued that concepts and terms "represent a terrain of struggle between groups and classes, development projects, and societies."[34] Thus, in relation to the political practice at work in the terminology of center-periphery theories, Brazilian sociologist Fernando Enrique Cardoso, queries: "Is the periphery a united whole? Is even the concept 'Third World' optional? There are many ways for the periphery to be integrated into the center. It is history which supplies the elements for an explanation."[35] Cardoso's questions can be usefully put to all theory: Who is using these terms and where? To whom and why do these categories seem useful? Clearly, ideas come together in one form in one location. Yet they may take another form in a different location. All these terms, whether we prefer to use them or argue against them, are equally products of specific discourses, and thus neither innocent nor neutral.[36]

Although it can be argued that the center-periphery model is difficult to sustain in a world structured by transnational cultural flows and multinational corporations, it is also problematic to think that this model worked well during the colonial, industrial period. For instance, such a model cannot account for the terrible conditions under which some people lived in the so-called center.[37] Nor does it explain the role of women in the West. In contemporary economic contexts, the model breaks down when we consider that the global economy is structured by five hundred multinational corporations that are headquartered across the world and not only in the United States and Europe. As Brian Berry suggests, in the wake of global telecommunications, many of these corporations have replaced the old center-periphery model with a new order of "specialized interdependence."[38] Furthermore, there is also the question of who owns what shares in these corporations. For instance, if SONY owns a Hollywood studio and if a Saudi Arabian investor owns the U.S. news organization

UPI, how do national distinctions reconfigure or maintain their conventional form?

Along with the world-system theory of center-periphery, the terminology "global-local" has emerged in popular and professionalized discourses of world-scale social relations. Barbara Abou-El-Haj accepts the formation "global-local" as a "qualitative step forward" in the search for an adequate vocabulary of power relations: "It suggests no charged hierarchical divisions, is less concordant with spatial boundaries or geographical regions, is capable of encompassing unequal distribution *within* as well as between national and regional entities."[39]

Although it is possible to use the terms in the sense that Abou-El-Haj suggests, the formation global-local is often used in a purely metaphorical sense, making the binarism even more problematic. For many critics in the United States, for example, the global-local binary opposition seems to make perfect sense because it corresponds to "reality"; that is, the relationship between "federal" and "local" governments in the United States. Yet for people in many other parts of the world such a division makes no sense at all. What is lost in an uncritical acceptance of this binary division is precisely the fact that the parameters of the local and global are often indefinable or indistinct—they are permeable constructs. How one separates the local from the global is difficult to decide when each thoroughly infiltrates the other.

Global-local as a monolithic formation may also erase the existence of multiple expressions of "local" identities and concerns and multiple globalities. In this particular way, global-local binaries dangerously correspond to the colonialism-nationalism model that often leaves out various subaltern groups as well as the interplay of power in various levels of sociopolitical agendas. For instance, the Subaltern Studies group, in rethinking Indian nationalist history, identifies several "dominant groups." First they demarcate the "dominant indigenous groups" from the "dominant foreign groups." Then they further subdivide the "dominant indigenous" groups into three parts: the "all-India level," and the "regional and local" levels.[40] In this instance the use of global-local begins to break down as what might be called "local" as opposed to "global" becomes "all-India," and "regional" as well as "local." These divisions are also problematic in that gender distinctions (which are not mentioned in Guha's definition of terms) seem to be diagonally located across these lines, although they do suggest that what counts as "local" may vary considerably.

Stuart Hall argues that global and local are two aspects of the same phenomenon. As the binary expression of a late-capital formation, the difference between global and local can mask the similarities or links in the process of globalization. Hall, however, does not simply condemn globalization as cultural homogenization. In seeking to understand how late capital requires differentiation and the stylistic markers of "otherness," Hall identifies the oppositional nature of postmodernity; the return to the local as a response to the seeming homogenization and globalization of culture can only work for social change if it does not become rooted in "exclusivist and defensive enclaves."[41] Hall argues against any mystification of the "local" as inherently purer or better than the "global":

> The homeland is not waiting back there for the new ethnics to rediscover it. There is a past to be learned about, but the past is now seen, and it has to be grasped as a history, as something that has to be told. It is narrated. It is grasped through desire. It is grasped through reconstruction. It is not just a fact that has been waiting to ground our identities.[42]

Hall finds the boundary crossing aspects of postmodernity, as expressed in transnational debates about identity and culture, imbued with contradictory but powerful possibility. So-called marginal groups, he argues, in reworking their relationship to "local" identities, must also "speak right across those boundaries" and "across those frontiers."[43]

Both center-periphery and global-local share a point of view that has been characterized as ethnocentric, if not specifically Euro-North-American-centric. Abou-El-Haj argues, for example, that "remnants of Eurocentrism" in center-periphery theories result in an overemphasis on local relations with global power brokers that ignores the complex class divisions and tensions on the local level: "Seemingly clear cases of local ambitions shaped by global interests can be profoundly local in their formation, for example, nationalism, a European creation and a European import."[44] Armand Mattelart has noted a lack of studies that differentiate elements within the "local." Without the cooperation and logistical backing of local mediators and agents, Mattelart argues, "transnational firms would not be able to exercise their power."[45] Any view of the relations between center and periphery (or global and local) that views the direction of influence, technology, and knowledge as one-way is not only ethno- or Eurocentric, therefore, but inaccurate.

Much of the debate about globalization is structured around the problematic notion of a homogenizing West. In this view, cultural flows are seen as unidirectional (i.e., from the "West" to the "rest"). Or the debate is structured in terms of assimilation or opposition to the West. What is not clear in such debates is what elements of which culture (including goods and services) are deployed where, by whom, and for what reason. Why, for instance, is the Barbie doll sold in India but not the Cabbage Patch doll? Why did the Indian Mattel affiliate choose to market Barbie dressed in a sari while Ken remains dressed in "American" clothes? Why is Barbie dressed in a sari (universalizing/national-izing a regional mode of dress) and not in other South Asian women's styles of dress? Which class buys these dolls and how do children play with them in different locations? Such questions underscore the need for research on links between multinational corporate strategies and dominant nationalist agendas. Getting away from what Mattelart calls "transnational centrism" acknowledges that local subjects are not "passive receptacles" who mechanically reproduce the "norms, values, and signs of transnational power."[46]

We use the term "transnational" to problematize a purely locational politics of global-local or center-periphery in favor of what Mattelart sees as the lines cutting across them. As feminists who note the absence of gender issues in all of these world-system theories, we have no choice but to challenge what we see as inadequate and inaccurate binary divisions.[47] Transnational linkages in-fluence every level of social existence. Thus the effects of configurations of prac-tices at those levels are varied and historically specific. The theories of cultural homogenization that often accompany analyses of cultural flows cannot ac-knowledge these historicized effects and transformations at various levels. Ar-jun Appadurai takes into consideration movements of people, technologies, capital, and cultures in order to describe these forces as a "model of disjunctive flows" from which "something like a decent global analysis might flow."[48] Ap-padurai also warns against cultural homogenization theories, particularly those that simply equate homogenization with Americanization. His concern is that these same theories are used by nation-states to mask the fact that the threat of global commoditization is "more real than the threat of their own hegemonic strategies."[49]

A cultural flow such as CNN has an undeniably hegemonic effect, but it would be a mistake to see such flows as unidirectional or uniform. Instead of constructing monolithic, hegemonic effects, we should ask: What aspect of a commodity gets utilized in what way and where? Can we see these commodi-ties as artifacts? How do we trace the cultural baggage of commodities from their point of origin (if this can be ascertained!)? For example, one scene that appeared on TV screens during the coup that ousted Ferdinand Marcos from the Philippines was that of the Marcos family at a party on their yacht, dancing and singing "We Are the World." We would not read this scene as the ludic play of postmodern syncretism. Rather, this scene signifies power and terror to a degree that insists that we examine the way in which the flows of cultural commodities are both linked and disjunctive.

Janet Abu-Lughod suggests that we have a "globalizing but not necessarily homogenous culture."[50] She cites the Salman Rushdie case as a "very concrete instance of how globalized and yet how unglobalized culture has become."[51]

Although Abu-Lughod does not critique the center-periphery binary formation, her statement alludes to the way in which anti-imperialist cultural criticism can both remain within binary structures and depart from them. Both Armand Mattelart and Ulf Hannerz study similarly paradoxical positions. Mattelart argues, for example, that subjects in the so-called peripheries, even if they appear entirely subordinated to transnational economic structures, "at least reformulate in accordance with the historical heritage and particular conditions the reception they give to these models."[52]

That such issues of localized reception will temper and vary the effects of cultural hegemony is the subject of Ulf Hannerz's work in cultural anthropology. Arguing against the current of conventional theories of culture, Hannerz asserts that a culture need not be homogenous, nor even particularly coherent.[53] In his view, if most cultures are "creolized" and are not based on isolation and autonomy then "Third" and "First" World societies can be seen as permeable, complex, and connected to other world societies. In fact, Hannerz suggests that most Western major metropoles are really extensions of other "home" communities and are increasingly less and less "Western." Hannerz's view of a world-system of cultures relies heavily on the center-periphery economic model but turns it inside out, as it were. Are there other powers, he asks, besides the "superpowers"? And where and how do these powers manifest themselves in culture? Hannerz argues that anything that comes from the West to diverse peripheries never remains intact or necessarily unaltered: "Imported cultural items which were at first to some degree in their unaltered, wholly alien forms would in time come to be taken apart, tampered and tinkered with, as people would evolve their own way of using them."[54]

We do not mean to suggest that all altered forms are in some sense subversive or oppositional to the "West." As historians of gender and nationalism amply demonstrate, such theoretical formations may also collaborate with agendas of exploitation.[55] Our point is that these tamperings are multifaceted. Perhaps the most constructive way to deal with a binary construction such as "First-Third" worlds is to insist, as Ella Shohat does, that the terms have a historically specific political significance. Thus, "Third World" has a more "activist aura," as opposed to the less confrontational "postcolonial." Yet both terms are products of particular eras and expressions of cultural tensions that must be read in relation to each other. The notion of the "three worlds," Shohat writes, "flattens heterogeneities, masks contradictions, and elides differences."[56] Yet substituting "postcolonial" for "Third World" without deconstructing the production and reception of the former term will result in a "flattening of heterogeneities" as well. The editors of *Public Culture* have also called for erasing the distinctions between First and Third worlds, not because these terms do not define significant differences, but because they enable the misrecognition of global multinational alliances. [57]

Inherent to these various challenges to standard Marxist or nationalist structures of power is a simultaneous commitment to changing unequal social relations and understanding the "explosion of cultural modernities" that make up the world today. Shohat argues that the current circulation of the term "postcolonial" has transformed a complex, historically specific concept into a literary and disciplinary signal for what comes after colonialism. Such a liberal appropriation of the term erases differences between distinct geographical regions, historical moments, and varied ideologies of nation and decolonization. It not only becomes impossible to assert neocolonial critiques of ongoing imperialisms but it becomes safe to study the "colonial" as a phenomenon of the "past" (thereby bypassing or displacing "race"). In its current usage in the humanities, "postcolonial" does not imply a critique of colonialism but a way of denying that colonialism continues in various forms at the present time.[58] Such a usage cannot connect the older colonial economic period to the one we live in now, a distinctly different yet related world economic system dominated by such entities as the International Monetary Fund and other global economic and cultural agencies. If colonialism is only "post," the diversity, vitality, and visibility of current liberation movements are minimized or erased.

What is the most accurate and useful way to use the term "postcolonial"? As a global, hegemonic term in contemporary cultural studies, it has to be critically accounted for and, certainly, historicized. To keep it subversive, one would have to insist on its use as a term that includes literary productions by First World subjects. Such a use resists a center/margin dichotomy that situates the "postcolonial" as geographically and culturally "other."[59] Another use of "postcolonial" that subverts appropriation draws upon Third World critiques of nativism and refusals of Orientalism (along the lines of Gayatri Spivak's work).[60] Because transnational economic structures affect everyone in the global economy, we need categories of differentiation and analysis that acknowledge our structurally asymmetrical links and refuse to construct exotic authors and subjects. Kobena Mercer suggests that we

> examine the unwieldy relationship between the Left and the new social movements because they both share problems made symptomatic in terms of "identity" and yet there is no vocabulary in which to conduct a mutual dialogue on the possibility of alliances or coalitions around a common project.[61]

"Postcolonial," therefore, can serve as a term that positions cultural production in the fields of transnational economic relations and diasporic identity constructions. It is particularly useful in projects that delineate fields of reception *in the West* (United States, Europe, and Australia). Critiques of Western reception can deconstruct the aesthetic and political mystiques that govern the marketing and distribution of cultural artifacts from the "Third World." For example, in this volume Robert Carr discusses the emergence of testimonial literature in the First World marketplace and the accumulation of knowledge (and power) by bourgeois readers of the "authentic" literature of the world's supposedly most underrepresented class—Third World working-class or peasant women. Carr's critique situates the "borderland" of testimonial as a complex location where contests for access are mediated by editors who broker "authenticity" and "real" stories. In raising questions about the function of the "real" and the politics of reception, Carr contributes to a more detailed mapping of the circulation of gendered commodities in the world system of culture.

Postcolonial diasporas also clearly problematize the center-periphery model, since they reflect the transnational circulation of populations. Complex analyses of diasporas help us to understand the relationship between movements of people and the mobility of information and capital in the world today. Caren Kaplan's essay in this volume addresses the proliferation of theories of location in recent Western feminist theory that do not challenge the center-periphery model or shift the power of representation beyond the West. These "politics of location" theorists vary widely in their feminist affiliations with women in diverse conditions and situations. Thus, what theorists of the diaspora often tend to forget is that location is still an important category that influences the specific manifestations of transnational formations. All diasporas are not alike; we must learn how to demarcate them, how to understand their specific agendas and politics. Furthermore, in order to problematize the separation of a pure "home" from a "contaminated" diasporic location, we have to pay attention to how people distinguish their diasporic location from their "home" location. For instance, Homi Bhabha's theories can be seen as emerging from Indian contexts as well as from those of the Indian diaspora in England. The manner in which his theories have been adopted by some U.S. mainstream theorists not only in reference to diverse colonial situations, but also to the analysis of race relations everywhere, suggests that the transnational flows of cultural ideas and effects also work to consolidate "theory" as an object of exchange.

We mean to address precisely this construction of inert, ahistorical generalizations. The relationship between "transnational," "postcolonial," "center-periphery," and "diaspora" in contemporary usage can be found in the way modernity masks particularities in favor of the appearance of universal categories. In theorizing transnational feminist practices we are suggesting not only that communities are much more multiply organized than the conventional usages of these terms have implied, but that gender is crucially linked to the primary terms and concepts that structure and inform the economic and cultural theories of postmodernity.

Postmodernism and Transnational Feminist Practices

If feminist political practices do not acknowledge transnational cultural flows, feminist movements will fail to understand the material conditions that structure women's lives in diverse locations. If feminist movements cannot understand the dynamics of these material conditions, they will be unable to construct an effective opposition to current economic and cultural hegemonies that are taking new global forms. Without an analysis of transnational scattered hegemonies that reveal themselves in gender relations, feminist movements will remain isolated and prone to reproducing the universalizing gestures of dominant Western cultures.

Notions such as "global feminism" have failed to respond to such needs and have increasingly been subject to critique.[62] Conventionally, "global feminism" has stood for a kind of Western cultural imperialism. The term "global feminism" has elided the diversity of women's agency in favor of a universalized Western model of women's liberation that celebrates individuality and modernity. Anti-imperialist movements have legitimately decried this form of "feminist" globalizing (albeit often for a continuation of their own agendas). Many women who participate in decolonizing efforts both within and outside the United States have rejected the term "feminism" in favor of "womanist" or have defined their feminism through class or race or other ethnic, religious, or regional struggles.

Yet we know that there is an imperative need to address the concerns of women around the world in the historicized particularity of their relationship to multiple patriarchies as well as to international economic hegemonies. We seek creative ways to move beyond constructed oppositions without ignoring the histories that have informed these conflicts or the valid concerns about power relations that have represented or structured the conflicts up to this point. We need to articulate the relationship of gender to scattered hegemonies such as global economic structures, patriarchal nationalisms, "authentic" forms of tradition, local structures of domination, and legal-juridical oppression on multiple levels.

Transnational feminist practices require this kind of comparative work rather than the relativistic linking of "differences" undertaken by proponents of "global feminism"; that is, to compare multiple, overlapping, and discrete oppressions rather than to construct a theory of hegemonic oppression under a unified category of gender. Kamala Visweswaran's essay in this volume undertakes such work; in examining the conjunction between nationalist discourse and ethnographic writing she raises the problematic of women's positionality as ethnographers and subjects of ethnographies. Both positions work within and against discourses controlled by the geopolitical context in which these particular women live and work. Visweswaran's critique of ethnographic practice enables her to explore the nuances of connection as well as the silences and betrayals in the acquisition of anthropological "information" in feminist contexts.

Feminists must continually question the narratives in which they are embedded, including but not limiting ourselves to the master narratives of mainstream feminism. As Kumkum Sangari and Sudesh Vaid assert:

> If feminism is to be different, it must acknowledge the ideological and
> problematic significance of its own past. Instead of creating yet another grand tra-
> dition or a cumulative history of emancipation, neither of which can deal with
> our present problems, we need to be attentive to how the past enters differently
> into the consciousness of other historical periods and is further subdivided by a
> host of other factors including gender, caste, and class.[63]

In this spirit of feminist self-examination, Fred Pfeil's essay in this volume looks carefully at the ways in which issues of difference are being addressed in contemporary feminist theory in the United States. Pfeil argues that, even among savvy and committed feminists, ahistorical relativism is in danger of replacing historical specificity as well as feminist solidarity. Feminist movements must be open to rethinking and self-reflexivity as an ongoing process if we are to avoid creating new orthodoxies that are exclusionary and reifying. The issue of who counts as a feminist is much less important than creating coalitions based on the practices that different women use in various locations to counter the scattered hegemonies that affect their lives. Norma Alarcón's essay addresses this issue in the area of identity politics and Latina women; examining how the figure of *Malinche* has been used by various Latin American writers, feminist and nonfeminist, she deconstructs the ideological formation of female cultural symbols. Demonstrating these shifts in representation, Alarcón delineates the limits of a feminist discourse that does not take into account the historically specific locations that construct the cultures that Chicanas, for example, or other women of color negotiate in their daily lives. "Despite some shared critical perspectives," Alarcón writes, "boundaries exist and continue to exist, thus accounting for differential experiences that cannot be contained under the sign of a universal woman or women." Acknowledging and specifying such differences must accompany any detailed articulation of links between women.

Part of any feminist self-examination necessitates a rigorous critique of emerging orthodoxies. In debates within the United States, for example, it is important to examine the ways in which race, class, and gender are fast becoming the holy trinity that every feminist feels compelled to address even as this trinity delimits the range of discussion around women's lives. What is often left out of these U.S.-focused debates are other complex categories of identity and affiliation that apply to non-U.S. cultures and situations. U.S. feminists often have to be reminded that all peoples of the world are not solely constructed by the trinity of race-sex-class; for that matter, other categories also enter into the issues of subject formation both within and outside the borders of the United States, requiring more nuanced and complex theories of social relations. For example, emerging theories of homosexual formations in various locations demonstrate that the category of sexuality can be multiply constituted in the context of transnational cultures, pointing the way for detailed feminist studies of cultural production and reception.[64]

The question becomes how to link diverse feminisms without requiring either equivalence or a master theory. How to make these links without replicating cultural and economic hegemony? For white, Western feminists or elite women in other world locations, such questions demand an examination of the links between daily life and academic work and an acknowledgment that one's privileges in the world-system are always linked to another woman's oppression or exploitation. As Cynthia Enloe's recent work demonstrates, the old sisterhood model of missionary work, of intervention and salvation, is clearly tied to the older models of center-periphery relations.[65] As these models have become obsolete in the face of proliferating, multiple centers and peripheries, we need new analyses of how gender works in the dynamic of globalization and the countermeasures of new nationalisms, and ethnic and racial fundamentalisms. Feminists can begin to map these scattered hegemonies and link diverse local practices to formulate a transnational set of solidarities. For instance, we need to examine fundamentalisms around the world and seek to understand why Muslim fundamentalism appears in the media today as the primary progenitor of oppressive conditions for women when Christian, Jewish, Hindu, Confucian, and other forms of extreme fundamentalisms exert profound controls over women's lives.

What is the relationship between transnational economies and the intensification of religious fundamentalism? For example, when the United States gave billions to General Zia of Pakistan to fight the Soviets in Afghanistan, the United States propped up a regime that was inimical to women. U.S. feminists need to fight against this kind of aid on their home ground instead of abstractly condemning Islam as the center of patriarchal oppression. Simultaneously, we need to examine how the importance of Christian fundamentalism within the Republican party in the United States affects the lives of millions of women worldwide through funding and development practices that structure reproductive and other politics. Transnational feminist approaches link the impact of such policies on women on public assistance in the United States and women who have little agency in their dealing with U.S.-sponsored clinics and health centers that have been established in the so-called peripheries. The concept of multiple peripheries, therefore, can link directly the domestic politics of a world power such as the United States to its foreign policies. Transnational feminist alliances can work to change these policies only when such congruencies are accounted for and transformed into the basis for multiple, allied, solidarity projects.

In calling for transnational alliances, our purpose is to acknowledge the different forms that feminisms take and the different practices that can be seen as feminist movements. We do not wish to dictate exactly who can stand as a feminist, for as Norma Alarcón argues, such dicta posit a standpoint epistemology that requires the construction of gender differences as the primary categories of analysis to the extent of "working inherently against the interests of non-white women."[66] In arguing against a standpoint epistemology, we are not arguing that this is an era of postfeminism. We believe that many white, bourgeois feminists have announced a postfeminist era precisely because their particular definitions of feminism (which often require universalization) have not been able to withstand critiques from women of color as well as the deconstructions of poststructuralist or postmodern theory. The bases of these two critiques of white, bourgeois feminism are sometimes different and sometimes collaborative, but that is not the issue here. What concerns us is that some feminist responses to postmodern critiques of the subject, of the decentered Self, of Marxist notions of class as applied to gender as a class, have signaled regressive moves.

Dismissing postmodern aesthetics may be easy for some feminist theorists but the cultural and economic implications of postmodernity should not be disregarded. In *Feminism Without Women*, Tania Modleski challenges postmodern theory by resurrecting a universal category of woman, citing "our cultural heritage as women" to discredit feminist theorists who argue for cultural specificity.[67] Representative of a certain feminist rejection of "postfeminism," Modleski does not examine fully the gendered terms of an era dependent on information technology and new forms of multinational domination. Thus she situates her reading of *Gorillas in the Mist* in relation to specific debates about race in the United States while "African civil wars" are abstractly and nonspecifically addressed (repeating the apolitical gestures of the film itself).[68] Similarly, some proponents of feminist psychoanalytic film theory in the United States now respond to critics who charge that they often ignore race not only by using Homi Bhabha's homogenizing theories of diaspora but by constructing "race" as a narrow category that erases differences between the United States and other countries and cultures as well as between regions within those countries. Such methods do not advance transnational affiliations between women and do much to prevent the examination of crucial links between diverse feminist practices.

Inasmuch as most feminist psychoanalytic or standpoint epistemology theories are wedded to modernist categories and agendas, they will remain Eurocentric. Such cultural snafus occur most often in the objectification of so-called Third World Women as privileged signifiers of difference. Cross-cultural analyses that position themselves within diasporas share a similar problem. Caught between critiques of modernity and assertions of authentic identities, some writers cannot see postmodern methodologies as a viable feminist practice. Inderpal Grewal's essay addresses this relationship between feminist discourses and postmodern aesthetic strategies, demonstrating that quite often even Third World writers who argue for postmodern, decentered, diasporic subjectivities become nostalgic for modernist verities.

While many feminists feel that postmodernism is detrimental to feminist projects, they fail to take issue with the conditions of postmodernity. We believe that critiques of modernity are necessary to feminism in any location. Often, the issue of postmodernism is formulated as a choice, that is, that feminists can choose to be either for or against postmodernism. Yet, recognizing the structure and dynamics of postmodernity is a necessity rather than a luxury or a simple choice. For world cultural, economic, and political conditions have become such that we must devise ways in which feminist practices can work against ever-changing, patriarchal collaborations all over the globe. However, many feminists who see the value of postmodern philosophies also forget the economic and material changes in this postindustrial era that have an impact on the movement of cultural flows such as feminism. For example, although Jane Flax acknowledges the validity of a critique of the Enlightenment philosophies and the "toleration" of ambivalence, ambiguity, and practice, her critique remains Eurocentric in its understanding of postmodernism as a Western literary phenomenon rather than as a critical practice that crosses cultural and economic boundaries.[69]

In fact, many postmodern feminists in the United States see postmodernism as a movement toward ambivalence, the decentered subject, and so on, rather than as a thorough critique of modernity and its related institutions. Thus the collection edited by Linda Nicholson, *Feminism/Postmodernism*, in many ways a ground-breaking and innovative contribution to these debates, does not address issues such as nationalism and therefore cannot participate in a critique of modernity. Instead, that collection sees postmodernism as a critique of aesthetic movements in modernist traditions. What gets left out of such considerations are the concerns of many women across the world regardless of whether or not they choose to describe themselves as "feminists": the place of women in the nation-state, resistance to revivals of "tradition," the complex issue of fundamentalism, the situation of workers in multinational corporations, and the relationship between gender, the nation-state, and mobile, transnational capital. Although both Linda Nicholson and Nancy Fraser suggest that postmodern feminism would be cross-cultural and comparative as the "practice of feminisms," there is little evidence of this effect in the theories produced in the West to date.[70]

Because we are arguing for an examination of modernity as an important part of transnational feminist practices and because modernity has participated predominately within discourses of the formation of nation-states, we feel that nationalism needs to be examined in relation to feminist practice. The essays in this volume by Mary Layoun, Lydia Liu, Nalini Natarajan, and Kamala Visweswaran examine the problematic of nationalism, showing how this construct places women in a symbolic relation to nation, leaving aside all those spaces in which women see nationalism as either outside or antithetical to their lives. While Liu's essay explores the different stakes at a particular point in Chinese history in reading a female writer's text as "nationalist" rather than concerned with other aspects of women's existence, Layoun explores the problematic of the metaphoric use of "woman" as "nation." Natarajan argues that most Indian narratives imagine a distinctly gendered nation through the representation of the female body. Visweswaran examines how Indian women are positioned between the master narratives of "Indian nationalism" and "Western feminism." What these essays reveal is that the concept of national identity serves the interests of various patriarchies in multiple locations and that these collaborations occur in different ways in different places.

When modernity takes shape as feminism, therefore, it collaborates with nationalism. In its nationalist guise, it cannot be oppositional. The need to free feminism from nationalist discourses is clear. Yet feminism is implicated in nationalism as well as in its counterdiscourses. Both Layoun and Liu's essays help us understand this paradoxical aspect of feminism, for feminism comes in many forms—sometimes as a hegemonic Western formation and sometimes as a threat to Western hegemony as well as to national and regional patriarchies. For example, Natarajan's essay argues that Rushdie's novel *Midnight's Children*, using the problematic symbolism of woman as nation that emerged in Bombay cinema in the 1960s and 1970s (well after India's independence in 1947), both writes against nationalist discourse and cannot refrain from using it. Rushdie's ambivalence reveals the role of nationalism and the concept of "home" in the Indian and Pakistani diaspora in England. In a sense, therefore, *Midnight's Children* cannot see a place for women outside the nation, even though nationalism is clearly delineated as a patriarchal formation. Liu's essay corresponds to Natarajan's assessment, showing that at least one Chinese woman writer does manage to see women as agents outside the discourse of nation. Therefore, Liu identifies a local practice of writing that positions women outside nation, something that feminist discourse has had trouble accomplishing.

What these critics bring into consideration is not only the transnational flow of ideas, concepts, and actions such as feminism and nationalism but the ways in which diverse practices that are also feminist can analyze, respond to, and assess these flows from different locations for different purposes. In these essays, the Chinese state, the Turkish-Cypriot conflict, and contemporary India are three very different sociohistorical locations that feminists respond to in linked but different ways.

Women's groups are practicing these methods of analysis and alliance in community and international political organizing. For example, Women Against Fundamentalism (based in England) and the group assembling the Women Living Under Muslim Laws dossiers are actively working against essentialist or conventional Western, bourgeois identities and categories in their efforts to resist religious fundamentalism and patriarchal elements in their communities. Rather than condemn the Iranian fundamentalist death penalty against Salman Rushdie as an attack against free speech, some feminists in England are criticizing it on entirely different grounds. Without collaborating with the construction of a "progressive" and "democratic" West against a "despotic" East, the Women Against Fundamentalism group has called for a struggle against all fundamentalisms, including Christian ones. They defend Rushdie's work by reading his text as an attack on fundamentalisms of all kinds, making the point that for fundamentalists of all persuasions there is no room for debate within religion or of religious texts.

In an important article in *Feminist Review*, "Washing Our Linen: One Year of Women Against Fundamentalism," Clara Connolly argues that fundamentalism is the "mobilization of religious affiliation for political ends" with detrimental results on women's lives.[71] Connolly chronicles the formation of the Women Against Fundamentalism group as a coalition of Asian, Black, and other ethnic minority feminists that struggles against every form of fundamentalism but, most importantly, critiques the Christian dominance of the English nation-state and the place of multiculturalism within it. Women Against Fundamentalism target "the *state* rather than the fundamentalists of any religion" and seek not only the complete separation of church and state but a "measure of legal and social protection against the efforts of fundamentalists to restrict our life-choices and sexualities."[72]

Many fundamentalist interests in states that have been through nationalist, supposedly decolonizing struggles present themselves as anti-Western and antimodernization even though such a West/non-West opposition is too simplistic a duality. Islamic fundamentalism, as Deniz Kandiyoti argues, has been a "constant vehicle for popular classes to express their alienation from 'Westernized' elites."[73] Yet certain "fundamentalist" dictums and beliefs are hardly "authentic" expressions of indigenous Islamic culture. For example, the well-publicized Islamic laws that prevent the prosecution of husbands who murder adulterous wives do not date from time immemorial but are borrowed from the nineteenth-century French Penal Code.[74] What needs to be examined in light of such transnational hegemonic "borrowings" are the ways in which various patriarchies collaborate and borrow from each other in order to reinforce specific practices that are oppressive to women.

Feminists have great stakes in understanding and theorizing these distinct fundamentalist formations. In the United States, for example, feminists need to examine how fundamentalist agendas pervade supposedly secular states, enabling Christian doctrines to masquerade as law. A transnational feminist practice, therefore, examines the ways in which Christian fundamentalism in different countries has an impact on women's lives in different ways, just as does Islamic, Jewish, or Hindu fundamentalism in different groups and locations. Each fundamentalism uses and disciplines women in different ways. As a result, we must examine the similarities and differences between anti-abortion politics sponsored by fundamentalists in the United States and the crackdown on reproductive rights in formerly socialist countries in Europe. In addition, the relationship between an entity like the Vatican and the practices of social control in Latin America may vary from the Baptist-oriented, U.S. TV evangelism that permeates the same geographical region.

We need to learn more about the varied ways in which a state becomes fundamentalist and how women fare in those locations. Although there are now twenty-three countries that can be considered to be Muslim fundamentalist, such states as Pakistan, Saudi Arabia, and Iran differ greatly in their political and global affiliations.[75] For instance, against the opposition of many women, Saudi Arabia gives aid to groups in Bangladesh that are fundamentalist, hoping to assist in the creation of an Islamic state.

Such transnational links between religious and state formations are the least clearly formulated. As Sara Diamond points out in her book on Christian fundamentalism, "many social science studies of right-wing movements ignore the national and international political context in which movement organizations operate."[76] U.S. Christian fundamentalism has an increasingly global reach through the development of televangelist broadcasting in Latin America and the Middle East. In addition, Diamond describes the comprehensive attempts by large evangelical denominations to win the allegiance of recent Latino immigrants to the United States who are particularly vulnerable to offers of assistance with immigration, language acquisition, and other valuable services. Spanish-language broadcasts "offering material success and a ready-made Christian 'family' to born-again believers," Diamond warns, are designed to increase dramatically the number of "Hispanic" churches throughout the decade.[77] In addition to studies on this domestic phenomenon, we need to examine the impact of the religious right on U.S. foreign policy. Diamond's work on the links between Christian fundamentalism and contra aid during the 1980s, for example, points the way for complex, multileveled, and interdisciplinary work on the transnational politics of cultures of fundamentalism.

Another coalition organized to address such transnational feminist issues is the international group constructing the Women Living Under Muslim Laws dossiers. By collecting dossiers on the condition of women in various Islamic countries, the women in this group gather information on the diverse political and social implications of Islamic laws as they are carried out in various countries. For instance, in some countries it is mainly poor women who feel the force of these laws while upper-class women have various means to escape them. Thus, these dossiers reveal that there is not one homogeneous Muslim world. Rather, as the introduction to Dossier 3 states:

> while similarities exist, the notion of a uniform Muslim world is a misconception imposed on us. We have erroneously been led to believe that the only way of "being" is the one we currently live in each of our contexts. Depriving us of even dreaming of a different reality is one of the most debilitating forms of oppression we suffer.[78]

What concerns this group of women is the widespread promulgation of the view that there is one interpretation of Islam and one way of living that reality as Muslim women. Yet, in only one instance of resistance to fundamentalism, Bangladesh women have organized by remembering what happened in Iran, where women participated in the revolution against the Shah only to find themselves outside the power structures once an Islamic state became established. One has only to look at the various essays in Deniz Kandiyoti's collection *Women, Islam, and the State* in order to see how differently Islamization becomes state law in various countries as it interacts with specific historical conditions, how varied the political interests are that are fostering Islamization, and the specific purposes that each of these groups of interests has in order to create Islamic states. As Kandiyoti writes:

> The legitimacy crises engendered by these processes have favored the rise of or-
> ganized oppositional movements with Islamist platforms, as well as attempts at
> social control by governments emphasizing their own commitment to orthodoxy.
> The arena in which these political projects can most easily be played out and
> achieve a measure of consensus is . . . the control of women.[79]

As Kandiyoti argues, the political interest Islamic fundamentalist groups have in common is that of basing their movements on the control of women; how and why they push this goal is specific and varied. The purpose of the dossiers is to record this variety of experiences. The documents that comprise the dossiers are not only collected by women in the countries themselves, they are used in any number of ways, including the documentation of oppressive conditions that can aid in some women's efforts to argue for refugee status. Reinterpreting the Koran, providing new translations and interpretations is, therefore, an important part of this movement. Such practices, of course, run counter to the various fundamentalist groups that wish to create a Muslim homogeneity. Therefore it can be argued that these practices refuse to play into the hands of both the U.S. "democratic, free-world" agenda as well as the Islamic fundamentalist states and groups. It is the collusion of interests and not their "authentic" homogeneity that needs to be examined, both in the patriarchies and in the groups that oppose them.

These examples suggest roles for women everywhere to play in the politics of solidarity in transnational feminist practices. Women in the United States can work on opposing various state policies that promote and collude with fundamentalisms (Christian, Muslim, Jewish, Hindu, or any other). Women from so-called minority communities can work to form alliances that oppose all these fundamentalisms (including Christian formations in the West) and to resist the agendas of a racist state. These activities do not collaborate with Eurocentric feminism, nor do they work for the patriarchal power groups within their own communities. Instead, they create affiliations between women from different communities who are interested in examining and working against the links that support and connect very diverse patriarchal practices.

An example of such a transnational affiliative group in the United States is the coalition of women from very diverse Asian communities in the San Francisco area who have organized the Asian Women's Shelter.[80] This group examines how the so-called cultural defense is used against women in the U.S. courts today. In focusing on what counts as "cultural defense," the group examines the implementation of this argument during sentencing for crimes committed by men from minority groups against women from minority communities, or committed by minority women who internalize and act upon the patriarchal ideologies of their particular cultures. It is part of this group's agenda to explore the links between who can define "culture," who can be legitimated as "expert" testifiers, and what kind of problematic, misogynist notions underlie this kind of authoritative legal testimony. The variety of "cultural defense" arguments highlights the diversity of the communities; from the Hmong woman who reports rape while the man involved claims marriage-by-capture, to the Japanese-American woman who attempts "*oyaku-shinju*" (parent-child suicide) in response to her husband's infidelity and is then accused of the murder of her children. In their analysis of the "cultural defense" argument, the Asian Women's Shelter group demonstrates how a patriarchal, Judeo-Christian legal system reinforces and institutionalizes racist stereotypes about Asian women rather than differentiating between the ethnic, regional, caste, and class practices of women of different cultures.

The Asian Women's Shelter group in San Francisco works from the assumption that women from diverse Asian cultures are constructed differently as women even though there are links between the ways that their communities and the dominant culture collaborate (although not always consciously) to oppress them. For example, in arguing that the "battered woman" syndrome is culture-specific rather than cross-cultural, the group is theorizing how U.S. immigration laws, historical circumstances, and cultural responses all figure in interpretations of domestic violence. In identifying these collaborations between powerful interests and by working collaboratively themselves, the members of the group can help to make changes in their communities. Although support for this project has not come from those feminists who view Asian culture as a monolithic category nor from women who participate in ethnic nationalist agendas, the example of such groups as Women Against Fundamentalism has been helpful in understanding how collaborative coalitions can be formed and maintained.

All three of the groups we have discussed acknowledge differences in women's lives as well as links between transnational power structures. Emphasizing a variety of cultural hegemonies, they are neither homogenizing nor relativistic in their use of the category "woman." Above all, how these groups use the term "woman" recalls Tani Barlow's argument that this category enables both oppression and opposition. Barlow's essay examines how the term "woman" comes into use in China in a variety of ways: through the state, through religious fundamentalism, or as an oppositional term. Barlow argues that "woman" as a universal term only came into use with colonialism and became a disciplinary category during state-deployed decolonization. As Barlow suggests, if the Chinese state's movements toward modernity can be seen in the creation of a category called "woman" that brought together all female persons, it did so also as a disciplinary, modernizing practice. Studies such as Barlow's clearly demonstrate that universalizing, anti-poststructuralist, anti-postmodernist movements toward an albeit nonessentialist but universal category called woman allows state power and the power of fundamentalist groups to mobilize forces against all female persons.

Given contemporary global conditions, transnational feminist practices will emerge only through questioning the conditions of postmodernity. Rather than attempt to account for or definitively circumscribe either "theory" or "practice," the essays in this collection engage political and narrative strategies as they proliferate in transnational cultures. The first section of the book, "Gender, Nation, and Critiques of Modernity," problematizes the relationship between feminism and nationalism, asking how feminist practices can exist outside certain master narratives. The second section, "Global-Colonial Limits," points toward feminist practices that acknowledge the scattered hegemonies that intersect discourses of gender. The essays in each section provide varied political engagements while deconstructing monolithic categories and mythic binaries. We hope this collection provokes further discussion and debate to rework the terms of theory and practice of gender across cultural divides.

Notes

1. For critiques of modernity see Caren Kaplan, *Questions of Travel: Postmodern Discourses of Displacement* (forthcoming, Duke University Press); Robert Young, *White Mythologies: Writing History and the West* (London: Routledge, 1990); Edward Said, *The World, the Text, and the Critic* (Cambridge: Harvard University Press, 1983); James Clifford, *The Predicament of Culture* (Cambridge: Harvard University Press, 1988); and see essays here by Lydia Liu, Tani Barlow, and Inderpal Grewal.

2. See *The Anti-Aesthetic: Essays on Postmodern Culture*, ed. Hal Foster (Port Townsend, Wash.: Bay Press, 1983); *Postmodernism and Politics*, ed. Jonathan Arac (Minneapolis: University of Minnesota Press, 1986); *Universal Abandon: The Politics of Postmodernism*, ed. Andrew Ross (Minneapolis: University of Minnesota Press, 1988); *Postmodernism and Its Discontents: Theories, Practices*, ed. E. Ann Kaplan (London: Verso, 1988); and *Feminism/Postmodernism*, ed. Linda J. Nicholson (New York: Routledge, 1990). Elizabeth Weed's collection, *Coming to Terms: Feminism, Theory, Politics* (New York: Routledge, 1989), begins to address our concerns but the discussion is limited primarily to one section.

3. See, for example, Terry Eagleton, Fredric Jameson, and Edward Said, *Nationalism, Colonialism, and Literature*, intro. by Seamus Deane (Minneapolis: University of Minnesota Press, 1990). Some discussion of feminist issues can be found in the collection *Nation and Narration*, ed. Homi K. Bhabha (London: Routledge, 1990).

4. We particularly applaud recent publications such as *Third World Women and the Politics of Feminism*, ed. Chandra Talpade Mohanty, Ann Russo, and Lourdes Torres (Bloomington: Indiana University Press, 1991); *Nationalisms and Sexualities*, ed. Andrew Parker, Mary Russo, Doris Sommer, and Patricia Yaeger (New York: Routledge, 1992); and *De/Colonizing the Subject: Politics and Gender in*

Women's Autobiographical Practice, ed. Julia Watson and Sidonie Smith (Minneapolis: University of Minnesota Press, 1992).

5. A relatively new concern with "race" and "colonial discourse" in the work of feminist theorists such as Tania Modleski, Kaja Silverman, Barbara Johnson, and Jane Gallop has resulted in interesting studies, but we would argue that the shift in the "content" of the analysis in question has not sufficiently transformed the structure of methodologies that resist acknowledging transnational feminist practices. See, for example, "Cinema and the Dark Continent: Race and Gender in Popular Film," in Tania Modleski, *Feminism Without Women: Culture and Criticism in a "Postfeminist" Age* (New York: Routledge, 1991), 115–34; Kaja Silverman, "White Skin, Brown Masks: The Double Mimesis, or With Lawrence in Arabia," *differences* 1:3 (Fall 1989): 3–54; Barbara Johnson, "Thresholds of Difference: Structures of Address in Zora Neale Hurston," in *"Race," Writing, and Difference*, ed. Henry Louis Gates, Jr. (Chicago: University of Chicago Press, 1985), 317–28; and Jane Gallop, *Around 1981: Academic Feminist Literary Theory* (New York: Routledge, 1992). Some feminist theorists who consistently integrate issues of race and gender in the context of poststructuralist issues include bell hooks, Wahneema Lubiano, Hortense Spillers, Hazel Carby, Donna Haraway, Ella Shohat, Gayatri Chakravorty Spivak, Barbara Harlow, and Rey Chow.

6. See Chandra Talpade Mohanty's critique of "feminist" development studies, "Under Western Eyes: Feminist Scholarship and Colonial Discourses," in *Third World Women*, 51–80.

7. See Kamala Visweswaran, this volume, and "Defining Feminist Ethnography," *Inscriptions* 3/4 (1988): 27–46; Deborah Gordon, "Writing Culture, Writing Feminism: The Poetics and Politics of Experimental Ethnography," *Inscriptions* 3/4 (1988): 7–26, and "The Politics of Ethnographic Authority: Race and Writing in the Ethnography of Margaret Mead and Zora Neale Hurston," in *Modernist Anthropology: From Fieldwork to Text*, ed. Mark Manganaro (Princeton: Princeton University Press, 1990), 146–62; Trinh T. Minh-ha, *Woman/Native/Other: Writing Postcoloniality and Feminism* (Bloomington: Indiana University Press, 1989); Mary E. John, "Postcolonial Feminists in the Western Intellectual Field: Anthropologists *and* Native Informants?" *Inscriptions* 5 (1989): 49–74; Dorinne K. Kondo, *Crafting Selves: Power, Gender, and Discourses of Identity in a Japanese Workplace* (Chicago: University of Chicago Press, 1990); Aihwa Ong, *Spirits of Resistance and Capitalist Discipline: Factory Women in Malaysia* (Albany: State University of New York Press, 1987); and Donna Haraway, *Primate Visions: Gender, Race, and Nature in the World of Modern Science* (New York: Routledge, 1989).

8. See Chandra Talpade Mohanty's critique of "global feminism" in "Feminist Encounters: Locating the Politics of Experience," *Copyright* 1 (Fall 1987): 30–44, and Chilla Bulbeck, *One World Women's Movement* (London: Pluto Press, 1988). See also such valuable early critiques as Gayatri Chakravorty Spivak, "French Feminism in an International Frame," in *In Other Worlds: Essays in Cultural Politics* (New York: Methuen, 1987), 134–53; Adrienne Rich, "Notes Toward a Politics of Location," in *Blood, Bread, and Poetry: Selected Prose 1979–1985* (New York: W. W. Norton, 1986), 210–32. For critiques of Western women's activities in the context of imperialism and the impact on feminist international politics see Cynthia Enloe, *Bananas, Beaches, and Bases: Making Feminist Sense of International Politics* (Berkeley: University of California Press, 1989); Margaret Strobel, *European Women and the Second British Empire* (Bloomington: Indiana University Press, 1991); Caren Kaplan, "Getting to Know You: Travel, Gender, and the Politics of Postcolonial Representation" (1994), *Postmodern Occasions*, ed. E. Ann Kaplan and Michael Sprinker (London: Verso); Inderpal Grewal, "Empire and the Movement for Women's Suffrage in Britain," in *"Home" and Harem: Nationalism, Imperialism, Feminism and the Culture of Travel* (forthcoming); Ella Shohat, "Gender and the Culture of Empire: Toward a Feminist Ethnography of Cinema," *Quarterly Review of Film and Video* 13:1–3 (May 1991): 45–84. See also "Theorizing Nationality, Sexuality, and Race," *Genders* 10 (Spring 1991).

9. Samir Amin, *Delinking*, trans. Michael Wolfers (London: Zed Books, 1990).

10. David Harvey, *The Condition of Postmodernity: An Enquiry into the Origins of Cultural Change* (Cambridge, Mass.: Basil Blackwell, 1990).

11. See Jean-François Lyotard, *The Postmodern Condition: A Report on Knowledge*, trans. Geoff Ben-

nington and Brian Massumi (Minneapolis: University of Minnesota Press, 1984); and Fredric Jameson, *Postmodernism, or the Cultural Logic of Late Capitalism* (Durham, N.C.: Duke University Press, 1992).

12. For a brief version of Jürgen Habermas's critique of postmodernism, see "Modernity—An Incomplete Project," in *The Anti-Aesthetic: Essays on Postmodern Culture*, ed. Hal Foster (Port Townsend, Wash.: Bay Press, 1983), 3–15.

13. Kobena Mercer, "Welcome to the Jungle: Identity and Diversity in Postmodern Politics," in *Identity: Community, Culture, Difference*, ed. Jonathan Rutherford (London: Lawrence and Wishart, 1990), 54.

14. bell hooks, "Postmodern Blackness," *Yearning: Race, Gender, and Cultural Politics* (Boston: South End Press, 1990), 27.

15. See Wahneema Lubiano, "Shuckin' Off the African-American Native Other: What's 'Po-Mo' Got to Do with It?" *Cultural Critique* 18 (Spring 1991): 149–86; Cornel West, "Postmodernity and Afro-America," *Art Papers* 10, no. 1 (Jan./Feb. 1986): 54; Michelle Wallace, "The Politics of Location: Cinema/Theory/Literature/Ethnicity/Sexuality/Me," *Framework* 36 (1988): 42–55.

16. Barbara Christian, "The Race for Theory," in *The Nature and Context of Minority Discourse*, ed. Abdul R. JanMohamed and David Lloyd (New York: Oxford University Press, 1990), 47.

17. bell hooks, "Postmodern Blackness," 23–24.

18. Ibid., 26.

19. Ibid., 27.

20. Inderpal Grewal, "The 'Post-Colonial' Question: South Asia Studies and Feminist Research in a Multinational World," paper delivered at the South Asia Conference, University of California at Berkeley, February 22, 1992.

21. For discussions of the construction of the "primitive" and the "modern" see James Clifford's work, in particular "Histories of the Tribal and the Modern," in *The Predicament of Culture: 20th Century Ethnography, Literature, and Art* (Cambridge: Harvard University Press, 1988), 189–214; Sally Price, *Primitive Art in Civilized Places* (Chicago: University of Chicago Press, 1989); and Marianna Torgovnick, *Gone Primitive* (Chicago: University of Chicago Press, 1991).

22. See S. P. Mohanty, "Us and Them: On the Philosophical Bases of Political Criticism," *Yale Journal of Criticism* 2, no. 2 (Spring 1989): 1–31.

23. See T. V. Reed, "Music/Politics/Spectacle: Rock 'n' Roll Music and/as Colonial Discourse" (presentation at the American Studies Association annual meeting, November 1991); Reebee Garofalo, "Understanding Mega-Events: If We Are the World, Then How Do We Change It?" in *Technoculture*, ed. Constance Penley and Andrew Ross (Minneapolis: University of Minnesota Press, 1991), 247–70; Steven Feld, "Notes on World Beat," *Public Culture* 1:1 (Fall 1988): 31–38; Andrew Goodwin and Joe Gore, "World Beat and the Cultural Imperialism Debate," *Socialist Review* 20, no. 3 (July-September 1990): 63–80.

24. Part of the "Vintage Departures" series, this memoir joins *Into the Heart of Borneo* by Redmond O'Hanlon and *Iron and Silk* by Mark Salzman in marketing travel nostalgia and the mystique of the "foreign correspondent" for a new generation of book buyers in an era of shrinking revenues for print. The blurb on the back of the paperback edition hails the potential consumer by stressing the hybrid, almost carnivalesque nature of the world through which this writer travels: "Mohawk haircuts in Bali. Yuppies in Hong Kong. In Bombay, not one but *five* Rambo rip-offs, complete with music and dancing. And in the new People's Republic of China, a restaurant that serves dishes called 'Yes, Sir, Cheese My Baby,' 'A Legitimate Beef,' and 'Ike and Tuna Turner.' These are some of the images—comical, poignant, and unsettling—that Pico Iyer brings back from the Far East in this brilliant book of travel reportage. A writer for *Time*, Iyer approaches his subject with a camera-sharp eye, a style that suggests a cross between Paul Theroux and Hunter Thompson, and a willingness to go beyond the obvious conclusions about the hybrid cultures of East and West." Actually, Iyer's text remains mired in the "obvious conclusions," particularly in regard to gender and tourism. See Pico Iyer, *Video Night in Kathmandu: And Other Reports from the Not-So-Far-East* (New York: Vintage Books, 1989).

25. For useful discussions on hybridity see Lata Mani, "Multiple Mediations: Feminist Scholarship

in the Age of Multinational Reception," *Inscriptions* 5 (1989): 1–24; and see essays in this volume by Inderpal Grewal and Caren Kaplan.

26. Nelly Richard, "Postmodernism and Periphery," *Third Text* 2 (Winter 1987/88): 11.

27. Ibid., 12.

28. Kumkum Sangari, "The Politics of the Possible," in JanMohamed and Lloyd, *The Nature and Context of Minority Discourse*, 222–23.

29. Ibid., 240.

30. Kwame Anthony Appiah, "Is the Post- in Postmodernism the Post- in Postcolonial?" *Critical Inquiry* 17:2 (Winter 1991): 342–43.

31. See Immanuel Wallerstein, *The Modern World-System: Capitalist Agriculture and the Origins of the European World-Economy in the Sixteenth Century* (New York: Academic Press, 1974). See also *The Modern World-System II: Mercantilism and the Consolidation of the European World-Economy* (New York: Academic Press, 1980); and *The Modern World-System III: The Second Era of Great Expansion of the Capitalist World-Economy, 1730–1840* (San Diego, Calif.: Academic Press, 1988).

32. See Janet Wolff's critique of Wallerstein, "The Global and the Specific: Reconciling Conflicting Theories of Culture," in *Culture, Globalization, and the World-System*, ed. Anthony D. King (London: Macmillan Education Ltd., 1991), 161–73; and Akhil Gupta, "The Political Economy of Post-Independence India—A Review Article," *The Journal of Asian Studies* 48:4 (November 1989): 787–97.

33. David Washbrook, "South Asia, the World-System, and World Capitalism," *The Journal of Asian Studies* 49:3 (August 1990): 479–508.

34. Armand Mattelart, *Transnationals and the Third World: The Struggle for Culture*, trans. David Buxton (South Hadley, Mass.: Bergin and Garvey Publishers, 1983), 150.

35. Fernando Enrique Cardoso, cited in Mattelart, *Transnationals*, 18.

36. See Janet Wolff's critique of the speakers at a symposium on culture globalization at SUNY Binghamton in April 1989, in particular her assertion that the speakers did not problematize or historicize their terms ("The Global and the Specific," 166).

37. Washbrook, "South Asia," 503.

38. Brian Berry, "Comparative Geography of the Global Economy: Cultures, Corporations, and the Nation-State," *Economic Geography* 65 (1989): 1–18.

39. Barbara Abou-El-Haj, "Languages and Models for Cultural Exchange," in King, *Culture, Globalization, and the World-System*, 143.

40. Ranajit Guha, "On Some Aspects of the Historiography of Colonial India," in *Selected Subaltern Studies*, ed. Ranajit Guha and Gayatri Chakravorty Spivak (New York: Oxford University Press, 1988), 37–44.

41. Stuart Hall, "The Local and the Global: Globalization and Ethnicity," in King, *Culture, Globalization, and the World-System*, 36.

42. Ibid., 38.

43. Ibid., 39.

44. Abou-El-Haj, "Languages and Models," 141.

45. Armand Mattelart, *Transnationals*, 3.

46. Ibid., 4.

47. This point has emerged in discussions with Tani Barlow.

48. Arjun Appadurai, "Disjuncture and Difference in the Global Cultural Economy," *Public Culture* 2, no. 2 (Spring 1990): 21.

49. Ibid., 6.

50. Janet Abu-Lughod, "Going Beyond Global Babble," in King, *Culture, Globalization, and the World-System*, 135.

51. Ibid., 136.

52. Mattelart, *Transnationals*, 17.

53. See Ulf Hannerz, "The World in Creolization," *Africa* 57, no. 4 (1987): 550.

54. Ulf Hannerz, "Notes on the Global Ecumene," *Public Culture* 1, no. 2 (Spring 1989): 74.

55. See *Recasting Women: Essays in Indian Colonial History*, ed. Kumkum Sangari and Sudesh Vaid (New Brunswick, N.J.: Rutgers University Press, 1990).

56. Ella Shohat, "Notes on the Post-Colonial," *Social Text* 31/32 (1992): 100.

57. "Editors' Comments," *Public Culture* 1, no. 1 (Fall 1988): 1.

58. In a recent essay, Anne McClintock argues that the term "post-colonialism," in reinforcing a logic of linear temporality, ressurects colonialism: "The term heralds the end of a world era, but within the same trope of linear progress that animated that era. . . . Colonialism returns at the moment of its disappearance." See Anne McClintock, "The Angel of Progress: Pitfalls of the Term 'Post-Colonialism,'" *Social Text* 31/32 (1992): 85. For another cogent discussion of the limits and possibilities of "post-coloniality" see Ruth Frankenberg and Lata Mani, "Crosscurrents, Crosstalk: Race, 'Post-coloniality,' and the Politics of Location," *Cultural Studies* 7 (Spring 1993): 292–310.

59. See Arjun Mukherjee's critique of the theory of the "postcolonial" associated with the work of Helen Tiffin, Bill Ashcroft, and Gareth Griffiths, best represented in their edited collection, *The Empire Writes Back: Theory and Practice in Post-Colonial Literatures* (London: Routledge, 1989). Arjun Mukherjee, "Whose Post-Colonialism and Postmodernism?" *World Literature Written in English* 30, no. 2 (Autumn 1990): 1–9. See also Simon During's "Postmodernism or Post-colonialism Today," *Textual Practice* 1, no. 1 (Spring 1987): 32–47.

60. See Gayatri Chakravorty Spivak, *In Other Worlds: Essays in Cultural Politics* (New York: Methuen, 1987); *The Post-Colonial Critic*, ed. Sarah Harasym (New York: Routledge, 1990).

61. Kobena Mercer, "Welcome to the Jungle," 45.

62. See in particular Chandra Talpade Mohanty's critique of Robin Morgan's *Sisterhood is Global*, "The Politics of Experience," 33.

63. Kumkum Sangari and Sudesh Vaid, "Recasting Women: An Introduction," in *Recasting Women*, 18.

64. See Katie King, "Lesbianism in Multi-National Reception: Global Gay Formations and Local Homosexualities," *Camera Obscura* 28 (1992): 79–99; Lourdes Arguelles and B. Ruby Rich, "Homosexuality, Homophobia, and Revolution: Notes toward an Understanding of the Cuban Lesbian and Gay Male Experience," Part I, *Signs* 9 (1984): 683–99, and Part II, *Signs* 11 (Autumn 1985): 120–36; Ana Maria Alonso and Maria Teresa Koreck, "Silences: 'Hispanics,' AIDS, and Sexual Practices," *differences* 1, no. 1 (Winter 1989): 101–24; and Lourdes Arguelles, *Homosexualities and Transnational Migration* (forthcoming).

65. Enloe, *Bananas, Beaches, and Bases*.

66. Norma Alarcón, "The Theoretical Subject(s) of *This Bridge Called My Back* and Anglo-American Feminism," in *Making Face, Making Soul/Haciendo Caras: Creative and Critical Perspectives by Women of Color*, ed. Gloria Anzaldúa (San Francisco: Aunt Lute, 1990), 358.

67. See "Some Functions of Feminist Criticism: Or, the Scandal of the Mute Body," where Modleski asserts that romance fiction is "the property of us all—and not of just white Anglo-Saxon and American women either." Citing the translation of Harlequin's and other romances into many languages, she suggests that "the limits of a 'sub-cultural' approach to women's romances ought to be clear, since the popularity of romances is a *cross*-cultural phenomenon, and romances provide women with a common fantasy structure to ensure their continued psychic investment in their oppression." Tania Modleski, *Feminism Without Women*, 43.

68. Tania Modleski, "Cinema and the Dark Continent: Race and Gender in Popular Film," *Feminism Without Women*, 115–34.

69. Jane Flax, "Postmodernism and Gender Relations in Feminist Theory," in Nicholson, *Feminism/Postmodernism*, 39–62.

70. Nancy Fraser and Linda J. Nicholson, "Social Criticism without Philosophy: An Encounter between Feminism and Postmodernism," in Nicholson, *Feminism/Postmodernism*, 34.

71. Clara Connolly, "Washing Our Linen: One Year of Women Against Fundmentalism," *Feminist Review* 37 (Spring 1991): 69.

72. Ibid., 76.

73. Deniz Kandiyoti, "Introduction," *Women, Islam and the State* (Philadelphia: Temple University Press, 1991), 8.

74. Melissa Spatz, "A 'Lesser' Crime: A Comparative Study of Legal Defenses for Men Who Kill Their Wives," *Columbia Journal of Law and Social Problems* 24 (1991): 600.

75. Spatz, "A 'Lesser' Crime," 597.

76. Sara Diamond, *Spiritual Warfare* (Boston: South End Press, 1989), 48.

77. Ibid., 42.

78. Cited in Pragna Patel, "Review Essay: Alert for Action," *Feminist Review* 37 (Spring 1991): 95–105.

79. Deniz Kandiyoti, "Introduction," 17.

80. We are indebted to the Cultural Defense Study group for their analysis of how cultural defense works in the U.S. courts. Thanks to Jacqueline Agtuca, Deanna Jang, Mimi Kim, Debbie Lee, Jayne Lee, Lata Mani, Leni Marin, Beckie Masaki, Alexandra Saur, and Leti Volpp. In particular, we would like to thank Jayne Lee for sharing her research and her work.

PART ONE

Gender, Nation, and Critiques of Modernity

TWO

The Female Body and Nationalist Discourse: *The Field of Life and Death* Revisited

Lydia Liu

Benedict Anderson's book *Imagined Communities* has exerted a good deal of impact on the study of nationalism in recent years.[1] Scholars of poststructuralist persuasion in particular find his idea of imagined political community rather useful for deconstructing established notions of national identity. But having understood that nation is a historical construct rather than a manifestation of some unchanging essence, is there anything else that we need to know about histories of the nation, nationhood, and national identity? For instance, has the notion of national identity ever been contested by alternative narratives of the self? If so, what historical possibilities arise as a result of their engagement and contention?

This essay will situate the problem of national identity in the intersecting area between the female body and nationalist discourse. In so doing, I intend to go beyond the current battle between essentialism and constructivism, and rethink the nation as a territory of struggle between competing subject positions, narratives, and voices where nationalism or nationalisms may win, as they have indeed won in many parts of the world, but cannot wipe out the traces of such struggles. On a theoretical level, I will try to answer some of the questions raised by recent postcolonial and feminist scholarship with regard to the rise of nationalism in non-Western countries; in terms of specific histories, I will focus on the relationship between gender and national literature in modern China. The central text to be discussed in this essay is a Chinese novel entitled *The Field of Life and Death* written by Xiao Hong, a female novelist from Manchuria. Published in Shanghai in 1935, this novel engages a crucial moment in modern Chinese history when nationalist discourse constitutes the female body as a privileged signifier and various struggles are waged over the meaning and ownership of that body. Those struggles, as I will try to demonstrate, open up an important avenue toward our understanding of the problematic of nationalism itself.

Xiao Hong (1911–42) lived in a time of national crisis and wrote novels, stories, and essays in response to contending discourses that were fought out on the symbolic terrain of the female body. Because of her ambivalent relationship with nationalism, her "canonical" status in modern (read "national") Chinese literature has been extremely controversial. My reading of her work, however, does not aim to improve her status in the canon so much as to bring into question the practice of nation-oriented and male-centered literary criticism. In that sense, I will be dealing with two levels of discursive practice surrounding her text: production and reception. The former involves Xiao Hong's engagement with nationalist discourse within the space of her novel and the latter a body of criticism that seeks to recuperate her text in the name of national literature. In so doing, I hope to help reframe the questions of nation, gender, and literary practice as first posed by postcolonial, poststructuralist, and feminist theories.

Chatterjee, Bhabha, and the Critique of Nationalist Discourse

Partha Chatterjee's book *Nationalist Thought and the Colonial World* may be taken as representative of the postcolonial position on the question of nationalism.[2] In his critique of Ernest Gellner, Elie Kedourie, and others, the author points out that both liberal-rationalist and conservative theories of nationalism operate within the ambit of Enlightenment philosophy and have proved incapable of situating either the problem or their own knowledge within a dialectic that relates culture to power.[3] It is for the purpose of elucidating the complex relation between nationalist discourse and colonial domination in the production of knowledge that postcolonial historians like Chatterjee reopened the issue for us and made it possible to approach it as a field of discourse.

Chatterjee's argument is that nationalism as a European discourse of domination is appropriated by Third World nations for self-empowerment in the struggle for independence. This lack of autonomy, however, marks a paradoxical situation, because the subjugated people who use nationalism to oppose the colonial rule or European hegemony invariably speak the language of colonialism—modernity, progress, development, and so on: "The very process of approximation means their continued subjection under a world order which only sets their tasks for them and over which they have no control."[4] Speaking in a dialectical framework, he points out that nationalism is, nonetheless, capable of producing a *different* discourse marked by political contests and struggles for power. Hence the historical possibility for the displacement of the dominant framework of knowledge and the subversion of its authority. This insight allows him to critique Benedict Anderson, who elides the twists and turns, the suppressed possibilities, and the unresolved contradictions in the complex process of nation making.

The dialectic of this theory lands him in certain difficulty, though. In the course of contrasting the claims of nationalist discourse with its paradoxical reliance on post-Enlightenment European thought, Chatterjee introduces two terms, the thematic and the problematic, to distinguish between "levels" within the structure of a body of knowledge where nationalist thought opposes the dominant colonialist discourse at one level (the problematic) and yet seems to accept the content of that discourse at another (the thematic). This schematization seems to me rather simplistic. By assigning the agency of the native intellectual primarily to the level of the problematic, he inevitably downplays the coauthorship of nationalist ideology within the perimeter of the thematic. It is not as if the author were unaware of the question of coauthorship; after all, his analysis of the thought of Bankimchandra Chattopadhyay gives us a good example of the way in which the agency of the local intellectual could work on both levels. The problem is that the cultural domination of the West is homogenized and totalized to such a degree that alternative narrative within the nation-space is virtually written out as a theoretical possibility.[5] Ironically, the consequence of his position, as is sometimes the case with other critics of colonialism, is that the hegemonic discourse of the West is made out as an absolute power in constituting the native.[6] It remains yet to be seen whether this dialectic of the problematic and the thematic, however subtly formulated, is capable of adequately explaining the contradictions and historical possibilities that arose from the complex process of nation building in the colonial and semicolonial world.

Take the rise of nationalism in late Qing China, for example. Here we find an extremely complex situation in which various narratives about the nation, including the European notion of nationalism, fought against one another. In its early stage, "Western" nationalism, in particular its racial theory, was deployed primarily by revolutionaries and the National Essence group to assert their Chinese identity against the non-Chinese Manchu court. The discourse helped them reinforce the native resistance movement that had contested the Manchu foreign regime long before Western powers invaded China. Even as they spoke in the language of the Western Enlightenment, modern intellectuals nevertheless appropriated some of the major tropes from the earlier resistance movement, such as the opposition between the Chinese and foreign barbarians.[7] So the idea that the meaning of Western knowledge (on the thematic level) cannot be changed or transformed when brought into contact with local traditions and local struggles is ahistorical at best and hegemonic at worst.

As Gyan Prakash reminds us, post-Orientalist historiography must move beyond the East/West binary and disclose that "which is concealed when issues are posed as India versus Britain. . . . The purpose of such disclosures is to write those histories that history and historiography have excluded."[8] This is the stance that Homi K. Bhabha adopts in his poststructuralist theory of the nation and nationalist discourse. Unlike Chatterjee, Bhabha refuses to locate Third World nations in a homogeneous space or make totalizing claims on their behalf. Instead, he suggests alternative interventions that would allow us to talk about the nation and cultural difference without reproducing the binaries of East/West and Self/Other, or refixing cultural boundary. In his introduction to *Nation and Narration*, he reads the nation as "an agency of *ambivalent* narration that holds culture at its most productive position, as a force for 'subordination, fracturing, diffusing, reproducing, as much as producing, creating, forcing, guiding.' "[9] Such a poststructuralist reading evokes the margins of the nation-space:

> To reveal such a margin is, in the first instance, to contest claims to cultural supremacy, whether these are made from the "old" post-imperialist metropolitan nations, or on behalf of the "new" independent nations of the periphery. The marginal or "minority" is not the space of a celebratory, or utopian, self-marginalization. It is a much more substantial intervention into those justifications of modernity — progress, homogeneity, cultural organicism, the deep nation, the long past — that rationalizes the authoritarian, "normalizing" tendencies within cultures in the name of the national interest or the ethnic prerogative.[10]

To foreground the margins of the nation-space is to question the legitimate politics of the state-representing-the-nation. Its purpose is to force open the totalizing boundaries of "imagined communities," and to problematize languages and symbolic systems — nationalist discourse — that designate the people as one. Bhabha borrows the term "occult instability" from Frantz Fanon to emphasize the continual slippage of cultural signification where meanings become ambivalent and unstable. Furthermore, he perceives the possibility of a nonpluralistic politics of difference in Kristeva's notion of "demassification of difference" and in the heterogeneous structure of Derridean supplementary in writing. In his view, women, the colonized, ethnic minorities, immigrants, and other marginal people occupy a place of "cultural undecidability" and may help establish the margins of the nation-space.[11] Once those margins are established, the threat of cultural difference is no longer a problem of "other people." "It becomes a question of the otherness of the people-as-one. The national subject splits in the ethnographic perspective of culture's contemporaneity and provides both a theoretical position and a narrative authority for marginal voices or minority discourse."[12]

The splitting of the national subject no doubt provides us with a useful point of entry to the contradictory space of nationalist discourse. But, as Henry Louis Gates, Jr., points out, Bhabha's reliance on the psychoanalytical explanation of culture—one that maps a problematic of subject-formation onto a Self-Other model—raises more questions than it solves, because his approach tends to collapse psychic repression with colonial repression such that history is virtually emptied of its concrete expressions.[13] Only within such an abstract framework, as can be seen in Bhabha's discussion of minority discourse, can women, the colonized, ethnic minorities, immigrants, and other marginal people be lumped together and leveled down to homogeneous totality. In her critique of Bhabha, Benita Parry warns that distinct and specific modes of oppression must not be conflated for the sake of another totalizing theory.[14] Each and every discursive system of discrimination, such as the one based on gender and sexuality, deserves an explanation specific to its own historical practice.

Chinese Woman and National History

It goes without saying that the question of woman in nationalist discourse must be treated on its own ground rather than that of the totalizing theory of oppression. But does it mean that one must rely on a universal idea of woman? When Kristeva brings the gendered body to bear on the national problematic in "Women's Time," she finds it necessary to dismantle the often-assumed term "woman" in contemporary feminism, which she sees as globalizing the problems of women of different milieu, age, civilization, and varying psychic structure.[15] But instead of pursuing a historical explanation for this problem, as critics of Eurocentric feminism have tried to do in various ways,[16] her critique of the notion of "Universal Woman" falls back on an essentialist view of the female body in Western culture and on a relativist notion of the Other that orientalizes her knowledge about women of the non-Western world.[17]

Historians of women's movements show, on the other hand, that national history is indeed capable of inventing a totalistic idea of woman (not necessarily by women themselves) and deploying it as a category in various local struggles. So the question is not so much whether one should reject the idea of "Universal Woman" as how to understand it as a theoretical problem. In most colonial and semicolonial countries, struggles for women's emancipation went hand in hand with national resistance movements and the "woman question" never failed to be part of the national agenda. Laura Nader points out that revolution in the context of modernity invariably sought gender hegemony in order "to change the traditional control over women as part of the transfer of power over women from the kinship group to the state."[18] Although the state had always been a dominant presence in imperial China, women as a social category never had a place on the state agenda. It was not until the late nineteenth and early twentieth centuries that the totalizing notion of *funü* (women) began to enter history and national politics, and became what Tani E. Barlow calls a state category.[19]

The story of women's liberation in China was as inextricably tied up with the concerns of nation building as it was in the rest of the colonial or semi-colonial world. For instance, during the late Qing Reform Movement, it was male nationalist/reformists like Kang Youwei, Liang Qichao, and Tan Sitong who acted as the chief spokesmen for oppressed Chinese women. Kang and Liang condemned the atrocity of inflicting corporal mutilation on women by footbinding and campaigned vehemently against the practice. In his "Memorial Requesting a Ban on the Binding of Women's Feet" (1898), Kang based his argument on the need to strengthen the nation:

> From the perspective of the government of the state, it [footbinding] punishes innocent women without justification. From the perspective of the kindness and love of the family, it is injurious to parental kindness and love. From the perspective of human health, it gives rise to needless sickness. From the perspective of increasing military strength, it weakens the race hereditarily. From the perspective of the beauty of our customs, it invites the slander of those other nations known as "barbarians."[20]

Kang's student, Liang Qichao, developed his position on women's liberation consistently on a nationalist basis. In an essay entitled "General Discussion of Reform" (1896–97), he attributed the nation's poverty and weakness partly to women's exclusion from productive labor and education. He advocated women's education mainly because it was directly connected with the survival of the nation. Prenatal care and maternal education were of primary concern because the country needed a strong military and the health of children was paramount to the task of "preserving the nation" and "preserving the race."[21] Clearly, the need to mobilize the nation in the face of imperialist powers gave rise to the totalizing notion of women from the first moment of Chinese modernity.

Ironically, when a young woman named Qiu Jin decided to cast her lot with the revolution, she ignored Liang's advice and left her children behind. Not only did this remarkable woman try to appropriate male identity by cross-dressing and behaving like a man, she also appropriated their nationalism. In a manifesto entitled "A Respectful Proclamation to China's 200 Million Women Comrades" published in *Baihua bao* (Colloquial Magazine), which she herself edited during her stay in Tokyo (1904–6), Qiu Jin exhorted Chinese women not to have their feet bound but to educate themselves: "The nation is on the verge of collapse. Men can no longer protect it, so how can we depend on them? If we fail to rouse ourselves, it will be too late after the nation perishes."[22] In her dangerous life as a political activist, Qiu Jin modeled herself on Madame Roland, Sophia Perovskaya, and Hua Mulan, and called herself the Female Knight. Her execution in 1907 by the Manchu government instantly turned her into a national heroine. But, as Ono Kazuko points out,

> The main point of her activities was less as an activist for women than it was as a woman revolutionary. There was something awe-inspiring in the look of this woman—sitting dashingly astride a horse and wearing a man's dark blue long-sleeved gown—that did not generally make one think of women.[23]

Between her split identity as woman and Chinese, Qiu Jin chose to be the latter, which she understandably equates with masculinity: "I want somehow to have a mind as strong as a man's. If I first take on the form of a man, then I think my mind too will eventually become that of a man."[24] Qiu Jin carries the patriarchal ideology of nationalism to its logical end when she vehemently rejects her female identity.

Xiang Jingyu, the first female member of the Central Committee of the Chinese Communist party, is another good example of women's involvement with nationalism. Representing the party line on the gender question in the 1920s, Xiang decided to subsume the specific issue of women's emancipation under the broader concerns of the nation. She argued that the liberation of women was not a separate issue and that women should not expect to be emancipated until the whole nation was liberated. In the manner of Qiu Jin, she accepted the totalizing claims of nationalist discourse and threw herself wholeheartedly into the labor movement.[25] To Xiang Jingyu and other revolutionary women who decided to sacrifice their lives for the national cause, revolution seemed to hold out the same promise as it did to their male comrades. But is the nation such a gender-neutral idea as it pretends to be? Xiao Jun's first novel, *Village in August*, provides an illuminating answer to this question by demonstrating that patriarchy is indeed capable of reinventing itself in multifarious forms. The novel is worth mentioning at this point not only because the author had a unique personal relationship with Xiao Hong (whose *Field of Life and Death* will be discussed below) as her common-law husband for many years, but because the two authors published under strikingly similar circumstances and yet their views on gender and nationalism contrast sharply.

Xiao Jun's novel epitomizes the ways in which nationalist discourse deploys gender during the war. It contains a story about a peasant widow named Li Qisao, who suffers the horrible fate of losing her husband, lover, and child to the war and, on top of all her bereavements, is raped by a Japanese soldier. As a sign of symbolic exchange, the raped woman often serves as a powerful trope in anti-Japanese propaganda. Her victimization is used to represent, or more precisely, to eroticize China's own plight. In such a signifying practice, the female body is ultimately displaced by nationalism, whose discourse denies the specificity of female experience by giving larger symbolic meanings to the signifier of rape: namely, China itself is being violated by the Japanese rapist.[26] Since the nation itself is at stake, the crime of rape does not acquire meaning until it is committed by foreign intruders. Li Qisao's tragedy is supposed to inspire average Chinese men and women to follow the path of revolution. But what exactly does the revolution mean in terms of women's liberation? As one of the guerrilla soldiers in this novel puts it in a conversation:

> Revolution? It means exterminating all those parasites that have lorded it on us since our ancestors' days. It means driving away all the Japanese soldiers that are now occupying Manchuria so that we would have our own land to farm. We wouldn't have to pay the excise tax to feed those bloodsucking parasites. You understand? Let me give you an example. Before the revolution, one rich guy alone has three, five, eight, or even ten wives, whereas you, in your thirties, cannot even afford a single one. *After the revolution, you could get a wife without having to pay a penny!*[27] (italics mine)

The prospect is certainly rosy enough to those lower-class bachelors. But what about women? Are they given any subject position at all? The picture is particularly poignant in light of the fact that this guerrilla soldier has learned his revolutionary theory from Anna, the only intellectual woman in the troop. One wonders if revolutionary women like Anna or Xiang Jingyu (had the latter survived to see the victory) would be able to escape the fate of being mere wives after the success of the revolution to which they have contributed so much.[28]

But what makes national history so fascinating is that nationalist discourse, which gave rise to the totalistic notion of *funü*, has not been able to consume women's subjectivity. In a way, it has opened up the possibility for women to assume historical agency and challenge the very authority of that discourse.[29] Thus, alternative narratives of the self became reality when women like Ding Ling began to protest against the subjugation of women by new forms of patriarchy.[30] In her story "When I was in Xia Village," Ding Ling explores the conflict between the female body and nationalist discourse. The protagonist Zhenzhen, who has been raped by numerous Japanese soldiers, is hired by the resistance forces as a spy. Her body becomes the battleground on which military men from the opposing camps engage each other in their bid for sovereignty, and thus generates contradictory meanings. In the eyes of her own village folks she is a whore, whereas to revolutionary fighters she is a heroine who gives her body to the noble cause of the nation. Yet neither reading makes sense to Zhenzhen herself. The woman refuses to be read as a rape victim and, in the end, she decides to leave her native village for good in pursuit of education, knowledge, and the right to define the meaning of her own existence. In this story, "rape does not signify woman,"[31] nor does it signify the victimization of China.[32]

Xiao Hong and *The Field of Life and Death*

Like Ding Ling's story, Xiao Hong's novel *The Field of Life and Death* radically subverts the trope of the raped woman in nationalist discourse. As if in deliberate parody of Xiao Jun's novel, the rape that occurs in Xiao Hong's work, which is also set on the eve of the Anti-Japanese War, turns out to be committed by a Chinese man rather than by a Japanese soldier. The appropriation of the female body by nationalist discourse is contested relentlessly throughout. The remarkable thing about this novel is that the mise-en-scène of nationalist myths is narrated in stark contrast to the uncertain status of peasant women as national subjects, which raises poignant questions about what it means to be Chinese/peasant/woman. Gender, class, and national identities clash rather than conjoin, resulting in woman's loss of one identity or another and in her fractured subjectivity with regard to the nation.

It is a profound irony that the reception of Xiao Hong's novel in China has been dominated by nationalist discourse since its publication in 1935. Like Ye Zi's *Harvest* and Xiao Jun's *Village in August* (two other works in the Slave Society Series that Lu Xun, the most influential leftist writer of the time, helped put in print), Xiao Hong's novel has been evaluated primarily on the basis of nationalism from the very beginning.[33] Most critics celebrate the work as a "national allegory," a quintessential anti-imperialist novel imbued with patriotic spirit, so much so that one can hardly read Xiao Hong today without being aware of the existence of a highly developed, institutionalized, male-centered critical tradition that has tried to frame and determine the meaning of her work. Yet the gendered politics in the practice of literary criticism has largely escaped the notice of well-intentioned scholars in the West, being themselves trapped in a similar situation, and thus greatly complicates the way in which orientalized knowledge is produced or perceived.

Fredric Jameson's controversial article "Third-World Literature in the Era of Multinational Capitalism" is a good example of this. The essay begins with an interesting preamble about non-Western intellectuals and their obsession with the nation. The author apparently assumes that those intellectuals represent the "Third World" to the West and their representation is transparent and unproblematic. This assumption enables him to arrive at the much-disputed hypothesis of the essay; namely, "Third World" literature is characterized by national allegory. In light of the author's unreflexive relationship with the non-

Western intellectual, his hypothesis becomes meaningful and revealing, rather than simply false, because it plays right into what I would call the nation-oriented and male-centered practice of literary criticism within some of the non-Western countries. It never occurs to him that this kind of critical practice, rather than "Third World" literature, is the stuff that the non-Western (male) intellectual represents so "authentically" to the West.[34] Jameson's attempt to establish "Third World" literature as national allegory elides the agency of literary criticism in the production of canons and texts within the national context. For instance, his choice and reading of Lu Xun is to a large extent predetermined by established readings that surround Lu Xun's text in the modern Chinese literary canon. So rather than just another instance of orientalism or "rhetoric of otherness," as his critics often suggest, I see in his essay an eloquent example of the coauthorship of nationalist discourse by Marxist intellectuals of the First World and the Third World.[35]

The allegorical readings of Xiao Hong's novel were initially framed by the views of Hu Feng and Lu Xun, who contributed an epilogue and a preface, respectively, to the first edition. As editor of the Slave Society Series, Hu Feng wrote his epilogue to praise the anti-Japanese spirit of the book and the awakening of the Chinese peasants to nationalism. "These antlike, ignorant men and women, sad but resolute, stood on the front line of the sacred war of nationalism," he says. "Once they were like ants, living in order to die. Now they were titans, dying in order to live."[36] Lu Xun does not force the epithet of nationalism onto the novel in his much quoted Preface, but he too obscures the fact that Xiao Hong's novel is more about the lives of rural women than "the tenacity of the people of northern China in their struggle for survival and resistance to death."[37] The field of *sheng* (birth, life) and *si* (death), as my analysis will show, primarily represents the experience of the female body—specifically, the two areas of rural experience relating to peasant women: childbearing and death from suicide, sickness, or abuse. Lu Xun's own national agenda, which comes out clearly in his allusion to the rumor of war in Shanghai's Zhabei district and to places such as Harbin, or the British and French Concessions, is responsible for the blind spot in his reading.

It is not surprising that nationalist interpretation of this novel is the rule rather than an exception in Xiao Hong scholarship.[38] In his Preface to Xiao's later novel, *Tales of Hulan River*, Mao Dun, a leading critic of the time, also judges the author on a basis of her commitment to the national cause, although his opinion runs counter to that of Hu Feng. In short, Xiao Hong is criticized for *not* participating in the national struggle this time. Reminiscing about the last moment of her life in Hong Kong, Mao says:

It is hard to understand how a woman with her high ideals, who had struggled against reaction, could "hibernate" in such stirring times as the years just before and after 1940. A friend of hers, trying to explain her frustration and apathy, ascribed them to a series of emotional shocks that confined this poet richer in feeling than intellect within the small circle of her private life. (Although she condemned that circle, some inertia kept her from breaking boldly with it.) She was cut off completely from the tremendous *life*-and-*death* struggle being waged outside. As a result, although her high principles made her frown on the activities of the intellectuals of her class and regard them as futile talk, she would not plunge into the laboring masses of workers and peasants or change her life radically. Inevitably, then, she was frustrated and lonely.[39] (italics mine)

It is true that Xiao Hong did not show the kind of enthusiasm for the national cause with which Hu Feng credited her. As a matter of fact, she did not even involve herself in the antiwar propaganda organized by the Chinese Writers' Anti-Aggression Association.[40] As a woman, denigrated as "richer in feeling than intellect" by Mao Dun, she was engaged in a different kind of struggle, a struggle that did not oblige her to share Mao's view of private and collective experience or, for that matter, male-centered notions of society, nation, and war. If, to the author of *The Field of Life and Death* and *Tales of Hulan River*, the meaning of "life" and "death" resides in the individual body – particularly the female body – more than in the rise and fall of a nation, then her lack of commitment to nationalism should by no means be construed as some kind of failure.

Not that Xiao Hong did not wish to resist Japanese aggression or feel attracted to the national cause. Her dilemma was that she had to face two enemies rather than one: imperialism and the patriarchy. This dilemma is vividly captured in an essay she wrote in August 1937, "A Night of Insomnia," where her ambivalent feelings about Manchuria contrast sharply with the nostalgia felt by her lover Xiao Jun. She finds it difficult to share the latter's passionate yearning for home and questions it from a female point of view. "But what about me?" she asks. "Would your family treat an outsider such as a *xifu* (daughter-in-law) equally well?"[41] Since a woman is condemned to permanent exile by the stigma of her gender, there is no need for her to identify with any particular place:

As far as I am concerned, it always comes down to the same thing: either riding a donkey and journeying to an alien place, or staying put in other people's homes. I am never keen on the idea of homeland. Whenever people talk about home I cannot help but be moved, although I know perfectly well that I had become "homeless" even before the Japanese set their feet on that land (Manchuria). (Ibid.)

Xiao Hong's life story illustrates a series of frustrated attempts to sort out the meaning of being a woman and Chinese. She had fled from her tyrannic father long before she and Xiao Jun escaped from Japanese-occupied Manchuria. In the subsequent years she spent with Xiao Jun in Shanghai and elsewhere, she had the misfortune of being repeatedly abused and physically assaulted by him. When she could no longer bear his violence, she would often run away. Once she went so far as to leave China for Japan in order to get away from Xiao Jun for a period of time. Given the deteriorating relationship between the two countries in 1936, the choice of Japan as her country of sojourn invites symptomatic reading. Whatever reasons might lie behind it, her choice indicates a strong desire to protect her body and mind from male domination even if it means exile from her homeland and loneliness in the enemy country.

In analyzing Xiao Hong's novel, I will be concentrating on the body of peasant woman as an important site of contestatory meanings. As a matter of fact, such a reading is partially suggested by the controversy over the cover design of the novel the author herself made in 1935. Needless to say, critics have a hard time trying to pin down the exact meaning of the drawing. Some say that the black shadow suggests an old fortress while the deep crimson in the background represents the blood of the people of Manchuria who died during the war of resistance. Others hold that the black area actually represents the map of Japanese- occupied Manchuria.[42] In an interesting article on Xiao Hong as an artist, Liu Fuchen points out that the black shadow is the profile of a woman's head while the diagonal line across the cover symbolizes the divided territory of China. He reads the uplifted face of the peasant woman as well as the firm lines of her neck and mouth as representing the anger and strength of the people of Manchuria in their struggle against the Japanese.[43] But Liu fails to explain why Xiao Hong uses a female head instead of a male head to represent the people of Manchuria. Having hinted at a possible reading from a gendered point of view, he immediately displaces it with nationalist discourse. If one takes the black shadow as representing a female head coinciding with (and parodying) the map of Manchuria, the diagonal line across the page may very well be interpreted as a symbol of the split national subject as well as the divided territory of China. As for the conjecture that the deep crimson may signify the color of the blood shed by the people of Manchuria, there is also strong evidence within the text that refers to women's blood specifically, because the female body in this novel is always linked with bleeding, injury, deformation, or death, be it from childbirth, beating, sickness, or suicide. The omnipresence of the female body casts an ominous shadow on nationalist discourse and insists on assigning its idiosyncratic meanings to the life-and-death struggle in rural Manchuria. Of course, one need not accept any of these read-

一九三五年版《生死場》封面

ings, but it is worth noting that the controversy surrounding the cover design calls into question the authority of a single nationalist interpretation that has heretofore prevailed in Xiao Hong scholarship and thus opens up a space for alternative reading.

What does the female body have to do with nationalism? Critics have often wondered about the fact that Xiao Hong's anti-Japanese novel is filled with details about women's lives in the village and does not begin to deal with the Japanese invasion until the last few chapters. Two Chinese women critics, Meng Yue and Dai Jinhua, have suggested in their book *Fuchu lishi dibiao* (Emerging from the horizon of history) that the meaning of *sheng* (birth, life) and *si* (death) should be perceived in terms of the experience of the female body, but their reading does not directly engage nationalist discourse.[44] In what follows, I intend to push their reading further by showing that the female body actually provides the critical angle for viewing the rise and fall of the nation rather than the other way around.

The boundary of the female body in this novel is chiefly defined by rural women's experience of childbirth, disease, sexuality, aging, and death. Despite the apparent allusion to the Buddhist concept of *samsara* in *sheng* and *si*, the novel does not espouse the Buddhist faith of some of its characters; on the con-

trary, it stresses the plight of the female body, locating the meaning of its suffering in the immediate socioeconomic context of this world rather than in a
world of *karma*. Death, for example, is the horrible disintegration of the body
rather than the ultimate escape from the distresses of life. Poverty, ignorance,
class exploitation, imperialism, and the patriarchy all conspire to reduce the rural people, especially women, to no more than animalistic existence.

As Howard Goldblatt points out, animal imagery is one of the most striking
features of Xiao Hong's language.[45] The mere fact that animals are part of any
rural scene can hardly account for the eerie power of those images in this novel.
What is emphasized is the sheer physicality of the animal existence, stubbornly
mute and intransigent, that parallels the condition of human existence in the
rural community. The body of the animal, which exists, decays, and falls apart,
often stands as a metaphor for the degradation of the human body. Xiao
Hong's language becomes particularly powerful when metonymy as well as
metaphor are used to evoke animals and humans contiguously so that the two
species are joined in the homogeneous space of the body. In chapter 3, for example, Mother Wang is ordered by her master to sell the old mare to the
slaughterhouse. The language with which the narrator describes her trip goes
as follows: "A falling leaf landed on Mother Wang's head. It lay there silently.
She drove her old mare ahead, wearing a yellow leaf on her head; the old horse,
the old woman, the old leaf—they were walking down the road that led into
the city."[46] The dying animal, the old woman, and the fallen leaf are coordi-
nated in a single syntactic sequence—reminiscent of classical Chinese song-
poetry—that emphasizes the process of aging involving all three. The presence
of the old mare evokes the oldness of Mother Wang metonymically, since the
two have grown old together serving the same master and have both loved and
suffered as mothers. The metonymy furthermore transforms itself into a metaphor when Mother Wang arrives at the slaughterhouse: "It was a short street,
at the end of which a double black door stood open. As she drew nearer, she
could see bloodstains splattered all over the door. The old lady was frightened
by the bloodstains and felt as if she herself were entering an execution
ground."[47] The hideous sight of coils of steaming intestines, the stench, dis-
membered leg bones, horse hooves, and animal hides bring home the most so-
matic aspect of death that connects the aging animal to the old woman.

The intimate experience of the body shared by female animals and women
alike is presented metonymically in chapter 6, which contains several shocking
scenes of childbirth:

> On the haystack behind the house a bitch was giving birth. Its limbs trembled,
> and its whole body shook. After a long period of time the puppies were born.

In the warm of the season the entire village was occupied with the birth of its young. Big sows were leading their litters of piglets squealing and running, while the bellies of others were still big, nearly scraping the ground, their many teats virtually overflowing.

It was evening. Fifth Sister's elder sister could delay no longer. She went inside and spoke to her mother-in-law. "Get one of the old women. I really don't feel well." . . .

Her mother-in-law gathered up the straw, stirring up clouds of dust. The naked woman squirmed on the *k'ang* like a fish.[48]

The bitch, the sows, and the woman whose naked body resembled that of a fish give birth in the same season, inhabit the same ritualistic space, and evoke one another contiguously. In their experience of the body, female animals and women have more in common than women and men do. The agony of having one's flesh torn apart, bones cracked, and life endangered generates a kind of knowledge impermeable to the male sex. What is worse for a woman like Fifth Sister's elder sister is that not only does her husband refuse to empathize with her pain but he hates her: "Feign death, will you? Let's see if you still want to feign death now." In a drunken state, he flings his tobacco pouch at the wife whose body is soaked in blood and already has the look of a corpse. The woman "dared not move a single muscle, for like the child in front of a patriarch, she lived in dread of her man."[49] In the end, she is delivered of a dead infant, whose body joins birth and death in an uncanny moment.

Entitled "Days of Punishment," chapter 6 casts an extremely negative light on the fertility of life. The excess of life certainly aggravates poverty in this rural village; more important, in the act of bringing forth new life the female body is severely punished. As the narrator describes this uniquely female world, her language is punctuated alternately with compassion for the agonizing body of the mother and bitter mockery of the self-inflicted disaster driven by man's instinct to continue the species. Her compassion shines forth in the following description: "The naked woman could no longer even crawl; she was unable to muster the final burst of effort in this moment of *sheng* [birth, life] and *si* [death]."[50] Besides Fifth Sister's elder sister, there are three more village women who give birth in this crowded chapter. Golden Bough's labor is rendered difficult because her husband demanded sex the night before her labor. With the help of Mother Wang, she gives birth to a baby daughter, who is dashed to the ground by her own father a month later. Second Aunt Li has a miscarriage that nearly costs her own life. Even the foolish wife of Two-and-a-Half-Li struggles in labor. The birth of her baby is followed by someone's sow giving birth outside the window at the foot of the wall. The narrator's insistence on drawing the parallel between animals and humans in sexuality and childbirth sometimes verges on sarcasm:

> Cows and horses in their ignorance plant the seeds of their own suffering. At night as the people sat in the cool breeze, they could hear odd noises coming from the stable or cowshed. A bull that was probably battling for its mate crashed out of the shed, breaking the fence. . . .
> In the village, folks and beasts busied themselves at *sheng* and *si*.[51]

If life and childbirth are horrible realities for women, death is hardly a desirable alternative. Innumerable deaths ranging from infanticide, fatal disease, war, and epidemic occur in the space of this short novel. Although men also die, the female sex seems to succumb to death more often and, in most of those cases, the narrator individualizes the female victim for us. Among those victims are, for instance, Mother Wang's three-year-old daughter, Xiao Zhong, and her grown-up daughter, the Feng girl; Golden Bough's little daughter, who is murdered by her own father; an old woman from North Village who hangs herself with her granddaughter; the beautiful Yueying, who dies of paralysis and neglect; and finally, Two-and-a-Half-Li's wife and her child, who die during the war. The deaths of the few men are meaningful only inasmuch as they affect the life of the women. When Golden Bough becomes a widow and is forced to make her own living, we are not told when, where, why, or how her husband died, whereas the manner of women's deaths, such as Mother Wang's suicide, receives extended treatment. Two women attempt suicide in this novel, Mother Wang before the Japanese occupation and the old woman from North Village after that. The reason is one and the same—namely, the loss of their beloved sons. Instead of elaborating on Mother Wang's inner sorrow when she hears the news of her son's execution by the government, the narrator plunges directly into the physical aspect of her suicide and on the deformation of her body, giving detail such as the froth gathered on her black lips, her expanded stomach and chest, her terrifying howling, and the ghostly stare of her eyes. Mother Wang's suicidal attempt is presented neither as a heroic act nor as social protest. It is the horrifying deformation of the body that is emphasized.

Since rural women live most intensely with their bodies, the transformation of the body in sickness is no less shocking than its deformation in death. Yueying was once a beauty. After she comes down with paralysis, her husband begins to lose patience and decides to give her up completely. He refuses to give her water and, to torture her further, he places a pile of bricks on her bed as a prop for her weak body. When village women come to offer their help, they discover that the poor woman is so neglected that the lower part of her body is soaked with excrement and that the former beauty is reduced to a horrible freak:

> The whites of her eyes had turned greenish, and so had her straight front teeth. Her frizzled hair stuck close to her scalp. She looked like a sick cat, abandoned and without hope. . . . With her legs like two white bamboo poles stretched out before her, her skeleton formed a right angle with the *k'ang*. It was a human shape composed of nothing but threads. Only the head was broader; it sat on the torso like a lantern atop a pole.[52]

Yueying's bottom is so rotten that it has turned into caves for maggots. Little white crawling creatures drop on the arms of Mother Wang as she tries to wipe the sick woman's buttocks. Yueying dies in the end, but not until witnessing the horrible decomposition of her own body in the mirror.

Finally, the precariousness of the female body in this novel lies in rural women's experience of sexuality, which is always interconnected with pregnancy. Compared with the male body, the female body signifies a woman's lack of control over her destiny, not so much because sexual desire is an animal instinct as because patriarchy determines the meaning of desire and chastity so it serves the interests of men. Golden Bough finds herself in deep trouble when she becomes pregnant before marriage, so she begins to fear and loathe her body:

> Golden Bough was in torment. Her stomach had become a hideous monstrosity. She felt a hard object inside, which, when she pressed hard on it, became even more apparent. After she was certain that she was pregnant, her heart shuddered as though it were retching. She was seized with terror. When two butterflies wondrously alighted on top of the other on her knees, she only stared at the two copulating insects and did not brush them off. Golden Bough seemed to have become a scarecrow in a rice field.[53]

It is common for a woman to perceive literal alterations of the boundaries of her body such as violence, disease, and maiming as extreme threats to selfhood. Pregnancy, however, occupies a rather ambiguous domain of signification where meaning must be decided according to the social codes that govern a woman's behavior through regulating her body. In this instance, Golden Bough experiences her premarital pregnancy as the body's deformation (monstrosity) and her illegal fetus as an alien intruder. The free copulation of the butterflies brings out, by way of contrast, the impasse a woman like herself faces in human society: the patriarchy desires her body, demands her chastity, and punishes her for her transgressive acts. Like a scarecrow, her body is emptied of its contents and reduced to a signifier of predetermined functions. This gendered knowledge is transmitted to the daughter through the mother, who forbids Golden Bough to go near the edge of the river where men seduce women: " 'The wife of Fufa, didn't she come to ruin at the edge of the river? Even the children in the village were talking about it. Ai! . . . What kind of woman is that? Afterwards she had to marry Fufa. Her mother suffered such terrible shame that she couldn't hold her head up among the villagers any more.' "[54] It turns out that not only does Golden Bough tread the path of the wife of Fufa but she is seduced by none other than Fufa's nephew Chengye. Like Fufa before him, Chengye does not care much for the woman he seduces. Whenever the lovers meet, he simply pulls her down onto the ground and pounces on her body. He neither kisses her nor says words of love, but is driven by a basic desire. Their marriage, arranged by Golden Bough's mother, who wants to cover up the daughter's shame, repeats the ancient story of conjugal hostility in the patriarchal Chinese family. The husband curses the wife—"You lazy wife, what were you doing during the day?"—whereas it does not take long for the wife to learn how to curse a husband and feel that "men are heartless human beings, a feeling shared by the rest of the village women."[55]

Among the rural women treated in this novel, Mother Wang deserves special attention. She commands the respect of the village women and, to some extent, that of her own husband for possessing unusual wisdom, verbal power, courage, and an independent mind. In her youth, she left the home of her first husband permanently in protest against his physical abuse. Her present husband, Zhao San, is the third she marries. The village women often gather in her home and absorb her stories. Mother Wang's profound knowledge about *sheng* and *si* comes from her personal experience of love, loss, poverty, and sorrow. When she tells stories, she speaks as an authority on woman's "history," and her audience, all women, are awestruck by her manner and her voice. As Chinese women are denied subject positions in male history, storytelling or gossip becomes the only means of transmitting women's unique knowledge about life and death among themselves. One of the stories Mother Wang tells in the novel concerns the fatal fall of her three-year-old daughter. As she speaks, a streak of lightning appears in the sky and the speaker is suddenly transformed into a disembodied voice:

> Ah . . . I threw her in the haystack, with blood flowing all over the hay. Her little hand was trembling and blood was trickling from her nostrils and her mouth. It was like her throat had been cut. I could still hear a rumbling in her stomach. It was like a puppy run over by a cart. I've seen that happen with my own eyes. I've seen everything. . . .
> My child's name was Xiao Zhong. For several nights I suffered. I couldn't sleep. What was all that wheat worth? From then on, grains of wheat didn't matter much to me. Even now, nothing matters to me. I was only twenty then.[56]

From her intimate experience of death, which is so vividly filled with bleeding nostrils, mouth, throat, hands, and stomach, Mother Wang learns about the precariousness of the human body. It is this knowledge that gives her a strong character and a compassionate heart as she goes about assisting the village women in childbirth, nursing sick women such as Yueying, or even walking the old mare to the slaughterhouse. But Mother Wang's plight as a woman in the patriarchal society is also the cause of her ultimate rejection of female identity. After her attempt at suicide fails, she sets out to teach her daughter to be a woman warrior in order to avenge the death of her son. On the arrival of the Japanese in Manchuria, Mother Wang joins men in their struggle for national survival. It is no surprise that, from then on till the end of the novel, her authority dwindles in proportion to the significant rise of the village males as nationalist fighters.

This brings us to Xiao Hong's position on nationalism, which Hu Feng emphasizes so much in his Epilogue. If we compare her treatment of the rural life prior to the Japanese invasion with that of Xiao Jun in *Village in August*, the ambivalence of her attitude immediately comes into focus. For Xiao Jun, the rural world before the occupation does not in the least resemble the sordid life that Xiao Hong depicts. *Village in August* contains the following description:

> He [Little Red Face] recalled the peaceful days in his past. Would he once again feel free to enjoy his plough and his pipe as before? How soon would all this happen? When that wonderful day came about, was it true that every one of those who had bullied him and every Japanese who had taken his land would have been shot and killed?[57]

The discrepancy between the visions of the two authors is clearly attributable to the role that gender plays in each novel. Xiao Jun's work concentrates on the soldiers' life and on their skirmishes against the Japanese enemy, whereas Xiao Hong deals primarily with the life of women whose oppression makes it difficult to idealize the patriarchal society before or after occupation. Whatever happens to the nation, it is always the female body that suffers most. The final chapters of her novel make it clear that national identity is largely a male prerogative, which allows the village men to acquire national consciousness and preach the new gospel to their women despite their own lowly status in society. Mother Wang's husband Zhao San, for example, shows great enthusiasm for nationalist propaganda and particularly enjoys preaching to the widows:

> That night old Zhao San came home very late. He had been talking to everyone he met about the loss of the country, about saving the country, about volunteer armies and revolutionary armies . . . all these strange-sounding terms. . . .

He roused his son from his slumber and, with pride, told him about the
propaganda work he had been doing: how the widow in the east village had sent
her children back to her mother's house so that she could join the volunteer
army, and how the young men were gathering together. The old man was acting
like an official in a magistrate's office, swaying from side to side as he spoke. His
heart was also swaying, and his soul was taking giant strides.[58]

Zhao San's propaganda work elevates his worth in his own eyes, for nationalism enables the poor village males to transcend their class status by giving them
a new identity. This empowered identity, however, does not seem so different
from that of the "official in a magistrate's office" because it reproduces the old
patriarchal relation by putting men in the subject position of a new discourse
of power. Interestingly enough, women joining the army, all widows, must reject their female identity in a suicidal manner to become Chinese and fight for
the nation. With men it is a different matter. Not only does nationalism give
them a new sense of identity but it enhances their manhood at the same time.
Li Qingshan's speech given during a solemn occasion at which the village people pledge their loyalty to the nation shortly before taking off on an expedition-
ary journey indicates that nationalist discourse is unequivocally gendered:
" 'Brothers, what day is today? Do you know? Today is the day we dare to
die . . . it is decided . . . even if all our heads swing from the tops of the
trees throughout the village, we shall not flinch, right? Isn't that right,
brothers.' "[59] When the widows respond to the call, they immediately lose
their gender and join the ranks of the brothers. Ironically, they are the first to
shout: "Yes, even if we are cut into a million pieces!"[60] One can hardly miss
the familiar tone of the tragic Qiu Jin in their vows.

Chapter 13 represents the height of anti-Japanese sentiments in the novel.
Instead of endorsing nationalism, it demonstrates how the national subject
comes into being. Over the past years of his life, Zhao San was merely the head
of a rural household like the rest of the rural men, and he was also a coward
who dared not even defy his landlord. He "had not understood what a nation
was. In prior days he could even have forgotten his own nationality."[61] It is
through a discourse—nationalist discourse—that Zhao (re)constitutes himself as
a national subject and is reborn. Speaking to the volunteer fighters, he pours
out torrents of nationalist emotions:

The nation . . . the nation is lost! I . . . I am old, too. You are still young, you
go and save the nation! My old bones are useless! I'm an old nationless slave,
and I'll never see you rip up the Japanese flag with my own eyes. Wait until I'm
buried . . . then plant the Chinese flag over my grave, for I am a Chinese!
. . . I want a Chinese flag over my grave, for I am a Chinese! . . . I want a

Chinese flag. I don't want to be a nationless slave. Alive I am Chinese, and when I'm dead, I'll be a Chinese ghost . . . not a nation . . . nationless slave."[62]

This is characteristic of all nationalist discourses in which the individual takes up a subject position ("I," "I am," etc.) in a homogeneous space ("Chinese," "nation") and thereby acquires a new identity and finds a new purpose in life ("save the nation"). Even Two-and-a-Half-Li, who cannot live without his goat, ends up joining in the revolution.

Unlike other men, Two-and-a-Half-Li is a cripple and is symbolically castrated from his own sex; moreover, his unusual attachment to the animal marks him out as someone closer to women in identity than men. Just like Mother Wang, who caresses and talks to her mare, Two-and-a-Half-Li treats his goat like a family member. It is his "feminine" character that prevents him from jumping to join the national cause at the outset. After the assembly persuades him to offer his goat for the sacrificial ritual, he manages to find a rooster somewhere in order to save his beloved goat from the blade. "He was the only person who did not take the oath. He did not seem particularly distressed about the fate of the nation as he led the goat home. Everyone's eyes, especially old Zhao San's, angrily followed his departure. 'You crippled old thing. Don't you want to go on living?' "[63] After the death of his wife and child, however, his "masculine" character begins to assert itself, and the novel closes with Two-and-a-Half-Li leaving home in search of the People's Revolutionary Army. His transformation from a self-absorbed peasant into a national subject once again demonstrates that the stakes involved in the process of becoming a national subject are very different for men and women. The patriarchy measures a man's power in terms of his possessions: wife, children, livelihood, if not in nobler forms of property. It is the loss of those possessions that turns Two-and-a-Half-Li against Japanese imperialism. Nationalist discourse enables this man to gain in manhood by giving him a new subject position. Compared with him, a woman who has lost her husband is left without many resources. The novel opens up two grim possibilities for rural widows: she either rejects her female identity, joins the ranks of the "brothers" without the comfort of the elevated sense of manhood that real brothers enjoy, and gets herself killed like Mother Wang's daughter, or, like Golden Bough, she subjects herself to rape and exploitation in order to survive.

After the death of her brute husband, Golden Bough decides to go to the city of Harbin to earn money as a seamstress. For fear of being caught by the Japanese, she smears her face with dust until she looks like an old, ugly beggar woman. On the road, she encounters a troop of Japanese soldiers who order her to stop, but when the soldiers see her appearance they let her go unharmed.

Having escaped from the Japanese, Golden Bough falls into the hand of a Chinese man in the city. As a seamstress she must visit the homes of her clients, and it is during one of those visits that she is raped. This experience gives her a new perspective on her life as a woman, so when Mother Wang discourses again on the atrocities of the Japanese soldiers such as their slitting of the bellies of pregnant women and killing innocent babies, "Golden Bough snorted: 'I used to hate men only; now I hate the Japanese instead.' She finally reached the nadir of personal grief: 'Perhaps I hate the Chinese as well? Then there is nothing else for me to hate.' It seemed that Mother Wang's knowledge was no longer the equal of Golden Bough's."[64] Golden Bough's knowledge is earned at the expense of her body. In order to protect her body from men, she decides to leave the job in the city and become a nun. To her disappointment, the Buddhist temple in the village has long been abandoned and she is left with no hopes for the future. The ending of the novel presents a sharp contrast between Golden Bough (in the penultimate chapter) and Two-and-a-Half-Li (in the final chapter). Despite her hatred for the Japanese, the woman never succeeds in becoming a national subject like the latter. The experience of her body at the hands of her husband and the rapist contradicts the national identity that the presence of the Japanese imposes on her.

The female body in this novel is the field of life and death as well as the ultimate source from which the work derives its meaning. The author's refusal to sublimate or displace the female body leads to a gendered position that intervenes in a nationalist discourse that the novel seemingly establishes but in actuality subverts. Nationalism comes across as a profoundly patriarchal ideology that grants subject positions to men who fight over territory, possession, and the right to dominate. The women in this novel, being themselves possessed by men, do not automatically share the male-centered sense of territory. "My home was dreary," says Xiao Hong's narrator in a refrain in a later novel, *Tales of Hulan River*. There are two temples in the narrator's home village, the Temple of the Patriarch and the Temple of the Immortal Matron, where even the immortals are subject to gender discrimination. The clay idols in the Temple of the Patriarch are given stern and imposing features whereas those in the Temple of the Immortal Matron look benign and submissive. We are told that the people who cast those clay idols are all men:

> It is obvious that for a man to beat a woman is a Heaven-ordained right, which also holds true for gods and demons alike. No wonder the idols in the Temple of the Immortal Matron have such obedient looks about them—this comes from having been beaten so often. It becomes apparent that obedience is not the exceptionally fine natural trait it has been thought to be, but rather the result of being beaten, or perhaps an invitation to receive beatings.[65]

Indeed, the reason that the author herself fled home at the age of twenty was that her father, who embodied the evils of the patriarchy in her eyes, tried to force her into an arranged marriage.[66] In "Chu dong" (Early Winter), published along with the author's other familiar prose in the 1936 collection *Qiao* (Bridge), Xiao Hong's narrator expresses her firm resolution to never set foot in her father's house again: "I will never think of going back to a home like that. My father and I are adamantly opposed to each other, and I simply cannot live on his charity."[67] This father figure haunted Xiao Hong throughout her short, stormy life as an exile in Qingdao, Shanghai, Tokyo, and many other places, terminating in Hong Kong in 1942.

Until recently, however, the history of Xiao Hong's reception in mainland China has been trying to tell a different story, one that is given to eliding or condemning her ambivalence about nationalism and erasing her subversion of nationalist appropriation of the female body. Of course, this is not something that happens to Xiao Hong and her works alone. The subcategory of the woman writer in modern Chinese criticism itself has been created and legitimized in the name of a "national" literature that patronizes women's writing and subsumes it under the category of the nation in much the same way as the state deploys the category of *funü* for political control. Such gendered practice of literary criticism, I want to emphasize, has been a major site for the production of nationalist discourse ever since China saw the introduction of the post-Enlightenment European notion that a nation cannot be a nation without a national literature.[68] Within this framework of knowledge, the long-standing practice of reading literary texts, traditional or modern, within a nation-oriented and male-centered critical tradition is easily justified or simply could not be brought into question.[69] So rather than establish *écriture féminine*, revisionary readings of women's works constitute an act of intervention into the hegemonic practice of modern literary criticism. It is a way of saying that national literature, nation-oriented literary criticism, discipline, and institution must be opened up, interrogated, and radically rethought.

Notes

I wish to thank Lisa Rofel, Tani E. Barlow, Ellen Widmer, Inderpal Grewal, and Mayfair Yang for their valuable comments and criticisms on an earlier version of this paper.

1. See Benedict Anderson, *Imagined Communities: Reflections on the Origin and Spread of Nationalism*, revised edition (London: Verso, 1991).

2. It is slightly ironic that this book, which deals with a local question, has been treated by many as theory with a capital T.

3. Partha Chatterjee, *Nationalist Thought and the Colonial World: A Derivative Discourse?* (London: Zed Books, 1986), especially chapter one, "Nationalism as a Problem in the History of Political Ideas."

4. Ibid., 10.

5. Inderpal Grewal's study of Indian women and nationalism shows that alternative narrative did appear under the colonial regime. Women such as Ramabai managed to operate in the space between nationalism and colonialism. See her forthcoming book *Home and Harem: Imperialism, Nationalism, and Women's Culture in Nineteenth Century England.*

6. See Benita Parry's critique of Gayatri Chakravorty Spivak in "Problems in Current Theories of Colonial Discourse," *Oxford Literary Review* 9 (1987): 34.

7. For a theoretical explication of this problem, see Prasenjit Duara's forthcoming article "Rescuing History from the Nation-State"; for a historical account, see Charlotte Furth, ed., *The Limits of Change: Essays on Conservative Alternatives in Republican China* (Cambridge: Harvard University Press, 1976).

8. Gyan Prakash, "Writing Post-Orientalist Histories of the Third World: Perspectives from India Historiography," *Comparative Studies in Society and History* 32:2 (1990): 401.

9. Homi K. Bhabha, "Introduction" to *Nation and Narration*, ed. Homi K. Bhabha (London: Routledge, 1990), 3–4. The quotation is from Edward Said, *The World, the Text, and the Critic* (Cambridge: Harvard University Press, 1983), 171.

10. Ibid., 4.

11. "Undecidability" is Fanon's word. See Bhabha, "DissemiNation: Time, Narrative, and the Margins of the Modern Nation," in *Nation and Narration*, 304.

12. Ibid., 301.

13. See Henry Louis Gates, Jr., "Critical Fanonism," *Critical Inquiry* 17:3 (Spring 1991): 457–70.

14. See Parry, "Problems in Current Theories of Colonial Discourse," 52.

15. Julia Kristeva, "Women's Time," in *The Julia Kristeva Reader*, ed. Toril Moi (New York: Columbia University Press, 1986).

16. See Gayatri Chakravorty Spivak's critique of Kristeva in "French Feminism in an International Frame," in *In Other Worlds* (New York: Routledge, Chapman & Hall, 1988). The essay first appeared in *Yale French Studies* 62 (1981): 154–84. For related works on non-Western women, see Trinh T. Minh-ha, *Women, Native, Other: Writing Postcoloniality and Feminism* (Bloomington: Indiana University Press, 1989); and Gloria Anzaldúa, ed., *Making Face, Making Soul/Haciendo Caras: Creative and Critical Perspectives by Women of Color* (San Francisco: Aunt Lute, 1990).

17. See Julia Kristeva, *About Chinese Women*, trans. Anita Barrows (London: Marion Boyars, 1977); and Spivak's critique of her in "French Feminism in an International Frame."

18. Laura Nader, "Orientalism, Occidentalism and the Control of Women," *Cultural Dynamics* 2:3 (1989): 337.

19. See Tani E. Barlow, "Theorizing Woman: Funü, Guojia, Jiating [Chinese Women, Chinese State, Chinese Family]," *Genders* 10 (Spring 1991): 132–60.

20. Kang Youwei, "Qing jin funü chanzu zou," in *Wuxu bianfa* (The 1898 reform movement), ed. Chinese Historical Association (Shanghai, 1953), vol. 2, 242–44; as quoted in Ono Kazuko, *Chinese Women in a Century of Revolution, 1850–1950*, ed. Joshua A. Fogel (Stanford: Stanford University Press, 1989), 33.

21. See Ono Kazuko's discussion of his "Bianfa tongyi" in *Chinese Women in a Century of Revolution, 1850–1950*, 26–27.

22. Qiu Jin, *Qiu Jin ji* (Writings of Qiu Jin) (Beijing, 1960); as quoted in Ono Kazuko, *Chinese Women in a Century of Revolution*, 63. For more studies of Qiu Jin in English, see Mary Backus Rankin, "The Emergence of Women at the End of the Ch'ing: The Case of Ch'iu Chin," in Margery Wolf and Roxane Witke, eds., *Women in Chinese Society* (Stanford: Stanford University Press, 1975), 39–66; and Jonathan D. Spence, *The Gate of Heavenly Peace: The Chinese and Their Revolution, 1895–1980* (New York: Viking, 1981), 83–93.

23. Ono Kazuko, *Chinese Women in a Century of Revolution*, 65.

24. Ibid., 60.

25. For a study of Xiang Jingyu in English, see Roxane Witke, "Woman as Politician in China of the 1920s," in *Women in China: Studies in Social Change and Feminism*, ed. Marilyn B. Young (Ann Arbor: Center for Chinese Studies, University of Michigan, 1973), 43.

26. This is not to deny the actual atrocities committed by Japanese troops against Chinese women during the war. What I am trying to do here is suggest the complexities in women's experience of nationalism as borne out by the discursive practices of that period.

27. Xiao Jun, *Bayue de xiangcun* (Village in August) (Beijing, 1954), 129. The translation is mine.

28. After the victory of the CCP, many women revolutionaries in the military were persuaded to retire to domestic life and take care of their husbands. Some were assigned unimportant positions in the government.

29. Reza Hammami and Martina Rieker's study of Egyptian peasant women who fought against the state's regulation of their bodies shows a similar case of women's subversion of nationalist ideology. See "Feminist Orientalism and Orientalist Marxism," *New Left Review* 70 (July/August 1988): 93–106.

30. See Ding Ling's essay "Thoughts on March 8" in Tani Barlow and Gary J. Bjorge, eds., *I Myself Am a Woman: Selected Writings of Ding Ling* (Boston: Beacon Press, 1989).

31. Tani Barlow, "Introduction," in *I Myself Am a Woman: Selected Writings of Ding Ling*, 38. Barlow gives an insightful analysis of Ding Ling's stories; and more important, she touches on the complex relationship between women, state, and nation in modern China.

32. What happens here is that women's resistance has too often been erased or condemned by the state and has yet to be rediscovered from national histories. In that sense, Lata Mani's work on the colonial eyewitness accounts of *sati* in India is a timely intervention, for she points out the manner in which modern official history has consistently effaced signs of women's agency and struggles. See her "Contentious Traditions: the Debate on *Sati* in Colonial India," in Kumkum Sangari and Sudesh Vaid, eds., *Recasting Women: Essays in Indian Colonial History* (New Brunswick, N.J.: Rutgers University Press, 1990), 88–126; and her essay "Multiple Mediations: Feminist Scholarship in the Age of Multinational Reception," *Feminist Review* 35 (Summer 1990): 24–41.

33. See *Xiao Hong yanjiu* (Studies of Xiao Hong), ed. Beifang luncong bianji bu (Harbin, 1983).

34. I will not take up his problematic use of the category "Third World" here. Aijaz Ahmad has already analyzed the issue in " 'Third World Literature' and the Nationalist Ideology," *Journal of Arts & Ideas* nos. 17–18 (June 1989): 117–35.

35. See Fredric Jameson, "Third-World Literature in the Era of Multinational Capitalism," *Social Text* 15 (Fall 1986): 65–88, and Aijaz Ahmad's rebuttal, "Jameson's Rhetoric of Otherness and the 'National Allegory,' " *Social Text* 17 (Spring 1987): 3–25.

36. Hu Feng, Epilogue, in *Sheng si chang* (The field of life and death) (Shanghai, 1935). Unless otherwise noted, the English translation used is that by Howard Goldblatt.

37. Lu Xun, Preface to *Sheng si chang*, 1. The English translation is mine.

38. Howard Goldblatt's study of Xiao Hong represents an interesting deviation from this critical tradition. In *Hsiao Hong* (Boston: Twayne Publishers, 1976), he is reluctant to treat the novel as an anti-imperialist work. However, a radical break with the nationalist reading of Xiao Hong did not occur until recently when two women critics from mainland China, Meng Yue and Dai Jinhua, began to read the work in light of the female experience it represents. See their *Fuchu lishi dibiao* (Emerging from the horizon of history) (Zhengzhou: Henan renmin chuban she, 1989), 174–99.

39. Mao Dun, Preface to *Hulan he zhuan* (Tales of Hulan River) (Shanghai, 1947).

40. Howard Goldblatt, *Hsiao Hong*, 78.

41. Xiao Hong, "Shimian zhi ye" (A night of insomnia), in *Xiao Hong daibiao zuo* (Major works of Xiao Hong), ed. Xin Fujun (Zhengzhou, 1987), 59.

42. Liu Fuchen, "Xiao Hong huihua suotan" (Xiao Hong as an artist), in *Xiao Hong yanjiu*, 209–10.

43. Ibid., 210.

44. See Meng Yue and Dai Jinhua, *Fuchu lishi dibiao*, especially 174–99.

45. See Goldblatt's Introduction to *The Field of Life and Death*, xxi.

46. Xiao Hong, *Sheng si chang* (Shanghai, 1953), 140. With minor modifications, the English translation used is that by Howard Goldblatt and Ellen Yeung in *The Field of Life and Death and Tales of Hulan River* (Bloomington: Indiana University Press, 1979), 37.

47. Ibid., 40.

48. Ibid., 69–70.

49. Ibid., 71. I have slightly modified Howard Goldblatt's translation of this sentence.

50. Ibid., 70. I choose to leave *sheng* and *si* untranslated to retain the ambiguity of the first word, which Goldblatt renders as "life." The rest of the quote is his translation.

51. Ibid., 74.

52. Ibid., 51–52.

53. Ibid., 30.

54. Ibid., 25.

55. Ibid., 73.

56. Ibid., 11–12.

57. Xiao Jun, *Bayue de xiangcun*, 4.

58. Xiao Hong, *Sheng si chang*, 114–15.

59. Ibid., 120.

60. Ibid.

61. Ibid., 119–20.

62. Ibid., 121.

63. Ibid., 121–22.

64. Ibid., 140.

65. Xiao Hong, *Hulan he zhuan* (Guilin, 1942), 174. The novel was finished in Hong Kong on December 20, 1940, and published posthumously.

66. In her memoir, "Yongyuan de chongjing he zhuiqiu" (Perpetual dream and pursuit), the author describes her father as a man totally devoid of human compassion and decency. He was an influential scholar and powerful landlord in Hulan, who despised his daughter and would often beat her up. Xiao Hong's mother was also cruel to her. The only family member that loved her was her grandfather, but he was powerless and virtually an outcast in the family. See *Baogao* (Report) 1 (1937): 164–70.

67. Xiao Hong, "Chu dong" (Early winter), in *Xiao Hong daibiao zuo*, 7.

68. For the relationship between nation building and literary practice in modern China, see my article in Chinese, "Wenben, piping yu minzu guojia wenxue" (Text, criticism, and national literature), *Jintian* (Today) 1 (March 1992): 165–79.

69. As I noted elsewhere, women critics in mainland China have recently begun to use words like "female literature" and "female tradition" to reclaim women's works from male-centered criticism. See my essay "Invention and Intervention: The Making of a Female Tradition in Modern Literature," in Ellen Widmer and David Der-wei Wang, eds., *From May Fourth to June Fourth: Fiction and Film in Twentieth-Century Chinese Literature*, forthcoming from Harvard University Press.

THREE

The Female Body and "Transnational" Reproduction; or, Rape by Any Other Name?

Mary Layoun

> Running in place at the speed of light, we defensively cling to cate-
> gories, our dilapidated signposts in a bleak landscape. . . . Reflections
> of control, they reassure us that there's a time and a place for every-
> thing. Declaring what's right and what's wrong. . . . Use them but doubt
> them. They are the rules of the game, but perhaps no longer the one
> being played.
>
> Barbara Kruger
> "What's High, What's Low—and Who Cares?"[1]

By way of a displaced footnote: I will not, in what follows, attempt yet another definition of postmodernism. I am interested here in the ways in which particular fictional narratives negotiate the conflicts and contradictions—both historical and literary—of nationalism in crisis. And within that context, my focus is more particularly the historical construction of categories of sexuality and gender, and in the specific instance of the literary and cultural production of post-1974 Cyprus, the striking and insistent textual concern with stories of female rape and its consequences—including potential reproduction, both literal and metaphoric. There, the literary articulation of historically constructed categories of sexuality and gender suggests a stance characterized by that which we have come to associate with postmodernism—the postmodern as parody,[2] pastiche, a "self-conscious, self-contradictory, self-undermining statement," one that "juxtaposes and gives equal value to the self-reflexive and the historically grounded."[3]

But, as Rob Wilson has aptly pointed out, there is a remarkable coincidence between the postmodern and the "post-nuclear."[4] That is, the virtual omnipresence of the possibility of indiscriminate, cataclysmic, and final destruction. And in contrast to earlier apocalyptic visions, the post-nuclear/postmodern can no longer postulate a primary mover in control on high who will selectively destroy the "evil" while encompassing the "righteous" in a messianic narrative of eternal life. It is, rather, something more ominously all-inclusive and encompassing— as the T-shirt with "That's all, folks!" written underneath an expanding mushroom cloud proposes with rather grim humor. The destructive potential of this configuration is brutally borne out in the conclusion of the Cypriot short story "Paralogic" ("*Paralogismos*"), discussed below. But simultaneously, there is a potential (however hesitant or implicit) for constructing or assembling other ways of knowing and being in the world, for shifts and transformations in modes of production (and reproduction). In post-1974 Cypriot fiction, the potential for alternative possibilities of *re*-production is both threat and promise. If boundaries (of nation, gender, ethnoreligious communities, class, patriarchy) are reaffirmed by violence and destruction, the crossing over of those boundaries is not necessarily an insurance of nonviolence. And yet, boundary crossings can also undermine violence, rigid identities, patrilineal production(s). Here too, in this undermining, the constructively "destructive" potential of the postmodern/post-nuclear is discernible.

By way of a nondefinition of postmodernism, then, I would only suggest that if postmodernism is "the cultural logic of late capitalism,"[5] in a world capitalist system, neither postmodernism nor postmodernity are phenomena restricted to or necessarily originating from a putative "center." The "First World" of late capitalism, contrary to what might be a preferred self-image, has no exclusive copyright. In fact, it is at least worth considering that the (social and economic) characteristics of what is called postmodernity have been increasingly apparent in the "Third World" in the post-World War II period and especially since the 1960s. In the case of postmodernism, of literary and popular cultural texts, this is perhaps not so difficult to distinguish. But it is also apparent, viscerally and visually, in the economic and social geography of the capital cities of, for example, Egypt or Greece or Brazil: with the juxtaposition of "traditional," "modern," and almost bizarrely futuristic architecture in the same immediate areas; of glossy American food franchises with working-class neighborhood restaurants; of "supermarkets" with open-air markets; of small (often closed) shops selling everyday items (to an increasingly diminished clientele) with those selling mass-produced tourist goods (and open long hours). That the "cultural logic" of postmodernity or late capitalism does not necessarily manifest itself in the "Third World" in the form of a Los Angeles shopping mall negates neither the cultural effects of postmodernity nor their social and economic situations. This assumption, then, of an international, unequally shared postmodernity and its overdetermined relations with "Third World" cultural production and consumption underlies the readings below of fictional narratives of nationalism in crisis. And it is perhaps in and through those narratives that we can sense the palpable longing for, the faint imagining of, other not-yetarticulable communities; other ways of producing and reproducing sexual, familial, and social relations; other ways of knowing and living differences.

If nationalism is articulated as a narrative, the tactical and strategic maneuvers *of* and *within* those narratives and *among* contesting narratives are a significant commentary on the workings of nationalism as it is told, heard, and retold. A crucial part of negotiating nationalism is located in the complexity of this narrative process and in the construction, deconstruction, and reconstruction of (parts of) the national narrative. The rhetorical attempt of nationalism-as-narrative—perhaps of narrative in general—is to give the impression of coherence, of the legitimate authority of the narrator (however that authority might be construed), of the "truth" of the story told, and, not least of all, to situate the implied narrative audience/listener/reader in a particular fashion. Clearly that attempt is always contradictory, full of slippages and gaps. Therein lies the vulnerability of nationalism-as-narrative, perhaps of any narrative. But there too—in those moments of narrative slippage and contradiction—lie possibilities of recasting or at least renegotiating the specific order (the "grammar") of nationalism. And it is not only historical, political, or legal narratives that engage in this process. Literary narratives, too, can be read as attempts to negotiate dominant narratives of nationalism in which they participate and the boundaries which those dominant narratives draw and seek to maintain. Such narrative negotiation is contestatory and acquiescent, often simultaneously.

In the Cypriot fiction discussed below, written following the Turkish invasion of Cyprus in the summer of 1974, the recasting, the renegotiation, of the order and boundaries of a dominant national narrative is underwritten by what might seem a familiar obsession with the body of a violated (Cypriot) woman. The metaphoric equation of inviolable woman and inviolable motherland is as unsurprising as it is fearfully problematic. For the moment, though, I am less interested in that vexed configuration than in the specifics of the cultural and literary responses to the *outcome* of that symbolic equation of violated motherland and violated women.

Certainly, bracketing literary texts for a moment, the political and social consequences of that metaphoric equation are instructive, even startling. The instances of rape of Cypriot women by the invading Turkish military and the resulting pregnancies were high enough that the distinctly conservative Cypriot Orthodox Church was compelled to sanction abortion in the fall and winter of 1974. And, at the same time, the Cypriot parliament passed a bill that ambivalently but open-endedly legalized abortion.[6] But it is the cultural interventions in and negotiations of the equations of invasion/rape and occupation/reproduction which suggest that far more was at stake than unwanted

pregnancies. For, as these narratives implicitly suggest, the abortion of unwanted pregnancies did not (and could not) abort the violations wrought on
the bodies of Cypriot women by the Turkish invasion and occupation – nor
the violations wrought by Cypriot society after the invasion.

> They say that one should love the homeland
> that's what my father always told me too.
> My homeland is divided in two
> Which half should I love?
>
> Nessié Yassin (1975)

Maria Abraamidou's "*Paralogismos*" – irrationality, illogicality, or miscalcula-
tion – was published in 1979, five years after a short-lived right-wing Cypriot
coup and the subsequent Turkish invasion and occupation of Cyprus.[7]
Abraamidou's short story opens in the Turkish-occupied northern port city of
Keryneia in the months immediately following the coup and invasion. A young
Greek Cypriot woman murmurs to herself, "I'm losing it, I'm losing it"
("*Paraloizomai, paraloizomaï*"), as she waters the flowers in the yard of her
mother's house in the evening darkness. She hears hesitant footsteps on the
dusty stone path that passes next to the house. The footsteps stop; someone
is watching her. She hears laughter and voices ("the others") and a Turkish love
song (*amané*) that sounds like a funeral dirge (*moiroloi*). It is then that she makes
out the body and face that belong to the footsteps:

> eyes like an owl, swollen with sleeplessness looking at her tensely as if he wanted
> to say something, as if he had finally decided to dissolve the pledge of silence
> that had existed between them for so long. (20)

"*Paralogismos*" narrates the story of an encounter between a Greek Cypriot
woman, Evtuxia,[8] and an unnamed Turkish soldier. And in telling that paralogic story, "*Paralogismos*" critically and daringly contests the dominant national order that would cast the Turkish occupying force and the Greek
Cypriots as implacable enemies: the former as brutal invader, the latter as innocent and uprooted victims. "*Paralogismos*" also – and perhaps even more daringly – contests the designated spaces for Cypriot women and sexuality. And yet,
within the narrative space of Abraamidou's short story, the contradictory and
uneasy national(ist) constructions that designate proper place – for men and
women, for Greek Cypriots and Turkish Cypriots, for Cypriots, (mainland)
Turks, and (mainland) Greeks – are taken up, momentarily recast, and arguably
rather brutally redrawn in conclusion. In that critical retelling of the dominant
national(ist) narrative and of an unthinkable relationship of sexuality and love
between a Turkish soldier and a young Greek Cypriot woman in occupied

Cyprus, *"Paralogismos"* is—as its title suggests—crazy, paralogic, unthinkable. Its paralogic attempt to remap gendered national(ist) spaces within the narrative is finally, though, impinged on, recontained by, the official national narrative, which can scarcely allow such subtleties of narrative maneuver.

Some of this uneasiness and ambivalence of ethnonational boundaries is linguistically played out in *"Paralogismos."* The narrative moves between the demotic Greek of the third person narrator and the Cypriot dialect of Evtuxia, her mother, and their co-villagers. The sometimes tense opposition between these two distinct versions of a single language—which in more than one account of the national story is also claimed as a single culture and nation—is punctuated by the repetition of two Turkish terms of endearment addressed by the Turkish soldier to Evtuxia. In a suggestive maneuver, they are the *only* words attributed to him in the story and the only Turkish words in the text. The presence of Turkish here, then, is, implicitly at least, a substantial textual recasting of the Turkish presence in Cyprus.

In a parallel of sorts to this linguistic movement, the narration itself moves back and forth between the everyday details of life under Turkish occupation for Evtuxia and her co-villagers and the dreamy nighttime sequences of Evtuxia's own attempted flight across the lines—lines between Turk and Cypriot, Muslim and Christian, occupier and occupied, man and woman. In this context of border crossings, it is of no little significance that Evtuxia's border movement is preceded and prompted by a series of memories of five men from within her own ethnoreligious community. Her memories of them are also the memory and present reality of her social and personal "failure"—as a still unmarried woman—to fill the (only) acceptable village role for young women as wife and mother. Evtuxia is neither; nor is she engaged to be married. And so, the overdetermination of her memories of the Greek Cypriot men is underscored by a narrative configuration in which she recalls those five men precisely as the Turkish soldier moves away from the wall of her mother's house where he had been standing, half hidden in the darkness:

> She saw him break away from the wall of the house, his large body like a threat in the twilight. The light of the moon rising over Peristeres was focused on his arms crossed awkwardly over his chest as if he were cold or like a vague gesture of offering or consolation. Later she saw him slowly uncross his arms and salute her. It was then, from his utterly and strangely appealing face, from a gesture foreign and hostile, that the memories leapt out at her, crowding the narrow pathway with their shadows. (21)

Contrary to what we might expect, it is not the shadowy threat of the Turkish soldier that leaps out of the darkness at Evtuxia but her own memories of five

Greek Cypriot men justifying why they did not—could not, they claim—marry her. Where does the most dangerous "threat" lie for Evtuxia? With the Turkish soldier who salutes her? Or with her own memories? Of course, the conventional answer is that the Turkish soldier will "leap out" of the shadows and attack the young Greek Cypriot woman. But, in fact, the rather more urgent threat is Evtuxia's memories of rejection and the consequences of that rejection. If the Turkish soldier is a threat here, he is a decidedly more ambiguous one. He is, perhaps, the threat of desire, of the very "consolation" and "offering" that Evtuxia attributes to him. Given the operative narrative (and extranarrative) boundaries, that is a threat indeed.

What is clear, then, is that Evtuxia's border movement—her attempt to recast herself in a different and less restrictive relationship both to her "own" community and to that of the "enemy"—is inextricably linked to her memories of the contradictions and impossibilities for herself as a young and conspicuously unmarried woman within the space of her own community, her own home. "Home" and "community" are here not self-evident and sustaining categories but problematic points of contention and limited possibility. It is in this context that the presence of the Turkish soldier can be a "foreign and hostile threat"—forcing Evtuxia's memories of "homelessness at home"—and, simultaneously, a "gesture of offering or consolation."

Still, Evtuxia's border movement is tenuous and problematic on its own terms. Some of its contradictions are apparent in her utopic account of Keryneia's "past" to the local schoolchildren. The children come to school full of anguished accounts of the occupation of their homes, neighborhoods, and village by the Turkish military. Evtuxia is unable to respond to their stories and worried questions about the future. Instead, she gathers the smallest of the children around her to tell them a story. It is, significantly, one infused with sunlight and whiteness:[9]

> She told them the story of how once the village was one gigantic garden that stretched to the plain below and within it strolled [Cypriot Orthodox] monks dressed in white because only white suited so much light, so much beauty. And their village was beautiful and they loved it, didn't they?
>
> And utterly unexpectedly she saw again, over the heads of the children, his face bending over hers. (24)

In addition to the loaded postulation of an ethnically and religiously exclusive narrative past, the dominant tropes of Evtuxia's story are in striking contrast to her flight into the "dripping dampness" of the "dark nights" and the virtual silence of her meetings with the Turkish soldier. Her movement *to* the Turkish soldier is *away from* what she herself narrates as "beauty," "light," and "whiteness" – religiously embodied, in her story, in the purity of the monks. But it is also, clearly, a flight away from boundaries of sexual repression, of rejection and loneliness. Away from the ethnonational and religious boundaries of her community. Away from the familial boundaries represented by her sick mother and extended family, for whom, in her dreams and out of them, she is "a whore" or "strangely nervous and excitable" – a hysteric. In a familiarly loaded move, then, the dreariness and "failure" of Evtuxia's daily life are countered in her "unthinkable" relationship with a forbidden other – the Turkish soldier.

Strikingly, "*Paralogismos*" does not specify the national origins of Evtuxia's "Turkish soldier." He could be either a member of the Turkish Cypriot community or from mainland Turkey. And, if the former, their relationship could conceivably predate the Turkish invasion. Is this, perhaps, the "pledge of silence that had existed between them for so long"? "*Paralogismos*" offers no clarification of such questions. It makes virtually no distinction between Turkish Cypriots and the invading Turkish army. In fact, in the passage that precedes Evtuxia's fantastic account of Keryneia's "history" to the young schoolchildren, the Turkish army and the Turkish Cypriots are both identified by the children as the "enemy." This narrative gesture calls up the ethnic chauvinism of a version of (Greek) Cypriot nationalism that, with no irony, calls for a free and independent Cyprus that is specifically "Greek."[10]

Still, the overwhelmingly predominant account of the encounter between Greek (and, less openly, Turkish) Cypriot women and the Turkish army that invaded and occupies Cyprus was not that of a weary soldier standing hesitantly off in the gathering darkness. It was rather that of rape. The right-wing coup, which preceded the Turkish invasion by little more than a week, proclaimed itself the defender of Cyprus against "foreign threats" – those threats being one of the purported pretexts for its takeover. In fact, the short-lived coup rather brutally located fellow Cypriots as "foreign threats," ironically illustrating, and not for the first time, the remarkable malleability of what is considered "foreign." And it is precisely in this context that the "paralogic" of Abraamidou's short story is illustrated as well. "*Paralogismos*" challenges, however ambivalently, the dominant social, political, and cultural definitions of Greek Cypriot nationalism. It retells the gendered national encounter between Cypriot and Turk, Christian and Muslim, woman and man.

Perhaps the most startling challenge of "*Paralogismos*," its potentially most radical recasting of the dominant national narrative, is located in Evtuxia's exultation in realizing that she is pregnant, a condition of which the Turkish soldier is also aware. As a result, she stops going to meet her lover at night. And she attempts to avoid his watchful gaze during the day, moving through the village via back streets and out-of-the-way paths. When the Turkish military orders "a weapons search" ("but everyone knew they weren't looking for weapons"), the Greek Cypriot residents of the neighborhood in which Evtuxia lives are herded out of their houses and into the square. And Evtuxia feels the "tense eyes" of the Turkish soldier "watching her from afar, hiding within them something of the helpless humility of an animal" (25). Although the homes of the other residents are vandalized, Evtuxia returns to her mother's home to find it "untouched with the key [still] in the door." Rejected by men from within her own ethnoreligious community, dismissed by her own family, pregnant with the child of her Turkish (or Turkish-Cypriot) lover, Evtuxia's account of the Turkish army's search concludes obsessively with a mournful description of young women's dowries thrown into the streets.

The realization that she is pregnant compels Evtuxia to reconsider what she had thought was "deadness inside her":

> How did it happen, since she was no longer alive? From where did this new life stir? . . . so there was finally hope, even for her; she could wait; it gave her some time on credit. (24)

But it is equally the untouched house of her mother that makes her "resolve to refuse everything":

> She would refuse her heart; that was the price she had to pay for the life that had been given back to her. (26)

Ominously, but not surprisingly, the "everything" that she will refuse—"her heart"—is precisely the Turkish soldier and her relationship with him. In what is a stark strategy of containment,[11] Evtuxia meets the Turkish soldier-become-lover-and-father-of-her-child one last time. And she bludgeons him to death with a garden hoe. Given the unsettling narrative propositions of the short story—about women and men, Cypriots and Turks, desire and repression, and not least of all about the internal dynamics of Cypriot society—that violent closure is virtually a strategic necessity for "*Paralogismos*." Thereby the potentially disruptive questions raised by the border negotiations of a Greek Cypriot woman and a Turkish soldier are rather brutally attenuated.

Nonetheless, it is the bloody conclusion of "*Paralogismos*" that points back to the fiercely ideological struggle at work throughout the narrative. The narration of the soldier's death is suggestive in this regard. Rather than cry out as Evtuxia strikes him, he falls to his knees, stretching out his hand to caress her swollen belly. Then he slips silently to the ground and dies. And rather than flee the scene, leaving his bloody body behind, Evtuxia performs funeral rites for him:

She stood for a moment, looking at him [lying] at her feet. Then she took water
from the yard and washed the blood from his face. She straightened his body
and crossed his arms over his chest as she had seen him do himself. She took the
hoe and began to dig in the damp soil. (27)

The next morning, Evtuxia bends over her mother's sickbed and promises that
for which her mother had been pleading and Evtuxia had been refusing for
months:

I'll go and find the Turkish Commanding Officer so that he can arrange our
papers and we can leave. All right, mother? (27)

The border crossing, the *"paralogismos"* — ambiguous, loaded, and impinged
upon as it was — is over. The Turkish soldier who emerged from the shadows
to contribute to the unspeakable story is effaced, beaten down, buried — literally. Evtuxia and her mother will leave their home with the dangerous and
paralogic negotiations that remaining there entail and become refugees in the
safe sameness of the southern, unoccupied part of Cyprus. Evtuxia momentarily retells her role in the Greek Cypriot narrative of Cypriot nationalism
with results that are only arguably fortuitous — even for her. Her role in the
dominant Cypriot national narrative will almost certainly now be cast as that
of an unmarried woman, pregnant but excusably so, with the child of a Greek
Cypriot man who died resisting the Turkish invasion. Evtuxia will no longer
be such an embarrassment to herself and others as a nonwife and nonmother.
She will now be able to fill at least one of those mandatory roles. But if Evtuxia's role is that of mother-to-be, it will also be that of a helpless and innocent
victim. A certain socially acceptable role as mother becomes available to her
while another impossible and paralogic role is utterly foreclosed.

Yet how else could *"Paralogismos"* possibly end? For its unspeakable story
is, in the dominant scheme of things, precisely paralogic. Dubious, attenuated,
and ambivalent, *"Paralogismos"* participates in the dominant narrative of
Cypriot nationalism as it simultaneously locates, explores, and negotiates a
contradictory fissure in the official narrative. That negotiation is precisely the
attempt to narrate a transgression, a momentary crossing-over of the lines. It
is, here, a fleeting temporal possibility of challenging and perhaps using
differently — of transgressing — dominant spatial organization.

That this transgression takes place across the reproductive space of a woman's body in *"Paralogismos"* is a gesture more than a little loaded.[12] That spatial construct and its correlative of Evtuxia-as-mother are, on the one hand,
scarcely a transgression of dominant gender roles. The body of woman is not
quite used differently — at least to the extent that it is the site of reproduction.

But the narrative agency of Evtuxia—strangely garnered as it is—is itself note-worthy. Does she use or instrumentalize her own body (and that of the Turkish soldier who is her lover) differently in establishing, maintaining, and definitively ending a relationship across ethnic, national, and religious boundaries? She does assume a kind of agency over her own body and desire, although with distinctly bloody consequences for the object of her desire. Still, her unborn child will be a tiny production of an impossible "transnationalism"—one based not on rape but on desire, seduction, and, arguably perhaps, love. That it is a costly production is indubitably indicated by the bloody corpse of the Turk-ish soldier. Yet if the violent conclusion of their relationship would seem to lend itself to a dominant nationalist reading, her attraction to, desire, and even love for the Turkish soldier simultaneously confound that reading.

> When I was a small child I wondered if she was Greek,
> the cat of our Greek neighbor.
> One day I asked my mother
> if cats are Turkish
> and dogs Greek.
> The dogs had snarled at our kittens.
> Days later
> I saw our cat
> eat the very kittens that she'd given birth to.
> Mehmet Yassin
> "The Myth of Our Own Cat" (1985)

Is there reproduction that allows another order of things? That allows for the agencies of female desire and sexuality and of reproduction? For the reconsideration of boundaries of the "nation" and of what they contain and exclude? One for which the violable/violated woman is not the site for and of the nation? Evtuxia's paralogic story comes as a provocative response (if not quite an answer) to such questions. Her reclamation of agency—limited, compromised, partial—clearly transgresses national *and* gender boundaries of "purity" and "integrity." Her story and its narration implicitly disrupt the equation of inviolable woman and inviolable nation.[13] In this transgression and disruption, her story implicates other stories as well, fictional and nonfictional. Evtuxia's story suggests that it is not only the violation of the female body that is at issue but also the violently gendered proscription of social agency and power. The violation of rape is evoked in a scheme of things in which women are pure, moral, and powerless; men are impure, aggressive, and powerful. It is precisely in that context that Evtuxia's story—her border negotiations—and its narration are conducted. She enters the "impure" and "contaminated" nocturnal zone, momentarily leaving behind the dazzling whiteness of pure and exclusionary narratives. In the "dark" she is the active agent of her own desires, body, and sexuality.

And the parameters of her story make utterly clear that this is not an isolated issue, a question of an individual woman's autonomy and inviolability. The very definitions and practices of the community of which Evtuxia is a part are at stake. And if, in conclusion, her paralogicality will be recontained by the dominant narrative of motherhood, nation, and reproduction as occurring within newly acceptable boundaries, nonetheless Evtuxia, the narrator, and we as readers, know that there is also a story of transgression to tell.

In conclusion, it is perhaps unnecessary to point out that the narrative representation of rape is not just the factual story of the violation of Cypriot women by the invading Turkish army. It is not—in a conflation of literary narrative with "anthropological realism"—some direct, inevitable, and unmediated literary reflection of historical fact. Foreign invasion and occupation do not inevitably or "naturally" produce a proliferation of cultural and literary narratives of female rape. The primacy of the story of rape is as striking in its occurrence in post-1974 Cypriot fiction as it is in its lesser significance in other social and cultural instances. Although gender and sexuality are inextricably involved in nationalism, the foregrounding of rape as the "national story" is not.

Rather than simply or primarily a literary refraction of historical instances of rape, I would suggest that the story of rape in post-1974 Cypriot fiction is a (potentially disruptive) marker in narratives of violently conflicted social and political relationships: the intercommunal relationships of Cypriot society between Greek Cypriots and Turkish Cypriots, between men and women; and the international relationships between Cyprus and its Mediterranean neighbors—Greece and Turkey, of course, as well as the Middle East. And further, these relationships are fiercely gendered—not just "naturally sexed" female. The narrative image and story of female rape, then, is not exclusively a "woman's" story. It is a social and political story. Something of that is suggested in Abraamidou's "*Paralogismos*." For, though it does not directly represent female rape, it is very much figured on the story of rape. Yet in narrating the transgression of (nonetheless firmly inscribed) gender and national boundaries, "*Paralogismos*" resituates rape to question social and national power and agency, not just bodily violation. Here the representation of rape is inextricably bound up with representations of national and religious, cultural and linguistic boundaries. This is not to diminish the violence and violation of the historical experiences of rape (or invasion). But it is to suggest that post-1974 Cypriot narratives do not simply replicate that "actual" experience. And it is also to suggest that the image or representation or story of the rape of woman figures something other than just the "rape of woman." Undoubtedly the penetration—national, sexual—by an invasive other is part of the story. But it is also, and equally, the sexual, political, and national issue of uncoerced female agency, of control over her body, sexuality, and reproduction and—equally—over her place(s) in society.

Narrating the female body as the site of purity and nation violated, as the site of an international maternal (re)production, is certainly a dubious gesture. It conjures figures of eternally fecund and nurturing woman, of the reproductive site of "natural" conciliation. Yet, simultaneously the narration of the (violation of the) female body in these texts also conjures the contradictions, the violatory representations, of the female body as national site. Those conflicting images mark—as threat *and* promise—many post-1974 Cypriot narratives, as they do a social and cultural discourse around them. But if that narration is a dubious gesture, it is also an indication of a different story beyond national boundaries that is yet to be told. For now, however, it can only be "paralogic," narrated in the dark silence of Evtuxia's midnight border movements.

Notes

Evolving versions of this essay were presented at an MLA panel (1990), "Disturbing the Piece: Narrative, Order, Gender"; at the University of Wisconsin at Milwaukee for the conference "Displacements: Cultural Identities in Question"; at Oberlin College; and at the University of California at Berkeley. I am grateful to the organizers—Jackie Byars (Wayne State), Angelika Bammer (Emory), Anu Dingwaney Needham (Oberlin), and Francine Masiello (University of California at Berkeley)—and to the audiences of those forums for their comments and suggestions.

1. Barbara Kruger. "What's High, What's Low—and Who Cares?" *New York Times*, Sunday, September 9, 1990, nat. ed.: H43. I am grateful to Jeff Shalan for bringing this article to my attention.

2. The literal sense of parody is worth recalling here. But if it is a usage derived from Aristotle's notion of imitation for ridicule or comic effect that we first recall, parody is also, as in Euripides, to "sing beyond the song," to sing indirectly and hint obscurely.

3. Linda Hutcheon, *The Politics of Postmodernism* (London: Routledge, 1989), 1–2.

4. Rob Wilson, "Postmodern as Post-Nuclear: Landscape as Nuclear Grid," in *Ethics/Aesthetics: Post-Modern Positions*, ed. Robert Merrill (Washington, D.C.: Maisonneuve Press, 1988), 169–92.

5. The phrase is, of course, Fredric Jameson's from his article "Postmodernism or the Cultural Logic of Late Capitalism," *New Left Review* 146 (1984): 53–92, and his more recent book of the same title. But the relations between late capitalism/postmoder*nity* and postmoder*nism* are less readily linked—more vexed, complex, and mediated—than the term "logic" might suggest. Otherwise, it is reminiscent of the pretext of realism—the link between the textual and extratextual is the former as "realistic" representation of the latter: postmoder*nism* as cultural logic, as a (parodically) "realistic" representation of postmoder*nity*.

6. The ambiguity of that bill has given rise to debate in recent years as to whether or not abortions are, in fact, legal in Cyprus. See, for example, "Abortion on the Increase" in *The Cyprus Weekly*, December 1–7, 1989: 6.

7. Maria Abraamidou, *"Paralogismos,"* in *O Teleutaios Horismos/The Final Separation* (Leukosia: Kypros Printing, 1979).

8. Literally, her name means "good luck."

9. The sunlight in her story here is in contradistinction to the moonlight that she notices illuminating the hands of the Turkish soldier.

10. There was, for example, a card and wall poster that circulated in Cyprus as late as 1989 to 1990 and that pictured a gold wreath behind a blue and white flag. The flag is that of Greece, not of Cyprus, and the message printed across the flag reads (as a holiday salutation among other things): "And on earth Peace." In smaller lettering underneath the flag are the words: "Cyprus—Free—Greek."

11. " . . . the story had begun and it had to end," Evtuxia observes.

12. The female body as the site of such transgression is, in the post-1974 Cypriot cultural and social context, scarcely peculiar to Abraamidou's short story. The point is precisely that rather than an isolated literary phenomenon, this configuration assumed the proportions of a dominant social trope. The fiction of Panos Ioannides, especially "The 'Uniforms'" ("*Oi stoles*") and "The Invisible Side" ("*E atheate opsi*"), or Christos Hatzipapa's novel *The Color of the Blue Hyacinth* (*To chroma tou galaziou iakinthou*) are particularly striking in this regard.

13. For a discussion of other Cypriot narratives invoking a virtually identical formulation, see "Fresh Lima Beans and Stories from Occupied Cyprus" in *Anthropology and Literary Study*, Val Daniel and Jeff Peck, eds. (forthcoming).

FOUR

Woman, Nation, and Narration in *Midnight's Children*

Nalini Natarajan

In Salman Rushdie's *Midnight's Children*, the midnight of Indian independence is represented through refraction of the colors of the Indian flag onto national celebrations (extravagant "saffron rockets" and "green sparkling rain") and the bodies of women giving birth: "green-skinned," "whites of eyes . . . shot with saffron" (*MC*, 132).[1] We may note significant juxtapositions and identities: woman's pain with communal joy, human with national birth, woman's body *as* the national tricolor flag.

Gender and Nation

The scene illustrates the centrality of gender in the space of the social imaginary that constitutes "nation" while indicating the dissimilar elements that comprise the collectivity of nationalism. The two women whose ordeal in labor is represented in national colors are from the more marginalized sections (by the dominant middle-class Hindu ethos) of Indian society: a Muslim woman and a humble street singer. The text provides an occasion for introducing my concerns in this essay: the spectacle or visual effect of woman as it shapes the national imaginary, the way woman functions as sign in the imagining of community, the relation of these aspects of woman as sign and spectacle (as figurations of the beloved, mother, and daughter) to the failure of the secularization project that "Indian" culture generally, and the Bombay cinema industry in particular, envisaged for itself in the early decades of Indian independence. I hope to offer the following: first, a reading of a postcolonial text in the context of other cultural productions from the postcolonial world, rather than against fashionable hegemonies that originate in the metropolis; second, a reading that can help to deconstruct essentalized images of "Third World" alterity that sometimes prevail. I focus here on the problematic power of the postcolonial state and the exclusions that go into the formation of the "Third World" nationalist subject; third, an examination of the shifting representations of the space of alterity occupied by women within the formation of nationalist subjectivities; finally, an investigation of the relation between film and fiction.

Rushdie's Text and Bombay Cinema: Elite and Mass Culture

My method is to focus on moments of the text that can be read as interrupting the dominant continuities of Bombay cinema. The juxtaposition of Rushdie's sophisticated and allusive text with the "mass cultural" Bombay cinema is deliberate.[2] For Rushdie's text is informed by Bombay cinema in a symbiotic relationship. Not only does the text allude often to Bombay cinema, its narrative reflects and parodies Bombay cinema. Stock narrative situations (such as the mistaken exchange at birth) and stock cinema figures (the good "ayah" Mary Pereira, for example) recall Bombay cinema to readers from the Subcontinent. In addition, the narrative parodies and reinvents some of Bombay cinema's fantasy operations. Sudhir Kakar has discussed the "splitting" that goes on in Bombay cinema as a "favored defensive activity to deal with the anxiety generated by disturbing relationships."[3] Thus, mother figures are either perfect (natural mothers) or evil (stepmothers), virtuous male protagonists are matched by evil counterparts, and so on. Women are either virgins or vamps. In Rushdie's text, Saleem's fantasies of love for and revenge against his mother bring together what cinema usually splits. Similarly Shiva, Saleem's alter ego combines the rebel-hero with the villain of Bombay cinema.

Bombay Cinema and the Imagining of India

At the outset, it is important to clarify somewhat the role of Bombay cinema in the postindependence national ethos. Although critically judged as escapist and conservative when juxtaposed to the more sophisticated "New Wave" film of the seventies and eighties, the reach of Bombay cinema is considerable. By sheer volume of production and star charisma, it dominates the market. What is more, it has broken into the anti-Hindi southern states so that it is an important agency for Hindi-speaking cultural hegemony in postindependence India.

Benedict Anderson's thesis about the fictional component of nation, the role of print in helping people imagine themselves as nationals along with others they have never seen, is powerfully pertinent to a consideration of cinema.[4] Many factors make it fairly difficult to project an imagined "India" in print. These are the institutionalization of English studies in India, many contending regional languages and literatures, illiteracy, and shortages in the resources that make wide reading possible. It is Bombay cinema that represents "India" for its audience and shapes (and reflects) the collective imaginary, however hegemonic and exclusive.

The transnational context of this collection provokes an analogy between Bombay cinema and Western mass media. Like the mass media, it displaces the role of older folk culture in people's lives. But the discrepancy between the ideology promulgated in modern mass culture in the West and the lives its consumers lead takes a different form in Bombay cinema.[5] While the material conditions represented are discrepant from Indian realities, the ideologies are not. Kishore Vallicha writes of Bombay cinema's psychological hold on the population, its reinforcement of "deep-seated beliefs that form the unconscious and semiconscious basis of the Indian psyche . . . attitudes to caste, to women, to manual work, to family."[6] Thus, ideologies such as the "purity" of women, the value of family life upheld by Bombay cinema remain powerful popular ideologies. Yet there are also wish-fulfillment components. The "dream life" of the moviegoer, for instance, revolves around the persons of the film actors and actresses who are, in Kishore Vallicha's words, "models of thought and feeling . . . psychological constructs which confirm the nature of the world and help to overcome fears, frustration, helplessness" (Vallicha, 26–27). The Bombay films' formulaic ingredients – elaborate romance plots and happy endings – are similarly aimed at wish fulfillment. In a society that strictly monitors male-female contact, these films are the audience's imaginary realm. They depict marriage between classes, and rags to riches transformations unimaginable in real life.[7] But they ensure the stability of the bourgeois status quo by disciplining desire. Wishes may be fulfilled but only if certain values identified as "traditional" – simplicity, filial duty, honesty – are adhered to. In this essay I read Bombay cinema as furthering the middle-class project of coordinating desire with power and control.

Spectacle, Gender, and Nation

Two aspects of cinema highlighted by Dana Polan, looking and dreaming, have an important role in engendering notions of community.[8] Cinema as spectacle can lend itself to popular influence to a much greater extent than print – its impact is immediate and engaging. And cinema's shadowy, ephemeral nature enables dreaming. Because, in its emphasis on presence, it is a world without background, and could even extinguish all traces of the past; it projects on the screen the audience's dreams and wishes, which invests "insubstantial material with a life and psychical force, and turn the emptiness of shadows into the fullness of the kingdom" (Polan, 57). If cinema, then, has, in Polan's words, made dreaming into "a social event" (57), individual subjectivity reinforces the social imaginary.

Looking and dreaming also become gendered (as male) activities. The viewing process, say critics of dominant cinema, constitutes the gaze as male. As object of the male gaze, woman is chief component of the spectacular (the present) and the dream (the absent/future) components of cinema. Because cinema has produced "forms of subjectivity that are individually shaped yet unequivocally social," it posits the *male* subject as the measure of desire and woman as one of the important signifiers in the collective male dream.[9] That women are so often identified in cultural studies as the ideal consumers of mass-produced fantasies provokes an interesting dialectic between "woman as subject and object, as spectator and character."[10] My viewpoint in this essay is that dominant Bombay cinema, like Hollywood cinema, grants greater space to male desires and fantasies even though women (mostly teenage, college-going girls) constitute, along with young males, a large bulk of the moviegoing population.[11] Because of the strict censorship restrictions on Bombay cinema, representations of sexuality are strictly policed. Nationalism is one of the areas where uninhibited passion may be displaced, and this essay is concerned with the symbolic use of woman in the erotics of nationalism.

Woman as Signifier for Nation

Woman functioned as a signifier in many ways in the contrary dialectic of stasis and change in the imagining of India. It was required not only to imagine one out of many, an operation requiring a relinquishing of the caste-based hierarchies to a pan-Indian modernity, but also to render this one ontologically stable, an effort that inevitably privileged the dominant cultural group–broadly speaking, the Hindu middle classes.[12] In reading narrative against this paradoxical cultural effort, I look at woman in three moments in nationalism: (1) the movement from regional to national in the "modernizing" process; (2) the threat of communal or civil rupture within the body politic; and (3) the rise of fundamentalism. Woman's body is a site for testing out modernity, in the first moment; in the second, as "Bharat Mata" or "Mother India," a site for mythic unity in the face of fragmentation; and in the third, as "daughter of the nation," a site for countering the challenge posed by "Westernization," popularly read as "women's liberation."

Woman and Nation in *Midnight's Children:* The Scopic and the Civic

> A nation which had never previously existed was about to win its free-
> dom, catapulting us into a world which . . . was . . . quite imaginary;
> into a mythical land, a country which would never exist except by the
> efforts of a phenomenal collective will–except in a dream we all agreed to
> dream–it was a mass fantasy.
> (*MC,* 129-30)

The text I am reading traces the fortunes of a Muslim family in complex allegorical relation to the fate of the nation. Woman occupies a minor role in
the narrative, but my argument foregrounds her marginality as a strategy of
reading. I have already indicated the symbiotic connection between *Midnight's
Children* and Bombay cinema. The representation of women is a startling instance of the connection, and it is possible to read the text as parodying Bombay cinema's use of women. At the same time, the text's own use of woman's
body as signifier for nation implicates it within a critique of male-dominated
culture.

My first argument links the scopic (that which is seen) with the civic. Synecdoche, the imagination of a whole from its parts, essential to nation construction, also becomes the way woman is perceived in *Midnight's Children.* The first
national subject textualized in Rushdie is the German-educated doctor Aadam
Aziz. He returns home with a void in his head–European skepticism has destroyed his faith in "Islam" and in "India." The void becomes the space of desire.
His reintegration occurs over the body of a woman patient, who later becomes
his wife. Because she is in purdah (veiled) she is shown to him through holes
in a sheet. As he treats her in parts he begins to imagine her as whole. This
coincides with his imagining a "whole" Indian identity for himself, instead of
his regional Kashmiri one.

The synecdochic process of discovery or construction of Naseem Aziz is a
camera technique familiar in Bombay cinema. The camera focuses on the
heroine's body part by part. On one level, this defers to the censors; on another,
it leaves the job of construction to the male hero and the audience. The popular
film *Mere Mehboob* (1963), for instance, depicts the hero's discovery (which is
also imaginative construction) of the woman he loves.[13] He, like Aadam Aziz,
has only seen her in parts–walking fully veiled on a university campus. The
woman's covering is a sign of orthodox values (here the national culture
exploits the titillations of Islamic restrictions on women as presented by many
producers who work in Bombay cinema) while the university campus is a
signifier for modernity. In another film, *Pakeezah* (1971), a viewing of the

heroine's feet takes place on a train.[14] The university and the train are both symbols and spaces of modernization and integration. The audience participates at once in the potential for female viewing offered by a modernizing India, as well as the retreat into traditional taboos that monitor the revealing of the female body. Such representations demarcate the space of desire as male. This imaginary uncovering/covering of woman becomes the site for national self-definition, a site where the contradictory facets of the national ideology are played out. Woman should fulfill the individual male psychic need for scopic/sexual gratification and yet be the figurehead for national culture, guarded by the censors. The contradictions in woman's position as spectacle may be seen in the social dramas of contemporary India—bride viewings by eligible males, the spectacles of lavish marriages financed by the fathers of brides, bride burnings caused by "inadequate" dowry, the resurgent spectacle of widow-sacrifice, or sati. In each case, the body of woman becomes a focus for the symbolisms of cultural and religious reaction.

While male discursive dismembering (such as Saleem's mutilated finger or bruised scalp) symbolizes national rupture, the representation of woman as parts in both fictional and filmic discourse provides an occasion for imagining wholeness. Although she is a symbol for wholeness, her own integrity remains secondary. The text announces within brackets "(he has told her to come out of purdah)," the punctuation indicating that woman's freedom is an aside in the narrative of nationalism. When the couple move to Amritsar, Naseem Aziz finds herself cruelly exposed to the multiplicity of the Subcontinent as Aziz sets fire to her purdah veils:

> Buckets are brought; the fire goes out; and Naseem cowers on the bed as about thirty-five Sikhs, Hindus and untouchables throng in the smoke-filled room.
> (*MC*, 33)

Imaginative construction of woman's body is a metaphor for constructing national identity from regional, and the exposure of woman's body is a signal for the melting pot of secular modernity. The text represents this modernity as a sexual threat for women—note the connotations of "bed," "throng." For in the political context of decolonization, modernity is required of Indian women. An Oedipal trace could be observed here—we recall that Aadam Aziz's mother also came out of purdah in order to finance her son's education. Aadam Aziz demands of his wife after the purdah-burning: "Forget about being a good Kashmiri girl. Start thinking about being a modern Indian woman" (*MC*, 33). Women are required to shed their traditional inhibitions; their reluctance to do this could indicate disjunctive articulations in the discourse of nationalism, which claims to construct one out of many. "You, or what?" says Naseem at Aziz's request that she come out of purdah. "You want me to walk naked in front of strange men" (*MC*, 33).

Incidentally, we may note the difference to woman in Western representations. In *Alice Doesn't*, de Lauretis quotes Mulvey's account of the paradigmatic film narrative where woman is first object of the collective male gaze and then reserved for the hero's eyes alone.[15] The movement of woman as scopic object between public and private spheres is mediated by the wider sociohistorical processes that affect gendering and by the specific anxieties of nationalism. Rushdie's text reveals how women are tied into the process of middle-class homogenization as India modernizes. As part and parcel of the new "nationhood" and its economic, social, and cultural coordinates, woman becomes an index of the erosion of discrete regional and caste cultures in the movement from regionalism to modernity. The class anxieties that imposed a "new kind of segregation" on women in the nineteenth century are modified so that women may emerge in public.[16] Thus in Rushdie's text, woman moves from man's individual gaze to the collective gaze of many. But this emergence into the public gaze is as problematic as women's seclusion.

Frantz Fanon has discussed the politics behind the veil in the colonizer's attempt to decimate the colonized culture. The battle to end purdah in the colonial context is inflected by the colonizer's wish to "rescue" the colonized woman from the "backward" colonized male.[17] Here in decolonization, the newly independent male demands what he resisted during colonialism, or conceded grudgingly in response to British accusations of "backwardness." In both cases, the uncovering of women's bodies is related more to the politics of men's power relations than any interest in female subjectivity.

Rushdie's text ironizes the formation of the national bourgeois imaginary through the relations of Aadam Aziz and Naseem. Although Bombay cinema retains for the male the scopic advantage, and consistently portrays woman as an entity to be discovered and protected in the formation of a new India of patriarchally monitored "progress" for woman, Rushdie's text unseats these confidences in the spectator/subject. For Aadam Aziz's attempt at mental construction fails—he misapprehends Naseem Aziz. Synecdoche allows a space for the imagined object to assert its autonomy. When the whole is assembled it turns out to be very different from the sum of its parts. Naseem Aziz emerges as the stronger partner in the relationship, defying her husband's desires by becoming fat and refusing to do his sexual bidding. Communication between the couple is forever curtailed through Naseem's silence; her body promises not cognitive wholeness, but rupture.

"Mother India"

Naseem Aziz's daughter Amina, though conventionally unattractive, is sexually precocious: she steals her older sister's fiancé. For the early chapters of her appearance, she lives underground with her fugitive lover—a textual absence. Like Naseem, unmarried women exist only partially in discourse. When she surfaces again, as wife and mother-to-be, national imagining goes side by side with Partition riots. In the Delhi sections of *Midnight's Children* the imagined India reappears in the visual space of the bioscope—the Dilli Dekho machine that shows children the collage of a unified India:

> Inside the peepshow of Lifafa Dass were pictures of the Taj Mahal, and Meenak-shi temple, and the holy Ganges . . . untouchables being touched; educated persons sleeping in large numbers on railway lines. (*MC*, 84)

We may note here the voyeuristic terminology: peepshow, the sight of untouchables being touched, of the educated homeless . . . the exclusions that help the bourgeois Indian child still dream of Indian unity. Meanwhile, in the geographical space of Delhi, attempts at unity are shown to be futile. A Hindu revivalist group (the Ravana gang) terrorizes Muslims, and the Muslim crowd turns on the lone Hindu Lifafa Dass. Once again, the spectacle of woman's body, Amina Sinai provides a national image and averts a riot:

> "Listen," my mother shouted, "Listen well, I am with child. I am a mother who will have a child and I am giving this man my shelter. Come on now, if you want to kill, kill a mother also and show the world what men you are!" (*MC*, 86)

Woman as spectacle of motherhood once again evokes dreams of unity and wholeness. Woman here is the dream of unified India, and her unborn child its hypothetical citizen. In pregnancy she is the symbol of the wholeness of the men themselves. Motherhood, which could be a privileged site for women and also a potential challenge to patriarchal systems through its admitting of, in Kristeva's terms, an "otherness within the self," is appropriated for nationalistic purposes. As Klaus Theweleit has said, "woman is an infinite untrodden territory of desire which at every stage of historical deterritorialization, men in search of material for utopias have inundated with their desires." He further adds that it is the lure of a freer existence that marks this territory of desire and is most often indulged in by men in search of power rather than those already dominant.[18]

How does the figure of Mother cement nation? She suggests common mythic origins. Like the land (which gives shelter and "bears"), she is eternal, patient, essential. National claims have always been buttressed by claims to the soil. The linking of "Mother" with land gains strength from Sita, who was the daughter of Mother Earth. During moments of "national" resurgence, the land is figured as a woman and a mother. In the era of militant Hindu resurgence in the late nineteenth century, Bankim Chandra Chatterjee's *Anand Math* captured the figuration through its famous slogan "Vande Mataram," Victory to the Mother. The film version of this work expressed the role of woman in the euphoria of a newly independent India. Thus, "Mother India" is an enormously powerful cultural signifier, gaining strength not only from atavistic memories from the Hindu epics, Sita, Sati Savitri, Draupadi, but also its use in moments of national (typically conflated with Hindu) cultural resurgence.

Figuring woman/mother as nation also suggests another of the sustaining analogies of the myth of nation. In an analysis of the foundational fictions of Latin America, Doris Sommer speaks of how the analogy of family helped to represent marriage between the different racial groups that comprised Latin American nations.[19] In India, however, exogamous marriage (across regions, religions, castes, and subcastes) was not a historical reality. Hence the analogy of nation as family could only lead to the appropriation and invisibility of minority groups in the hegemonic Hindu national narrative.

Let us now see how this appropriation of the maternal body as the "imaginary site where meaning (or life) is generated,"[20] which excludes women from being meaning makers in their own right, is cemented by film. We have said that Hindi film took upon itself the task of covering the fissures in Indian society through an "India" it represented for its viewers. This "India" was best captured by its "values" figured in woman. Mother as presiding over the link between nation and land/family found its classic expression in a film of the late fifties. I refer to *Mother India*, a film released in 1957, still said to be screened in India every day of the year. Here the nation gains its strength and validity from its metonymic identification of woman with land and family. In *Mother India*, the mother Radha works the land as a serf and is exploited by the forces of capital in Sukhilala the moneylender. She works the land and provides for her family after the death of her husband. And she stands for woman celebrated in the mythic Hindu narratives—of Sita in the *Ramayana* and Draupadi in the *Mahabharata*, who encounter privations (and in Sita's case rejection and expulsion) in the service of their hero-husbands. Her younger son Birju joins the dacoits in order to avenge his family's ruin. This has been read as an allegory of radical action.[21] But the mother kills her own son, using her moral authority within the family and the nation to uphold the law, making the figure a force for conservatism.

In conflating the maternal with the national, the film extinguishes the heterogeneity of Indian women in favor of the Hindu model. The potential of different cultural formations to interrupt one another and reduce the tendency to privilege man's version of woman over historical women is thereby lost. This stereotyping of Hindu Woman as Mother India gives great impetus to the Hindu fundamentalist project, and makes woman's body the very site of fundamentalism.

Feminist criticism has stressed this need to distinguish between woman as sign and women as historical subjects in their own right.[22] Here feminist perception intersects that of critics of Hollywood cinema who argue that by relying on the primacy of the visual, cinema manages to efface real women in its representation of the image of woman. The image privileges what is present over that which is absent. As Christian Metz has said, the mastery of technique in cinema "underlines and denounces the lack on which the whole arrangement is based (the absence of the object, replaced by its reflection), an exploit which consists at the same time of making this absence forgotten."[23]

This disguised lack in cinema has a communal as well as sexual dimension in the case of the film *Mother India*. In this archetypal film of nationalism, the Muslim identity of the actress who played the recognizably Hindu character symbolizing the nation is at once appropriated and emptied of significance. The main actress who played Mother India was the Muslim actress Nargis, and she has always been associated in the minds of the public with Mother India. Her marriage to the Hindu Sunil Dutt, who played her son in the film, cemented her image as Mother India. The cultural message of the film has always been seen as Hindu, with its echoes of Radha, Parvati, Sita, with all of the traditional self-sacrificing virtues ascribed to these women.[24] We have, then, a nationalist articulation of Hindu religion and culture focusing on the figure of a Muslim actress.

Woman, symbol of Hindu nationalism, covers real *women* in India, heterogeneous, various, of many castes, religions, and geographical regions. As spectacle on screen, the regional identity of the actress is usually subsumed under the hegemonizing cultural sway of the Hindi heartland, the Indo-Gangetic plain. The metonymic representation of all women—whatever their cultural identity—as Hindu women is a recurring feature in Hindi film. Indeed, a large majority of popular film actresses have in fact come from the "minority" sections, but rarely are these sections the subject of the national film industry. Because in Indian popular culture, attention is focused on the person of the actor or actress (gossip magazines about these characters constitute a major popular discourse), such metonymic representations obscure, at the level of individual actor, the fissures in Indian society, and may work to appropriate minority groups.

Read against the cultural politics of the Bombay film industry, the spectacle of Amina as Mother India in *Midnight's Children* yields interesting ironies. The conflations of mother with origin, land, family, and Rule of Law, upheld in the Bombay cinema, are exposed in Rushdie's text. Amina is mother but not to her own son, sharing the raising of Vanitha, the street singer's son, with Mary Pereira. The text is much more interested in maternal betrayal. When Saleem's telepathic gifts give him an inside view of women, he uncovers maternal adultery. But this adultery can be read in terms of national anxiety, suggesting the text's complicity with the imaginary of Bombay cinema. His mother, auntie Pia, and Leela Sabarmati become the collective scapegoat for the emergence of militancy and national heroism, especially significant in the context of the Indo-Pakistani war of 1965. Once again it is the expulsion of Sita enacted. The graphic scene linking women's purity with national events is conveyed textually through the letter Salim sends to a Commander Sabarmati. He cuts out words from national newspapers relating current events to phrase a letter of warning. Once again, over the body and morality of woman, national events take shape. There is a public unanimity in the reaction to Commander Sabarmati's murder of his wife ("We knew a Navy man wouldn't stand for it" [*MC*, 314]). The ironies are obvious—woman's shame, dispensable in the urge to modernize, becomes a mystified area once the crisis has passed, and India, from being victim, is now the aggressor and victor in subcontinental politics (the two wars with Pakistan, the second over the creation of Bangladesh, established this position for India).

Woman in Postindependence Anxieties

In *Midnight's Children*, the dream image of woman as embodying the desire for nation becomes subjected to greater ironies even as male desire (represented first in Saleem's erotic attraction to his Auntie Pia and then to his sister, Jamila Singer) continues to provide the narrative's impetus. Each time this desire is deflated. Women recur as different kinds of bodies: the body in adultery, the body aging.

But the myth of nation is in fast decay, especially in the context of partition and war, and with it the dream image of woman. Male dismembering—as Saleem loses first hearing, then hair, then finger—is symptomatic of deep national anxiety. But this, too, happens in relation to the anxiety aroused by women. The description of the other children of midnight allows the narrator to imagine many versions of women who are no longer idealized or a dream, but victims of the brutal realities of poverty. There is Sundari, the beggar, whose face is slashed because her beauty blinds people, but now "was earning a healthy living" and because of her story "received more alms than any other member of her family" (*MC*, 236), and Parvati the witch, who "stood mildly amid gasping crowds while her father drove spikes through her neck" (*MC*, 239). In contemporary India, poverty drives women to present a different kind of spectacle. Wee Willie Winkie's wife Vanitha, the street singer, is a common sight in India's big cities, her rags barely covering the body that in other circumstances is so mystified a site. In poverty, woman's shame is dispensable.

And woman's shame is the cornerstone of Islamic fundamentalism. The status of woman as a sign constantly subordinated to male-dictated contexts is demonstrated in the transformation of Saleem's once uninhibited sister the Brass Monkey into Jamila Singer when the family moves to Pakistan. The Brass Monkey, like the Monkey God Hanuman in the *Ramayana*, has entered the world of corruption (read as Western influence on women). Thus she is friendly with the "hefty" Europeans of Walsingham School and plots with them to discredit the young boys. Later she (temporarily) embraces Christianity. But she can hold her own against these girls—she defeats Evie Burns in a street fight. Saleem's narrative adopts the male-oriented rhetoric of the nation—women are the electorate to be wooed by those in power (*MC*, 221).

Woman becomes the site of the East-West cultural battle so often depicted in Bombay cinema. The classic example in this genre is the film *Purab aur Paschim* (East-West) (1970), where Indian values for women are reiterated over European. The "Westernized" heroine (played by the actress Saira Bano) smokes, wears miniskirts, and is reformed into Indian womanhood by her love for the hero (played by Manoj Kumar, a recognized "nationalist" filmmaker).[25] *Purab aur Paschim* uses woman to vent cultural anxiety in the wake of war and migration. The film targets Indian immigrants in Britain (metonymically represented by women who wear short dresses, smoke, and drink) and the nationalist message of the film is the containment of the threat to national culture (once again represented by Hindu ideals for women) from diasporic Indian populations. In other films of the seventies heroines are similarly reformed or punished for daring convention (*Thodisi Bewafai* and *Do Anjane*, for example).

So too, in *Midnight's Children*, the taming of Jamila Singer, which now involves not the exhibition but the extinguishing of woman as spectacle. As a child, the Brass Monkey was at the center of spectacle—she set fire to shoes. In the cosmopolitan world of Bombay her exuberance was irrepressible, but now, in fundamentalist Pakistan, she is captive to the Pakistani nationalist rhetoric and its view of women. She becomes martyr to the idea of nation. The wheel has come full circle when Jamila's voice, dream/imaginary of the Pakistani nation, is dissociated from her body. Heard by all on the Voice of Pakistan, she is placed during public appearances behind a perforated sheet; "this was how the history of our family once again became the fate of a nation . . . being the new daughter-of-the-nation, her character began to owe more to the most strident aspects of the national persona than to the child-world of her monkey years" (*MC*, 375). As inspirer of men's souls, she must hide her body: "Jamila, daughter, your voice will be a sword for purity; it will be the weapon with which we shall cleanse men's souls" (*MC*, 376). Because "no city which locks its women away is ever short of whores," Saleem Sinai acts on his country's dual view of woman, as saint and whore. While the sister he desires sings of holiness and hides her body, Saleem's lusts drive him to "women of the street"—latrine cleaners, Tai Bibi, whore of strange odors, and eventually Padma, the muscular pickle maker, whose hairy and strong forearms fascinate him.

Midnight's Children represents and ironizes not only the dream image of woman really servicing the psychic needs of the male subject constructed at the time of decolonization, but also her flip side, fat, gross, dirty but strong, as, from the male narrator's point of view, the dream of nation turns to nightmare in the wake of Indo-Pakistani postcolonial history. The text thus demonstrates woman's body's continued exploitation as a sign (albeit not a fixed one—the role of shame, and of spectacle, for instance, keeps changing), and the shifting space it occupies in the tentative process of decolonization and nation forming imaginatively represented in *Midnight's Children*. Reading Rushdie against Bombay cinema reveals gender as a trope in the narrative imagining of nation. This analysis hopes to reveal how all narratives imagining nation—sophisticated postmodern as well as mass cultural—collude in the engendering of nation as male through their representation of the female body. Thus, though Rushdie's representation parodies this engendering, moments in the text are complicit with Bombay cinema's signifying practices on women.

Notes

1. Quotations from *Midnight's Children* are cited in the text with page numbers in parentheses using the abbreviation *MC*: Salman Rushdie, *Midnight's Children* (New York: Avon, 1980).
2. For a useful discussion of mass culture see Irving Howe, "Notes on Mass Culture," *Mass Culture*, ed. B. Rosenberg and D. M. White (Glencoe, Ill.: Free Press, 1957).
3. Sudhir Kakar, "The Cinema as Collective Fantasy," *Indian Cinema Superbazar*, ed. Aruna Vasudev and Philip Lenglet (New York: Advent, 1983), 89–97, 97.
4. Benedict Anderson, *Imagined Communities* (London: Verso, 1983).
5. T. W. Adorno, "Television and the Patterns of Mass Culture," Rosenberg and White, *Mass Culture*, 474–88, 477.
6. See Kishore Vallicha, *The Moving Image: A Study of Indian Cinema* (Bombay: Orient Longman, 1988), 26–27. Subsequent references to Vallicha include page numbers in parentheses.
7. See Vasudev, *Superbazar*, and Kobita Sarkar, *Indian Cinema Today: An Analysis* (New Delhi: Stirling, 1975).
8. Dana Polan, " 'Above All Else to Make You See': Cinema and the Ideology of Spectacle," in *Postmodernism and Politics*, ed. Jonathan Arac (Minneapolis: University of Minnesota Press, 1986), 55–69, 56. Subsequent references to Polan are indicated in parentheses.

9. On the gendering of cinema see Teresa de Lauretis, *Alice Doesn't: Feminism, Semiotics, Cinema* (Bloomington: Indiana University Press, 1984), 8. On the relation of psychoanalysis to desire and viewing see E. Ann Kaplan, "Is the Gaze Male?" *Women and Film: Both Sides of the Camera* (New York & London: Methuen, 1983), 23–35.

10. On the complex mechanisms in women's looking, see Lidia Curti, "What Is Real and What Is Not: Female Fabulations in Cultural Analysis," in *Cultural Studies*, ed. Lawrence Grossberg, Cary Nelson, and Paula Treichler (New York: Routledge, 1992), 143.

11. On female viewing see Jean Franco, "The Incorporation of Women," ed. Tania Modleski, *Studies in Entertainment* (Bloomington: Indiana University Press, 1986), 119–37.

12. Throughout this essay I refer to "Hindu middle classes" not as an essentialized religious or cultural group, but as a construct of a cultural production relying on recognizable Hindu symbolisms. For the recent political use of Hinduism, see Tapan Basu, Pradip Datta, Sumit Sarkar, Tanika Sarkar, and Sambuddha Sen, *Khaki Shorts, Saffron Flags* (Delhi: Orient Longman, 1993). By "modernization" I mean the postindependence changes caused by increased intranational mobility of the professional and clerical sectors, and the legal changes in women's status with the widespread education and visibility of women. These are distinct from the role of women in modernization during reform and nationalism. See Partha Chatterjee, "The Nation and Its Women," in *The Nation and Its Fragments: Colonial and Postcolonial Histories* (Princeton: Princeton University Press, 1993), 116–58. See Immanuel Wallerstein's discussion of "modernity" and Westernization, "Culture as the Ideological Battleground of the Modern World System," *Global Culture*, ed. Mike Featherstone (London, Newbury Park, and New Delhi: Sage, 1990), 45.

13. Made by H. S. Rawail, this film was very popular in the sixties, chiefly because of its music. The sixties was a decade of euphoric nationalism, centering in the early half around the figure of Nehru, and fueled by the war with China and the two wars with Pakistan.

14. Although released in 1971, this is essentially a film of the late fifties as it took twenty years to complete. In mood and representation of women, it echoes the earlier period of filmmaking. The fifties and sixties were notable for the preponderance of Muslim themes. See Hameeduddin Mahmood, *The Kaleidoscope of Indian Cinema* (New Delhi: East West Press, 1974), 84.

15. Teresa de Lauretis, *Alice Doesn't*, 139.

16. See Kumkum Sangari and Sudesh Vaid, "Recasting Women: An Introduction," in *Recasting Women: Essays in Colonial History*, ed. Sangari and Vaid (New Brunswick, N.J.: Rutgers University Press, 1990), 10–11.

17. Frantz Fanon, *Studies in a Dying Colonialism* (New York: Monthly Review Press, 1959), 35–67.

18. Klaus Theweleit, *Male Fantasies* (Minneapolis: University of Minnesota Press, 1987), 294.

19. Doris Sommer, "The Foundational Fictions of Latin America," *Nation and Narration*, ed. Homi Bhabha (New York: Routledge, 1990), 71–98.

20. Mary Jacobus, *Body/Politics: Women and the Discourses of Science*, ed. Mary Jacobus, Evelyn Fox Keller, and Sally Shuttleworth (New York and London: Routledge, 1990), 7.

21. Vijay Mishra, "The Texts of 'Mother India,'" *Kunapipi* 11, 1 (1989): 119–37, 134.

22. Mary Poovey, "Speaking of the Body: Mid-Victorian Constructions of Female Desire," in *Body/Politics*, 29.

23. Mary Ann Doane, "Technology, Representation, and the Feminine," in *Body/Politics*, 170–76.

24. Mishra, "Texts," 125–26.

25. The director is noted for his interest in nationalist themes. The film in question deals with the protection of Indian values for women in an era of change. To assess the nationalist mood at the time, it is useful to note that this era was framed by the two wars with Pakistan—1965 and 1971 (Sarcar, *Indian Cinema*, 147).

FIVE

Betrayal: An Analysis in Three Acts

Kamala Visweswaran

> Instead of interrogating a category, we will interrogate a woman. It will at
> least be more agreeable.[1]

Introduction

In this paper, I attempt to confront some of the dilemmas within recent contemporary feminist theorizing of difference by reading a series of specific social relations ("betrayals") as allegory for the practice of feminist ethnography.

Such a theme is poignantly suggested by Judith Stacey's (1988) article, "Can There Be a Feminist Ethnography?" Here Stacey argues that "feminist researchers are apt to suffer the delusion of alliance more than the delusion of separateness,"[2] and that such delusion may lead to what she calls "the feminist ethnographer's dilemma" in which the ethnographer inevitably betrays (or I might add, is betrayed by), a feminist principle. Stacey concludes by asserting that there can be no fully feminist ethnography.

In Stacey's narrative, the paired terms "betrayal" and "innocence" metonymically recall one another. Feminist innocence is betrayed by relations of power; betrayal signals the loss of innocence. The terms recur as place markers for the loss of an earlier moment in feminist thinking that theorized a sisterhood without attending to the divides that separated women. Donna Haraway has recently noted that the costs for feminist theory of maintaining such moments of innocence are great, especially in the questioning of what is meant by feminism.[3] If, for example, one exchanged Stacey's definition of feminism based upon assumed affinity and identity for a contested field of meanings around issues of specificity and difference, how would a feminist ethnography be reconstituted?

I suggest that "betrayal," rather than signaling the impossibility of a feminist ethnography, can more appropriately be read as allegory for its practice at a moment when feminist theory is repositioning itself along the lines of difference.[4] Allegory, as James Clifford has reminded us, "draws special attention to the narrative character of cultural representations, to the stories built into the representational process itself."[5] It generates multiple levels of meanings, and further allows us to say that "this is a story about that."

If this is a story about "betrayal," then the central, unspoken betrayal here is, of course, my own assumption of a universal sisterhood between women. At crucial junctures, this assumption both informs and is interrupted by the analysis that follows, forestalling, I hope, any reading of this piece as redemptive allegory. There are places where the analysis is deliberately uneven, points at which I stray from definitive reportage, moments when I undercut my own authority, moments when readers inevitably challenge my authority. The response of many a disciplinary practitioner confronted with questions of authority posed by experimental ethnography has been to attempt a more authoritative account. My response has been the contrary: to offer a decidedly less authoritative account so that readers continually question it as ethnography.

This analysis takes a dramaturgical form. Allegorical in the Shakespearean sense, it opens with a betrayal and ends with a death.[6] As such it is a story about loss and transgression; violation and disappointment. The three acts outlined here are themselves social performance, which, as Turner has argued, "enact powerful stories providing social process with a rhetoric and mode of emplotment and meaning." This analysis is framed as theater, not only to emphasize agency as performance, but as a means of underscoring the constructedness and staging of identity.[7] Identities are constituted by context and are themselves asserted as partial accounts.

Agreeing with Marilyn Strathern's analysis of the differences between feminist anthropology and experimental ethnography,[8] Stacey herself posits a certain rapprochement between feminist ethnography and experimental ethnography on the notion of "partial accounts." In this paper, however, there is a deliberate concatenation of the partial account with the partial(ly revealed) identity. For this reason, I attempt a move from the history of the fragment (or partial account) to its epistemology.

Let me then indicate the shape of this analysis in three acts. The key characters are two women, Janaki and Uma, who met when they were imprisoned together in the days of the Indian nationalist movement for committing acts of individual satyagraha. The first act of analysis attempts an "accountable positioning," an effort to situate a series of "betrayals" within an organization of knowledge in order to recuperate it within the parameters of a feminist epistemology that describes the production of knowledge as situated and relational.

Act II attempts to work this feminist epistemology into a feminist ethnography by stressing temporality, silence, and the multiple identities set into play by silence. Here my reading shifts to a reading of betrayal as symptomatic of an inequality and power differential between women, as well as a marker for women's agency. I examine how Janaki's identity in particular is partial, contradictory, and strategic; how her silences can be read as both resistance and capitulation.

Act III of the analysis situates this emergent feminist ethnography in the specific ideological context of its production. It traces the influence of the master narrative of Indian nationalism upon individual narratives as an attempt to locate other sources of ideological subject positioning. I emphasize the importance of Janaki and Uma's silences, their refusals to speak, by situating them in a larger arena of nationalist silence: the family. Finally, I demonstrate the potential of women's agency to defy the containments of Indian nationalist discourse.

ACT 1, SCENE 1

First Interview with Uma
Q: At what age were you married?
A: At age 16.
Q: That's late for those days?
A: Yes, but my mother married young and she was determined I should marry later.

Second Interview with Uma
Q: What are your ideas about child marriage and widow remarriage?
A: There should be no child marriages. My mother's mother was married when she was one. My mother's sister was married when she was five. That is wrong. At that age what do they know about marriage? These people would act as if marriage was doll's play. Then after ten or twelve years, they would make the marriage legal. After marriage they would put the couple together. This is wrong. It can't be done like that. So a law brought the age of marriage to 14. But that was also wrong, so a new law brought the age of marriage to 18.
Q: Have you seen any widow remarriages?
A: I have seen. It was very good, but we should not force them. We can do it only if it's their choice. It's a good thing.

ACT 1, SCENE 2

A few days later I met Janaki. A friend of Uma's from her jail days, I had first met Janaki in Uma's home. This time I was meeting Janaki in the cramped quarters of the CPI-M (Communist Party of India-Marxist) office in Washermanpet, a congested area of North Madras, several miles from the orthodox Triplicane neighborhood where Uma stayed.

It was now the end of a long (three-hour) interview. I had run out of tape and was getting ready to leave.

"By the way," asked Janaki with a twinkle in her eye, "did Uma tell you she was a child widow?"

I was stunned and shook my head in confusion. At first I thought I'd misheard her. Janaki gave me a triumphant grin. "Yes, that Subramaniam is her second husband, the one she married when she was 16."

"No," I said slowly, "she didn't tell me that. I always assumed Subramaniam was her first husband."

"Well, she was married when she was five or six, then that man died. This Subramaniam was very progressive—a Congressman—he didn't mind marrying a child widow. That's why he married Uma."

"Don't tell her I told you so," warned Janaki as she sent me out the door. I could only nod my head in mute agreement.

ACT 2, SCENE 1

First Interview with Janaki
Q: When you were selling khadi in Madras, did people say anything about your being unmarried?
A: I left that work when the Congress Socialist party came; no one knew I was unmarried. At first there was talk. There were problems when I stayed with my brother and his family. He had three girls. He used to ask, "Why are these girls still unmarried?"
Q: Did your family ask you to leave for the sake of the three girls' marriages?
A: Nobody said anything. I left the house on my own.

Second Interview with Janaki
Janaki speaking:
Didn't they think that all women who lived in the city were prostitutes? Even if there is a party, there are obstacles to joining politics. We changed that today. The reason is I myself have stood for election. I told my sister that after making a chain I am going to wear it. Seeing it, people thought it was the "Tali" (marriage necklace), and I stood for election.

ACT 2, SCENE 2

I was sitting in the Egmore Archives looking at Janaki's jail file. Getting the record itself had been quite an achievement. Files were often misplaced, or the harried and overworked staff often simply said that file did not exist. That was what they had told me the first time I requisitioned the file. The second time I requested it, I received it along with nine other files. So now I was looking through it and trying to make sense of the information it held. There was the report from the Inspector of Police, Intelligence Section, on the occasion of Janaki's sentencing January 1, 1941. It said:

> Mrs. P. R. Janaki is the wife of a Brahmin priest but has not been living with him.

But the text of the judgment given a day earlier read:

> Accused is Mrs. P. R. Janaki, wife of one Mr. Ramachandran Iyer, who is reported to be employed in a film company at Calcutta and who is a four anna Congress member.

And then to confuse matters more there was an appeal to the Chief Secretary of the Government of Madras from one T. N. Ramachandran, "Playwright and film director," protesting the sentencing of his wife P. R. Janaki to "C" class, the lowest designation in the British prison classification scheme.

The final document in the file was a letter addressed to a T. N. Ramachandran Pillai from the General Secretary of the Madras All-India Hindu Mahasabha stating his inability to make inquiries into Janaki's sentencing.

I was left to wonder: Who was the Brahmin priest? Could it have been the Ramachandran Iyer referred to in the judgment? But two documents said that Ramachandran Iyer was involved in films—a strange occupation for a priest, if that was really what he was. Or perhaps the British officials had just confused the caste name with his occupation (a common enough occurrence). "Iyer" was a Brahmin name and Brahmins were the priestly caste.

But the letter from the Hindu Mahasabha addressed Janaki's husband as "Pillai," a different caste altogether, and a non-Brahmin one at that. There was something disturbing about the way the records almost, but not quite, meshed.

Then I remembered that Janaki had not told me she was married at all.

ACT 3, SCENE 1

The next time I met Janaki was in Tangam's house. Tangam was a friend who also worked in the women's wing of the CPI-M and who knew Janaki well. In fact, Janaki frequently came over to play with Tangam's two children (they called Janaki "patti" or grandmother). Tangam said she often grew impatient with Janaki's stories, but Tangam's husband liked to listen to her, and so she would seek him out in particular.

I had told Tangam about the record I had discovered in the archives. Tangam knew the whole story. "We'll ask her about it," she said. "But I don't know if she'll be frank with you." "That's all right," I said. "If she doesn't want to talk about it, I have to respect her decision."

ACT 3, SCENE 2

Tangam nudged me. "So tell her about the record you found." Already uncomfortable about the interview, I hesitated before I began.

"Janaki, I found a record at the Archives which said 'Mrs. P. R. Janaki. . . .' What does that mean? Why does it say Mrs.?"

"Oh," said Janaki blithely, "we often told the jail authorities we were married so that they would give us more respect and not harass us."

I should have stopped there. But I did not and I could not. "But the record says you were married to a Brahmin priest—who was it?"

"No one."

Tangam looked at Janaki. "Why don't you tell her about it? Tell."

Janaki tried another tack. "Oh, yes, as a child I was married to an old man, but we were poor and my family could not pay the groom's family the dowry we promised. As I myself was against getting married, we left it."

"Really?" I asked.

Tangam said to me in English, "She is not going to be frank. I don't know why, but she is not telling you the truth."

"Leave it," I said. But Tangam had grown impatient with the old lady. "Tell her about Ramachandran," she insisted.

Betrayal flickered in Janaki's eyes; they seemed to plead with Tangam not to expose her. Instead, Tangam turned to me and said, "Tell her about the letters Ramachandran wrote."

Janaki's eyes sparked and then her face deflated. Her secret was out.

Some things of course were clearer, but a high price had been paid for that clarity. The Brahmin priest referred to in the records was Janaki's first husband-to-be. As an arranged marriage, it would have been an in-caste affair. Ramachandran, on the other hand, had been the partner of her choice and was not necessarily a Brahmin. As one document suggested, he could have been a Pillai (a prominent non-Brahmin regional caste).

I had wanted to stop, but now I could only see what I had started to its painful conclusion. I did not know the exact nature of Janaki's relationship to Ramachandran—whether they had actually been married or not. I knew only from Tangam that at a certain point Janaki left him to live alone again. Yet it was possible that Janaki had never known of Ramachandran's efforts to get her status reclassified in jail, and perhaps that knowledge would be of some small consolation.

"Did you know," I began, "that someone named Ramachandran had been very concerned about you when you were in jail in 1941? He wrote a lot of letters to people trying to get you into B class."

"No," said Janaki, sulking. But I noticed that her face had brightened a little. Then she abruptly turned to Tangam and asked, "Why does she want to know these things?"

Tangam told her: "Only if she knows what it was like for women of that time can she write about it accurately. What were the problems women faced? What were their difficulties? Kamala is very sympathetic; she is not going to blame you. She only wants to understand."

Janaki stared briefly at the wall, then changed the subject.

I thought of the foreword to Le Roy Ladurie's book, *Montaillou*: "From Inquisition to Ethnography."[9] Was I, to use his terms, "ethnographe et policier?" "A kind of obsessive and compulsive Maigret?" What kind of knowledge was I policing anyway? And what kind of confession did I hope to produce?

In playing detective, I searched for hidden facts, hoping to fit together different pieces of a puzzle. Then followed the interrogation in which I sought confirmation of facts uncovered. "Facts," as we know, are compelling. And facts were compelling me. A will to knowledge had been set into play, but whose will was it? It was a will that was at once alien to me, and one in which, with some shock, I felt myself sentient.

I could not help wondering: Had I been "simply" a cultural anthropologist, would I have gone to the archives to detect the record that gave me the conflicting information about Janaki? And had I been only a historian, would I have imagined that the women I encountered in the archives might choose to tell me a story at odds with documented "facts"?

Of course these were ruminations as confused as they were reductive. Anthropologists have been struggling with the interpretation of history, as of social life, for many years. And, of course, oral historians in particular have had to address issues of the construction of evidence, and questions of narrative veracity, from the beginning. No, what happened was not the result of an unforeseen confluence between the methods of history and anthropology, between reading narratives and hearing them.

An Inquisition had been set in motion, and I was its naive if unwilling architect. The questions were not merely, "Why did Janaki betray Uma, and Tangam betray Janaki?" or even "Why was Tangam's help enlisted in confronting Janaki?" for indeed, would anyone have betrayed anyone else had the anthropologist not provided the opportunity? For a year or longer I was paralyzed by this set of incidents. The horror of my trespass lingered on. I did not know how I could or should, write about it. Indeed, I thought more that I could not, and should not.

I recognize that the issue extends beyond my own agency and culpability; it has to do with the very organization of knowledge and the structure of inquiry. Still, I want neither to imply a kind of complete, self-willed agency (I only am responsible); nor a kind of total overdetermined agency (what happened was solely the product of my training). The answer, I think, lies somewhere between the two extremes. I had witnessed one betrayal and staged another, but it was equally clear that I was a secondary character in a drama that existed before my arrival, and that would continue after my departure.

The three ethnographic acts I have described—Janaki's revelation of Uma's secret and Janaki's story about pretending to be married; my consequent discovery of Janaki's marriage in the archives; and finally my confrontation of Janaki with Tangam—converge to produce a questioning of the interlocutor. Yet I narrate these events of "betrayal," not with the aim of producing a more vivid confessional ethnography, nor with the object of rehearsing the timeworn ethnographic formula that it is only after talking to our informants over a period of time that we eventually learn the "truth." My concern is rather one of epistemology. How do we arrive at what we call the "truth"? And conversely: What is the truth produced by a specific kind of epistemology?

This analysis of betrayal is not a philosophical point about the perversity of information retrieval, nor is it intended as a fable about my loss of innocence as a feminist researcher.[10] It is an attempt to locate myself in a field of power (the West) and in the production of a particular knowledge (about the East). It is an effort at "accountable positioning" (to use Donna Haraway's term), an endeavor to be answerable for what I learned to see, and for what I have learned to do. Here I want to advance the case for a critical feminist epistemology that finds its stakes, as with other interested and subversive epistemologies, in limited location and, as Haraway puts it, "situated knowledge." This feminist way of knowing sees the process of positioning itself as an epistemological act.

Situated accounts by definition exclude some analytic elements from their purview while focusing intensely on others. Acts of omission are as important to read as the acts of commission in constructing the analysis. A partial account also locates one of the ideological processes of subject positioning within the production of knowledge itself: both for the "I" who investigates and the "I" who is investigated. It assumes that the relationship of knower to known is constituted by the process of knowing.[11] Conversely, the process of knowing is itself determined by the relationship of knower to known. Such a focus leads us to ask how the terms of our current discussion, betrayer and betrayed, are implicated in the relationship between some women's refusal to be subject(ed), and my own subject position. Indeed, this paper is perhaps more about the proliferation of a certain kind of subject position that enables me to write as it is about the subject positions of the Tamil women about whom I write.

And what of this subject position, my own location, intellectually and otherwise? It has become almost commonplace to rehearse inventories that begin with middle-class and end with Western or Western-educated.[12] Nor can I better specify the peculiarities of my own positioning (more "second generation" than "postcolonial") by characterizing the contours of my audience. Although the questioning shifts from "who speaks" to "who listens,"[13] such a maneuver has also become increasingly sterile, for it is clear that I write for an audience narrowly constituted by the academy, be they feminists, anthropologists, or postmodern critics.

Then there are the expectations and demands of this Western, if not largely American, audience, its hunger for news of the "Third World Woman," which as Trinh Minh-ha has noted, "came to listen to that voice of difference."[14] Gayatri Spivak has likewise dubbed this the (Third World) "information retrieval system."[15] My admittedly limited strategy as a member of this system is to resist at the junctures I am able, even as I knowingly (if not always willingly) perpetuate it.

Although one of my identities was that of anthropologist, such a term had no currency among the people with whom I spoke. Janaki perceived me as a historian, and as such, a writer of "official history," an official history of which she was aware and in which she wanted to be included. As I argue later, her choice to stage for me only certain aspects of her life has as much to do with the censoring power of official history and nationalist ideology as it has to do with her "own reasons." Perhaps, along with the situated knowledges Donna Haraway advocates, we can also speak of "situational knowledges"—knowledges produced both in and for a specific context. That is, these acts of "betrayal" can also be read as a series of moments of self-staging and fashioning: Uma's, Janaki's, and my own. Thus I am not concerned with whether Janaki lied to me; I want more to understand why she told me what she did. For Janaki tells me not about being married, but about *pretending* to be married, and it is this staging I want to apprehend.

It is important to recognize that, confronted with facts at odds with her story, Janaki does not "confess." For her the secret closest to her heart was not that she was married, but that she was married to Ramachandran. She reveals the facts about her marriage strategically, and in the end, when she sees I know of Ramachandran, refuses to either confirm or deny that knowledge. It is also significant that what I learned about Janaki outside of what she herself told me in no way altered the substance of her self-representation as a courageous and independent woman. If anything, it deepened and enriched it.

In the end I can only speculate on certain aspects of Janaki's life. That moment of shock when I saw myself reflected in the panopticon has become the space in which Janaki has reclaimed the integrity of her secrets. She is no longer a puzzle for me to solve but a woman with her reasons, not so unlike me. Finally, there is a complicity between different kinds of refusals: Janaki's in refusing to tell me what I wanted to know; and my own as ethnographer, in refusing to tell my audience all it wants to know about Janaki. This strategized complicity between subjects unequal in power unfolds into a peculiar form of knowing, one in which the confounding yet tactical junction of disclosure and exposure is dramatized. In interrupting a Western (sometime feminist) project of subject retrieval, recognition of the partially understood is not simply strategy but accountability to my subjects; partial knowledge is not so much choice as necessity.

My first act of analysis has been to suggest that a set of betrayals is emblematic of the unequal power relations involved in the production of ethnographic knowledge. Now let me shift gears and move to another level of analysis. Consider the question, What are the tactics a feminist epistemology can deploy to develop a different kind of ethnography? I want to claim shifting identities, temporality, and silence as tools of a feminist ethnography.

First, a feminist ethnography can consider how identities are multiple, contradictory, partial, and strategic. The underlying assumption is, of course, that the subject herself represents a constellation of conflicting social, linguistic, and political forces.[16] Individual narratives can be seen as both expressive and ideological in nature. However, the category "experience" is utilized not to pin down the truth of any individual subject, but as a means of reading ideological contradictions.[17] It could gauge the processes of subject constitution in the articulation of individual with master narratives.

Experimental ethnography has argued that we play with voicing, but let me suggest that we look not only at language, or how things are said, but also at when and where things are said. The partiality of identity is seen to be inextricable from the contingency of speech. In locating the temporality of speech, we gain another lens on the constitution of subjectivity. Further, understanding gender as a temporal construction underscores what it means to be "at times a woman."[18]

But who said what to whom is equally important, for knowledge is also relational. Here the "truth" is refracted through a series of unequal relationships of power: that between myself and Uma, between myself and Janaki, between Uma and Janaki, between Janaki and Tangam. Janaki's reluctance to speak is framed by Tangam's betrayal of her and her own betrayal of Uma. Interpretation was now seriated through a chain of relationships, although one of those relationships, that between Janaki and Tangam, remains outside the purview of this analysis.

Elsewhere, I have described some of the difficulties in merging feminist theorizing too quickly with strategies of experimental voicing. There I suggested that polyphony and multiple voicings are not a solution to the vexed problems of power and authority, and that we should be attentive to silence as a marker of women's agency. I argued that a feminist ethnography cannot assume the willingness of women to talk, and maintained that "One avenue open to it is to investigate when and why women do talk; to assess the strictures placed on their speech; the avenues of creativity they have appropriated; the degrees of freedom they possess."[19] Perhaps, then, a feminist ethnography can take the silences among women as its central site for the analysis of power between them. We can begin to shape a notion of agency that, while it privileges speaking, is not reducible to it. My aim is to theorize a kind of agency where resistance can be framed by silences, a refusal to speak.[20] In this my task is partly, as one critic has suggested, one of "measuring silences."[21]

Ofttimes our theorization is limited in its formulation of resistance as speech. Bourdieu's notion of heterodoxic discourse is a good example. He says:

> Private experiences undergo nothing less than a change of state when they recognize themselves in the public objectivity of an already constituted discourse, the objective sign of recognition of their right to be spoken publicly. . . . This is true not only of establishment language, but also of the heretical discourses.[22]

But Bourdieu has failed to theorize the third term between the "what goes without saying" and the "what cannot be said." This is the "refusal to say," that which is willfully not spoken. Indeed, it is this third term that most interests me.

Acts 1 and 2 reveal decisive silences in Uma and Janaki's narratives of their marriages. Of course I have dramatized these silences, but this does not mean that listening is not a part of the process of speaking. If we do not know how to "hear" silence, we cannot apprehend what is being spoken, how speech is framed.

It is possible that both Uma and Janaki did not experience their child marriages as something "real," and therefore do not remember them. In this sense, Uma's words "At that age, what do they know of marriage?" can be taken to be somewhat self-referential. But we cannot rule out the force of social opinion and nationalist ideology; the former regarded child widows as objects of fear and disgust, and the latter depicted child brides as objects of pity and reform. Uma and Janaki's refusal to speak of their child marriages reflects the stigmatized nature of this category, and perhaps considerable affective distress as well.

In speaking of her grandmother's child marriage, Uma avoids speaking of her own, just as in "betraying" Uma's child marriage, Janaki avoids speaking of her own. Here women's silences about their early marriages are bordered by their descriptions of other child marriages. It is almost as if they are unable to think of the fate so narrowly escaped, and this kind of nonremembrance occurs with a kind of sublated reference to specific women—child widows—with whom they disavow any identification. This disavowed identification, however, is also the means through which they are able to articulate some agency. For a child widow is not in control of her own destiny. She is incapable of acting to change her fate. Indeed, the very source of her widowhood is the sin she has committed in another lifetime, for which she is now paying with the death of her husband. Janaki, for example, talked scornfully of her older sister, widowed at age eleven, who refused to try and change her fate by going to the widow's home:

> She was shaved. After she was shaved, she was given a white sari to wear and could not eat in the evening. She must only sleep on a grass mat, she could not eat hot food. Like this, everything was so strict then. . . .
> The family was very orthodox. I ignored the old ways. I joined the women's organization. And my sister, I also opposed her. Always the hypocrisy, if you touched like that she would wash, so orthodox. So I joined. I wanted to do something besides sitting in the house like her.

Of course, Uma avoids the fate of the child widow only because she is remarried to a man who is willing to marry a widow. Janaki, on the other hand, avoids her fate first because of her family's poverty, and second because of her own insistence that the marriage not be finalized. This is the factor that I think triggers Janaki's "betrayal" of Uma.

Yet was Janaki's betrayal of her friend Uma really a betrayal? It was no accident, I think, that the tape recorder was off, or that I was on my way out the door before Janaki made her revelations. In a sense, Janaki had preserved her friend's secret in the moment of its utterance. Was Janaki not, after all, playing by the rules of official history? The tape recorder was off, and the notebook was closed. Therefore what she told me could not be recorded as "fact." And, as I was on my way out the door, I had no further opportunities to question her about what she had told me.

I read Janaki's exposure of her friend, then, as a partial exposition of her own agency. It is by laying bare the aspects of Uma's life to which I did not have access that the contrast to Janaki's own life is heightened.

During the course of the second interview, Janaki parodies married women like her friend Uma. In asking her about the difficulties married women might have encountered in jail, Janaki had replied, "Once the husband was arrested, he became so concerned about his wife's chastity that he sent her to jail too so he didn't have to worry that she would run off with another man!" Weeks earlier I had asked the same question of Uma and she had commented that "Husbands and wives both used to go to jail so they didn't have any problems." Thus Janaki's response to this question reveals a critical deconstruction of nationalist ideology even as Uma's recapitulates it. Gandhi, for example, always emphasized the importance of women securing permission from their father or husband before going to jail. Janaki's betrayal of Uma, then, is a way of emphasizing her own agency at the same time that she undercuts Uma's, who, she insinuates, went to jail because her husband sent her there.

In this way, Janaki again constructs her own agency through the projected nonagency of another woman, her friend Uma. In Janaki's eyes, Uma was what she was because of her husband. Had Subramaniam not married Uma, Janaki implies, Uma would have lived the rest of her life as a child widow and would not have joined the nationalist movement. Janaki, on the other hand is presented as a woman of her own self-fashioning.

Is my audience disturbed at the claim that a woman's agency is constructed in reference to other women, but at the same time resists that reference? Is it uneasy that I see a contrast not between active men and inactive women, but between active women and inactive women? Is it concerned that a woman's own volition could be contrasted with the lesser—or lack of—volition of other women?

What I describe now is a specific relationship of power between two women that hinges in part upon class difference. For although Uma and Janaki are friends, and both are Brahmin women, their friendship is not impermeable to the effects of class, which radically alter their life experiences. Both women begin their lives as the subjects of child marriages and end their lives alone, though it is not clear whether Janaki can exactly be called a widow. But there the similarity ends. Uma has lived a life of comfort, in a nice house, surrounded by family. Janaki, on the other hand, has lived much of her life as an activist alone, in a shifting, hand-to-mouth existence. Her narratives are punctuated with references to hunger.

The class-differentiated nature of Janaki's and Uma's experiences is suggested by Janaki's account of her first political demonstration:

> I was on a march with Ambujammal, Manjubashini, and others that happened to pass by my street. I felt very proud to be marching with them. Then I saw my brother and tears on his face. He was crying, "If women start participating in the Freedom Struggle, where will the country go?" When I saw the tears on his face, I thought the reverse—that they were tears of happiness. But when I came home, he threw me inside a room and slammed the door. He shouted, "Pavi! (Sinner!) We are only poor Brahmins. They are all rich people educated abroad. What does it matter if they are arrested—they will get A class. You will get a warrant in your name and you'll get C class along with the prostitutes." So saying, he bolted the door.

In the prison classification scheme of that time, "A" class was reserved strictly for the nationalist elite, those who could prove they had great wealth or status. "B" class was more subject to negotiation. One had to have some means, but often one's status was enough to be granted "B" class, particularly if one had had an English education. Class "C" was for those with neither means nor status and included the category "common criminal." Much energy was expended by nationalists on getting the British to accept the category "political prisoner" in order to be granted minimum "B" class status. Thus when Uma goes to jail, she has both class and gender privilege. The first because she receives "B" class, and the second because she is a married, respectable woman who has her husband's support. It is this differential that is underscored by Janaki's narrative.

For Uma, marriage is a proudly acknowledged aspect of her identity. But marriage for Janaki is something that she is continually playing with, repudiating in one moment and appropriating in the next. At times she is a married woman when she is not, as when she buys a gold chain she knows will be taken for a *tali* while campaigning for election. She is the city woman who is bold enough (and here again the reference to prostitutes) to run for election. Yet she gains respect while campaigning by wearing a gold chain, which implies she is married. At other times she is married, but keeps this a secret, possibly because of Ramachandran's occupation, acting, which was not then considered a respectable activity.

However, in disavowing her status as wife, Janaki forfeits the only identity available to her through nationalist ideology. If it is true that the multidimensional nature of Janaki's subjectivity is clearly shown in relief to other women, it is equally true that Janaki is ineligible for many of the identities claimed by women that are posited by nationalist ideology: that of mother, daughter, and sister. Janaki has no children so she is denied the status of "mother." She loses both of her parents in early childhood, so she is not the "dutiful daughter." She loses contact with her three brothers after the oldest one disowns her for moving too freely in nationalist circles, so she is no more a sister.

Although Gandhi attempted to open up the subject position of "wife" by arguing that the terms of the marriage contract be changed and women allowed to choose their own husbands, such a move can still be seen as a strategy of containment, an attempt to keep women within defined roles. Janaki's rejection of the only remaining term in this gendered sign-chain—that of "wife"—is perhaps her attempt to forge a different identity for herself as a single woman outside of known familial relationships; thus her appropriation of "unmarried" status through a kind of silence or refusal to speak about her marriage(s).

Nationalist ideology, of course, translated the status of "unmarried woman" into "spinster" or "widow"—both of which are defined by their failure at marriage: the former through a failure to achieve it, and the latter through a failure to maintain it. Janaki avoids both of these identifications, even though Gandhi himself tried to carve out a space for the spinster as celibate, unmarried woman. But in Janaki's self-representation, she has never desired marriage and therefore cannot be called a spinster. She has never been married and therefore cannot be called a widow. Janaki, then, resists with her silences and refusals to speak the negative subject positions nationalist ideology would slot her into—widow or spinster—even as she plays with the only positive subject position accorded to her: that of wife. Janaki's experimentation with the role of wife reveals the strategic construction of her subjectivity and the partiality of her identity.

Yet Janaki's resistance is not unproblematic. At times she is trapped by the oppositional subject position she occupies. Uma has lived her life with all the privileges and security of a married woman. Uma's chastity was never in doubt. By virtue of this recognized status she earned the title "chaste woman." The status conferred on Janaki as an unmarried woman is quite different. She struggles to achieve recognition as a chaste woman; her narratives are marked by references to prostitutes and threats to her sexual integrity. Class and status are collapsed in Janaki's narratives to identify her as a lower-class, unmarried woman. Consider, for example, the end of Janaki's second interview:

> Q: Is there any memorable incident in your life during the freedom struggle?
> A: There are so many. I can't say which one in particular . . . . Well, in Congress there was one Baliah. He was from Trichy. He would come to my house often. But since I was alone he thought he could do whatever with me. I would do stitching. When he came he would give 5s and 10s [rupee notes]. From 1935 to '36 I did needlework. Afterwards, when party work came I left it. I am not worried about money. He would come at night to talk about politics. He was a Congress MLA [Member of the Legislative Assembly]. He thought I should go with him when he went to meetings. One day, as soon as I saw him I knew

there was something strange. "Sir, please go to my brother's house," I said just like that. They called me to a meeting in Rajapalayam. He insisted I must not go. I gave him the keys and sent him outside.

At my brother's house they had gone to a movie. "I'll stay here," he said. "I am stubborn." "You are a pervert," I said, and locked the door and left. When I returned from the cinema he asked why I was not coming to my room. "I am going to my brother's house; I'll stay there only," I said. "I'll come along," he said. I saw the broom and gave him a lot of whacks. An MLA, but then how awful he should be! It happened then, when I was 17 or 18 years old. When I lived on Govinda Naickka Street.

It is significant that Janaki narrates this episode at the end of the interview. Janaki's response to a question about the memorable incident in her life during the Freedom Struggle is unusual. Most respond with a description of their first meeting with Gandhi or of various other freedom fighters encountered. The fact that Janaki closes this narrative with an episode that marks her vulnerability as a young woman is particularly striking.

It is my contention that the silence irrupted by the betrayals I have described tells us much about the expressive and ideological lived experiences of these two women. The "betrayals" themselves define the parameters of women's agency and identity. They reveal how women who fell outside the sign-chain of possible nationalist subject positions could be compelled to construct themselves as lone individuals, even in relationship to their friends. I have discussed the exposition of Janaki's agency in relation to Uma, as well as the relationship of Janaki's agency to the gendered ideological subject positions of nationalism. For the third act of analysis, let me try to look in more detail at how women's narratives are produced both through and against the master narrative of Indian nationalism. Here I would like to move from an analysis of women's silences to a discussion, however limited, of their speech.

One of Gandhi's interventions in nationalist discourse was to gender it by inscribing the rule of the family into politics; the family is written again as metaphor for the nation. He says, for example, that the "doctrine of satyagraha is not new: it is merely an extension of the rule of domestic life to the political."[23] Yet with "family" now a metaphor for the nation, the term becomes discursively fixed, leaving relations within the family pointedly undiscussed.

Even such a schematic understanding allows us to reply more clearly to the historians of India who are puzzled by why the family does not appear to change under nationalism. They are concerned with "the absence in every phase of any significant struggle by women themselves to change relations within or outside the family."[24] Yet the family does not appear to change, because seen discursively, it is the point of nationalist silence. As Partha Chatterjee has himself suggested, it cannot change precisely because the home is the realm of nationalist victory over colonialism when the world has been lost to the West.

But there is no simple reproduction of the family and nation through marriage. Ideological discourses can be interrupted, if only briefly, by individual agency. For marriage is a term negotiated by women in different ways. It is by being married *differently* that women displace the family/nation metonymy and assert their own agency.

This, then, is the ideological context for understanding Uma's and Janaki's agency. Their refusal to speak of their marriages must be measured against this larger silence. Uma, for example, is eclipsed in its shadow; she capitulates. She reproduces the nationalist silence on the "woman question" (read: the family) when she is questioned about whether she was able to take up issues of widow remarriage while doing District Congress Committee work. She says:

> There was no time to take them up. Then in our Congress Committee we discussed what we would do and how we would act after freedom came. In that time, how to get freedom, how to send the Raj out of the country, how to win rule of our country. For us this was the main point. Dr. Muthulakshmi Reddy, Subbalakshmi, women like this only did these things. In the party there was no time to think of this. Then it was, "In which village should we have a meeting? What to say, what to do? In which village should we make propaganda?" Those kinds of things we were doing.

Where issues concerning women and the family disappear in Uma's account, Janaki's by contrast foregrounds and questions the nature of the family. Here, Janaki's speech confronts discursive hegemony. Upon her first arrest she describes her sentencing by the district magistrate:

> Then the question of my caste arose. I said I couldn't say. "Well, then, what is your parents' caste?" they asked. I said my mother is of the woman caste and my father of the man caste. "No, no. A family has to have a caste," they insisted. "Is that so?" I said. "In my family there are two castes: a man caste and a woman caste. Nothing else." I was sentenced to three more months in prison because I would not tell my caste. They said they would give me A class just for telling them. If I refused I would get C class. "You can put me in a class even lower than C class," I said. "I am here for my country's freedom, and not for my personal convenience."

Janaki's account is radical. Yet even as it breaks boundaries it is at the same time constrained by them. She questions the caste system by insisting on her gendered status, appropriating a popular saying of the Tamil woman saint, Avvaiyar, itself instructive.[25] Avvaiyar, known for her teachings emphasizing wifely duty, was herself unable to square a wifely role with that of the wandering teacher, and failed to reconcile devotion to a cause with service to the husband.[26] Janaki, however, utilizes Avvaiyar to problematize the family by marking it as a site of power. Although families contain both males and females, it is the male that rules the family. Thus gender is like caste, which exists in a state of relational inequality. (Indeed, even the counterhegemonic moments in Gandhi's own thinking often collapsed the status of women with that of the most deprived caste, harijans, in order to show the baseness of their oppression.) On the other hand, as Janaki's own brother implies, she was likely to get "C" class along with the prostitutes in any case. But Janaki's refusal to tell her caste is still a way to assert her agency, even if it is to choose what would necessarily be given to her. There can be no total resistance, but neither is there total capitulation.

I want to emphasize, finally, that Janaki's speech with me, her interlocuter, was as strategic as her silences. She told me the story of her first sentencing on three different occasions, each time with relish and humor. She was disappointed with me the first time; my Tamil was not good enough, I was listening too closely, and I missed the punch line. The second time, she was impatient with me; I had heard the story before and had laughed without fully appreciating her skill as an orator. But for her third performance I caught all her rhetorical flourishes, the significant pauses, her powerful gestures, and we laughed together for what seemed like a long time.

Close Curtain

Uma died unexpectedly shortly before I left Madras in September 1988. Unexpectedly, because she was a full ten or twelve years younger than Janaki, and she had been in good health. Her death was a shock to everyone.

It was the thirteenth day after her death, and this Brahmin family was marking the end of a formal period of mourning by inviting friends to join them for a ritual meal. This was the Subha Sveekaram, the day for the family to push aside sorrow and disbelief with acceptance of the death of their loved one.

Mountains of food were piled on our plantain leaves, and though I did not feel much like eating, I did my best to conform to the idea of the day. Uma's brother was entreating the guests to eat more food, and his wife hovered nearby with an ever-ready platter of rice.

True to the spirit of the occasion, none of Uma's family showed anything but positive emotions, except her young niece, who was openly crying (and was later gently reproached for it). The other guests were chatting and sharing pleasantries, except for Janaki, who sat a little way off from the rest.

Janaki watched the others eating, then stared at the food on her leaf. She took a few bites, then pushed the plate away from her in disgust. It was the day of acceptance, but as usual Janaki was not going to accept anything. "I'm not hungry," she said. And for me those simple words expressed how much she missed her friend.

Notes

I would like to thank Jane Collier, Dipesh Chakrabarty, Nasser Hussein, Dorinne Kondo, Renato Rosaldo, David Scott, Rajeshwari Sunder Rajan, and Sylvia Yanagisako for their comments on various versions of this paper. I am especially indebted to Caren Kaplan, Ruth Frankenberg, Debbie Gordon, Inderpal Grewal, Marlene Hidalgo, Mary John, and Lata Mani for their insightful and supportive close readings.

1. E. P. Thompson, *The Poverty of Theory*, cited in Denise Riley, *Am I that Name?* (Minneapolis: University of Minnesota Press, 1988).

2. Judith Stacey, "Can There Be a Feminist Ethnography?" *Women's Studies International Forum* (1988) 11(1): 21–7.

3. Donna Haraway, "Situated Knowledges: The Science Question in Feminism and the Privilege of Partial Perspective," *Feminist Studies* 14, no. 3 (Fall 1988): 575–99.

4. See Norma Alarcón, "The Theoretical Subject(s) of *This Bridge Called My Back* and Anglo-American Criticism," in *Making Face, Making Soul/Haciendo Caras: Creative and Critical Perspectives by Women of Color*, ed. Gloria Anzaldúa (San Francisco: Aunt Lute, 1990); Teresa de Lauretis, "Eccentric Subjects: Feminist Theory and Historical Consciousness," *Feminist Studies* 16(1) (Spring 1990): 115–50; Donna Haraway, "A Manifesto for Cyborgs: Science, Technology and Socialist Feminism in the 1980s," in *Coming to Terms*, ed. Elizabeth Weed (New York: Routledge, 1989); Audre Lorde, *Sister/Outsider* (Freedom, Calif.: Crossing Press, 1984); Chela Sandoval, "U.S. Third World Feminism: Oppositional Consciousness in the Postmodern World," *Genders* 10 (Spring 1991); Elizabeth Spelman, *The Inessential Woman* (Boston: Beacon Press, 1988); Trinh T. Minh-ha, "Not You/Like You: Post-Colonial Women and the Interlocking Questions of Identity and Difference," *Inscriptions* 3/4 (1988): 71–8; and *Woman/Native/Other* (Bloomington: Indiana University Press, 1989).

5. James Clifford, "Introduction: Partial Truths" and "On Ethnographic Allegory," in *Writing Culture*, ed. James Clifford and George Marcus (Berkeley: University of California Press, 1986).

6. I would like to thank Elena Feder for her comments on this subject.

7. See Edward Bruner, ed., *Text, Play and Story: The Construction and Reconstruction of Self and Society* (Washington, D.C.: AES, 1984), and Clifford Geertz, "Blurred Genres," in *Local Knowledge* (New York: Basic Books, 1983), 27.

8. Marilyn Strathern, "An Awkward Relationship: The Case of Feminism and Anthropology," *Signs* 12(2) (1987): 276–92.

9. LeRoy Laudurie, *Montaillou* (New York: George Braziller, 1978). See also Renato Rosaldo, "From the Door of his Tent: The Fieldworker and the Inquisitor," in *Writing Culture*, 77–97, and Carlo Ginzburg, "The Inquisitor as Anthropologist," in *Clues, Myths and the Historical Method* (Baltimore: Johns Hopkins University Press, 1989).

10. I am of course skeptical of the "feminist as hero" tone that runs through some analyses; cf. Frances Mascia-Lees, Patricia Sharpe, and Colleen Cohen, "The Post-modernist Turn in Anthropology: Cautions from a Feminist Perspective," *Signs* 15(1) (Autumn 1989): 7–33.

11. See Mary E. Hawksworth, "Knowers, Knowing, Known: Feminist Theory and Claims of Truth," *Signs* 14(3) (Spring 1989): 533–57, for a different discussion of these terms.

12. See Mary John, "Postcolonial Feminists in the Western Intellectual Field: Anthropologists and Native Informants?" *Inscriptions* 5/6 (1989): 49–74.

13. Gayatri Spivak, *The Post-Colonial Critic* (New York: Routledge, 1990), 59.

14. Trinh T. Minh-ha, *Woman/Native/Other*, 88.

15. Gayatri Spivak, *The Post-Colonial Critic*, 77.

16. See Hawksworth, "Knowers, Knowing, Known."

17. See Elizabeth Weed, "Introduction: Terms of Reference," in *Coming to Terms: Feminism, Theory, Politics* (New York: Routledge, 1989), ix–xxxi.

18. Denise Riley, *Am I that Name?* 6.

19. Kamala Visweswaran, "Defining Feminist Ethnography," *Inscriptions* 3/4 (1988): 27–44.

20. See Trinh T. Minh-ha, *Woman/Native/Other*, and Susan Gal, "Between Speech and Silence: The Problematics of Research on Language and Gender," in *Gender at the Crossroads of Knowledge*, ed. Michaela Di Leonardo (Berkeley: University of California Press, 1991), 175–203.

21. Gayatri Spivak, "Can the Subaltern Speak?" in *Marxism and the Interpretation of Culture*, ed. Cary Nelson and Lawrence Greenberg (Urbana: University of Illinois Press, 1988), 296.

22. Pierre Bourdieu, *Outline of a Theory of Practice* (New York: Cambridge University Press, 1977), 170.

23. Mahatma Gandhi, "Congress Report on the Punjab Disorders," *Collected Works of Mahatma Gandhi* (Delhi: Government of India Ministry of Information and Broadcasting, 1958), 170. See also Kamala Visweswaran, "Family Subjects: An Ethnography of the 'Woman Question' in Indian Nationalism" (Ph.D. thesis, 1990, Stanford University).

24. Partha Chatterjee, "The Nationalist Resolution of the Women's Question," in *Recasting Women*, ed. Kumkum Sangari and Sudesh Vaid (Delhi: Kali for Women Press, 1989), 235.

25. I wish to thank Sampath Kannan for this observation.

26. Uma Chakravarti, "The World of Bhaktin in South Indian Traditions and Beyond," *Manushi*, Special Issue on Women Bhakta Poets (January-June 1989): 18–29.

SIX

Traddutora, Traditora: A Paradigmatic Figure of Chicana Feminism

Norma Alarcón

> When the Spanish conquistador appears, this woman [a Mayan] is no
> more than the site where the desire and wills of two men meet. To kill
> men to rape women: these are at once proof that a man wields power and
> his reward. The wife chooses [*sic*] to obey her husband and the rules of
> her own society, she puts all that remains of her personal will into
> defending the violence [of her own society] of which she has been the
> object . . . Her husband of whom she is the "internal other," . . . leaves
> her no possibility of asserting herself as a free subject.
>
> Tzvetan Todorov, *The Conquest of America*

In his splendid book *Quetzalcóatl and Guadalupe*, Jacques Lafaye gives a fascinating account of the roles those two divine and mythic figures played in the formation of the Mexican national consciousness.[1] Quetzalcóatl was an Aztec god
whose name, so the missionaries argued, was the natives' own name for the
true Messiah. Guadalupe, on the other hand, was the emerging Mexican people's native version of the Virgin Mary and, in a sense, substituted for the Aztec
goddess Tonantzin. By the time of Mexican independence from Spain in 1821,
Guadalupe had emerged triumphant as the national patroness of Mexico, and
her banner was often carried into battle. In a well-known article, which may
have inspired Lafaye, Eric R. Wolf comments that

> the Mexican War of Independence marks the final realization of the apocalyptic
> promise . . . [T]he promise of life held out by the supernatural mother has be-
> come the promise of an independent Mexico, liberated from the irrational
> authority of the Spanish father-oppressors, and restored to the chosen nation
> whose election had been manifest in the apparition of the Virgin at
> Tepeyac. . . . Mother, food, hope, health, life; supernatural salvation from op-
> pression; chosen people and national independence—all find expression in a single
> symbol.[2]

There is sufficient folklore, as well as documentary evidence of a historical
and literary nature, to suggest that the indigenous female slave Malintzin

Tenepal was transformed into Guadalupe's monstrous double and that her "banner" also aided and abetted in the nation-making process or, at least, in the creation of nationalistic perspectives. On Independence Day of 1861, for example, Ignacio "El Nigromante" Ramírez, politician and man of letters, reminded the celebrants that Mexicans owed their defeat to Malintzin – Cortés's whore.[3] Moreover, Malintzin may be compared to Eve, especially when she is viewed as the originator of the Mexican people's fall from grace and the procreator of a "fallen" people. Thus, Mexico's own binary pair, Guadalupe and Malintzin, reenact within this dualistic system of thought the biblical stories of our human creation and condition. In effect, as a political compromise between conquerors and conquered, Guadalupe is the neorepresentative of the Virgin Mary and the native goddess Tonantzin, while Malintzin stands in the periphery of the new patriarchal order and its sociosymbolic contract.[4]

Indeed, Malintzin and the "false god" and conqueror Hernán Cortés are the countercouple, "the monstrous doubles," to Lafaye's Quetzalcóatl and Guadalupe. These two monstrous figures become, in the eyes of the later generations of "natives," symbols of unbridled conquering power and treachery, respectively.[5] Malintzin comes to be known as *la lengua*, literally meaning the tongue. *La lengua* was the metaphor used by Cortés and the chroniclers of the conquest to refer to Malintzin the translator. However, she not only translated for Cortés and his men, she also bore his children. Thus, a combination of Malintzin-translator and Malintzin-procreator becomes the main feature of her subsequently ascribed treacherous nature.

In the eyes of the conquered (oppressed), anyone who approximates *la lengua* or Cortés (oppressor), in word or deed, is held suspect and liable to become a sacrificial "monstrous double." Those who use the oppressor's language are viewed as outside of the community, thus rationalizing their expulsion, but, paradoxically, they also help to constitute the community. In *Violence and the Sacred*, René Girard has observed that the religious mind "strives to procure, and if need be to invent, a sacrificial victim as similar as possible to its ambiguous vision of the original victim. The model it imitates is not the true double, but a model transfigured by the mechanism of the "monstrous double."[6] If in the beginning Cortés and Malintzin are welcomed as saviors from, and avengers of, Aztec imperialism, soon each is unmasked and "sacrificed," that is, expelled so that the authentic gods may be recovered, awaited, and/or invented. While Quetzalcóatl could continue to be awaited, Guadalupe was envisioned, and her invention was under way as the national Virgin Mother and goddess only twelve years after Cortés's arrival. Guadalupe, as Lafaye himself suggests, is a metaphor that has never wholly taken the place of Tonantzin. As such, Guadalupe is capable of alternately evoking the Catholic and meek

Virgin Mother and the prepatriarchal and powerful earth goddess. In any case, within a decade of the invasion, both Cortés and Malintzin begin to accrue their dimensions as scapegoats who become the receptacle of human rage and passion, of the very real hostilities that "all the members of the community feel for one another."[7] In the context of a religiously organized society, one can observe in the scapegoating of Cortés and Malintzin "the very real metamorphosis of reciprocal violence into restraining violence through the agency of unanimity."[8] The unanimity is elicited by the chosen scapegoats, and violence is displaced onto them. That mechanism then structures many cultural values, rituals, customs, and myths. Among people of Mexican descent, from this perspective, anyone who has transgressed the boundaries of perceived group interests and values often has been called a *malinche* or *malinchista*. Thus, the contemporary recuperation and positive redefinitions of her name bespeak an effort to go beyond religiously organized Manichaean thought. There is nothing more fascinating or intriguing, as Lafaye demonstrates, than to trace the transformation of legends into myths that contribute to the formation of national consciousness. However, by only tracing the figures of transcendence—the recovered or displaced victims of the impersonators—we are left without a knowledge of the creation process of the scapegoats, whether it be through folklore, polemics, or literature. An exploration of Cortés's role as monstrous double shall be left for another occasion. It is clear that often his role is that of the conqueror, usurper, foreigner, and/or invader.[9] In the course of almost five centuries Malintzin has alternately retained one of her three names— Malintzin (the name given her by her parents), Marina (the name given her by the Spaniards), or Malinche (the name given her by the natives in the midst of the conquest). The epithet *La Chingada* has surfaced most emphatically in our century to refer to her alleged ill-fated experience at the hands of the Spaniards.[10] The epithet also emphasizes the sexual implications of having been conquered—the rape of women and the emasculation of men.

Guadalupe and Malintzin almost always have been viewed as oppositional mediating figures, though the precise moment of inception may well elude us. Guadalupe has come to symbolize transformative powers and sublime transcendence and is the standard carried into battle in utopically inspired movements. Always viewed by believers as capable of transforming the petitioner's status and promising sublime deliverance, she transports us beyond or before time. On the other hand, Malintzin represents feminine subversion and treacherous victimization of her people because she was a translator in Cortés's army. Guadalupe and Malintzin have become a function of each other. Be that as it may, quite often one or the other figure is recalled as being present at the "origins" of the Mexican community, thereby emphasizing its divine and sacred constitution or, alternately, its damned and secular fall. The religiously rooted community, as Girard notes, "is both attracted and repelled by its own origins. It feels the constant need to reexperience them, albeit in veiled and transfigured form . . . by exercising its memory of the collective expulsion or carefully designated objects."[11] Although Guadalupe is thought to assuage the community's pain because of its fall from grace, Malintzin elicits a fascination entangled with loathing, suspicion, and sorrow. As translator she mediates between antagonistic cultural and historical domains. If we assume that language is always in some sense metaphoric, then any discourse, oral or written, is liable to be implicated in treachery when perceived to be going beyond repetition of what the community perceives as the "true" and/or "authentic" concept, image, or narrative. The act of translating, which often introduces different concepts and perceptions, displaces and may even do violence to local knowledge through language. In the process, these may be assessed as false or inauthentic.

Traditional nonsecular societies, be they oral or print cultures, tend to be very orthodox and conservative, interpreting the lifeworld in highly Manichaean terms. It is common in largely oral cultures to organize knowledge, values, and beliefs around symbolic icons, figures, or even persons, which is a characteristic of both the Spanish and the natives at the time of the conquest, and one that in surpising numbers continues to our day in Mexico/Chicano culture.[12] In such a binary, Manichaean system of thought, Guadalupe's transcendentalizing power, silence, and maternal self-sacrifice are the positive, contrasting attributes to those of a woman who speaks as a sexual being and independently of her maternal role. To speak independently of her maternal role, as Malintzin did, is viewed in such a society as a sign of catastrophe, for if she is allowed to articulate her needs and desires she must do so as a mother on behalf of her children and not of herself. Because Malintzin the translator is perceived as speaking for herself and not the community, however it defines itself, she is a woman who has betrayed her primary cultural function—maternity. The figure of the mother is bound to a double reproduction, *strictu sensu*—that of her people and her culture. In a traditional society organized along metaphysical or cosmological figurations of good and evil, cultural deviation from the norm is not easily tolerated nor valued in the name of inventiveness or "originality." In such a setting, to speak or translate in one's behalf rather than the perceived group interests and values is tantamount to betrayal. Thus, the assumption of an individualized nonmaternal voice, such as that of Chicanas during and after the Chicano movement (1965–75),[13] has been cause to label them *malinches* or *vendidas* (sellouts) by some, consequently prompting Chicanas to vindicate Malinche in a variety of ways, as we shall see. Thus, within a culture such as ours, if one should not want to merely break with it, acquiring a "voice of one's own" requires revision and appropriation of cherished metaphysical beliefs.

The Mexican poet and cultural critic Octavio Paz was one of the first to note—in his book *The Labyrinth of Solitude*[14]—a metonymic link between Malintzin and the epithet *La Chingada*, which is derived from the Hispanicized Nahuá verb *chingar*. Today *La Chingada* is often used as a synonym for Malintzin. Paz himself reiterates the latter in his introduction to Lafaye's book by remarking that "entre la chingada y Tonantzin/Guadalupe oscila la vida secreta del mestizo" (the secret life of the mestizo oscillates between La Chingada and Tonantzin/Guadalupe).[15]

Although Paz's views are often the contemporary point of departure for current revisions of the legend and myth of Malintzin, there are two previous stages in its almost five-hundred-year trajectory. The first corresponds to the chroniclers and inventors of the legends; the second corresponds to the development of the traitor myth and scapegoat mechanism, which apparently comes to fruition in the nineteenth century during the Mexican independence movement.[16] In this study I would like to focus on the third, modernistic stage, which some twentieth-century women and men of letters have felt compelled to initiate in order to revise and vindicate Malintzin.

In writing *The Labyrinth of Solitude* to explicate Mexican people and culture, Octavio Paz was also paying homage to Alfonso Reyes's call to explore and discover our links to the past as put forth in *Visión de Anáhuac* (1915).[17] In that work Reyes suggested that Doña Marina, as he calls her, was the metaphor par excellence of Mexico and its conquest, oppression, and victimization, all of which are very much a part of Mexican life and "historical emotion."[18] Although Reyes's vision was somewhat muted by the decorous language of the beginning of the century, Paz exploits the modernistic break with the sacred in order to expand and clarify Reyes's Doña Marina by transfiguring her into *La Chingada*. In the now-famous chapter "The Sons of La Malinche," Paz argues, as Reyes did before him, that "our living attitude . . . is history also"[19] and concludes that La Malinche is the key to our Mexican origins. In his view, Malintzin is more properly our historically grounded originator and accounts for our contemporary "living attitude." However, Paz is not interested in history per se but in the affective and imaginary ways in which that history is/has been experienced and the ways in which we have responded to it. Paz explores the connections between Malintzin and *La Chingada*, that is, the sexual victim, the raped mother. He argues that as taboo verb (and noun), *chingar* lacks etymological documentation, yet it is part of contemporary speech. Independent of any historical record, the word's existence and significance seem phantasmogorical, illusory. In Terry Eagleton's terms, then, Paz goes to work on the apparently illusory, "The ordinary ideological experience of men,"[20] and tries to demonstrate its connection to historical events and, by implication, men's attitudes toward the feminine. In doing so, however, he transforms Malintzin into the Mexican people's primeval mother, albeit the raped one. To repudiate her, he argues, is to break with the past, to renounce the "origins."

Paz believes that he is struggling against "a will to eradicate all that has gone before."[21] He concludes by saying that Cortés's and Malintzin's permanence in the Mexican's imagination and sensibilities reveals that they are more than historical figures: they are symbols of a secret conflict that we have still not resolved. Through the examination of taboo phrases, Paz makes Malintzin the Muse/Mother, albeit raped and vilified—hence, also *La Chingada*. In calling attention to the fact that Malintzin and Cortés are more than historical figures, Paz in effect is implying that they are part and parcel of Mexican ideology—our living attitude; thus they have been abducted from their historical moment and are continuing to haunt us through the workings of that ideology. In a sense, by making Malintzin the founding mother of Mexicans, Paz has unwittingly strengthened the ideological ground that was there before him while simultaneously desacralizing our supposed origins by shifting the founding moment from Guadalupe to Malintzin. Paradoxically, Paz has displaced the myth of Guadalupe, not with history, but with a neomyth, a reversal properly secularized yet unaware of its misogynistic residue. Indeed, Paz's implied audience is male— the so-called illegitimate mestizo who may well bristle at the thought that he is outside the legitimate patriarchal order, like women! In Paz's figurations illegitimacy predicated the Mexican founding order. It is a countersuggestion to the belief that Guadalupe legitimized the Mexican founding order. The primary strategy in Paz's modern (secular) position is to wrest contemporary consciousness away from religious cosmologies.

Unlike Reyes, Paz mentions that "the Mexican people have not forgiven Malinche for her betrayal."[22] As such, he emphasizes the ambivalent attitude toward the origins despite the need for acceptance and a change of consciousness. Carlos Fuentes, too, pleads for acceptance of the "murky" and knotted beginnings of the Mexican people in *Todos los gatos son pardos*.[23] However, if Paz implicitly acknowledges the asymmetrical relationship between that of slave (Malintzin) and master (Cortés) by saying that our neosymbolic mother was raped, Fuentes privileges Malintzin's attributed desire for vengeance against her people—hence her alliance with Cortés. Subsequently, Fuentes has Malintzin reveal herself as a misguided fool, thus becoming the ill-fated Mother-Goddess/Muse/Whore, a tripartite figure who possesses the gift of speech. The gift, in the end, makes her a traitor. She self-consciously declares herself *la lengua*, "Yo sólo soy la lengua," adding that objects ultimately act out the destiny that the logos proposes.[24] In this instance, Fuentes, along with such contemporaries as Rosario Castellanos, Elena Poniatowska, José Emilio Pacheco, and Octavio Paz, is portraying through Malintzin the belief that literature is the intention, through the power of language, to recover memory by recovering the word and to project a future by possessing the word.[25] The underlying assumption is that history, insofar as it obeys ideological and metaphysical constraints, does not truly recover human events and experience, nor is it capable of projecting change—thus literature is allocated those functions. Simultaneously, however, and perhaps unknowingly, this point of view ironically suggests that literature (language) also narrates ideological positions that construct readers. In suggesting that their literary production is a theory of history, these Mexican writers also appear to suggest that it is capable of effecting historical changes. It is clear that both Paz and Fuentes view themselves as catalysts, as movers and shakers of the "academic" historians of their time and country. From a secular perspective Paz and Fuentes see themselves as more radical and as providing a cultural critique. They explode myths with countermyths, or narrative with counternarrative.[26]

In Fuentes's play, Malintzin is the narrator who is in possession of speech. She is, as a result, given the task of recovering the experience of the conquest by spanning the confrontation between powers—that of Cortés and Moctezuma. Thus, for Fuentes, narration is a feminine art in opposition to the masculine "arts of power," a bridge for disparate power brokers, who thus make use of Malintzin's mediating image. One can observe here a romantic artifice—woman the Mother-Goddess/Muse/Whore who is knowledge itself—if only the male artists can decipher it; in this Fuentes falls in line with many other writers from Goethe to Paz. It is, of course, ironic that the narrative should be viewed even symbolically as a feminine art, or an art embedded in the feminine, since few women have practiced it throughout history. But as the fallen goddess in Fuentes, Malintzin recalls patriarchy's Eve, the first linguistic mediator and the primeval biblical mother and traitor, who, of course, is later replaced by the Virgin Mary, alias Guadalupe—the "go-between" mediating two cultural spaces that are viewed as antithetical to each other.

To suggest that language itself, as mediator, is our first betrayal, the Mexican novelist and poet José Emilio Pacheco writes a deceptively simple yet significant poem entitled "Traddutore, traditori" ("Translator, Traitor"). In the poem, Pacheco names the three known translators involved during the time of the conquest—Jerónimo Aguilar, Gonzalo Guerrero, and Malintzin. Pacheco claims that we are indebted to this trio for the knot called Mexico ("el enredo llamado México").[27] For Pacheco, what might have been "authentic" to each cultural discourse before the collision has now been transformed by language's creative and transformative powers. The translators, who use language as their mediating agent, have the ability, consciously or unconsciously, to distort or to convert the "original" event, utterance, text, or experience, thus rendering them false, "impure." The Mexican cultural and biological entanglement is due to the metaphoric property of language and the language traders. By translating, by converting, by transforming one thing into another, by interpreting (all meanings suggested by the dictionary), the "original," supposedly clear connection between words and objects is disrupted and corrupted. The "corruption" that takes place through linguistic mediation may make the speaker a traitor in the view of others—not just simply a traitor, but a traitor to tradition that is represented and expressed in the "original" event, utterance, text, or experience. In Pacheco's poem the treacherous acts are rooted in language as mediator, language as substitution, that is, as metaphor.

It is through metaphor and metonymy that Reyes, Paz, Fuentes, and Pacheco have been working to revise, reinterpret, or reverse, Malintzin's significations. In the twentieth century, they are the first appropriators "rescuing" her from "living attitudes." To cast her in the role of scapegoat, monstrous double, and traitor, as other men have done, is to deny our own monstrous beginnings, that is, the monstrous beginnings of the mestizo (mixed-blood) people in the face of an ethic of purity and authenticity as absolute value. By recalling the initial translators and stressing the role of linguistic mediation, Pacheco's revisions are the most novel and diffuse the emphasis on gender and sexuality that the others rely on for their interpretive visions. Paz and Fuentes have patently sexualized Malintzin more than any other writers before them. In so doing they lay claim to a recovery of the (maternal) female body as a secular, sexual, and signifying entity. Sometimes, however, their perspective hovers between attraction and repulsion, revealing their attitudes toward the feminine and their "origins." For Fuentes, Malintzin's sexuality is devouring, certainly the monstrous double of Guadalupe, the asexual and virginal feminine.

Chicano writers have been particularly influenced by Paz's and Fuentes's revisions of Malintzin. The overall influence can be traced not only to the fascination that their writings exert but to the fact that their work was included in early texts used for Chicano studies. Two such texts were *Introduction to Chicano Studies* and *Literatura Chicana: Texto y Contexto*.[28] The Chicanos, like the Mexicans, wanted to recover the origins. However, many Chicanos emphasized the earlier nationalistic intepretations of Malintzin as the traitorous mediator who should be expelled from the community rather than accepted, as Paz and Fuentes had suggested. In their quest for "authenticity" Chicanos often desired the silent mediator—Guadalupe, the unquestioning transmitter of tradition and deliverer from oppression. Thus, it should not have come as a surprise that the banner of Guadalupe was one of those carried by the Chicano farm workers in their strike march of 1965.[29]

In discussing woman's role in traditional cultures, anthropologist Sherry Ortner has stated:

> Insofar as woman is universally the primary agent of early socialization and is seen as virtually the embodiment of the functions of the domestic group, she will tend to come under the heavier restrictions, and circumscriptions surrounding the unit. Her (culturally defined) intermediate position between nature and culture, here having the significance of her mediation (i.e. performing conversion functions) between nature and culture, would account not only for her lower status but for the greater restrictions placed upon her activities. . . . [S]ocially engendered conservatism and traditionalism of woman's thinking is another – perhaps the worst, certainly the most insidious – mode of social restriction, and would clearly be related to her traditional function of producing well-socialized members of the group.[30]

The woman who fulfills this expectation is more akin to the feminine figure of transcendence, that is, Guadalupe. In a binary, Manichaean society, which a religious society is almost by definition, the one who does not fulfill this expectation is viewed as subversive or evil and is vilified through epithets the community understands. If one agrees with Adrienne Rich, not to speak of others since Coleridge, that the imagination's power is potentially subversive, then for many Chicanas, "to be a female human being trying to fulfill traditional female functions in a traditional way [is] in direct conflict"[31] with their creativity and inventiveness, as well as with their desire to transform their cultural roles and redefine themselves in accordance with their experience and vision. If literature's intention is, in some sense, the recovery or projection of human experience, as the Mexican writers discussed also suggest, then linguistic representation of it could well imply a "betrayal" of tradition, of family, of what is ethically viewed as "pure and authentic," since it involves a conversion into interpretive language rather than ritualized repetition. It is not surprising, then, that some of the most talented writers and intellectuals of contemporary Chicana culture should be fascinated with the figure most perceived as the transgressor of a previous culture believed to be "authentic." It is through a revision of tradition that self and culture can be radically reenvisioned and reinvented. Thus, in order to break with tradition, Chicanas, as writers and political activists, simultaneously legitimate their discourse by grounding it in the Mexican/Chicano community and by creating a "speaking subject" in their reappropriation of Malintzin from Mexican writers and Chicano oral tradition – through her they begin a recovery of aspects of their experience as well as of their language. In this way, the traditional view of femininity invested in Guadalupe is avoided and indirectly denied and reinvested in a less intractable object. Guadalupe's political history represents a community's expectations and utopic desires through divine mediation. Malintzin, however, as a secularly established "speaking subject," unconstrained by religious beliefs, lends herself more readily to articulation and representation, both as subject and object.[32] In a sense, Malintzin must be led to represent herself, to become the subject of representation, and the closest she can come to this is by sympathizing with latter-day speaking female subjects. Language, as Mikhail Bakhtin has noted,

> becomes "one's own" only when the speaker populates it with her own intention, her own accent, when she appropriates the word, adapting it to her own semantic and expressive intention. Prior to this moment of appropriation, the word does not exist in a neutral and impersonal language (it is not, after all, out of a dictionary that the speaker gets her words!), but rather it exists in other people's mouths, in other people's contexts, serving other people's intentions: it is from there that one must take the word, and make it one's own. . . . Language is not a neutral medium that passes freely and easily into the private property of the speaker's intentions; it is populated—over populated with the intentions of others. Expropriating, forcing it to submit to one's own intentions and accents, is a difficult and complicated process.[33]

Expropriating Malintzin from the texts of others and filling her with the intentions, significances, and desires of Chicanas has taken years. Mexican men had already effected the operation for their own ends; it was now women's turn. (Although in this essay I only deal with the efforts of Chicanas, some Mexican women writers such as Juana Alegría and Rosario Castellanos have also worked with this figure and have contested male representations.)

One of the first to feel the blow of the masculine denigration of Malintzin was Adelaida R. del Castillo. It was a blow that she apparently felt personally on behalf of all Chicanas, thus provoking her to say that the denigration of Malintzin was tantamount to a defamation of "the character of the Mexicana/Chicana female."[34] For Chicanas, as del Castillo implies, Malintzin was more than a metaphor or foundation/neomyth, as Paz would have it; she represented a specific female experience that was being misrepresented and trivialized. By extension, Chicanas/Mexicanas were implicated; del Castillo's attempt to appropriate Malintzin for herself and Chicanas in general involved her in vindication and revision. It is not only Malintzin's appropriation and revision that is at stake, but Chicanas' own cultural self-exploration, self-definition, and self-invention through and beyond the community's sociosymbolic system and contract. The process, however, is complicated by Chicanas' awareness that underlying their words there is also a second (if not secondary) sociosymbolic order—the Anglo-American. She leaves herself open to the accusation of "anglicizing" the community, just as Malinche "hispanicized" it, because her attempts at self-invention are "inappropriate" to her culture and her efforts are viewed as alien to the tradition. In other words, changes wreak havoc with the perceived "authenticity." Each writer, as we shall see, privileges a different aspect of Malintzin's "lives"—that is, the alleged historical experience and/or the inherited imaginary or ideological one.

Adaljiza Sosa Riddell, in "Chicanas in El Movimiento," an essay written in the heat of the Chicano movement of the early seventies, views Malintzin as a cultural paradigm of the situation of contemporary Chicanas.[35] She thinks that the relationship of Chicanas to Chicanos in the United States has paralleled Malintzin's relationship to the indigenous people in the light of the Spanish conquest. Riddell concludes that Chicanas, like Malintzin before them, have been doubly victimized—by dominant Anglo society and by Mexicano/Chicano communities. In turn, these factors account for some Chicanas' ambiguous and ambivalent position in the face of an unexamined nationalism. Riddell's passionate attempt at revision and appropriation is both a plea for understanding some women's "mediating" position and an apology—an apologia full of irony, for it is the victim's apologia!

Victimization in the context of colonization and of patriarchal suppression of women is a view shared by Carmen Tafolla in her poem "La Malinche."[36] Tafolla's Malintzin claims that she has been misnamed and misjudged by men who had ulterior motives. In Tafolla's poem Malintzin goes on to assert that she submitted to the Spaniard Cortés because she envisioned a new race; she wanted to be the founder of a people. There are echoes of Paz and Fuentes in Tafolla's view, yet she differs by making Malintzin a woman possessed of clear-sighted intentionality, thus avoiding attributions of vengeance.

As Tafolla transforms Malintzin into the founder of a new race through visionary poetry, Adelaida R. del Castillo effects a similar result through a biography that is reconstructed with the few "facts" left us by the chroniclers. In her essay del Castillo claims that Malintzin "embodies effective, decisive action. . . . Her actions syncretized two conflicting worlds causing the emergence of a new one, our own. . . . [W]oman acts not as a goddess in some mythology"[37] but as a producer of history. She goes on to say that Malintzin should be "perceived as a woman who was able to act beyond her prescribed societal function (i.e., servant and concubine) and perform as one who was willing to make great sacrifices for what she believed to be a philanthropic conviction."[38] Del Castillo wants to avoid the mythmaking trap by evading "poetic language" and by appealing to "historical facts." In a sense, unlike the male Mexican writers reviewed, she privileges history as a more truthful account than literature. (This may spell the difference between del Castillo's Anglo-American education and experience and that of Mexican nationals for whom history often is reconstructed anew with each new regime, thereby encouraging a cynical attitude. Perspectives on the disciplines of history and literature differ according to our location, experience, and education.) However, notwithstanding her famed translating abilities, Malintzin has left us no recorded voice because she was illiterate; that is, she could not leave us a sense of herself and of her experience. Thus our disquisitions truly take place over her corpse and have no clue as to her own words, but instead refer to the words of the chroniclers who themselves were not free of self-interest, motive, and intention. Thus, all interpreters of her figure are prey to subjectivized mythmaking once they begin to attribute motives, qualities, and desires to her regardless of the fact that they have recourse to historical motifs regarding her role, a role seen through the eyes of Cortés, Bernal Díaz del Castillo, Tlaxcaltecas, and many others present at the time.

For Adelaida R. del Castillo, then, Malintzin should be viewed as a woman who made a variety of *choices* (*sic*) because of a "philanthropic conviction," that is, her conviction that Cortés was Quetzalcóatl and, subsequently, that Christ was the true Quetzalcóatl, or that the true Quetzalcóatl was Christ—hence Malintzin's role in converting the indigenous population and her "sense of deliverance when she recognized that the Spaniards resembled Quetzalcóatl."[39] In other words, Malintzin initially fell victim to a mistaken identity but subsequently recognized Quetzalcóatl in Christ and displaced her devotion onto Cortés, onto Christ, and, subsequently, onto the child who would represent the new race. I think there is as much a revision of Paz and Fuentes as of history (i.e., the chroniclers) in del Castillo's intepretation, as well as a repudiation of Paz's views of woman's passive sexuality. In short, as del Castillo revises a "mythology" (as she names it in opposition to history) with which she feels implicated, she appears to be reading two texts at once, the purported "original" one (the chroniclers) and the "mythology of the original" (Paz and Fuentes). These texts are separated by almost five centuries; however, del Castillo wants to appropriate Malintzin for herself, as one whose face reflects her vision— Malintzin as agent, choice maker, and producer of history. Actually, the whole notion of choice, an existentialist notion of twentieth-century Anglo-European philosophy, needs to be problematized in order to understand the constraints under which women of other cultures, times, and places live. In trying to make Malintzin a motivated "producer of history," del Castillo is not so much reconstructing Malintzin's own historical moment as she is using her both to counter contemporary masculine discourse and to project a newer sense of a female self, a speaking subject with a thoroughly modern view of historical consciousness.

A similar strategy is used by Cordelia Candelaria in the essay "La Malinche,

Feminist Prototype."[40] For Candelaria, Malintzin is the feminist prototype because she "defied traditional social expectations of woman's role."[41] Candelaria enumerates a variety of roles that she enacted: "liaison, guide to region, advisor on native customs, and beliefs, and strategist . . . [T]he least significant role was that of mistress."[42] Although the roles described by the chroniclers may fit within such a description, the verb "defied" does not. It is difficult to know to what extent it was possible to defy either native or Spanish cultures since both adhered to the trinitarian worldview of Authority, Religion, and Tradition. The defiance Candelaria speaks of is rooted in contemporary existentialist philosophy, which has been as yet an unfinished revolt against the former worldview.[43] In revising the image of Malintzin, Candelaria privileges a self capable of making choices and of intellectual acumen over a self-manifesting sexuality and polyglotism, thus avoiding in effect the two most significant charges against her. Since sexuality, especially as ascribed to the maternal, and language are such powerful aspects of culture, it is in my opinion inadvisable to avoid them; they must be kept in view by the newer sense of a self who challenges traditions.

It is as a redeeming Mother/Goddess that Sylvia Gonzáles awaits Malintzin's return in her poem "Chicana Evolution."[44] In this poem Gonzáles views the self as a "Chicana/Daughter of Malinche."[45] Gonzáles claims to await Malinche's return so that she may deny her traitorous guilt, cleanse her flesh, and "sacrifice herself" in "redemption of all her forsaken daughters"[46] – the New World's Demeter, perhaps, who shall rescue all Chicana Persephones. Whereas Fuentes will have Malintzin redeem the latter-day sons/Quetzalcóatl, Gonzáles will have her redeem the daughters. This redemptory return will empower Gonzáles's creativity; she admires those women who have stripped themselves of passivity with their "pens."[47] At present, however, she feels overwhelmed by her definitions – "a creation of actions/as well as words."[48] For Gonzáles, writing itself is empowering, yet she postpones the daughter's actual enablement, as if the appropriation of language were still to take place. As a result, her revision is gloomy – we still await. Our deliverance is viewed in apocalyptic terms, but Malinche has been substituted for Guadalupe.

The intertextual debate between women and men raises the following question implicitly: does Malintzin belong to the sons or the daughters? Each answers for himself or herself, narrowing the quarrel to a struggle for the possession of the neomaternal figure. Malintzin's procreative role is privileged in one way or another by most of these rites. Who shall speak for her, represent her? Is she now the procreator of the new founding order? Who will define that order?

In the face of patriarchal tradition Malintzin as Mother-Goddess/Muse/

Whore is viewed by some as the daughters' own redemptress. In the recently published three-part poem called *La Chingada*, Alma Villanueva envisions Malintzin as the displaced and desecrated prepatriarchal goddess who has returned to redeem and empower her daughters and to transform the sons. Villanueva states in a short preface to the poem: "This poem is a furious response centuries later to masculine culture, that is, a patriarchal destructive power that threatens all existence . . . "; the destructiveness emanates from "a strange, disembodied, masculine God" through whom men first "discredited the first raped woman, when the feminine was forced to abdicate its sacred power."[49] In the previsionary section, Villanueva suggests that the Mexican/Chicana Malintzin, also known as *La Chingada*, is a recent reenactment and parody of the more ancient routing of the Goddess, one of whose names was Demeter.

Within the poem itself, the goddess Malintzin/Demeter calls upon the sons to transform themselves into "loving men capable of reinventing love." That feat can only be achieved by evoking the "girlchild inside" of them, by healing all the nameless wild animals that they killed and watched die because of some masculine quest or ritual.[50] In Part II, titled "The Dead," in opposition to Part I, which was titled "The Living," the Goddess, who is now conflated with *La Llorona/Mater Dolorosa*, mourns her dead daughter.[51] The daughters were prepared for their defeat through socialization. The malediction "*Hijos de La Chingada*" is reserved for the sons, who in profound irony have been birthed to kill the mourned daughters. Subsequently, the Goddess calls upon the daughters to give birth to themselves, to renew their being. Both sons and daughters are forbidden to look back to old religious models and are urged to recreate themselves with her help. She is willing to sacrifice herself so that "You are born, at last, unto / yourself!"[52] In her representation of Malintzin, Villanueva tries to fulfill Adrienne Rich's view of the daughter's desire for a mother "whose love and whose power were so great as to undo rape and bring her back from death."[53]

Villanueva's interpretation of Malintzin draws on elements from Paz, who, along with Rich in *Of Woman Born: Motherhood as Experience and Institution*, is one of the epigrammatic voices preceding the poem.[54] She also borrows elements from Fuentes; however, she replaces his view of a vengeful Malintzin with a redeeming one, who will not be still until she is recognized as patriarchy's suppressed woman, the one upon whose body Western civilization has been built--hence, the call for erasing religious models that hold daughters and sons back from newer senses of self. In her feminist revision Villaneuva differs from Paz and Fuentes in that she does not "plead" for acceptance of Malintzin as Goddess/Raped Mother. On the contrary, Malintzin speaks on her own behalf and is enraged over her suppression, desecration, and rape, all of which have disenabled the female line. A crime has been committed against the Mother/Goddess, and she demands retribution and justice. Villanueva addresses directly the sexual and linguistic aspects of Malintzin's so-called betrayal, precisely what Candelaria avoids in her representation. In reading Villanueva's poem, one is made aware of the powerful charge effected when the speaking subject appropriates language and expresses her rage at the suppression of maternal self-representation.

Lucha Corpi refers to Malintzin by her Spanish name, Marina. This factor is significant because Corpi inscribes Marina into biblical discourses rather than prepatriarchal ones. Thus, it follows that she should be called Marina as the Spaniards baptized her. For Corpi, Marina is a parody and reenactment of Eve and Mary, a woman who has sacrificed herself for the latter-day daughter and who, because of her experience, presages a renewing and enabling cycle. In four poems, or one poem consisting of four parts, which are in turn titled "Marina Mother," "Marina Virgin," "The Devil's Daughter," and "She (Distant Marina)," Corpi revises the story of Marina/Malintzin.[55] Marta Sánchez, in *Contemporary Chicana Poetry: A Critical Approach to an Emerging Literature*, views Corpi's cycle of poems accurately, I think, when she observes that "Corpi's cultural paradigm leaves readers no alternative but to accept a passive Marina who can do nothing about her situation."[56] "Marina Madre" is perceived as victim of her own feminine condition. That is, insofar as women are women and mothers, they are incommensurably vulnerable. Using images that allude to the Old and New Testaments, Corpi imagines a Marina made of the "softest clay" by the Patriarchs ("los viejos"): in biblical inscription and creation as either Eve ("her name written on the patriarchal tree") or as Mary ("the fruit of her womb stolen") and, nearer to us in time, the Marina abandoned and vilified by father, husband, and son. The latter three may be seen as an allusion to the male triad in one God—Father, Son, and Holy Ghost—as the Catholic tradition holds. By planting the soul in the earth, Corpi's latter-day Marina reinscribes herself and awaits her own renewal. The "she" in the fourth poem—"She (Distant Marina)"—is that contemporary daughter who is imagined as a "mourning shadow of an ancestral figure" crossing a bridge leading to a new time and space, a reconstructed self. The passive, victimized Marina of the first two poems is left behind. Marta Sánchez has also suggested that the bridge is the boundary crossed "between Mexico and the United States."[57] Both Corpi's reinscription and Sánchez's interpretation of it continue to emphasize the mediating function assigned to Marina, though from a Chicano point of view in which the Spaniards, harbingers of a different existence, are now replaced by Anglo-Americans. It is important to reiterate the value placed by many Chicanas on a primary identification with the indigenous people or recuperations of that identity and the rejection of a Spanish one, despite the use of the language. However, these rhetorical strategies are now often undertaken to underscore our differences from Anglo-Americans.

For Gonzáles, Villanueva, and Corpi the forced disappearance of the Mother/Goddess leads to the daughter's own abjection. The daughter is doomed to repeat the cycle until the ancient powers of the goddess are restored. Of the three, however, Villanueva is the only one who, in appropriating Malintzin, makes her a speaking subject on her own behalf and on behalf of the daughters in a truly powerful way. Gonzáles and Corpi objectify her and leave us with a promise of vindication.

Cherríe Moraga also explores the significations of Malintzin in her recent book *Loving in the War Years: lo que nunca pasó por sus labios*.[58] Moraga feels, on the one hand, a need to recover the race of the biographical mother so that she may recover her ethnosexual identity and, on the other, a need to appropriate her political and literary voice.[59] Simultaneously, however, a search for the identity of, and relation between, self and mother also requires an exploration of the myth of Malintzin, who is our "sexual legacy."[60] That legacy is inscribed in cruel epithets such as "*La Chingada*," "*La Vendida*," "Traitor." These epithets are in turn used on women to stigmatize, to limit the quest for autonomy, and to limit "the Chicana imagination . . . before it has a chance to consider some of the most difficult questions."[61] Moraga points to the double bind of the Chicana who defies tradition; she is viewed as either a traitor to her race or a lesbian. As such, not only is the lesbian in the Chicano imagination *una Malinchista*, but vice versa. Feminism, which questions patriarchal tradition by representing women's subjectivity and/or interjecting it into extant discursive modes, thereby revising them, may be equated with *malinchismo* or lesbianism. Even as she recognizes the double bind, Moraga proceeds to identify herself as a lesbian who, as such, represents the "most visible manifestation of a woman taking control of her own sexual identity and destiny, who severely challenges the anti-feminist Chicano/a."[62] Moraga thinks that if she were not a lesbian she would still be viewed as one by a culture that does not understand the pursuit of a sexual identity beyond heterosexism.[63] In a sense, for Moraga, lesbianism in our culture is the ultimate trope for the pursuit of newer gender identities, for anything that smacks of difference in the face of traditional gender values. Rather than try to revise the myths of Malintzin, Moraga has no choice but to declare that, indeed, she comes "from a long line of vendidas."[64] One could, however, opt for Lorna D. Cervantes's sarcastic view of the usual male perception of Malintzin's figure by stating ambiguously, as does the title of her poem, "Baby, You Cramp My Style."[65] Baby is, of course, a double allusion—

to him who would impose his notions on her and to Malinche, whose historical existence and subsequent interpretations are a burden.

Moraga and Cervantes, in a sense, become the heroines of their own individualized vision and revision, for it is through their appropriations that we
proceed beyond Malinche. However, have they truly integrated the "treacherous" Malintzin whose ascribed attributes are the source of contention – the
speaking subject and procreator? Cervantes's sarcasm is a dismissal of the subject
in favor of her own future self-creation. On the other hand, if one follows
Moraga's reasoning and takes it one step further, then one would have to say
that the ultimate trope for the pursuit of new gender identities is not so much
lesbianism as it is the speaking subject who is also a lesbian mother, or perhaps
one who articulates and visualizes herself and procreation beyond heterosexism. If newer racial and gendered identities are to be forged, the insight arrived
at in writing needs to be communicated to millions of women who still live
under such metaphoric controls. How are they to be persuaded to accept these
insights if they still exist under the ideology "Guadalupe-Malintzin"?

If, for Mexican male writers, the originating rape is of paramount importance because it places in question their legitimacy as sons, Chicanas – with the
exception of Villanueva, who accept Paz's view – do not even mention rape in
connection with Malintzin. Paz, as far as I can discern, was the first writer to
advance forcefully the metonymic relations between three terms – Malintzin,
La Chingada, and rape. Although pillage and rape are almost by definition factors of conquest and colonization, there is no trace of evidence that Malintzin
suffered the violent fate of other indigenous women, strictly speaking – though
her disappearance from the record is troublesome and puzzling. One may even
argue that she performed as she did to avoid rape and violence upon her body,
to "choose" negatively between lesser evils. Clearly, in patriarchal and patrilineal societies – which these were – sons stand to lose a great deal more if they
are illegitimate offspring of rapes. Daughters, like their mothers, would still
have to struggle to protect themselves from rapists. "Legitimacy" under these
circumstances at best grants a female protection from rape; it does not make
a woman her father's heir nor even give her a sure claim to her offspring. For
the men, the so-called rape is largely figurative, a sign of their "emasculating"
loss; for the women, it is literal. There is irony in Paz's insistence that Malintzin
should also serve as the figure for "our" rape since it may well be that she saved
herself from such a fate through diligent service. There are no choices for
slaves, only options between lesser evils.

Because Malintzin's neosymbolic existence in the masculine imagination has
affected the actual experience of so many Mexicanas and Chicanas, it became
necessary for "her daughters" to revise her scanty biography. Through revi-

sions, many undertaken in isolation, contemporary Chicana writers have helped to lay bare Malintzin's double etymology, which until recently appeared illusory and hallucinative: one privileges the sociosymbolic possibilities for signification; the second, the existential and historical implications. Some of the writers discussed have actually, as speaking subjects, reemphasized the patriarchal view of the maternal/feminine as mediator, even though they wish to represent her themselves. Others have transformed her into the neomyth of the goddess. Still others have foregrounded qualities such as "choice maker," "history producer," and "self-aware" speaking subject, all of which are part of modern and contemporary experience and desire. In a sense, they sidestep the image of Malintzin as raped mother and part of the feminine condition. Except for Villanueva, who follows Paz in this respect, no one has explored the full impact—imaginary or not—that such an image may have for us. It emphasizes that our beginnings, which took place barely half a millennium ago, are drenched in violence, not simply symbolic but historically coinciding with European expansionist adventures. It implies that the object of that violence was/has been feminine (or feminized) and that it barely begins to be recovered as subject or even object of our history. Since the European expansionists of the time were Christians, it implies that indeed the ancient putative suppression of the goddess was reenacted; the missionaries did not have a problem assimilating Quetzalcóatl into their discourse but suppressed Tonantzin. However, since Chicanas have begun the appropriation of history, sexuality, and language for themselves, they find themselves situated at the cutting edge of a new historical moment involving a radical though fragile change in consciousness. It is an era in which we live in simultaneous time zones from the pre-Colombian to the ultramodern, from the cyclical to the linear. The latter is certainly a theme in the work of Carlos Fuentes, Rosario Castellanos, Octavio Paz, and other contemporary Mexican writers. However, I think that the objectified thematics have now passed onto a more consciously claimed subjectivity in the work of Chicanas such as Gloria Anzaldúa.[66] Moreover, such subjectivity is capable of shedding light on Chicanas' present historical situation without necessarily, in this newer key, falling prey to a mediating role but, rather, catching stunning insights into our complex culture by taking hold of the variegated imaginative and historical discourses that have informed the constructions of race, gender, and ethnicities in the last five hundred years and that still reverberate in our time. Issues of "class" and "color" (i.e., race and ethnicity) per se have not entered the appropriation because, I think, the historical person and textual figure of Malintzin (indigenous female slave in her own society as well as in the one taking shape under the Spaniards) implicitly subsume those as part of her condition—hence the possibility of her suppression as feminine/maternal speaking subject. It could very well signify that anyone *completely* deprived of voice within the Anglo-European and Spanish imperialist projects has by definition been an impoverished and/or enslaved woman of color.

Here, then, is a powerful reason why the notion of the "literature of women of color" in the United States is one of the most novel ideas to have arisen in the Anglo-European imperialist context. Such a notion is yet to be part of Mexican or Latin American criticism; we have yet to see how women there begin to resolve their struggle for self-representation. Mexican writers Elena Poniatowska and Rosario Castellanos have many a heroine who is a woman of color. Consciously or unconsciously, they have tried, as upper-class Mexican writers, to understand the complexity of the relationship between a woman of color (or a native one) and Anglo-European patriarchical history and thought. It is in the vibrations of that distance between them that the appropriation of the many transformations of a woman of color lies.

In a more recent appropriation of Malintzin, Tzvetan Todorov appears to agree with some of the Chicanas discussed, which is an interesting phenomenon since for each the work of the other was unavailable at the time of writing. The agreement appears coincidental for those of us who have been forced for historical, political, and economic reasons to become perennial migrants in search of "home." For Todorov, Malintzin is the

> first example, and thereby the symbol, of the cross-breeding of cultures; she thereby heralds the modern state of Mexico and beyond that, the present state of us all, since if we are not invariably bilingual, we are inevitably bi- or tri-cultural. La Malinche glorifies mixture to the detriment of purity . . . and the role of the intermediary. She does not simply submit to the other . . . ; she adopts the other's ideology and serves it in order to understand her own culture better, as is evidenced by the effectiveness of her conduct (even if "understanding" here means "destroying").[67]

The reconstruction of ourselves as women or as exiles from "home" due to subjugations is fraught with paradox, contradiction, and unlikely partners, such as Mexican male writers and Todorov. Although Todorov does not mention the role of gender and sexuality in his interpretation, he readily finds a point of identification for himself.

As historical subject, Malintzin remains shrouded in preternatural silence, and as object she continues to be on trial for speaking and bearing the enemy's children and continues to be a constant source of revision and appropriation— indeed, for articulating our modern and postmodern condition. The "discovery" and colonization of what is presently called the Third World could just as well be said to have started when the Spaniards conquered Mexico as at any other moment—and also as a time when a significant portion of Europe was about to inaugurate the modern epoch, that is, the Reformation, Copernicus, Galileo, Cartesian philosophy, and so on. Thus the quarrel over the interpretation of Malintzin serves not only as a heuristic device for the assumption of feminism in a traditionalist and essentialist setting where men refuse to let women speak for themselves, or women feel constrained from speaking, but also as the measurement of discursive maneuvers in the effort to secularize or appropriate thought for oneself. It is noteworthy that these have to be undertaken under the auspices of a woman—the one who did not remain the "internalized other" of the European's other. And what about the women who remain the "internalized others," that is, the ones who submit or are "offerings" to the colonizers? What can we make of such gifts? Do they become, like the Mayan woman in the epigraph at the beginning of this essay, a woman in the service of violence against herself?

Much of the Chicana feminist work of the seventies, like Anglo-American feminist work, was launched around the assumption of a unified subject organized oppositionally to men from a perspective of gender differences. The assumption that the subject is autonomous, self-determining, and self-defining has been a critical space shared by many feminists because it opens up vistas of agency for the subject. Often that critical space has generated the notion, especially among Anglo-Americans, that women's oppression can be described universally from the perspective of gender differences, as if boundaries of race, ethnicities, and class had not existed. The fact that Todorov also shares that critical space makes it possible for him to project onto La Malinche observations similar to those of some Chicanas, ironically even more similar than those of Mexican men. Mexican men do not forget that she is an Indian and a woman, thus making it possible for them to understand the "betrayal" on the grounds that she would not want to remain "in the service of violence against herself." However, to the extent that we know it, the story of La Malinche demonstrates that crossing ethnic and racial boundaries does not necessarily free her from "violence against herself"; moreover, once her usefulness is over she is an Indian and a woman. She crosses over to a site where there is no "legitimated" place for her in the conqueror's new order. Crossings over by "choice" or by force become sporadic individual arrangements that do not necessarily change the status of Indian women or women of color, for example. The realization that the "invitation" to cross over, when it is extended, does not ameliorate the lot of women of color in general has led, in the eighties, to a feminist literature by Chicanas and women of color which demonstrates that, despite some shared critical perspectives, boundaries exist and continue to exist, thus accounting for differential experiences that cannot be contained under the sign of a universal woman or women. Yet for Mexicans, Guadalupe is a symbol that continues to exist for the purpose of "universalizing" and containing women's lives within a discrete cultural banner, which may be similar to those of other cultures. On the other hand, the diverse twentieth-century interpretations of La Malinche rupture the stranglehold of religion by introducing the notion of historical, sexual, and linguistic agency, though not necessarily available to La Malinche herself at the beginning of the Mexican colonial period.

Postmodern feminist theories have arisen to supplant gender standpoint epistemology and to diffuse explanatory binarisms. However, the critical question arises: do they free women of color from the "service of violence against themselves," or do they only rationalize it well? For those of us who simultaneously assume a critical position and a kinship with "native women" and women of color, the "philosophical bases of political criticism"[68] and cognitive practices are as important as the deployment of critical theories: do they also function to help keep women from doing service against themselves—if not, why not?

Notes

Reprinted from *Cultural Critique* 13 (Fall 1989): 57–87.

1. Jacques Lafaye, *Quetzalcóatl y Guadalupe: La Formación de la conciencia en México (1531–1813)*, trans. Ida Vitale (Mexico City: Fondo de Cultura Económica, 1983).

2. Eric R. Wolf, "The Virgen de Guadalupe: A Mexican National Symbol," *Journal of American Folklore* 71, no. 279 (January-March 1958): 38.

3. Cited in Gustavo A. Rodríguez, *Doña Marina* (Mexico City: Imprenta de la Secretaría de Relaciones Exteriores, 1935), 48.

4. I borrow the notion of "sociosymbolic contract" from Julia Kristeva. She uses the notion in the essay "Women's Time," trans. Alice Jardine and Harry Blake, *Signs* 7, no. 1 (Autumn 1981): 13–35. I take it to mean a kind of contract within which the social life of women (and some men) is expected to conform or live up to a metaphysical (essential) configuration of who we ought to become in the socialization process. These metaphysical configurations are accompanied by culture-specific "semantic charters." Pierre Maranda suggests that "semantic charters condition our thought and emotions. They are culture specific networks that we internalize as we undergo the process of socialization." Moreover, these charters or signifying systems "have an inertia and momentum of their own. There are semantic domains whose inertia is high: kinship terminologies, the dogmas of authoritarian churches, the conception of sex roles." See his essay "The Dialectic of Metaphor: An Anthropological Essay On Hermeneutics," in *The Reader in the Text: Essays on Audience and Interpretation*, ed. Susan R. Suleiman and Inge Crosman (Princeton: Princeton University Press, 1980), 184–85.

5. The "natives" that came to hate Cortés and Malintzin are the mestizos—the mixed-blood offspring—since the indigenous people at the time of the conquest often welcomed them as liberators. It is of interest to note that throughout the Mexican colonial period the missionaries staged secular plays for the indigenous population in which Cortés and Malintzin were represented as their liberators. Some parishes, even today, continue to reenact these plays in dispersed communities. I draw the preceding comments from Norma Cantú's work in progress, "Secular and Liturgical Folk Drama," presented at the National Association of Chicano Studies, Los Angeles, March 29-April 1, 1989.

6. René Girard, *Violence and the Sacred*, trans. Patrick Gregory (Baltimore: Johns Hopkins University Press, 1977), 273.

7. Ibid., 99.

8. Ibid., 96.

9. Cortés's misfortunes with the Spanish Crown may be linked to the need of the successor colonizers and the colonized to extirpate him from their relations with Spain. Certainly, he has been expelled from public life in Mexico, where no monuments or mementos to his role in the conquest may be seen. Ironically, he is very much in everyone's mind.

10. *La Chingada* is used to refer, literally, to a woman who is "fucked" or "fucked over." Thus, Paz and others suggest a metonymic relation to rape. When used in the past participle, passivity is implied. The verb and its derivatives imply violent action, and much depends on context and the speaker's inflection. To refer to a masculine actor, the term *chingón* is used.

11. Girard, *Violence and the Sacred*, 99.

12. I draw on the work of Walter J. Ong for parts of this discussion, especially *The Presence of the Word: Some Prolegomena for Cultural and Religious History* (New Haven: Yale University Press, 1967) and *Orality and Literacy: The Technologizing of the Word* (New York: Methuen, 1982).

13. These dates are highly arbitrary, especially the closing date. There is consensus among Chicano critics that the production of contemporary Chicano literature began in conjunction with César Chávez's National Farm Workers' Association strike of 1965, noting the fact that Luis Valdez's Teatro Campesino was inaugurated on the picket lines. See Marta Sánchez's *Contemporary Chicana Poetry: A Critical Approach to an Emerging Literature* (Berkeley and Los Angeles: University of California Press, 1985), 2–6. For the recuperation of the term *vendida* (sellout), see Cherríe Moraga's essay "A Long Line of Vendidas," in her *Loving in the War Years: lo que nunca pasó por sus labios* (Boston: South End Press, 1983), 90–117.

14. Although the Spanish original was published in 1950, I use the Lysander Kemp translation of Octavio Paz, *The Labyrinth of Solitude: Life and Thought in Mexico* (New York: Grove Press, 1961).

15. Lafaye, *Quetzalcóatl y Guadalupe*, 22.

16. These stages have suggested themselves to me in reviewing Rachel Phillips's essay "Marina/Malinche: Masks and Shadows," in *Women in Hispanic Literature: Icons and Fallen Idols*, ed. Beth Miller (Berkeley and Los Angeles: University of California Press, 1983), 97–114. See also Rodríguez's *Doña Marina* and the work of Norma Cantú, "Secular and Liturgical Folk Drama."

17. Although the work was originally published in 1915, I use Alfonso Reyes, *Visión de Anáhuac* (1915) (Mexico City: El Colegio de México, 1953).

18. Reyes, *Visión de Anáhuac*, 61–62.

19. Paz, *Labyrinth of Solitude*, 71.

20. Terry Eagleton, *Marxism and Literary Criticism* (Berkeley and Los Angeles: University of California Press, 1976), 19.

21. Paz, *Labyrinth of Solitude*, 87.

22. Ibid., 86.

23. Although originally published in 1970, I use Carlos Fuentes's *Todos los gatos son pardos* (Mexico City: Siglo XXI, 1984).

24. Ibid., 64, 99.

25. Ibid., 5–6.

26. An interesting study of Paz's and Fuentes's work is presented by Edmond Cros, *Theory and Practice of Sociocriticism*, trans. Jerome Schwartz (Minneapolis: University of Minnesota Press, 1988), 153–89.

27. José Emilio Pacheco, *Islas a la deriva* (Mexico City: Siglo XXI, 1976), 27–28.

28. For example, Octavio Paz's "The Sons of La Malinche" may be found in *Introduction to Chicano Studies: A Reader*, ed. Livie Isauro Durán and H. Russell Bernard (New York: Macmillan, 1973), 17–27, and Carlos Fuentes's "The Legacy of La Malinche," in *Literatura Chicana: Texto y Contexto*, ed. Antonia Castañeda Shular, Tomás Ybarra-Frausto, and Joseph Sommers (New York: Prentice-Hall, 1972), 304–6.

29. For a perspective on men's implicit or explicit use of oppositional female figures whose outlines may be rooted in Guadalupe-Malintzin, see Juan Bruce-Novoa, "One More Rosary for Doña Marina," *Confluencia* 1, no. 22 (Spring 1986): 73–84. In the eighties some Chicana visual artists began ex-

perimenting with the image of Guadalupe. Ester Hernández, for example, depicts the Virgin executing a karate kick. Santa Barraza depicts a newly unearthed Coatlicue (Mesoamerican fertility goddess) pushing Guadalupe upward and overpowering her. The contrastive images tell the story of the difference between them—the one small, the other huge. See reproductions of these works in *Third Woman* 4 (1989): 42, 153, respectively. Yolanda M. López has portrayed "Guadalupe Walking" in high-heel sandals. The reproduction that *Fem* 8, no. 34 (June-July 1984) carried on its cover provoked a large amount of hate mail, accusing the editors of being "Zionists." According to Hernández's personal communication, the exhibit of her Guadalupe ink drawing caused a minor scandal in a small California town. She had to leave the exhibit to avoid violent attack. Community leaders had to schedule workshops to discuss the work and the artist's rights. Modern revisions of Guadalupe are fraught with difficulty and may well be the reason why Chicana writers have bypassed her. She still retains a large, devoted following.

30. Sherry B. Ortner, "Is female to male as nature is to culture?" in *Woman, Culture, and Society*, ed. Michelle Zimbalist Rosaldo and Louise Lamphere (Stanford: Stanford University Press, 1974), 85.

31. Adrienne Rich, *On Lies, Secrets and Silence: Selected Prose, 1966–1978* (New York: W. W. Norton, 1979), 43.

32. For the notion of the "speaking subject" I am guided by Julia Kristeva's work, especially "The Ethics of Linguistics," in *Desire in Language: A Semiotic Approach to Literature and Art*, trans. Thomas Gora, Alice Jardine, and Leon S. Roudiez, ed. Leon S. Roudiez (New York: Columbia University Press, 1980), 23–25.

33. I have taken the liberty of changing all of the "he's" in Bakhtin's text to "she's" (Mikhail M. Bakhtin, *The Dialogic Imagination: Four Essays*, trans. Caryl Emerson and Michael Holquist, ed. Michael Holquist (Austin: University of Texas Press, 1981), 293–94.

34. Adelaida R. del Castillo, "Malintzin Tenepal: A Preliminary Look Into a New Perspective," in *Essays on La Mujer*, ed. Rosaura Sánchez and Rosa Martínez Cruz (Los Angeles: Chicano Studies Center Publications, University of California, Los Angeles, 1977), 141.

35. Adaljiza Sosa Riddell, "Chicanas and El Movimiento," *Aztlán* 5, nos. 1–2 (1974): 155–65.

36. Carmen Tafolla, "La Malinche," in *Five Poets of Aztlán*, ed. Santiago Daydi-Tolson (Binghamton, N.Y.: Bilingual Press, 1985), 193–95.

37. Del Castillo, "Malintzin Tenepal," 125.

38. Ibid., 126.

39. Ibid., 130.

40. Cordelia Candelaria, "La Malinche, Feminist Prototype," *Frontiers* 5, no. 2 (1980): 1–6.

41. Ibid., 6.

42. Ibid., 3.

43. The unfinished revolt is discussed by Hannah Arendt, *Between Past and Future: Eight Exercises in Political Thought* (London: Penguin Books, 1978).

44. Sylvia Gonzáles, "Chicana Evolution," in *The Third Woman: Minority Women Writers of the United States*, ed. Dexter Fisher (Boston: Houghton Mifflin, 1980), 418–22.

45. Ibid., 420.

46. Ibid.

47. Ibid.

48. Ibid., 419.

49. Alma Villanueva, "La Chingada," in *Five Poets of Aztlán*, 140.

50. Ibid., 153.

51. In "La Llorona, The Third Legend of Greater Mexico: Cultural Symbols, Women, and the Political Unconscious," *Renato Rosaldo Lecture Series Monograph*, no. 2 (1984–85) (Tucson: Mexican American Studies and Research Center, University of Arizona, Spring 1986): 59–93, José Limón has argued that La Llorona (The Weeping Woman) would make a more effective feminist cultural symbol for women of Mexican descent. In fact, he argues that Chicanas have failed to recognize her potential feminist political importance. In my view, La Llorona fails to meet some of the modern and secularizing factors that Chicanas have felt they have needed in order to speak for themselves. The so-called second

wave of global feminism forces contemporary women to deal with the notion of the self and subjectivity that previous feminisms have often bypassed in favor of women's rights on the basis of being wives and mothers. The current debate on La Malinche goes beyond that.

52. Villanueva, "La Chingada," 163.

53. Ibid., 142.

54. Adrienne Rich, *Of Woman Born: Motherhood as Experience and Institution* (New York: W. W. Norton, 1976).

55. Lucha Corpi, "Marina Mother," "Marina Virgin," "The Devil's Daughter," and "She (Distant Marina)," in her *Palabras de Mediodía/Noon Words: Poems*, trans. Catherine Rodríguez-Nieto (Berkeley: El Fuego de Aztlán Publications, 1980), 118–25.

56. Sánchez, *Contemporary Chicana Poetry*, 190.

57. Ibid., 194.

58. Cherríe Moraga, *Loving in the War Years*.

59. For a complementary essay on the way Chicana writers have reconstructed the relationship between self and mothers in order to redefine their feminine/feminist identity, see Norma Alarcón, "What Kind of Lover Have You Made Me Mother?" in *Women of Color: Perspectives on Feminism and Identity*, ed. Audrey T. McCluskey (Bloomington, Ind.: Women's Studies Monograph Series, no. 1, 1985), 85–110.

60. Moraga, *Loving in the War Years*, 99.

61. Ibid., 112.

62. Ibid., 113.

63. In charging the Chicano community with heterosexism, Moraga relies on Adrienne Rich's sense of the term in "Compulsory Heterosexuality and Lesbian Existence," in *Women — Sex and Sexuality*, ed. Catharine R. Stimpson and Ethel Spector Person (Chicago and London: University of Chicago Press, 1980), 62–91.

64. Moraga, *Loving in the War Years*, 117.

65. Lorna D. Cervantes, "Baby, You Cramp My Style," *El Fuego de Aztlán* 1, no. 4 (1977): 39.

66. Gloria Anzaldúa, *Borderlands/La Frontera: The New Mestiza* (San Francisco: Aunt Lute, 1987).

67. Tzvetan Todorov, *The Conquest of America: The Conquest of the Other*, trans. Richard Howard (New York: Harper and Row, 1985), 101.

68. The gulf between criticism and politics or criticism and cognitive practices is examined by S. P. Mohanty, "Us and Them: On the Philosophical Bases of Political Criticism," *Yale Journal of Criticism* 2, no. 2 (1989): 1–31; Mary E. Hawkesworth, "Knowers, Knowing, Known: Feminist Theory and Claims of Truth," *Signs* 14, no. 3 (Spring 1989): 533–57; Edward W. Said, *The World, the Text, and the Critic* (Cambridge: Harvard University Press, 1983); and Chandra T. Mohanty, "Under Western Eyes: Feminist Scholarship and Colonial Discourse," *Boundary 2* 12, no. 3, and 13, no. 1 (Spring and Fall 1984): 333–58.

PART TWO

Global-Colonial Limits

SEVEN

The Politics of Location as Transnational Feminist Critical Practice

Caren Kaplan

In the winter of 1936–37, Virginia Woolf wrote: "As a woman I have no country. As a woman I want no country. As a woman my country is the whole world."[1] In the decades since Woolf wrote these words, Western feminists have extended them to justify the dream of a global sisterhood of women with shared values and aspirations. It is, perhaps, no accident that the author of these lines about a common world of women also wrote the essay "A Room of One's Own," the classic exposition of modern Western feminism's efforts to expand the conditions for work and a life of the mind to women. Juxtaposing these two images, a world of women and a room of one's own, underscores Woolf's modernist concern with space and location, with articulating the need for physical place as a matter of material and spiritual survival as well as with the expansion and contraction of colonial worlds. Such a concern with location and space, with rooms of one's own, with expanding "home" from the domestic to the public sphere, has been one of the hallmarks of Western feminist practice. Drawing upon Woolf's powerful metaphors of claiming and imagining space for women, Western feminists have conceptually refurbished rooms and staked out worlds in the name of women everywhere.

The claiming of a world space for women raises temporal questions as well as spatial considerations, questions of history as well as of place. Can such claims be imagined outside the conceptual parameters of modernity? Can worlds be claimed in the name of categories such as "woman" in all innocence and benevolence, or do these gestures mark the revival of a form of feminist cultural imperialism? Chandra Mohanty has argued that any "naturalization" of analytic categories such as "woman" that are supposed to have cross-cultural validity end in a mystification of difference, more particularly in the production and reproduction of discourses of difference between men and women, between women, and certainly between countries and peoples.[2] The discourses of "global feminism" have naturalized and totalized categories such as "Third World women" *and* "First World women." If such naturalizations have begun to be deconstructed in the name of an anti-imperialist and antiracist feminism, what conceptions of location replace Woolf's worlds and rooms?

It is in the complex and often paradoxical practices of a "politics of location" that the postcolonial and postmodern discourses of feminism emerge as intertwined subjects of criticism. First coined by Adrienne Rich in a series of essays presented and published in the early 1980s, the term "politics of location" has traveled far afield to alight in the proceedings of the Modern Language Association as well as various humanities conferences, publications, and other cultural forms of articulation. As sketched out in Rich's work throughout the early eighties when she most forcefully examined the limits of feminism and the effects of racism and homophobia in the women's movement in the United States, her notion of a politics of location deconstructed hegemonic uses of the word "woman" within a context of U.S. racism and elite or academic feminist practices. As this concept moved beyond Rich's articulation, it began a process of cultural translation and transformation. At the present moment, it both functions as a marker of Western interest in other cultures and signals the formation of diasporic identities. Whether it encourages resistance to hegemonic formations, whether it becomes its own academic reification—turning into an instrument of hegemony itself—or whether it marks important shifts in discourses of location and displacement depends, not surprisingly, upon who utilizes the concept in what particular context.

A politics of location that investigates the productive tension between temporal and spatial theories of subjectivity can help us delineate the conditions of transnational feminist practices in postmodernity. It can be argued that postmodern theories that link subject positions to geopolitical and metaphorical locations have emerged out of a perception that periodization and linear historical forms of explanation have been unable to account fully for the production of complex identities in an era of diaspora and displacement. Yet, any exclusive recourse to space, place, or position becomes utterly abstract and universalizing without historical specificity. A politics of location that theorizes the histories of relationships between women during colonial and postcolonial periods, that analyzes and formulates transnational affiliations between women, requires a critical practice that deconstructs standard historical periodization and demystifies abstract spatial metaphors. We need critical practices that mediate these most obvious oppositions, interrogating the terms that mythologize our differences and similarities.

In order to understand how different versions or uses of a politics of location create conflicting or diverse critical practices and to sort out the repercussions of these contradictions, it is necessary to focus on the production and reception of feminist theories in transnational cultures of exchange.[3] Too often, Western feminists have ignored the politics of reception in the interpretation of texts from the so-called peripheries, calling for inclusion of "difference" by "making room" or "creating space" without historicizing the relations of exchange that govern literacy, the production and marketing of texts, the politics of editing and distribution, and so on. Most important, feminists with socioeconomic power need to investigate the grounds of their strong desire for rapport and intimacy with the "other." Examining the politics of location in the production and reception of theory can turn the terms of inquiry from desiring, inviting, and granting space to others to becoming accountable for one's own investments in cultural metaphors and values. Such accountability can begin to shift the ground of feminist practice from magisterial relativism (as if diversified cultural production simply occurs in a social vacuum) to the complex interpretive practices that acknowledge the historical roles of mediation, betrayal, and alliance in the relationships between women in diverse locations.

A politics of location is most useful, then, in a feminist context when it is used to deconstruct any dominant hierarchy or hegemonic use of the term gender. A politics of location is not useful when it is construed to be the reflection of authentic, primordial identities that are to be reestablished and reaffirmed. We should be suspicious of any use of the term to naturalize boundaries and margins under the guise of celebration, nostalgia, or inappropriate assumptions of intimacy. A politics of location is also problematic when it is deployed as an agent of appropriation, constructing similarity through equalizations when material histories indicate otherwise. Only when we utilize the notion of location to destabilize unexamined or stereotypical images that are vestiges of colonial discourse and other manifestations of modernity's structural inequalities can we recognize and work through the complex relationships between women in different parts of the world. A transnational feminist politics of location in the best sense of these terms refers us to the model of coalition or, to borrow a term from Edward Said, to affiliation.[4] As a practice of affiliation, a politics of location identifies the grounds for historically specific differences and similarities between women in diverse and asymmetrical relations, creating alternative histories, identities, and possibilities for alliances.

Western Feminist Theory in Transit: Rich's Politics of Location

The term "politics of location" emerged in the early 1980s as a particularly North American feminist articulation of difference, and even more specifically as a method of interrogating and deconstructing the position, identity, and privilege of whiteness. Adrienne Rich's examination of a concept of a "politics of location" stems from more than a decade of struggles over the defining and positioning of feminism in the United States. Racism and homophobia in the U.S. women's movement in general, and in academic feminist discourses in particular, brought such painful splits between women that the white feminist mainstream was forced to turn its attention away from assertions of similarity and homogeneity to examinations of difference. The uneven, divisive, and slow process of these shifts, shifts that remain incomplete and unfinished, testifies to the difficulties mainstream academic feminism has encountered in moving from theory to practice. Simultaneous to struggles within U.S. women's movements and the emergence of an activist agenda of articulating difference, the introduction of poststructuralist methodologies also brought new value to explorations of difference within academic feminism. Rich's essays on a "politics of location," therefore, can be read as eruptions of "difference" in both activist and academic discourses at a pivotal moment in white, North American feminist practices.

In several essays published in her collection *Blood, Bread and Poetry* in 1986, Rich describes how she began to formulate the concept of a politics of location during her travel as a delegate from the United States to a conference in Sandinista-governed Nicaragua in the early 1980s. She is quite explicit about the effects of this material displacement on her consciousness of power differences between countries and between people. Rich argues that "going there" changed her perception of her location as a North American. Yet, rather than conduct missionary movements to dictate correct feminist attitudes and practices in other countries, Rich argues for U.S. feminists to mobilize around a much broader range of issues than ever before, including foreign policy. In the early 1980s this line of argument was new to many white, Western feminists, marking a postcolonial moment of rupture from the agendas of modernity.

The key to Rich's politics of location lies in her recognition that as marginal as white, Western women appear to be in relation to the real movers and shakers in this world—white men—there are others made marginal by white, Western women themselves. Rich desires "us" to take responsibility for these marginalizations, to acknowledge "our" part in this process in order to change these unequal dynamics. "The movement for change," she writes, "is a changing movement, changing itself, demasculinizing itself, de-Westernizing itself, becoming a critical mass that is saying in so many different voices, languages, gestures, actions: it must change; we ourselves can change it."[5]

How does a feminist movement for social change "de-Westernize" itself? Rich proposes a politics of location in which white, Western feminists explore the meaning of "whiteness," "recognizing our location, having to name the ground we're coming from, the conditions we have taken for granted."[6] Rich had been moving in the direction of such a deconstructive moment for some time, yet without the critiques of Audre Lorde, Barbara Smith, Michelle Cliff, and other U.S. women of color with whom Rich worked throughout this time period, a "politics of location" would not have been as fully formulated. "De-Westernizing," then, could be seen to begin at "home." Yet her fullest critique of her earlier "chauvinism" is written out not within the parameters of domestic conversations but in the aftermath of a trip abroad. In its first articulation as a term, therefore, a politics of location could be seen as a suppression of discussions of differences between white women and women of color *within* the geographical boundaries of the United States in favor of a new binary—North American, white women and the victims of North American foreign policies.

Despite her efforts to account for the politics of location, Rich remains locked into the conventional oppositions between global and local as well as Western and non-Western. Rich deconstructs the equalizations of "global feminism" (the "common world of women" scenario) by homogenizing the location of "North American feminist." Yet, in her earlier deconstructions of North American differences between women Rich had seemed to ignore or discount global distinctions. Such oscillations are predictable in binary constructions that depend upon generalized polar opposites. The root of the particular problem at work in Rich's essays on a politics of location can be traced to her attachment to the conventional belief in travel as transformation. Unable to critique the inherently binary nature of Western travel paradigms, Rich completely rewrites her "home" in terms of "away." Yet, over ten years of coalition work with women of color in the United States might account for many of the ideas found in the politics of location essays. The issue of accountability is not only between North and South American women, then, but between women at home in the United States as well.

Transnational Reception: The Limits and Possibilities of Location

Rich's essays on the politics of location can be read as a decentering move, as a call to U.S. feminists to examine their investments in geopolitics. Parting ways with "global" feminism's vision of a unitary world of women, Rich asks Western feminists to acknowledge the problematic power of mapping, naming, and establishing agendas. This practice of a politics of location, however, conflates "Western" and "white," reinscribing the centrality of white women's position within Western feminism. A further danger lies in the removal of the term from the context of debates about feminist accountability to celebrations of cultural relativism, expressing a transnational "fiesta" of differences that mystify and codify power relations. While friendly readings of Rich (such as Chandra Mohanty's 1987 essay on the politics of experience)[7] have integrated this specific formulation into feminist, anti-imperialist cultural criticism, the circulation of Rich's notion of a politics of location also reveals the complexities of transnational reception.

The limits of such a politics of location can be read in some of the published presentations from the "Third Scenario: Theory and Politics of Location Symposium" held in conjunction with the Fourth Birmingham Film and Television Festival in 1988. In his introductory remarks, John Akomfrah directly quotes Adrienne Rich, referring to the passage in her essay "North American Tunnel Vision," where she stresses the need for a "conscious grasp on the particular and concrete meaning of our location here and now."[8] Akomfrah draws upon the notion of a politics of location to articulate a "new space," or "third scenario," for black and Third World film without falling into "militant and nationalist pretensions" of certainty.[9] In arguing that the "certainty" of "place, location, and subjectivity" — the traditional signposts of militant nationalist rhetoric — are no longer possible, Akomfrah positions his concerns about cinema within "postcolonial" contexts, in alignment with both poststructuralist deconstructions of humanist categories as well as Western feminist interrogations of the politics of location.

Akomfrah's complex theoretical bridgings were not universally endorsed by the conference speakers, who included Coco Fusco, bell hooks, Stuart Hall, Laleen Jayamanne, and Michele Wallace. Wallace's remarks enact the sharpest, most particular rupture with fusions of poststructuralist and feminist "location" theories. Beginning her presentation with a story about her resistance to the conference's adoption of Rich's terminology, Wallace's anger stems from her identification of the powers at work within the institutions of academia and publishing, institutions that erase or obstruct the recognition of some writers even as they validate others. Wallace acknowledges that she has been placed in a dilemma: the "postmodern critique mirrors the outsider's or the migrant's or the nomad's sense of being in the world" and she therefore feels an interest and a kinship with such a powerful discourse.[10] On the other hand, the representatives of these discourses rarely turn out to be the outsider, the migrant, or the nomad (to borrow Wallace's figures of marginality) but the insiders, the Western and/or white cultural critics. Rich, Wallace specifies, is "the gatekeeper," "somebody who defines the inside," keeping Wallace "out."[11] Wallace's critique of Rich, therefore, does not so much argue that Rich is *wrong* as that Rich remains unself-conscious of her position's own centrality. Rich "may be appropriating black feminist analysis," Wallace writes, "even as she seems to be sponsoring and defending it."[12]

In describing her trajectory as a writer as "schizophrenic" and "unlocated," Wallace proposes an account of location that reads quite differently from

Rich's. As astutely aware of the pitfalls of nationalist rhetoric as Akomfrah, Wallace refuses to situate herself as searching for substance or certainty. On the other hand, she does not romanticize her feelings of fragmentation. More specifically, in detailing her politics of location, Wallace articulates the multiplicity of positions and allegiances that characterizes the contemporary diasporic or marginal subject. "By schizophrenic," she writes, "I mean that it is more than one process, more than one location, perhaps three or four, none of which necessarily connect in a self-evident manner."[13] Within the context of her multiple positions, writing is clearly the method that gives Wallace some power: "writing is travelling from one position to another, thinking one's way from one position to another."[14] Michele Wallace's consideration of the terms of a politics of location forcefully reminds us that the context of theoretical language is part of the sociohistory of cultural criticism.

Presenting a paper at the same 1988 film conference in Birmingham, U.S. black feminist cultural critic bell hooks used the notion of a politics of location to expand upon her own work on the powerful possibilities of the margin. Hooks imagines a dialectical space of dynamic interplay between repression and resistance. Such a margin, a space of radical openness, creates a critical subject, in this case a black cultural critic who invents multiple points of view and discourses. For hooks, considering a politics of location is an identification of the "spaces where we begin the process of revision":

> I have been working to change the way I speak and write, to incorporate in the manner of telling a sense of place, of not just who I am in the present but where I am coming from, the multiple voices within me . . . When I say then that these words emerge from suffering, I refer to that personal struggle to name that location from which I come to voice—that space of theorising.[15]

Hooks is not advocating identity politics in this passage. The struggle to "name" locations occurs in language: "Dare I speak to oppressed and oppressor in the same voice? Dare I speak to you in a language that will move beyond the boundaries of domination—a language that will not bind you, fence you in, or hold you?"[16] Rather than construct a static "home" or center, hooks describes a process of moving "beyond boundaries," an embracing of multiple locations.

Both hooks and Wallace have articulated the complex nodes of identity that are staged by a politics of location even as they refuse to be boxed into simplistic essentialist positions. These theorists read Rich in complicated ways, adding their own particular and powerful valances to the notion of a politics of location. In identifying marginal space as both a site of repression and resistance, location becomes historicized and theoretically viable—a space of future possibilities as well as the nuanced articulation of the past.

Western Feminist Literary Criticism: The Politics of Location as a Poetics of Relativism

At the very center of academia, a different reading of Rich's politics of location takes place, a practice that can be most generally described as an Anglo-American feminist poststructuralist reading. As poststructuralist feminist theory has responded to critiques of racism and ethnocentrism, the notion of a politics of location has provided an opportunity to expand the ground of what counts as "theory" and who can be considered a "theorist." Recourse to a politics of location, however, does not always result in a transformative feminist critical practice. The theoretical celebration of difference and pluralism that marks much of feminist poststructuralist criticism in the United States more often has led to a relativism that masks appropriation than to significant changes in the theory and practice of criticism.

One way to follow the course of this gesture of emulation and appropriation is to track the citation of Rich's politics of location essays in current work produced by academic, poststructuralist, feminist literary criticism. The popularity of Rich's recent work on location speaks to a strong desire on the part of many poststructuralist feminists to expand their ideas about who and what constructs feminist theory and where and how these theories come into being. This desire can lead to transformative moments of methodological and epistemological change. Unfortunately, despite critiques of humanist categories, poststructuralist methodologies are no less prone to desiring the "other" or exoticizing difference. It is crucial that we seek to understand how poststructuralist feminist theorists fall into modes of appropriation and relativism through strategies of equalization or superficial inclusion. Why or when does a politics of location enable such acts of critical domination rather than feminist alliance?

One recent example can be found in Nancy Miller's book *Getting Personal*. Miller's chapter "Dreaming, Dancing, and the Changing Locations of Feminist Criticism, 1988" begins by invoking Adrienne Rich's "Notes Toward a Politics of Location" through a long citation. The premise of the chapter rests on Miller's attempt to open up the terms of her study of feminist criticism to more diverse voices and influences. The resulting text is a pastiche of Miller's contextual and interpretive comments with citations from other critics. The prominence of Rich's citation (the first quotation of another writer in the text) suggests that Miller will emulate the gestures of Rich's politics of location in this consideration of feminist criticism. Yet, from the beginning, Miller extends Rich's "politics" to a "poetics of location" as a "mode of theorization and self-inscription": "From within the university . . . I read Rich reading the world."[17]

Such a distinction between Rich "reading the world" and Miller "reading Rich," the divide between politics and poetics, is particularly fraught in the history of feminist theories. Marking such a strict boundary between action in the world and in language erases or fails to acknowledge bell hooks's argument that language is a place of worldly struggle—that is, hooks struggles to bring the world into language, to bring her worldly locations into the realm of poetics. Miller's theory of location keeps poetics apart from the world except in carefully controlled doses. Her citational practices are, perhaps, what could be called "the small doses."

Miller's effort to diversify her field of references arises from her consideration of Rich's destabilization of the pronoun "we" in the context of feminist theory. "What are the conditions," Miller asks, "under which as feminists one (not to say 'I') can say 'we'?"[18] Miller's "map" of these conditions includes the location of the female reading subject (presumably white?) under poststructuralist erasure and the figure of Sojourner Truth, endlessly posing the question: "Ain't I a woman?" Miller's path among these subject positions consists of a series of citational bridges. She writes that she intends to bring together "voices that don't normally address each other."[19] Yet Miller's citation practice of "difference" produces a form of pluralist relativism where cultural asymmetries and historically specific distinctions are subsumed into another unitary formulation of containment. As a poststructuralist, Miller wishes to avoid the essentialist excesses of feminist "identity politics." Rejecting the politics of location in favor of poetics, Miller constructs a citational pluralism that refutes essentialism by engaging in relativism.

For Miller, resisting the unitary identities (and labeling practices) of identity politics requires resisting politics pure and simple along with humanist constructions of identity. We have returned to the questions posed by John Akomfrah at the Birmingham conference when he asked the participants to consider precisely how to acknowledge and generate the contradictions of poststructuralism and antiracist politics in the context of film studies. Miller's response, in the context of feminist literary criticism, is to conflate essentialist identity politics and *all* politics.

Despite Miller's efforts to produce an open text, her chapter on locations in feminist criticism asserts an apolitical relativism that replicates feminist textual mastery in the name of inclusiveness. Location in this exposition is institutionally situated in the center, that is, in the heart of Anglo-American academic literary and feminist criticism. From this central location, Miller has invited in, as it were, materials from the margins. Yet Miller's attempt to "travel" through different or peripheral locations of feminist criticism ends in a return to theory as elite institutional practice.

Another invocation of Rich's politics of location in the context of Anglo-American feminist poststructuralism occurs in Elizabeth Meese's book, *(Ex)tensions*. Not unlike Miller, Meese cites Rich in order to call attention to a need to bridge divisions between center and periphery in feminist writing. Yet Meese's commitment to a unitary, "global" feminist theory enacts yet another version of Western feminist cultural imperialism.

Meese structures her fifth chapter, "(Dis)locations: Reading the Theory of a Third-World Woman in *I, Rigoberta Menchú*," as a discussion of the theory/practice divide that has splintered feminist communities over the last two decades. In particular, Meese intends to use her reading of Rigoberta Menchú's *testimonio* to transcend several oppositional factors: theory/practice, Western/non-Western, and feminist/nonfeminist. As a self-proclaimed deconstructionist, Meese is careful not to make overt truth-claims or bids for authority, yet her reading of this complex text not only fails to deconstruct the binary oppositions that she correctly identifies as problematic but also is unable to demonstrate the grounds for a responsible, nonimperialistic "global" feminism.

As I have argued elsewhere, romanticizing nomad or guerrilla cultures is a frequent practice in contemporary poststructuralist theories.[20] Meese reproduces this practice when she describes feminist literary criticism's power as an ability to remain "dis-located, without a home in culture's institutions."[21] Likening the location of feminist criticism to the "some place" of guerrilla revolutionaries "like the *campañeros de la montaña* who steal, hide, attack, and set up camp somewhere else," Meese's metaphors for feminist practice stress unpredictability, mobility, and flux. Such an adherence to modernist myths of extreme dislocation and refusal of "home" ground can result in an appropriation of the margins by the center in the name of a supposedly radical theoretical practice. Meese's discussion of *I, Rigoberta Menchú* repeats this very move.

Readings of *I, Rigoberta Menchú* (something of a textual icon in feminist criticism) demonstrate both the weakness of certain poststructuralist versions of "global" feminism and the necessity for more detailed feminist analyses of transnational economies of texts and theories.[22] Briefly, *I, Rigoberta Menchú* presents the life story of a Guatemalan Indian woman, Rigoberta Menchú, as recounted to Elizabeth Burgos-Debray. The testimonial genre is an increasingly popular and vital part of South American literary production and is in evidence in other parts of the world where "subaltern" or less-literate subjects come to collaborate with literate allies to generate interest and inspire aid in political struggles for liberation. While appearing to be "authentic" oral accounts set directly into writing, however, most of these texts are the product of complex, hybrid authorial strategies. Thus, the *testimonio* participates in the discourse of individual autobiography while utilizing a different technology from conventional first-person Western accounts. Recent critical work on the testimonial genre by John Beverly, Doris Sommer, Robert Carr, and others stresses the complex, highly mediated aspect of this genre of life-writing.[23]

Although Meese addresses Burgos-Debray's editorial role in the production of the *testimonio* and the political question of translation, her analysis assumes Rigoberta Menchú to be a unitary, autobiographical subject. Thus, although Meese acknowledges the impact of editorial mediation and translation, she constructs an "authentic" figure, "Rigoberta Menchú," with whom she desires to find common ground even as she admits to a complete failure to be able to "know" her.

In a discussion of the contradictory position of current feminist theory, Meese extends Rich's statement that "white middle-class feminism" cannot "know for 'all women,' " to a generalized "Feminism": "Feminism's double bind is that it cannot speak 'for' other women, nor can it speak 'without' or 'apart from' other women."[24] Meese argues that feminist critical practice can resolve this double bind through negotiation and through a refusal to fully "know" or appropriate the "other."

Yet, while asserting the contradictory, partial nature of feminist criticism, Meese equalizes aspects that may have historically distinct manifestations. For example, in arguing that Rigoberta Menchú's writing is "feminist theory" despite Menchú's arguments against both a certain type of intellectual activity and the gender-centered politics of Western feminism, Meese is fashioning similarity out of difference. Meese's creation of a "space" where women who are not "white, middle-class Anglo-American or European feminists" can speak or write assumes that she has the power to make such cultural expressions occur. Granting "theory" status to "activist" texts such as *testimonios* might matter only to those who have the social power to discriminate between critical and cultural practices.

Meese's politics of location—a seemingly respectful "I can never fully know or account for the other" stance—occasions a feminist appropriation or theoretical totalization. Rather than leave the text "open," as it were, Meese admits to a "struggle of competing denominations." The struggle, as Meese describes it, lies between "Rigoberta's rejection of the words 'feminism' and 'theory,' and my desire, admittedly violent and imperialistic, but also admiring and loving, to attach those names to her."[25] In honestly acknowledging the epistemic violence of her "desire," Meese has improved upon standard Western feminist critical practice. But her acknowledgement seems calculated to absolve her of any further responsibility in her project of constructing Menchú as a producer of Third World women's "theory" for the First World feminist. Menchú's text is required to bear witness not only to a contiguity between Quiché Indians and First World women's liberation, but to a future rapport, even "love" between those who are situated unequally in world economies.

The struggle between Rigoberta Menchú's resistance to being "named" a feminist theorist and a theorist's characterization of her insistent desire to "name" as an act of "love" cannot be dismissed simply as the incompatibility of Western feminist theory and the liberation struggles of the world's poor. As a deconstructive critic, Meese is keenly aware of the power of her acts of naming and she has tried to account for partial rather than total knowledges. Both Meese and Miller have recognized the role of accountability to be a crucial aspect of any politics of location. Yet, both Meese and Miller end with the equalizations of pluralistic difference or remystifications of objectified "others" rather than differentiations of transnational feminist politics.

Theorizing Feminist Transnational Practices as Critiques of Location

In a transnational world where cultural asymmetries and linkages continue to be mystified by economic and political interests at multiple levels, feminists need detailed, historicized maps of the circuits of power. As superpowers realign and markets diversify, many of the conventional boundaries of earlier eras have been dismantled. Yet our critical languages and methodologies continue to refer to these older constructs. Location, or the local, is tied both to older, modern conventions and to postmodern critiques of modernity. For instance, universalizing "location" appropriates points of view and modes of expression from the so-called margins and mystifies the very workings of power that enable such appropriations. Thus, in an effort to deconstruct hegemonic, global universals, quite often theorists of "difference" have reinstituted hegemonies. Nevertheless, recognizing the limits of a politics of location does not obviate the need for terms and concepts that help us address the tensions between conventional oppositions such as global/local and West/non-West. Feminist theorists continue to revise the concept of location, stressing and stretching its "original" meaning in working toward more progressive practices of transnational cultural politics.

Elspeth Probyn suggests that we not abandon the local, but that we "work more deeply in and against it."[26] Such a revision of critical practice produces the grounds for a rejection of unitary feminism in favor of solidarity and coalitions that are not based on mystified notions of similarity or difference. Or, as Lata Mani articulates this shift, a "revised" politics of location demonstrates that "the relation between experience and knowledge is now seen to be not one of correspondence but one fraught with history, contingency, and struggle."[27]

Chandra Mohanty has also called for a modified and extended practice of the politics of location that includes the "historical, geographical, cultural, psychic and imaginative boundaries which provide the ground for political definition and self-definition."[28] Both Mohanty and Mani emphasize the need for an analysis of the production and reception of discourses of difference in feminist theories. Mohanty asks: "How does location . . . determine and produce experience and difference as analytical categories in feminist 'cross-cultural' work?"[29]

This question is echoed in Probyn's critique of postmodern theories of location, particularly in her attention to the social construction of feminist knowledge. Probyn asks feminist theorists to analyze location as a question of "where we speak from and which voices are sanctioned."[30] In this analysis, reference to location is not transformative in and of itself. Specifying location, Probyn argues, is a standard gesture in the West, part of the production of value and knowledge that creates canons, races, genders, and a host of other marked categories. In Probyn's work, the term "local" signifies a more particularized aspect of location—deeply connected to the articulation of a specific time—and a potentially transformative practice. The local, Probyn writes, does not exist in a pure state. Retrieving or recuperating the local cannot immediately transform the contradictory politics of feminist theory, nor is recourse to the local an instant panacea. Probyn writes:

> Living with contradictions does not necessarily enable one to speak of them, and in fact for concrete reasons, it may be dangerous to do so. The recognition that the subaltern works across her positioning does not immediately entail a form of free agency.[31]

Norma Alarcón supports this critique of poststructuralist celebrations of paradox, writing in relation to the contradictory discourses surrounding the figure of La Malinche in Mexican and Chicano/a cultures that "crossing ethnic or racial boundaries" does not necessarily free the subaltern or marginal woman from "violence against herself" nor from hegemonic feminist constructions of sisterhood.[32]

Boundaries or asymmetrical differences continue to exist despite the celebration of contradiction or theoretical affirmations of hybridity. Both Probyn and Alarcón caution us, therefore, to acknowledge boundaries, not as mythic "differences" that cannot be "known" or "theorized" but as the sites of historicized struggles. Donna Haraway's description of borders as "productive of meanings and bodies" encourages us to think about boundaries as specific kinds of location, as places where the spatial-temporal tension can be examined in its full complexity.[33] Looking at a border or boundary as a zone that deconstructs its difference through historicization does not revive either an aestheticized postmodern "play" of difference or a feminist standpoint epistemology based on a fixed, universalized notion of gender.[34] Rather, as Gloria Anzaldúa's work shows us, "borderlands" generate the complicated knowledges of nuanced identities, the micro-subjectivities that cannot be essentialized or overgeneralized.[35]

Maria Lugones has theorized this complex operation as " 'world'-travelling," a process of simultaneous displacement and placement that acknowledges multiple locations. These locations are not necessarily equally accessible, assimilable, or equivalent. Lugones argues that women of color must value this familiar form of "travel" without depoliticizing the compulsory nature of much of this displacement. "Racism," she writes, "has a vested interest in obscuring and devaluing the complex skills involved in this."[36]

In her conception of theoretical travel, Lugones argues that there are alternatives to cultural imperialism and appropriation:

> Through travelling to other people's "worlds" we discover that there are "worlds"
> in which those who are the victims of arrogant perception are really subjects,
> lively beings, resistors, constructors of vision even though in the mainstream con-
> struction they are animated only by the arrogant perceiver and are pliable, folda-
> ble, file-awayable, classifiable.[37]

The simultaneous worlds of resistant, lively, and diverse subjectivities that Lugones locates are not reducible to the common world of women that Virginia Woolf called for in *Three Guineas*. In rejecting the conventional myth of travel as a quest for rapport and unconditional acceptance, Lugones articulates a feminist theory of location that acknowledges "different temporalities of struggle" and that situates the grounds of knowledge in the realms of politics and history. Lugones's critical practice of " 'world'-travelling" articulates connections between women based on the material histories of their differences. Such a politics of location undermines any assertion of progressive, singular development and alerts us to the interpellation of the past in the present. A politics of location in this mode is a method of critiquing the limits of modernity without overvalorizing the possibilities of postmodernity.

Notes

1. Virgina Woolf, cited in Adrienne Rich, "Blood, Bread, and Poetry: The Location of the Poet," in *Blood, Bread, and Poetry: Selected Prose, 1979–1985* (New York: W. W. Norton,1986), 183.

2. Chandra Talpade Mohanty, "Feminist Encounters: Locating the Politics of Experience," *Copyright* 1 (Fall 1987): 31.

3. Inderpal Grewal and I discuss definitions of transnational culture and the politics of its applicability to feminist issues in the introduction to this volume.

4. See Edward Said, *The World, the Text, and the Critic* (Cambridge: Harvard University Press, 1983).

5. Rich, *Blood, Bread, and Poetry*, 225.

6. Ibid., 219.

7. Mohanty, "Feminist Encounters," 30–44.

8. Rich, cited in John Akomfrah, "Introduction to the Morning Session," *Framework* 36 (1989): 5.

9. Ibid., 6.

10. Michele Wallace, "The Politics of Location: Cinema/Theory/ Literature/Ethnicity/Sexuality/Me," *Framework* 36 (1989): 53.

11. Ibid., 48–49.

12. Ibid., 45.

13. Ibid., 49.

14. Ibid., 64.

15. bell hooks, "Choosing the Margin as Space of Radical Openness," *Framework* 36 (1989): 16.

16. Ibid.

17. Nancy K. Miller, *Getting Personal: Feminist Occasions and Other Autobiographical Acts* (New York: Routledge, 1991), 74.

18. Ibid., 75.

19. As a sample of diversity, Miller cites or refers to Donna Haraway, Zora Neale Hurston, Hazel Carby, Teresa de Lauretis, Jacques Derrida, Christie McDonald, Susan Suleiman, Hélène Cixous, Toril Moi, Cherríe Moraga, Luce Irigaray, Hortense Spillers, Naomi Schor, Annette Kolodny, Ellie Bulkin, Rena Grasso Patterson, Jane Marcus, Gayatri Spivak, bell hooks, Barbara Omolade, Barbara Smith, Audre Lorde, Barbara Christian, Barbara Johnson, Minnie Bruce Pratt, Biddy Martin, Chandra Mohanty, Evelyn Torton Beck, Sondra O'Neale, Blanche Gelfand, Woody Allen, and Edward Said.

20. See my "Deterritorializations: The Rewriting of Home and Exile in Western Feminist Discourse," *Cultural Critique* 6 (Spring 1987): 187–98; and a chapter on Baudrillard, Deleuze, and Guattari and "nomad thought" in my forthcoming book *Questions of Travel: Postmodern Discourses of Displacement*.

21. Elizabeth A. Meese, *(Ex)tensions: Re-Figuring Feminist Criticism* (Urbana: University of Illinois Press, 1990), 127.

22. For a full discussion of *I, Rigoberta Menchú*, see Robert Carr's essay in this volume. See also, my "Resisting Autobiography: Outlaw Genres and Transnational Feminist Subjects" in *De/Colonizing the Subject: Politics and Gender in Women's Autobiographical Practice*, ed. Julia Watson and Sidonie Smith (Minneapolis: University of Minnesota Press, 1992), 115–38.

23. See John Beverley, "The Margin at the Center: On *Testimonio* (Testimonial Narrative)," *Modern Fiction Studies* 35, no. 1 (Spring 1989): 11–28; Doris Sommer, " 'Not Just a Personal Story': Women's *Testimonios* and the Plural Self," in *Life/Lines: Theorizing Women's Autobiography*, ed. Bella Brodzki and Celeste Schenck (Ithaca: Cornell University Press, 1988), 107–30; and Robert Carr's essay in this volume.

24. Meese, *(Ex)tensions*, 98.

25. Ibid., 127.

26. Elspeth Probyn, "Travels in the Postmodern: Making Sense of the Local," in *Feminism/Postmodernism*, ed. Linda J. Nicholson (New York: Routledge, 1990), 186.

27. Lata Mani, "Multiple Mediations: Feminist Scholarship in the Age of Multinational Reception," *Inscriptions* 5 (1989): 4.

28. Mohanty, "Feminist Encounters," 31.

29. Ibid.

30. Probyn, "Travels in the Postmodern," 178.

152 / Caren Kaplan

31. Ibid., 182.

32. Norma Alarcón, "Traddutora, Traditora: A Paradigmatic Figure of Chicana Feminism," *Cultural Critique* 13 (Fall 1989): 86–87.

33. See Donna J. Haraway, "Situated Knowledges: The Science Question in Feminism and the Privilege of Partial Perspective," in *Simians, Cyborgs, and Women: The Reinvention of Nature* (New York: Routledge, 1991), 201.

34. See Inderpal Grewal's critique of feminist standpoint epistemology in her essay in this volume.

35. See Gloria Anzaldúa, *Borderlands/La Frontera: The New Mestiza* (San Francisco: Aunt Lute, 1987).

36. Maria Lugones, "Playfulness, 'World'-Travelling, and Loving Perception," in *Haciendo Caras/Making Face, Making Soul*, ed. Gloria Anzaldúa (San Francisco: Aunt Lute, 1990), 390.

37. Ibid., 402.

EIGHT

Crossing the First World/Third World Divides: Testimonial, Transnational Feminisms, and the Postmodern Condition[1]

Robert Carr

Reading (in) the Divides: History, Geography, and Textualizations of the Third World

> The Questions: What administers the souls of the dead? What is the euphoria of the panorama? What is the neatly voluptuous plenitude which, arranging sequences and ordering events, locks in the world? What revels in the site of the so-called objective with the abandon usually reserved for the body, but has no body?
> The Answer: History.[2]

In their prefatory remarks to *Remaking History*, Barbara Kruger and Phil Mariani approach the crisis in what passes for historical knowledge. Such crises seem endemic to postmodernism in the First World, where the rule of the country is debated in terms of public images circumscribing and institutionalizing privatized violence, interpellating increasingly divergent communities into the national psyche. To better understand the manifestations of "the postmodern condition" in the First World, as much as its relation to an imaging of the Third World, we need to dethrone postmodernism's stature as an artistic tour de force and explicitly examine this phenomenon in terms of the interlocking systems of economic and governmental control.

Even as the rise of Japan, the collapse of the USSR and the Second World as a viable economic bloc, the unification of Europe, and the U.S. national debt combine to squeeze the masses and managerial classes of Latin America and the Caribbean out into the United States, for a spectrum of liberal and leftist critics the subject of the peoples of the Third World has begun to form a conceptual vanguard, assuming the function of a cutting edge by taking on value as capital in the fund for agendas of national reconceptualization. What is perhaps most seductive in these texts for leftist academics is the idea of access to the "Third World" — in the case of testimonials, access to the "subalterns" in the Third World — which too easily becomes a substitute for the "thing-itself," the (left's) transcendental signifier. I want to begin, then, by raising questions about the function of the "real" in our understandings of geography and historical narratives.

Writings about and from the "New World" have historically occupied a tenuous position in relation to the dominant cultures coming out of Europe in the wake of 1492. Because differences of place, culture, and ideology are translated into terms the Anglo-American/European can understand, the history of citizens of the First World reading the textualizations of the Third World provides an important historical context: since the sixteenth century, such writings have been read and rumored about by Anglo-Europeans in the safety of the Old World's emerging bourgeois social text, and the "knowledge" so gained was integral to the heated debates in the "mother" countries about the development of modern Europe, as well as the value and nature of the aboriginal inhabitants, the New World territories, African slaves, and eventually the leaders of industry in the New World.

To engage more specifically with the U.S. context, from the occupation of North America by European forces through the emergence of the United States as a world power, exponentially from World War II to the 1980s, government and media in the United States have implemented strategies of interested representation as the United States took the role of a primary imperialist power. Narratives of geography collapse into narratives of history to create an understanding of, at first, the Anglo-Europeans' natural right to any land and value they stumbled across or took by force. With the spread of Anglo-Americans across the continent and the containment if not extermination of Native American tribes, as well as the annexation of half of Mexico, narratives of the history and geography of North America changed from justifications of genocide to histories and images of Anglo-Americans on the continent that erased the original peoples altogether, collapsing them with the value of the landscape as capital, barriers to it, or outmoded people-species destined for extinction in the ineluctable march of "progress" (read history).[3] The continued project of Native American genocide and Chicano-American labor exploitation, as much as the New World Order, will make such narratives of the middle-class Anglo-American as anchoring the term "American" ring more true. Thus narratives of geography are at stake in narratives of history, and vice versa, as both are caught up in the imperialist agenda of remapping the world on the basis of the "real" and the "true" in terms of First World interests in controlling the centralization of value (money, intelligence) in the metropoles.

We can broach the problematic of a double vision in reading texts from the other side of the international division of labor by raising the question of difference in interpellations of the worlded viewing subject of Perry Henzel's *The Harder They Come*. Where the Jamaican subject in viewing this film re-cognizes an Othering in the (imported) figure of the lone "gunslinger" of U.S. and Italian Westerns, the U.S. subject finds itself Othered by the (exported) subaltern Jamaican language and culture the characters inhabit.

By way of an analogy for the problems of reading the text of subaltern culture—and the film is about a world on the margins of the (inter)national flow of capital—imagine the image goes dark, the speakers fall silent, and all that is left is the crude translations of the subtitles. Something of the erasures necessary for the production of international cultural capital representing the subaltern emerge here. Given that English is the language of the Jamaican middle and ruling classes, and as a result Patwah[4] and English speakers must constantly negotiate across the two languages, we can recognize the complex erasures in the inclusion of subtitles provided in the exported version of the film as a site of international cultural negotiations. The subtitles preempt local actualities and further marginalize the Patwah-speaking subaltern in the periphery. The grafting of English reductions of subaltern speech onto the image thus undercuts the destabilizing reminders of a lack in English speakers' mastery over the meanings of the world, undercuts the radical possibilities of the film. In its place, we have the security of something between a Jamaican picture book (images of the land- and cityscape) and the violent, ganja-selling, exotic Jamaican subaltern as unintelligible.

This example points to the (elided) geopolitical investments of cultural production and consumption. As the debates surrounding media access in the "bloodless" Persian Gulf war amply demonstrated, U.S. government policy and the blackout of information characteristic of the First World mass media in relation to the Third World work to foster and encourage the imperialist agenda in the cultural construction(s) of an accommodating allegory of consciousness of the Third World in the First. As a result, the movement for the liberation of women has much to gain by breaking the silence surrounding the international division of labor, the flow of multinational capital, the global networks of capitalist patriarchy at work to exploit women in the periphery. Subaltern women in the periphery, East and West, are incorporated into the plans for global reorganization only as cheap, surplus labor to be superexploited in the production of surplus values (money, leisure, sex) for the comforts of ruling-class men, their allies, their wives, and their patriarchal, middle-class managers, male and female alike.

The emergence of testimonial literature in the First World marketplace (geographically defined) is thus involved in an ongoing history of mappings of Otherized communities and their worlds (dehistoricized and deterritorialized) for the accumulation of knowledge and power by bourgeois/ruling-class Anglo-Americans and their descendants. In the rest of this paper, I want to ask three questions of a number of social and printed texts—who speaks, where do they speak from, and for whom?[5] Two bridges from the Third World to the First that I will read very carefully are the "Introductions" to Elizabeth Burgos-Debray's *Me Llamo Rigoberta Menchú*[6] and Honor Ford-Smith's *Lionheart Gal*.[7] I will approach all of these texts from different perspectives in order to map my overarching concern: the process of translation, of speaking across culture and ideology for the sake of international and intercultural alliances.

Reading Testimonials and the Voice of the Other

John Beverley's catalytic "The Margin at the Center: On *Testimonio* (Testimonial Narrative)" raises the critical issues of "truth-value," appropriation, political urgency, and commodification at stake in studying testimonials in the academy, particularly the difficulties of re(-)presenting the subaltern—crossing the divides—that present a point of departure given the First World scene of writing.[8]

Negotiating such a differential relationship between reading testimonial from the Third World and reading literature in the First is an important point in Beverley's agenda. His analysis of *Rigoberta Menchú*, however, works against his desired distinctions in what he himself described as "a symptomatic slip" when he refers to Menchú's long descriptions of the torture and death of her mother and brother as having "a hallucinatory and symbolic intensity different from the matter-of-fact narration one expects from *testimonio*. One could say this is a kind of testimonial expressionism or 'magic realism.' "[9] Beverley follows this foray into a testimonial analysis that treats descriptions of torture and death in terms of literary styles with an argument against deconstructing his categories for the sake of political urgency. Ultimately, he seems caught between his desire for a transparent subject and the fact that he is faced with words on a page, transcribed, edited, and arranged for mass production on the open market whose use in academia he advocates for a political agenda of representation, albeit with last-minute reservations.[10]

In configuring the space between "testimonial" and "literature" I would foreground politicizing "literature" rather than aestheticizing testimonials. In order to combat the reproduction of imperialist agendas of silencing and marginalizing members of the exploited community, it is crucial to work with the differences between literature and testimonial. Within the context of *testimonio*, and this is the first set of issues that will condition my readings, such processes involve the speaker from an exploited, oppressed community working with someone who has or can gain access to the managers of the mass media to produce a commodity that can be marketed. Such a text inevitably draws on a

"Third World" experience produced for consumption. It is thus important to recognize that First World/Third World relations are also implicated in the text of the "testimonial subject(ivity)" constructed within and through these interventions.

The importation of these written texts into the First World then raises a second set of issues: as the speaker from a marginalized community, the subject thus occupies a consistently slipping place within the discourse of the First World. Although it has become standard operating procedure to assume an easy metonymic relation between the subject of testimonial and the ethnic group from which she or he comes, such closure on difference within the group celebrates the elite reader's ignorance as the group is conversely constituted as infinite duplicates of the "original" subject presented in the pages of the testimonial.

A careful reading of the testifying subject's positioning of herself/himself, however, suggests the complex position of the "I" within this metonymic relation, revealing ways in which the speaking subject must negotiate her/his relationship within the oppressed group. The voice of testimonial that speaks for "her people" speaks specifically about the experience of a particular person working for and within a particular group, in a particular period, in a particular country, centering around one person's life/story, though alliances can be and are often made.

What I am arguing for is a notion of the female subaltern subject constructed with(in) a heterogeneous and disruptive contextualization concerned to acknowledge the agenda of Third World women's liberation movements, recognizing that as critics and citizens we operate within a U.S. academic scenario complicit with the disenfranchisement and exploitation of peoples of color. Resisting this process requires careful and extensive reading of Third World women's texts, always with an eye to the almost definitional status of the subaltern woman as outside the sphere of literacy historically constructed by and for the middle and ruling classes.

My negotiations should make clear that I do not mean to suggest that testimonials hold no value: rather, I mean to insist that that value — of representation (*Vertretung*/speaking for) manufactured and distributed in the form of representation (*Darstellung*/speaking about) — is itself caught up in the mechanisms of production, the shift of value/labor power from a Third World to a First, and the operations of a deep capitalist, patriarchal structure working to produce a commodity that may ultimately help to undo it.

I would add, then, to Beverley's definition of testimonial literature the tracks of the international flow of capital, First World/Third World relations, and the locus of the borderland of the testimonial. By the borderland I mean to invoke at once the issues raised in Anzaldúa's text,[11] the complexity of the place of testimonials and their introduction in the extraction of value from the Third World for the benefit of the First, the status of the genre as between "literature" and "reality," and the status of the subject of the testimonial as on the margins of the subaltern class s/he seeks to represent, since access to the text requires some degree of re-presentation to support our assumption of a parametric distortion.[12] What First World and Eurocentric strategists need to broach is the reality of the subaltern Third World Other in its seeming "madness," "excess," and "nonsense," the hallmarks of specific epistemic and ontological alterity that complicate – if not block – First World analogizing. As the educational aspects of Sistren's projects suggest, essentialist celebrations of "Third World difference" are not, at the same time, a useful response. Given the existence of many other subaltern epistemologies and ontologies hidden behind the term "Third World" alone – consider Peru, India, New Guinea – we approach here the enormity of the task of a transnational movement for the liberation of women.

Configurations of the Divide 1: Reading Burgos-Debray

Working with the issues of the place of the speaker and the status of the text between fiction and history, I want to turn to Elizabeth Burgos-Debray's "Introduction" to *Me Llamo Rigoberta Menchú*. I want to stress at the outset that I choose this text because its English translation, *I, Rigoberta Menchú*, is likely to be a familiar example, whereas *Lionheart Gal*, whose "Introduction" I also want to read, is not. Against *Me Llamo Rigoberta Menchú*'s multiple translations and editions, we can place the interrupted publication history of *Lionheart Gal*, whose first two publishers could not maintain a sufficient profit level.[13] The reasons for this are no doubt complex, but it seems safe to point to the rise in academic interest in Latin and Central America as against interest in the English-speaking Caribbean. Media-generated images and narratives of Fidel Castro and Daniel Ortega as metaphors for the evils and failures of a monolithized Communism in the right-wing and liberal press are supplemented by a nationalist cultural history that includes Carmen Miranda and Ricky Ricardo as the benevolent Latin spirit anxious to perform for white audiences. The effects of this history reaped by government can be seen in the manufacturing of consent to the 1989 invasion of Panama.

In contrast, Jamaica is barely picked up in the media, except minimally as the home of reggae, a beautiful beach populated by female sex objects and men peddling drinks and ganja for the tourist, with a brief flurry of stories about Jamaican drug gangs immediately prior to the national Jamaican elections that leftist Michael Manley was slated to win. The diversion of the drug mafia narrative to Colombia and Africa and Latin America suggests the extent of white U.S. anxiety (not limited to the ruling classes) over the increasingly politicized and represented peoples of color within U.S. territory. Such diversions of media capital, then, may have an effect on cultural capital generated in the U.S. academies increasingly supported by military research grants, government contracts, and major grant-giving institutions funded by global corporations and their investors. The critique I will offer works with the specifics of Burgos-Debray's introduction, but similar critiques could be made of innumerable essays, reviews, articles, and introductions.

The real Rigoberta, we are told, is a Quiché-speaking Indian who "tells her story" in Spanish, a language she has been learning for "only three years."[14] Immediately she is constructed as the transcendental signified, via the Latin American subaltern gendered woman:

> Her life story is an account of contemporary history rather than of Guatemala itself. It is in that sense that it is exemplary: she speaks for all the Indians of the American continent.[15]

In the ensuing preface, the "Rigoberta" signified slips between the speaking subaltern, the land itself, and all indigenous peoples in the Americas. Histories collapse as Menchú stands not just for the living but also the dead:

> The cultural discrimination she has suffered is something that all the continent's Indians have been suffering ever since the Spanish conquest. The voice of Rigoberta Menchú allows the defeated to speak.[16]

Five pages later, when Menchú makes breakfast, Burgos-Debray describes it as "a reflex that was a thousand years old."[17] The figure is not so much Menchú cooking, but all the indigenous people, dead and alive, throughout the Americas, throughout the centuries, cooking tortillas in the kitchen of Burgos-Debray's Paris apartment where the interviews took place. In the construction of the transcendental signified, we can note, the instances of guerrilla warfare, labor exploitation, and genocide that dominate *Me Llamo Rigoberta Menchú* dissolve into thin air.

The ideological complexity of author/redactor relations are further exacerbated by Burgos-Debray's positioning of herself in relation to the production of the marketable text. Whereas for Rigoberta and her community not only agendas but lives are on the line, Burgos-Debray proceeds to construct an analogy of the exiled Guatemalan revolutionary Menchú's relationship to bourgeois Venezuelan social scientist cum editor/redactor Burgos-Debray in her Paris apartment as a way of (re)investing the surplus of her involvement in the project, domesticating "Rigoberta" and "radicalizing" herself:

Within seconds, perfectly round, paper thin tortillas would materialize in her hands, as though by a miracle. . . . By chance, I had pickled some hot peppers in oil shortly before Rigoberta's arrival. She sprinkled her beans with the oil, which almost set one's mouth on fire. "We only trust people who eat what we eat," she told me one day as she tried to explain the relation between the guerrillas and the Indian communities. I suddenly realized that she had begun to trust me. A relationship based upon food proves that there are areas where Indians and non-Indians can meet and share things: the tortillas and black beans brought us together because they gave us the same pleasure and awakened the same drives in both of us.[18]

Given Menchú's difficulty in explaining to Burgos-Debray guerrilla-*campesino* community relations as she has experienced them under repression, the power of the editor, drawn from Menchú's involvement, is abused in the attempt to construct the fantasy of the two women as operating within an equal exchange. As the mountain guerrillas are to the subaltern communities, so, we are to think, Menchú is to Burgos-Debray, though eating and pleasure are more desirable contexts than the "evolution" of civilization from the Third World to the First.

Spivak's concern regarding a "psychoanalytic allegory that can accommodate the third-world woman to the first"[19] returns as Burgos-Debray elides specificities of class, race, psyche, and history, watching with astonishment the "miracle" of Rigoberta Menchú making "perfect" tortillas three times a day. The fact that Menchú is employing a skill exploited by the *caporales* and landowners on the *fincas* as well as the urban bourgeoisie—related in the very *testimonio* Burgos-Debray is editing—is lost as she further elides difference not just in terms of "pleasure" gained, but the very drives of a perfectly known "ethnic unconscious."[20]

After her experience of producing Menchú's *testimonio*, given all she has "Rigoberta" stand in for, Burgos-Debray's "American self is no longer something 'uncanny.'"[21] As a result of having "lived in Rigoberta's world" for a week[22]—note the erasure of the Paris apartment—she decides to "delete all my questions," becoming at the end of this process

what I really was: Rigoberta's listener. I allowed her to speak and then became her instrument, her double by allowing her to make the transition from the spoken to the written word.[23]

It seems contradictory, then—though less so if we follow the tracks of power, profit, and desire—that Burgos-Debray's *Me Llamo Rigoberta Menchú* identifies a chronology supporting "major themes (father, mother, childhood, education)" explicitly confounded in Menchú's re(-)presentations, with balanced digressions, chapter headings that isolate "important" incidents in that passage, and an epigraph or two for every chapter.[24] The contents page thus reads like a Euro-American biographic timetable, putting the difference of Quiché epistemologies and ontologies – Burgos-Debray's "cultural discrimination" ongoing "since the Spanish conquest" – under erasure.

Within the hinges of the text, we can still find the traces of an ontological fragment whose assumptions are in conflict with the project of the testimony turned bildungsroman: "Rigoberta" also found it strategic to blow up the Costa Rican embassy in Guatemala City. We broach here again the possibilities in the spaces of deferred difference between the agenda of "representation" (Vertretung) and the project of "re-presentation" (Darstellung).[25] Thus, while on the one hand the revolutionary Rigoberta Menchú stands at several strategic removes from Me Llamo Rigoberta Menchú, on the other hand, by an elaborate fantasy of the text, Burgos-Debray finds a relation to the "Rigoberta" of her text something like the papal relation to god, mystifying the participants, the text they construct, and the various political, economic, and cultural contexts in which their relations take place.

This situation is further exacerbated by an English translation that works to make "Rigoberta" more comprehensible, lest "the wealth of memories and associations that come tumbling out in this spontaneous narrative leave the reader a little confused as to chronology and details of events,"[26] and deletes a Committee of Campesino Unity (CUC) press release/manifesto (denouncing capitalist imperialism, the exploitation of campesinos and poor ladinos as well as Guatemala's natural resources by a repressive oligarchy supported by multinational corporations and the governments of Europe, Japan, and the United States of America) that amounts to a re-view of the scene of writing from the other side of the international division of labor (see the appendix to this paper for a translation). What is silenced is a historical specificity that opens onto the role of First World economic interests in the superexploitation described in the book, and a call to arms.

Again, I am not especially interested in picking on Burgos-Debray per se beyond her narrative investment in the (cultural) logic of (academic complicity with) multinational capitalism. In complex and hidden ways, the production of texts like I, Rigoberta Menchú – with introductory claims to a full, transhistorical, and transparent reality, even as that "reality" is caught out in the gaps in the process of transubstantiation – is itself caught up in the flow of capital and the construction of an "at best" pre- or nascent-capitalist/socialist/barbarian Third World where all manner of chaos, repression, and corruption exist in opposition to a First World in which Anglo-American and European culture and its consorts stand as a mark of Progress, Development, and Civilization.

The danger of cohering with the work of imperialist subject-constitution returns in an English translation called *I, Rigoberta Menchú*, which is to stand in as the voice of all indigenous Americans throughout history. In the process of fetishization, the text is marketed as outside (before?) the tracks of the flow of capital and the military powers backing it that maintain the "Third World" as a source of cheap labor and mineral resources in the extraction of value for First World enrichment, which includes the realms of culture maintained in the academic industry.

First World (mis)readings of Trinh T. Minh-ha's provocative suggestion that "there is a First World in every Third World and a Third World in every First"[27] can reduce the Third World to a synonym for abject poverty. This can only assist the imperialist agenda by presenting the Third World as also contained in the First World, erasing the complex realities of living in Third World territories. One of the marks of Third World economies left out in such misreadings, for example, is limited access to goods and services. Even the poorest in the urban United States, given the money or food stamps, can buy a variety of foods readily available in supermarkets. In the Third World, there is often little variety of food to buy, and what there is is expensive. In Georgetown, the capital of Guyana, for example, the price of a pound of chicken is G$100.[28] A loaf of bread is G$40-G$50. Gas—when the government has the U.S. currency needed to pay for it—is G$210 a gallon. The average wage is G$300 a week, based on a minimum wage of G$60 a day with a five-day workweek. Further, most of Guyana lives without electricity: Georgetown alone requires an estimated 30 megawatts of power, but since the government can only supply 12 to 20, there is no electricity for 12 to 15 hours a day on the average. The public hospital is a compound of two-story wooden buildings. When the socialist government announced devaluations in accordance with an IMF loan agreement to be signed, there were strikes, cane-field burnings, marches, and arrests.

While the implications of such differences of histories and agendas in "Third World" territories determine the testimony Burgos-Debray is editing, the subject/consciousness she invokes emerges in the imperialist countries of the First World with its silences put under erasure in the rhetoric of imperialism—the noble savage of the Latin American bourgeoisie. If the project of political representation is to supersede aesthetic re-presentations in discussions of testimonial literature, then historical, cultural, and textual specificities must be foregrounded, and the flows of capital in its various forms must be opened onto. To erase differences is to celebrate elite ignorance and cohere with the imperialist constitution of the Third World subject: "they are just like us, they want what we want," gives way to "they want what we have," the forced insertion of the subalterns in the periphery into the production side of the international division of labor for, purportedly, their own good. The situation is worsened by Third World capitalists and politicians eager to benefit from the process of exploitation. U.S. invasions of other "New World" territories are thus advertised as the will of "the people," the subaltern class. The installation of a "democracy" loyal to the U.S. agenda, combined with capital employed for the benefit of global corporations and the U.S. military personnel to protect it, become the gifts of the First World to the Third.

Configurations of the Divide 2: Reading Honor Ford-Smith

In light of Burgos-Debray's configurations of passage, we can read Honor Ford-Smith's careful participation in the production of *Lionheart Gal: Life Stories of Jamaican Women*. Perhaps the most important aspect of Ford-Smith's role as presented in her "Introduction" is her immediate acknowledgment of the effect of class, education, and history on the production process, the difference it makes, and their importance to producing the text. Recognizing the difficulties of her editorial situation, Ford-Smith is careful in her "Introduction" to define her role not as an equal voice, but as an educated, middle-class participant constantly struggling to displace herself from the center to the borders, whose editorial interventions must be approved by the community of Sistren.

Ford-Smith grounds the questions of fiction, history, and geography within the context of events in the women's lifetimes, and their response to local oppressions within the context of national investments in the language of "development":

> The voices in Lionheart Gal echo across the last forty years of Jamaica's history, reverberating with the impact of so-called 'development' on women. The stories chart the terms of resistance in women's daily lives and illustrate ways in which women can move from the apparent powerlessness of exploitation to the creative power of rebel consciousness. They reveal the humour and courage released in this process and project fragments of the future it envisions.[29]

Thus, rather than representing the span of imperialist invasion in the Americas, the subjects of *Lionheart Gal* are immediately historicized. Ford-Smith goes on to give analyses of the site-specific conditions surrounding the production of the testimonials of the women of Sistren. Such conditions include an examination of how relations of class, gender, race, nationality, and political mo(ve)ments conflate in multiple ways to construct and oppress poor Jamaican women. The oppressive constructions help to cover up the increasingly diversified exploitation of these women on the margins of the labor market for the value of their labor in the (re)production of more workers, the labor power of these workers, and leisure time for the middle and ruling classes:

The exploitation of girl children extends from the household, out into the labor market where women can still exist in the strange half-slave, half-serf existence of the domestic worker in the late twentieth century. . . . Untouched by any of the legislation of the 1970s such as minimum wage, or by labor organisation, these forms of 'hidden' exploitation stubbornly persist. They do not disappear when new social institutions are introduced, as used to be thought. Instead they merely continue to exist as before. To change this situation clearly requires careful study and special consideration. So far, however, these issues have remained low priorities for most organisations in [Jamaican] society who complain about the difficulty of organising domestic workers and about the divisive potential of organising women in their own interest.[30]

In her narrative of the production of *Lionheart Gal*, Ford-Smith discusses ways in which the crucial effects of class and education leave their marks on the languages, forms, and scripting of the testimonies. At one stage the life stories were all to be recorded oral narratives structured around three questions: "How did you first become aware of the fact that you were oppressed as a woman? How did that experience affect your life? How have you tried to change it?"[31]

For the two "middle-strata" women in the group, the interviews did not work well because they were "accustomed to standard English and conventions of academic expression."[32] Thus two of the testimonies are in standard English, twelve are in Patwah, and one, "Ava's Diary," is written and printed in both. The form and textual heterogeneity of "Ava's Diary" is explained in material terms that open onto the multiple jeopardies in "Ava's" life and constellate on the question of language and power for women:

> 'Ava's Diary', for example, began from a detailed statement she had written about her experience of domestic violence to give to the police. We decided to keep the diary she had created herself and to extend it back through the other interviews.[33]

By positioning this voice almost at the end of the volume (there is a glossary), Sistren with Ford-Smith open onto several different sets of issues. Space constraints allow me to point to only one here: the way in which the language and form of the "diary" operate to construct a speaking/writing/written subject on the borders of Jamaican class strata and point to a notion of the politicized Jamaican collective subject gendered woman, the "we" of Sistren. To make my argument, further contextualization of the relations of language and power in the Caribbean is needed.

Patwah is the language spoken by lower-class Jamaicans. The official language of the government and the bourgeoisie is English. This means, among other things, that poor children are faced with another language altogether in the educational system, whereas for middle-class children it is a question of reading and writing in the language they and their families speak. Patwah, then, is a mark of culture/class identity rigorously expelled from official discourse and tolerated only as a mark of a casual class alliance within what passes for (bourgeois, cultural) nationalism in the strata of the neocolonial elite. It is the language of an economic stratum that maintains in the face of extreme poverty indigenous cultural forms, concepts, assumptions, and strategies for survival in an oppressed and oppressive society. It is a language initiated in the emergency economy of slave culture, where alliances had to be made and a language/culture constructed that could maintain a sufficiently broad base of intertribal African understandings to keep each other alive and able to go on.

In the one hundred and fifty-odd years since slaves and maroons like Ni, the Maroon guerrilla "general," won emancipation, many Jamaicans have continued to live under crushing poverty on the margins of a (hostile) plantation and urban economy, despite a long history of participation in anticolonial uprisings, agitation for home rule, and the elections of a range of labor-oriented administrations; and women have predictably had the worst of it. We begin to glimpse here again the view of the subaltern woman from the other side of the division of labor, but through something approaching class and regional specificity. To be unable to speak English is to be found lacking in a society dominated internally by a postcolonial patriarchy controlled by the English-speaking elite/bourgeoisie, and externally by patriarchal imperialist countries like the United States, Japan, China, and England. Access to the English language and institutional education allows one to enter the track of upward mobility in the private and public spheres. The situation is much more complicated than this initial sketch allows, but it is perhaps sufficient to register some of what is at stake in the heterogeneous flow of language(s) in the borderlands between oral/written Patwah and written English that constitute "Ava's diary."

In the penultimate moment of the "diary," before the glossary that translates Patwah at its most illegible for the benefit of English-speaking readers, there are acknowledged parameters of difference in the relation of oral to written culture that leave their marks on the transcription of the life stories of the Sistren community, the configurations of the "rebel consciousness" of Lionheart Gal. The epistemologies and strategies of oral culture, as part of the heritage of the Patwah community, are invested in the oral interweaving of life stories. The effect of institutional education is to foreground the issues of writing's relation to and implication in consciousness and speech, the need to construct subjectivity within the discourse of the written/printed word. In the difference of the two displaced middle-strata stories in English, class and culture leave their marks, openly, on the construction of the Lionhearted subject and her geogra-

phy in the printed text as a final product. The "diary" also foregrounds this by
the privacy of the diary context and its relations to the survival of generally
middle- and upper-class women's culture in many parts of the world, including
the Caribbean, a forum often recording hidden scenes of domestic violence
against women.

In this, however, "Ava's diary" again oscillates on the borderlands as it is
meant for public consumption – initially by a police force notoriously uncon-
cerned with victims of domestic violence, then by a national and international
readership of *Lionheart Gal*. Ford-Smith's structurations are not always this suc-
cessful, as in the subtitles that attempt to fill in the hinges of the story " 'Exodus'
A Run": faced with breaks in the text, she inscribes phrases from the upcoming
passage to make the silences speak. These catchphrases can serve no purpose
other than to calm the bourgeois reader's anxiety over what might lie behind
the silences. However, if the politicized collective Jamaican subject signaled by
the voice of the diary and the "we" of *Lionheart Gal* is problematically utopic,
it is at least problematized in terms of class, race, world, history, ideology, and
culture, and always only pointed to in the process of performing specific healing and empowering activities. The image of the "rebel consciousness" becomes
a space where differences can be acknowledged and sifted to interact produc-
tively for change. The infusion of privatized violence into the (inter)national
public sphere constellates with the political urgency of their lives/stories and
the (re)cognition of the class interests hidden in the Patwah/English division
to create a challenge for transnational feminist practices within the contexts of
postmodernism and globalization: a heterogeneous space for collective and
radicalized sister subjectivities, working as Sistren for the liberation of women
and the disruption of a racist and (inter)national capitalist patriarchy.

APPENDIX

Translated by Paul Miller

COMMITTEE OF CAMPESINO UNITY (CUC)[34]

PRESS BULLETIN

THE COMMITTEE OF CAMPESINO UNITY (CUC) to all field and city
workers, to all organizations of workers and campesinos and other sectors that
suffer exploitation and repression, and to all the means of communication
united with the workers' struggle.

We Manifest:

1. That during the days of April 19, 20, 21, and 22 of 1979 we have called to order the National Assembly of the CUC. Our committee, representing the different zones in which we are organized in assemblies of workers, leagues, unions, groups, and communities, has convened with three objectives: to review our progress as we approach the end of our first year of organized, combative, and unified struggle; to analyze the situation of the *pueblo* and especially that of the Guatemalan field-worker, thereby structuring the principal bases and points of battle that we are to push forward; and, finally, to organize our participation in the First of May celebration.

2. That we want our analysis and accords to be officially communicated to the media, since it is contingent on all the workers' organizations to make known to the people their thought, and thus all the people's struggles are better integrated.

3. That the National Assembly of the CUC, reunited in its third session, has arrived at various conclusions that will be discussed as we proceed:

FIRST. – The situation of exploitation among our people has become more and more harsh. The foreign bankrollers, along with their accomplices, the Guatemalan bankrollers, become every day more powerful thanks to urban and rural labor. We live in destitution so that they may amass millions with our blood and the blood of our families.

Panzós is an example of the theft of our land and of the repression to which we are subjected by the bankrollers and their government, utilizing the army and all their repressive bodies.

Those that forcibly remove field-workers from the land that we have worked for years, those that pay us starvation wages or leave us stranded and without work on the coastal farms, those that unjustly dismiss us as in Santa Rita, those that snatch away from us the lands that until recently we used to cultivate our *milpa*, are slowly murdering us. They murder us with the debt from BANDESA, the lies of INTA and of INDE, the unfair politics of IN-AFOR that gives away our forests to the powerful, but does not allow us to gather firewood. They murder us when they transport us in trucks to the coastal farms, when they poison our crops and the lives of our women and children with fumigation. In this way slowly and surely in our daily lives they are murdering us.

And with the money we generate for the bankrollers, they continue their exploitation and can pay for their repression. Thousands of brave indigenous campesinos and *ladinos* are persecuted, tortured, and murdered for having denounced the abuses that are committed against us and for having waged a decided battle for our rights: thus it has been in Panzós, Cotzal, Izcán, Olopa, in many of the villages in the southern coast and in all the corners of the country. In the capital union members are persecuted, murdered, or forced into exile. Not even the innocent lives of children are respected. The bread of Lucas and the lies of the social pact have turned into bullets and repression.

We, the indigenous peoples, who constitute the majority of the population, also suffer from discrimination, in addition to exploitation and repression, humiliation and suffering. They humiliate and discriminate against us. They steal our wealth; they do not respect our customs or our rights. But they commercialize and proudly display our cultural wealth to foreigners.

SECOND. – The Committee of Campesino Unity (CUC), an organization of young people, children, older people, men, women, indigenous peoples, and *ladinos*, is a hope that takes upon itself the decision, the will, and the best interests of the workers of the field. We have spent several years in search of the best methods of organization to fight for our rights. The CUC must be the *clear head* that analyzes well the situation of the field-workers and their allies that are united in the struggle, and that recognizes their enemies to combat them.

The CUC must be the *united heart*, since it was born to unite together all the workers of the field and wishes to unite itself with all the organizations that participate in the same struggle and seek the same results. The CUC is a step toward a worker-campesino alliance, an alliance that should be the motor and the heart of the struggle of all the Guatemalan people for their liberation.

The CUC must be the *combative fist*. We have learned that the exploited workers acquire their rights only through the force of organized action, and not by humiliating themselves before the promises, laws, and lies of those who oppress them.

THIRD. – By a sense of duty and in light of the needs of all workers of the field, the CUC will fight for the following rights:

a) For our *right to life*: by bravely confronting whoever represses us in order to defend our organization, our families, our communities, and our people.

b) For our *right to land*: by fighting in an organized and militant way against any attempt at eviction, denouncing the traps and legal theft of land, against the chicanery of the INTA and the bankrollers that would like to rob us of our land. By fighting so that the big landowners give us plots to cultivate our *milpa* in conditions favorable to the campesinos. By fighting against the moneylenders and against BANDESA that choke us with interest rates. By fighting against INAFOR for the defense of our forests and for the right to have our firewood.

c) For our *right to work and fair salaries*: against unfair dismissals, for year-round work, against the deductions in salaries and in the weights and measurements of the work. By fighting for double pay on holidays and overtime hours and for payment for the seventh day and to recover whatever forced deductions that amount to robbery of the farm workers.

d) For our *right to fair prices*: demanding that they pay us well for the product of our labor and that fertilizers, tools, and whatever else we have to buy from the big companies and businesses owned by the bankrollers are fairly priced.

e) For our *fair and safe work conditions*: for an eight-hour workday, for good and safe transportation, adequate housing, food, and medical attention. Against the poisonous effect that fumigations have on us.

f) For our *right to organization*: to be able to organize, unite, demonstrate, and act freely wherever and whenever we decide, so as to defend our rights and our interests, without having to humiliate ourselves before the laws of the bankrollers and the permits of the authorities, whose only function is to impede the unity and organization of the workers.

g) By fighting for our *right to culture* against all forms of discrimination and for equality of all the existing indigenous and *ladino* groups in Guatemala, and the right to have our languages and indigenous customs fully respected. By fighting for the right to receive necessary and useful education, to be able to live and work fully.

And, in all our vindications, by fighting for the equality of women and children and all their rights.

With respect to the above, we agree:

FOURTH:

1. To implement our plan of battle.
2. To strengthen our organization, making it more militant and uniting it with the thousands and thousands of campesinos from the different regions of Guatemala, so that our just struggle will triumph and our voice will be heard, and so that those who exploit, discriminate against, and repress us will withdraw.
3. To form alliances with remaining organizations to increase solidarity among all the workers, organized and unorganized.

4. To extend our organization to more regions and more locales.
5. To reaffirm our active participation in the National Committee of Labor Unity (CNUS), which brings together the most important organizations of exploited workers, and is beginning to fight to bring together laborers and campesinos. The CUC will work together actively with the CNUS, carrying the voice of the organized field-workers, so that all the pursuits of the CNUS may be consistent with the interests of the exploited.
6. To reaffirm our active participation in the Democratic Front Against Repression, this being the largest national tool that we have to fight against criminal repression committed by the bankrollers and their government against all the popular sectors.
7. To pursue further our international labor and solidarity relations with parallel organizations in Central America, Latin America, and the rest of the world, since ours is a struggle united with the exploited of the world.

FIFTH. – Finally, the CUC makes a call to all its members, to all its bases, sympathizers, and collaborators to actively participate in the First of May celebration by taking part in our activities of liberation proposed by our organization and the CNUS.

CLEAR HEAD, COMBATIVE FIST, UNITED HEART
OF ALL THE WORKERS
OF THE FIELD.
THE STRUGGLES OF THE CUC WILL REAP LIFE
WORK, LAND, AND LIBERTY
FOR THE FIRM CONSTRUCTION OF OUR ORGANIZATION
LET US ALL PARTICIPATE IN THE DEMONSTRATION
OF THE FIRST OF MAY

From the Guatemalan countryside, April 22, 1979
Committee of Campesino Unity (CUC)
Active member of the CNUS and of the Democratic Front Against Repression

THE NATIONAL COMMITTEE OF LABOR UNITY (CNUS)[35]

ON THIS FIRST OF MAY OF 1979,
TO THE PEOPLE OF GUATEMALA

MANIFESTS

The capitalist world continues its oppressive and exploitative expansion
Capitalist development has carried on its steady growth in Guatemala, based on the exploitation of laborers, campesinos, and workers in general, as well as on the political oppression of the popular sectors. But this development has its own characteristics, since ours is a dependent country. We can point out that in Guatemala, capital goods are not produced, since the whole of the industry is of a manufacturing and transformation-of-goods nature. This causes our country to depend on the imperialist powers, since all the capital goods necessary for production (machines, machinery, and raw materials like iron, etc.) must be consumed. But our industry is oriented to cover the deficient existing market of the region of Central America through investments by monopolistic foreign capital. As to the extractive industry (extraction of minerals), it is an undeniable fact that foreign capital has its investments guaranteed for the appropriation of our natural resources.

Notes

This paper could not have been written without the help of the following community: Sharon Groves, Ileana Rodríguez, Carla Peterson, Angela Pérez, Maria Lima, Caren Kaplan, and Paul Miller.

1. A greatly extended version of this essay appeared in Spanish in *Revista de Crítica Literaria Latinoamericana 36* (1992): 73–94.

2. Barbara Kruger and Phil Mariani, eds., "Introduction," *Remaking History* (Seattle: Bay Press, 1988), ix.

3. See Noam Chomsky, *Necessary Illusions* (Boston: South End Press, 1989); for details of government destabilization of Native American civil rights groups, see Ward Churchill and Jim Vander Wall, *Agents of Repression: The FBI's Secret Wars* (Boston: South End Press, 1990).

4. I use "Patwah" to refer to the specifically Jamaican "patois."

5. Edward Said raises just these questions in "Opponents, Audiences, Constituencies," in *The Anti-Aesthetic*, ed. Hal Foster (Port Townsend, Wash.: Bay Press, 1983), 142–43.

6. Rigoberta Menchú, with Elizabeth Burgos-Debray, *Me llamo Rigoberta Menchú y así me nació la conscienca* (Barcelona: Editorial Argos Vergara, 1983); see also *I, Rigoberta Menchú, An Indian Woman in Guatemala*, trans. Ann Wright (New York and London: Verso, 1984).

7. Sistren, with Honor Ford-Smith, *Lionheart Gal: Life Stories of Jamaican Women* (London: Women's Press, 1986).

8. John Beverley, "The Margin at the Center: On *Testimonio* (Testimonial Narrative)," *Modern Fiction Studies* 35, no. 1 (Spring 1989): 11–28.

9. Beverley, letter to the author; "Margin," 21.

10. Paul Miller suggests that mass reproduction of the original tapes might be the best compromise, given that the moments surrounding the recording are irretrievable (conversation with the author). Beverley chooses to exclude this possibility in his definition of *testimonio* as a transcribed document (12). One of the crucial questions at stake is the difference between the object and its use for the leftist and radical agendas.

11. Gloria Anzaldúa, *Borderlands/La Frontera: The New Mestiza* (San Francisco: Aunt Lute, 1987).

12. See Ranajit Guha, "The Prose of Counter-Insurgency," *Subaltern Studies II* (Delhi: Oxford University Press, 1983), 294–95.

13. Publishers were first Women's Press, then Canada's Sister Vision, now Barbara Smith's Women of Color Press, although the book is distributed through Inland Book Company, which can at least afford an 800 telephone number.

14. Burgos-Debray, *I*, ix.

15. Ibid., xi.

16. Ibid.

17. Ibid., xvi.

18. Ibid.

19. See Gayatri Spivak, "Can the Subaltern Speak?" in *Marxism and the Interpretation of Cultures*, ed. Cary Nelson and Lawrence Grossberg (Urbana: University of Illinois Press, 1988), 294–95.

20. Burgos-Debray, *I*, xvi.

21. Ibid., xxi.

22. Ibid., xv.

23. Ibid., xx.

24. Ibid.

25. See Karl Marx, "Eighteenth Brumaire of Louis Bonaparte," in *Karl Marx and Frederick Engels: Selected Works* (New York: International Publishers, 1986); also Spivak, "Subaltern."

26. Burgos-Debray, *I*, viii.

27. Trinh T. Minh-ha, *Woman/Native/Other: Writing Postcoloniality and Feminism* (Bloomington: Indiana University Press, 1989), 98.

28. Figures quoted in Guyanese dollars, as of October 1991.

29. Ford-Smith, *Lionheart Gal*, xii.

30. Ibid., xix.

31. Ibid., xxviii.

32. Ibid.

33. Ibid.

34. In March of 1978 the break was completed between the Guatemalan National Headquarters of Workers (CNT) and the Latin American Workers' Central (CLAT), because of the former's opposition to the latter's "reformist" and "thirdist" orientation as well as its line of work, which was markedly against socialist currents. Many of the Campesino Leagues of the CNT found themselves at the same time integrated in the Federation of Campesinos of Guatemala (FCG), whose leaders continued directly under the influence of CLAT. This originated an inevitable falling-out among the different leagues of campesinos. At this juncture, around the middle of April 1978, the Committee of Campesino Unity (CUC) emerged, with the purpose of grouping together all the campesino organizations and pushing forward the joint worker-campesino struggle.

The CUC defines itself not as a federation or a new headquarters, but rather a "Committee whose only demand made on its members is that they give themselves with honor, decision, sacrifice, and consistency to the collective tasks, to the interests of the field-workers and also be willing to fight for the interests of other exploited peoples in Guatemala."

35. The National Committee of Labor Unity was established in April 1976, not long after an earthquake, based on the ample presentation of organized workers, campesinos, and diverse labor groups including representatives of the National Headquarters of Workers (CNT), the Autonomous Labor Federation of Guatemala (FASGUA), and the Federation of Guatemalan Workers (FTG). Since its reemergence, the CNUS has been present in the majority of important workers' struggles and has therefore also been one of the primary permanent targets of repressive forces.

On repeated occasions it has declared its independence from political parties and from the guerrilla movement. It fights, of course, for a change of system and for the promotion of real measures of social transformation, although according to the judgment of some observers, it has not suffiently defined its proposed social alternative.

NINE

Theorizing Woman: *Funü, Guojia, Jiating* (Chinese Women, Chinese State, Chinese Family)*

Tani Barlow

> What narratives produce the signifiers of the subject for other traditions?
>
> Gayatri Spivak[1]

> It would make no sense . . . to define gender as the cultural interpretation of sex, if sex itself is a gendered category. *Gender ought not to be conceived merely as the cultural inscription of meaning on a pregiven sex . . . [but as] the very apparatus of production whereby the sexes themselves are established.*
>
> Judith Butler[2]

This essay critically rethinks some assumptions made in previous anglophone histories of Chinese women. Primarily, I see historical context as literally producing not reflecting realities. That is why I parse historical texts rather than deploying abstract, ahistorical, prediscursive "woman."[3] The essay also suggests an outline for a genealogy of concrete female subject positions in sinophone texts over the last two centuries. I desire a feminist politics rooted in difference without identity, what Chandra Mohanty calls a "non-imperialist feminism . . . a real space for the articulation, interpretation, theorization, and reflection about the historical specificity of the construction of women."[4]

The essay's historical lesson is that *funü*, the preeminent Chinese, female, subject position between about 1940 and 1985, was in fact a catechrisis, that is, an imaginary master word with very real political effects and power. I document my point by investigating the history of contests over signifiers of the subject "modern Chinese woman." I suggest that between the mid-Qing dynasty and the 1920s cultural revolution, the dominant formula *funü* signified kinswomen within a discursive economy that circulated power via a specialized, patrilineal, canonical rhetoric. In the "semifeudal, semicolonial" 1920s, when post-Confucian cultural revolutionaries rewrote the past as dead Tradi-

---

*Chinese is not inflected. All nouns are both singular and plural and are read according to the sense of the English syntax.

tion/*quantong*, intellectuals and activists made Woman/*nuxing*–a neologism that Chinese intellectuals produced as a consequence of their encounter with global colonial discourse in the semicolony world of the treaty ports–into a privileged site of struggle. Eventually, the Chinese Communist party inherited the organized women's movement. An alternative, massified, politicized subject known within the CCP *nomenklatura* as *funü* superseded *nuxing*/Woman, which was then redesignated as "Westernized," "bourgeois," erotic. Under the triumphant Maoist state's centralizing discourses, *funü*/women got situated first in *guojia*/state and then, through the magic of metonymy, within the modern *jiating*/family. Modern People's Republic of China *funü*/women thus provided one site for state socialist transformation.

Staging my argument in this way accomplishes several objectives. First, history emerges from this productive textuality to make genealogical claims about the past and its persistence. But although it is true that the Chinese monarchy had long been concerned with hegemonizing female subject positions,[5] the key words of the socialist imaginary's rhetoric–*guojia*/nation-state,[6] *jiating*/family, and female subject/*nuxing*–show the marks of intense struggle in modern rhetoric: they do not directly partake of older, dynastic social formations. Second, this argument locates *funü*/women synchronically in discursive constellation with other modern state categories, like "worker/*gongren*" and "youth/*qingnian*" and "proletariat/*wuchanjieji*." *Funü*, that is, forms a part of the "system of designations by . . . which," until the repudiation of Maoism, party "political authorities regulate[d] all important social relationships."[7] Third, the project explains gendered subject positionalities in social-political rather than psychodynamic terms. The Women's Federation, Fulian, has sustained *funü* as a political category since the 1940s and ensured that gender inscription remained a province of the state–at least until very recently.

Producing Virtuous Mothers and Good Wives

In late-imperial Chinese discourses, *funü* signified female family members. In his *Jiaonu yigui* or "Inherited Guide for Educating Women," the eighteenth-century scholar Chen Hongmou neatly illustrated what I mean:[8]

> When *fu*1 [persons, sages, women of rank] are in the *jia* [lineage unit] they are *nu* [female, woman, daughter]; when they marry they are *fu*4 [wives] and when they bear children they are *mu* [mothers]. [If you start with] a *xiannu* [virtuous unmarried daughter/female] then you will end up with a *xianfu* [virtuous wife]; if you have virtuous wives, you will end up with *xianmu* [virtuous mothers]. Virtuous mothers insure virtuous descendants. Civilizing begins in the women's

quarters. Everyone in the *jia* benefits from female chastity. That is why educating women is so important.[9]

Chen's statement usefully demonstrates why later cultural radicals found colonialist categories worth borrowing and even, perhaps, why the Maoist state's recuperation of *funü* had such nativist overtones.

My first point involves categories. The citation presents a *fu*1 who marries a husband, has children, is her father's daughter ("she" appears in quotation marks since Chinese pronouns are not gendered). Chen says that the *fu*1 is a person of rank within the differential patrilineal sublineage group, the *jia*. The point, however, is that the text's very specificity concerning *fu*1 forecloses a general category of generic woman, a category that would incorporate *fu*1, *nu*, *fu*4, *funü*, *xiannu*, plus all poor women of no rank and *nu*2/slaves. In other words, I could render the passage into English as follows: "before [women] are married they are *nu*/female/daughters, when they get married they are *fu*/wives, and when they give birth to children, then they are *mu*/mothers." But as soon as I did so I would substantiate a category—Woman—*that does not appear in the syntax of the sentence*.

What does this imply? The subjects Chen's passage situates and addresses are primarily wives and daughters or *fu*4*nü*. (They are "women," of course, but, as I will demonstrate momentarily, by virtue of protocols specific to their subject positions and not necessarily or even in the first case by reference to a physiological ground.) *Funü* is a frame of differential *jia*-relation, while Woman is a transcendental signifier. There exists no moment in Chen's text where "woman" operates as a framing category outside of *jia* or the relationality implied in *funü*. Another way to phrase this point is that Chen Hongmou assumes no foundational status for Woman. Rather than frame kin-specific situations as instances of "things women do," Chen explains that acting within specified ethical-practical boundaries produces a recognizably female person.

So *funü*/female kin was the (con)text that produced subject positions like *xianmu*/virtuous mother as always already gendered.[10] But what made it work? How did this discursive context magically deploy positionalities of kin like *xianmu* and make them stick? To develop a response I turn to Elizabeth Cowie, who argued a decade ago that rather than theorizing women as prediscursively "*situated* in the family" we ought to grasp that "it is in the family—as the effect of kinship structures—that women as women are produced."[11] Cowie sought to understand "kinship" not as a system of exchange but as a production line for subjectivities. I agree: relational nomenclature produce subject positions. Cowie also sought to expose the ways Victorian anthropological discourses had essentialized Man and Woman into binaried, exclusionary, sexist reductions from the start. Reading Chen with Cowie in mind, I can argue that the exchange of actual women in patrilineal, patrilocal Chinese kin fields produced not the sign Woman, but a profusion of signs with one thing in common: though they all accommodated "real" women, none could be reduced to a prediscursive *hegemonic sign*.

Yin/yang logic structured disciplinary gendering in Chen Hongmou's world just as it structured religious, generational, and many associated juridical relations.[12] To cast my point negatively, Chen Hongmou's texts do not refer to women's bodies, nor to their body parts, as proofs of their social existence. Rather, his text argues that appropriately disciplined behaviors for *funü* constrained within the capacious relations of *yin/yang* logic (remaining within, filial caretaking, service to parents, moral instruction of children, individual normative practice) all contribute to the coherence of human culture.[13]

When I refer to these processes as social-cosmological activities enacted on the never stable or fully boundaried primary site of the *jia*, I am rendering into my own language the point the late-sixteenth-century physician, Li Shichen, made in his *Materia Medica*. "Normally *qian* and *kun* make fathers and mothers; but there are five kinds of nonmales/*feinan* who cannot become fathers and five kinds of nonfemales/*feinu* who cannot become mothers."[14] Now *qian* and *kun* are the first and last hexagrams of the *I Ching* or *Book of Changes*, since the Song dynasty the foundational text of hegemonic Confucian studies. *Qian* and *kun* refer to forces operating in *tiandi*, the realms extrinsic to human culture, as well as the realm of *wen*, of human social life. The forces *yin* and *yang* are many things: logical relationships (up/down, in/out, husband/wife), practical forces, "designations for the polar aspects of effects," and, in a social sense, powers inscribing hierarchy (i.e., *yang* subordinates *yin* because it encloses the lesser force within itself), but *yin/yang* is neither as totalistic nor as ontologically binaried a construct as current cliché would have it. What Li says is that the dynamic forces of *yin/yang* do "produce"—only not women and men (themselves subject positions but in another discourse) so much as subject positions named mother and father, husband and wife, brother and sister, and so on.

The anomaly confronting the physician in the cases Li cites rests on the general instability of bodies in most Confucian discourse. Here the nonman and the nonwoman, whose defective bodies forestall production, as well as the castrated, impotent, vaginally impenetrable, and bodies known to change from female to male and from male to female, *all* present to the physician unstable surfaces that resist customary "gendering." In Li Shichen and Chen Hongmou's time, Simone de Beauvoir's odd notion that "women are not born Women but become Women" makes sense. Why? Because the surface onto which

eighteenth-century Chinese subjectivities were inscribed (i.e., Li Shichen's fecund body) were more flexible than the (gendering) subject positions that
producing sons and daughters enabled women to occupy and possess.[15]

What appear in Chen's texts are not the "sexes" but a profusion of relational,
bound, unequal dyads, each signifying difference and positioning difference
analogically. A *nu* is a daughter, unequally related to parents and parents-in-
law. A *xiaozi* or filial son is differentially unequal to mother and father, *yin* to
their *yang*. A *fu* is a wife, tied in a secondary relation to her husband. A *xianfu*
is a wife who, grasping the powers visited upon the secondary *yin* term, masters
her domain through familiarity with protocol.[16] Obviously (invoking Cowie's
point), subjects got produced within the *jia* (more properly *jia*-ist or familist
discourses). Chen Hongmou's definition of *nu*, *fu*4, and *mu* makes it clear that
while (good) women in the *jia* did effect social relations outside the family, no
position existed for female persons (or for male persons, for that matter) outside
of the *jia* boundaries. The *fu*1 exists within the kin world of reciprocal inequality, by virtue of her father's high standing.

Chen Hongmou advocated educating women to produce more *xiannu* and
enhance the *jia*. Learning to act virtuously is coterminous with acting "like a
woman," in Chen Hongmou's view, and "acting like a woman" required the
maintenance of difference.[17] "[Just as] the *yin* and the *yang* are different quali-
ties/*shuxing*, so males and female/*nan nu* should act differently," as Chen's text
puts it.[18] In the view of Lu Jingxi, Chen Hongmou's own cited authority,
"there is a difference between the *li*/ritual of men and women/*nan nu*. If you
do not maintain the distinction, then you will cause gossip."[19] Protocols consisted primarily of *li*—behaviors, scripted actions, and normatized manners—
that shaped appropriate, proper, good behavior. Social norms and gendered experience were inextricable.[20] In the cadence of the texts: when the daughters
act on the *li* of daughterhood, married women act on the *li* of wives, and so
on, then the distinction between men and women is accomplished and gendering is effected.

Protocols took virtually everything into consideration. "As a kins-
woman/*nuzi* you must establish yourself in life/*lishen*," for instance. "In behavior don't turn your head from side to side; if you wish to speak do so without moving your lips; if you wish to sit, do so without moving your knees,
and if you stand do not wiggle your skirt. If you are happy do not giggle, if
you are unhappy, do not yell aloud. Within and without/*nei*/*wai* [the *jia*]
women and men (*nan*/*nu*) should be separate." Chen Hongmou cited reams
of text from ancient times describing in minute detail the *lishu* (body etiquette)
he felt would allow people in the present, through their physical actions, to
resurrect the splendid world of the Confucian past.

Protocol effected "gender" relationally by linking good behavior to correct enactment of texts that inscribed kin difference. "The father-in-law/*ahweng* and mother-in-law/*agu* are the heads of the husband's family," a typical specimen reads. "You are their daughter-in-law when you marry your husband, so you must support them as you supported your own parents" (i.e., specified practices enumerated in concrete detail: serve parents only when properly dressed, listen attentively while remaining in a standing posture, prepare their wash water and towels in the morning, premasticate their food, prepare their bedding, and avoid disorder, criticizing, or neglecting their comfort).[21] Such protocols were neither mere code, nor maps or roles. They instructed in the fashion of advice literature and they provided continuously reinforced subject positions because they linked the archaic past, where culture heroes had inititally written them down, to contemporary texts. Protocol formed a bulwark of order against the undoing of difference and positioned subjects in social narrative.[22]

Producing *Nuxing*/Woman

Western imperialism forced into crisis the text protocols Chen Hongmou and those like him had (re)produced. The Manchu dynasty's long, slow implosion and the imperialists' relentless penetration of the heartland via "treaty ports" transformed the political elite's social configuration and powers. Where previously the monarchy's texts enabled Confucian officials to regulate the meaningful world, gargantuan pressures dispersed the older stacked powers; they collapsed in 1905 when the Qing throne abolished the civil-service examination system. Eager to replace Chen Hongmou, who hegemonized the Confucian production of gendering, a modern, post-Confucian, professionalized intellectual emerged, who oversaw the appropriation of foreign signs into the new, domestic, urban, mass-market, print economy, an "intellectual" who signaled a shift from the widely diffused textuality of the old society to the scriptural economy of realist representation in a peripheralized world economy.[23]

In the early twentieth century a new social formation arose calling itself *zhishi jieji* or intellectual class, later to become *qiming xuezhe* ("enlightened scholars"), and finally, under the same forces that produced *funü*/women as a political category, *zhishifenzi* or Chinese intellectual under Maoist inscription. *Zhishifenzi* were the "Western"-educated offshoot of the tiny, very significant new commercial bourgeoisie, who monopolized the appropriation of Western ideas forms, signs, discourses. In their hands, peripheralization of signs proceeded as new missionary-educated and college-graduated professionals imported, translated, republished, and commented on texts from foreign languages. Historically, this group constituted itself as a colonialized elite, meaning two things: that the imperialist semicolonization of China forced into existence "new intellectuals," and that these elements did not just "import" neologisms from Japan and the European West, they redrew the discursive boundaries of elite social existence. In this way *zhishifenzi* occupied (thereby further valorizing) a new, modernist, social field of *shehui* or "society." Situated inside the treaty ports in a crude material sense – the palladian English banks and French boulevards, the German beer, American YMCAs, and Japanese factories – terms like *shehui* acquired concrete referents. The powerful older terms *guan*/official, *gong*/common, and *si*/singular from Chen Hongmou's time increasingly gave up ground. Once-robust conventions were gradually reduced into something intellectuals of the 1920s would call "tradition/*chuantong*" and regarded with either painful nostalgia or contempt and fear.[24]

A longer project would require far more comment on colonialist discourses among the treaty port *zhishifenzi*. Here let it suffice that the discourses of "semicolonialism" had an effect on older Chinese gendering practices. A rash of masculinist interest in the universal sign of woman had surfaced as early as the 1830s, when there occurred what Mary Rankin calls an efflorescence of "profeminine" male writing. Male reformers in the 1860s spoke admiringly of "enlightened" relations between women and men in Western countries. Antifootbinding and pro-female academy arguments held key positions, in the late 1890s and the first decade of the twentieth century, in the work of major male new-style intellectuals.[25]

Indeed, masculinist redeployment of *nu* initiated, according to Charlotte Beahan, an unprecedented female journalism within the slackening old-world discourses between 1890 and 1910.[26] Calling themselves "sisters/*jiemei*," female writers reversed the strategy Chen Hongmou had adopted when he argued for female literacy on the grounds that ethical women in families produced strong states. "Why isn't China strong?" one asked. "Because there are no persons of talent. Why are there no persons of talent? Because women do not prosper."[27] Late-Confucian women sought liberty on "nationalist" grounds. The sisters' publications contributed to what rapidly emerged as "myths of the nation."[28] That is to say, writers positioned themselves as citizens of the Chinese nation, as advocates of national emancipation from Western imperialism and Manchu occupation, and as different from men of their own "Han Chinese" nationalist group. On those unimpeachable grounds they sought to mobilize China's "beloved but weak two hundred million women . . . the direct slaves of slaves."[29]

The expression "slaves of slaves" as a term for Chinese women signified a noteworthy change in the theorization of *nu*. "Slave" referred to male Han Chinese "enslaved" to the Manchu monarchy and thus signaled democratic patriotism. Women, as the "slaves of slaves," reached into domestic units to recategorize all Chinese women in a patriotic unity against the myriad imperialists seeking to "divide China up as though it were a melon," as people put it then. The kin-inflected category of *funü* began the referential shift. Writers offered Chinese *nuren* (female person) as one specific instance of a universal category consisting of all women, and they did so under a patriotic inscription. An example of the mechanics of the referential shift comes from Zhen Ziyang's *Nuzi xin duben* (New Study Book for Women), a collection of stories about virtuous women linked generically to narratives in the Chen Hongmou book I cited earlier. The older text had celebrated "just mothers," "ethical stepmothers," and other situated kinswomen who had managed the *jia* sphere well, thereby effecting, through their adept use of protocol under difficult circumstances, the space beyond their own *jia*, that is, the *gong* or general world. The modern text, in contrast, provided not one, but two sets of ethical narratives about good women, set off from each other in two separate "books." [30]

Book 1 retold stories familiar to readers even before Chen Hongmou's time, like the story of Mencius's mother, who sacrificed to provide her son an appropriate ethical environment; Yue Fei's wife Liang, who personally fought the Nuzhen barbarians on behalf of the Song dynasty; and Hua Mulan of the Liang dynasty, who masqueraded as a filial son and fought as her father's proxy for twelve years. It also included examples of women who had, in the hoary past, transgressed unfairly gendered boundaries or had been unjustly ignored in masculinist histories. Huang Zongjia, for instance, "was born a girl but did not want to be a woman [*nuzi*]" so she masqueraded as a man, served as an official; Suo Maoyi taught the master calligrapher Wang Xizi his calligraphy style; and so on.

Book 2 assembled a set of parallel stories about famous women of the West who matched or exceeded Hua Mulan's filial devotion, because they served not father, husband, or patriline but the nation. "Sha Latuo" or Charlotte Corday, according to the Chinese version of her story, studied at a nunnery for six years, became engrossed in a particular book (I cannot figure out who "Puluhua" might have been in a European language) about national heroes. The book's inspiration sent Sha Latuo to Paris, where she surprised the tyrant Mala (Marat) while he was with his concubine. In prison for his murder, she sent her father a filial letter declaring that tyrannicide was not a crime, and met her death with "Puluhua's" book clutched in her hands. Another narrative venerated Madame Roland, who studied "the Confucianism of her country" but who preferred the example of the Greeks and Romans. After marrying Roland for his politics, she inspired her timid husband to resist Robespierre's "People's Party/*mindang*." When Robespierre executed Madame Roland her husband committed suicide and their servants, overcome, also petitioned execution; their requests were carried out.[31]

The juxtaposition of "Chinese" and "Other" stories engendered meaning in two significant ways. First, obviously the reworked "Chinese" stories and the "Western" parallels jointly showed female heroes shifting their loyalties from husband or father to "nation," without directly requiring that they abandon the prior object. A certain "Frances" (Frances Willard, perhaps) appears to have been selected because, following her father's death, she remained unmarried and devoted herself to the improvement of North America through a renovation of the family, the nation, and finally the entire world. Nation rose up to peripheralize Father, never precluding his importance at the personal level.[32]

Second, the bilateral mutual exchange of "Western" signs and "Chinese" narrative had the effect of producing a category of universal womanhood. "Chinese" narratives changed in a generic sense, that is, when the subjects of their interest became "Western" women. When Zhen located Chinese female heroes in the company of European women-of-the-state like Joan of Arc, Charlotte Corday, and Madame Roland, the effect was to legitimate and universalize *nuzi* within a statist, universal (i.e., Europeanized) world history. Zhen sought to conjoin bourgeois state revolts like the Glorious Revolution, the French and Italian Revolutions, to the expected Chinese Revolution (the Xinhai Revolution occurred a decade later in 1911). Giving such remarkable prominence to Western women in their national revolutions, moreover, granted universality to heroic female actions of whatever kind, at whatever time. Remarkably, the "Chinese" section of the text went so far as to legitimate Wu Zetian of the Tang dynasty, previously reviled as a female usurper and defiler of her husband's throne. Changes in pro-feminine discourses did condition the form that *nuxing* eventually took. Before the 1920s, however, female heroes continued to rest securely in the inherited binarism familiar from Confucian contexts of hero and the throne. The term *nuxing* (literally, female sex) erupted into circulation during the 1920s when treaty-port intellectuals overthrew the literary language of the Confucius canon. Critics replaced the *wen*/culture of the old world with *wenxue*/literature, inscribed in a hybrid (part colloquial Chinese, part "European" syntax garnered reading Western fiction in Chinese translation) literary language. *Wenxue* consisted of an appropriated realist representationalism, and thus supported the production of modernist subjectivities. The field of *wenxue* unfolded in the 1920s as a general terrain of combat for intellectuals. The May Fourth Movement of 1919 established *wenxue* as a field of realist referentiality: the second-most significant major figure of that new textuality, after the "hypertrophied self" of the writer himself, was *nuxing*.[33]

Women did not deploy *nuxing*. Like the recuperation of *nu* as a trope of nationalist universality in masculinist discourse, *nuxing* constituted a discursive sign and a subject position in the larger frames of anti-Confucian discourse. When intellectuals overthrew the Confucius canon they sought the total transformation of "Chinese culture." The same modernist revolution that invoked new, modern signs—"society/*shehui*," "culture/*wenhua*," "intellectuals/*zhishifenzi*," "individualism/*geren zhuyi*," and innumerable other Westernized Chinese words—gave *nuxing* or "Woman" wide discursive powers. *Nuxing* played a particularly significant role in two separate textual streams: literary representation and the body of writing known as Chinese feminism. Historically, women writers did not predominate in either one.[34]

"Historical languages constitute classes," Talal Asad has argued, "they do not merely justify groups already in place according to universal economic structures."[35] So *nuxing* coalesced as a category when, as part of the project of social class formation, Chinese moderns disavowed the older literary language of power. After the May Fourth Movement, Chinese writers wrote in a newly modernized, westernized, semicolloquial language in which *nuxing* played the part of a subject of representation and an autonomous agent. *Nuxing* operated as one half of the Western, exclusionary, male/female binary. Within the *zhishifenzi* as a class, the sign of the sex binary had enormous utility. *Nuxing* and its correlate *nanxing*, or male sex, acted as a magnet, attracting around its universal, sexological, scientific core a psychologized personal identity that allowed its possessor to act as the fulcrum for upending Confucianism and all received categories. Chinese translations of European fiction and social theory also relocated agency in the individual at the level of sex-opposition and sex-attraction. In particular, colloquial fiction established sex as the core of an oppositional personal identity and woman as a sexological category.[36]

The career of *nuxing* firmly established a foundational womanhood beyond kin categories. It did so on the ground of European humanism. That is, when it introduced the category of "woman" as a universal category of *nuxing*, Chinese feminist writing flooded texts with representations of women as the "playthings of men," "parasites," "slaves"; as dependencies of men or simply as degraded to the point of nonexistence. Feminist texts accorded a foundational status to physiology and, deploying the Victorian ideology of Europe in the last century, they grounded sexual identity in sexual physiology. Indeed, the most shocking of all of Chinese feminism's arguments substituted sexual desire for reproductive service to *jia* as the foundation of human identity. The secret attraction of European texts was their emphasis on what Foucault termed "sexuality" as historical artifact. Yet when the leading male feminist Yeh Shengtao spoke of women, even while he granted foundational status to male/female, it was often in terms of Chinese women's lack of personality or human essence.[37] In other words, when Chinese translators invoked the sex binary of a Darwin or an Ellis, they valorized notions of female passivity, biological inferiority, intellectual inability, sexuality, and social absence through reference to the location of these "truths" in European social scientism and social theory. Thus, Chinese women became Women/*nuxing* only when they become the other of Man in the Victorian binary.[38] Woman was foundational only insofar as she constituted a replication of Man, his other.

Ching-ku Chan's recent exploration of *nuxing* in the literature of major male May Fourth realist writers makes this point at the level of literary texts. When the intellectual or *zhishifenzi* turned to European-style realism, Chan argues, "the classical mimetic function of realism" required that the writer represent himself through his own representations of the Other, and the Other of male realist choice was Woman. *Nuxing* was first and foremost a trope in the discourses of masculinist Western-inspired realist fiction. As Chan puts it, "textually speaking," *nuxing* appeared in realist texts, "but as an innocent scapegoat, paying for the crimes that society has committed." Indeed, Woman appeared within a cruel equation: "The root of *your* [female] suffering is to be found in *my* [male writer's] inability to right the wrongs that society has done *me*."[39]

Chan's point can also be made in a slightly different way. When the modernist female writer Ding Ling began producing texts in the late 1920s she too had to struggle with the self/other dynamic coded into the sex binary Man/Woman. Ding Ling's texts sought to take Woman as a subject position and social psychology. Yet the texts she produced during that period of her career invoke a *nuxing* who either must die, commit suicide, or lose herself in sexual excess and mental disorder. No positivity, no universal Woman independent of Man could exist under the terms of the sex binary. In the end Ding Ling, who continued to write but not as a Woman, simply abandoned psychological realism.[40]

The social history of the trope *nuxing* requires more space than I am allotted here. Once it entered elite *zhishifenzi* discourses, *nuxing* as a representation took on a life of its own. Her image appeared in popular movies, in pulp fiction, in photographs and fashions, schools and parks. These indigenous representations of *nuxing* constructed a universal category of Woman in the image of an object of consumption, to paraphrase Annette Kuhn, and *nuxing* "enter[ed] cultural and economic circulation on [its] own accord."[41] It ceased to be a "Western" sign, and became a sign of modernity in bourgeois New China. Once recontextualized, the sign Woman/*nuxing*, had a career and a politics of its own.

Producing *Funü*/Women

The sex binary Man/Woman and the sign Woman/*nuxing* never went uncontested. Carolyn Brown has vividly shown Lu Xun criticizing the initial formulation, arguing that the physical body of modern Chinese women "had become the repository of a meaning—the signified, that it did not rightfully bear."[42] Social critique from Chinese Communist party theorist Xiang Jingyu, who employed *funü*/women as a Marxist trope, contested the pervasive irrationalization of *nuxing*.[43] Xiang lost no time classifying *nuxing* as a product of bourgeois preoccupations, and her comments in the early 1920s set the tone of Communist theorizing for decades. Regardless, Xiang Jingyu's early Communist *funü* entered discourse the same way as sex-opposed *nuxing* had, through *zhishifenzi* appropriation. In the process of transmitting social theory, Communists retranslated out of the European revolutionary heritage the Woman of their political theory as *funü*. The bourgeois social sciences, political rights theory, and nineteenth-century patriarchal-theory left-wing *zhishifenzi*/intellectuals found valuable also shared elements of the sex essentialism manifest in realist fiction. But appropriators shaped their critique to emphasize social production, thus weighing historical and institutional teleology over organic, biogenetic time. Moreover, the *funü*/woman of early Chinese Marxist categories could never exist as more than half of her potential within the all-encompassing revolutionary equation of theory/praxis. So unlike *nuxing*, Marxist *funü* found its referential framework in revolutionary practice and in the historical woman that future world historical teleology would produce.

The Chinese translation of Bebel's *Women and Socialism* established *funü* in its political usage. Its chiliastic tone and the systematic use of *funü* as the figure par excellence of general social revolution relied on a conjuncture of woman and society that attracted Chinese Marxists from the start. Joining it later in CCP theory were Engels's "Origin of the Family, Private Property, and the State," Lenin's "Soviet Political Power and Women's Status," "International Women's Day," and "On the Freedom to Love," and Stalin's "International Women's Day."[44] *Nuxing* had taken over the foundational sex binary Man/Woman from Victorian literary texts and feminist theory in translation. The Communist inscription of *funü* engaged other colonialist discourses, the Euro-Marxist machinery of production/reproduction, teleology, stage theory, state/society binarism, and, of course, the discourse's universal, international referentiality.

A social history of Chinese Marxist discourses on *funü* substantiates how thoroughly the history of "women" in China had by the early 1950s become, for all intents and purposes, a subsidiary to the history of the European working class. Du Zhunhui's 1949 *Funü wenti jianghua* (Lectures on the Woman Problem), exemplified how, when Europe gets placed at the hegemonic center of "universal" theories of capital, Chinese history is inevitably reduced to being a subsidiary, local growth, possessing historical significance only as a semicolony of Europe, following a two-thousand-year dark night of "feudalism." Significantly, Du's sophisticated historical critique berates the Chinese women's movement's "failures" measured against the "universal" European women's movement.[45]

State-building supplanted bourgeois consolidation in both the "white" as well as the Communist camps, as the Japanese advanced in the late 1930s. Socialist *funü* obviated *nuxing* once the right allowed the discourses of national salvation [*jiuguo*] to fall into the left's special province. The reactionary right rescinded its pallid remaining feminist rights arguments and dissolved the women's movement into a "feminine mystique." Socialist mobilization politics targeted *funü* as a tactical object, eventually a triangulating category mediating modern state and the modern Chinese family. But in the provinces during the late twenties and thirties an increasingly Maoist CCP grafted elements appropriated from local categories to its international Marxist teleology of women in social production/reproduction.

"Keep in mind," said a 1932 activists' organizing manual for party cadre doing women's work under the auspices of the Jiangxi Soviet, "what world revolutionary leader Lenin said [to the effect that] 'socialism cannot succeed without the participation of women.' At the same time we must keep in mind *that the liberation of Chinese women and the victory of soviet state power are inseparable.*"[46] The Communist party's fugitive state projects ("fugitive" in the sense that during these years the CCP decamped from its various territories) made the *funü* of Chinese Marxism into a category of political praxis. In so doing it reversed and canceled the earlier relationship of theory and practice.

Thus, the "universal" woman of Euro-Marxism, an agent in the "universal" history of capital, not only relinquished her theoretical centrality to the women of practical village mobilizations, but Chinese Communist practices canceled out the existence of that older European woman and she simply vanished. The peripheralized sign of woman realized its own independent local politics, to put it another way. Context revised text. The Jiangxi Soviet (1930–34), for instance, identified "woman" as a political subject who was over 14 years of age; had been emancipated from the *tongyangxi*, prostitution and female slave systems; had recourse from family violence; whose physical body did not bear the marks of "feudalism" (no earrings or footbinding); and named herself as a *funü* in liberating political praxis.[47]

This subject existed inside a structured sphere of politics beyond the rural calender of fieldwork and beyond village social relations. She labored according to schedule,[48] and according to protective laws.[49] A rudimentary bureaucracy concerned itself with her welfare,[50] and insured her freedom of marriage.[51] Political networks, such as the Working Women's Congress,[52] operated to rationalize her political outlook.[53] The symbolic center of this Woman as a subject was undoubtedly the effort to propagandize "Women's Day."[54]

Discourse of woman under the fugitive state had a proto-mass-line role that allowed activists, party Central Committee, and local women to speak in different voices and that opened a large range of positions to local people.[55] These included *qingfu*/young women, *ludai de tongyangxi*/oppressed wives by virtue of infant bride sale, *da pinku laodong funü*/the large suffering masses of laboring women, *nongcun zhong di laodong funü*/laboring women of the rural villages, *nugong nongfu*/women workers and peasants. Even the heterogeneous *funü* of this period, however, was always already a subject-effect of state discourses and a by-product of its legal, ideological, and organizational apparatus. It is just that before 1949 the "line" did not attempt political closure. *Funü* appeared in it as a range of subject positions inside the Soviet state, beyond the reach of family and feudalism. As one document put it, village women do not understand the agitation for liberation and need to have explained to them the link between victory in class struggle and the liberation of women. They must be taught that their self-interest is connected to the state not the family.[56]

Thus the ideological ideal was a healthy semiliterate woman of 18 to 35 who could "destroy her familist outlook and serve [the state even when called upon to make] government transfers."[57] She was expected to act out of self-interest/*benshen liyi* for personal rights/*quanli*,[58] "representing" herself through grass-roots mass organizational work.[59] The *funü* encountered in these texts appeared never to have understood what was meant by "women's self-interest" until propagandists explained the stakes in concrete detail.[60] The natural interests women theoretically possessed, in other words, had first to be inscribed via the actions of recruiting, educating, nurturing, and mobilizing. *Funu's* proper field was "the organizational sphere of the party/*dang di zuzhi fanwei*,"[61] where she sustained herself in the political space of the CCP through election/*xuanzhi*, mobilization/*dongyuan*, and various organizational/*zuzhi* practices.[62] Maoism in the late thirties and forties constantly reformulated *funü*, always retaining the statist slant.[63] The formula that emerged in the early 1940s, consequently, involved a synecdochic process of exchange between two, interpenetrated, objects of political discourse: the state/*guojia* and the family/*jiating*. Rather than posit independent *funü* as an agent of politics outside domestic closure, as the brief earlier experiments had done, the later

Soviets' praxis emphasized production of *funü* through political processes that retained women and men in a sphere of politicized domestic relations.

After 1943 the party's line turned to the transformation of the family itself. By 1947 Maoist state policy had shifted – in contradistinction to Marxist theory and socialist practices elsewhere – toward a reinvented family, which appears in these texts as *jiating*. The homily of the Zhu Fusheng family conference, for instance, treats the "history" of domestic politics as a party historiographer might chronicle a Central Committee meeting. The women of the Zhu family, though oppressed, did not have the "habit of democracy, and did not know how to speak, ask questions, or actually say a thing." After Zhu Fusheng explained democratic procedure to them they collectively transformed themselves from an autocracy/*jiazhang zhuanzhi* into a "democratic family/ *minzhu jiating*." In the subsequent months family members instituted political-democratic policies such as self-criticism/*ziwo piping*, domestic production of thread and cloth, and planning, all domestic production activities the CCP promoted at the time. The homily of the Zhu family nicely exhibits how statist political practices interpenetrated family relations, lodging *funü* through democratic rhetoric in a renovated statist *jiating* or nucleating family.[64]

The recuperation required that the politicized new family reconstitute itself in the language of politics. Leading party officials promoted domestic political construction, as Zhou Enlai did, for instance, when he argued that women did not need emancipation from family, that men needed to take family responsibilities as seriously as women.[65] As Patricia Stranahan has argued, it was precisely this reorientation of woman policy that provided the stable base peasant women eagerly accepted; the resulting line both reflected "peasant realism" and achieved revolutionary transformation through social production.[66] The resulting collaboration of village women and Central Committee, was, I want to stress, neither "traditional" nor universally "Marxist." It was syncretic and as "modern" as any alternative.[67]

The newly minted Maoist metonymic interpenetration of state/family made the body of women a field of the state at the same time that it opened the state to inflection by kin categories.[68] The entry point was reproductive science. Woman-work *ganbu*, armed with medical knowledge, brought to political activity the power/knowledge of sanitation, physiology, and scientific midwifery. Texts drilled village women in reproductive physiology ("it's just like your farm animals") and dispensed information on bodily functions like menstrual cycle and hygiene (don't borrow pads, don't drink cold water, stay away from the dirty menstrual blood that carries disease, don't have intercourse during your period, visit the doctor for irregularities, etc.). Scientific midwifery connected reproduction to politics.[69]

The dawning of the golden era of Chinese Communist familism in the 1950s found the modern Chinese *jiating* sandwiched between a pre-1949 peasant-inflected formation and idealized revolutionary images flooding in from the more advanced socialist USSR. By that time the *jiating* had become the nineteenth-century Europeanized family of *zhishifenzi* idealization: mommy, daddy, and me.[70] So *jiating* grounded social production in a context heavily marked with traces of older formations, just as the nation did. The modern socialist *jiating* and Maoist *guojia* coexisted in synecdochic unity, as concept metaphors of each other. That, at least, is how I interpret mobilizations like the 1957 campaign "Industrious and Frugal in Establishing the Nation, Industrious and Frugal in Managing the Family," where state and family are virtually synonymous; what operates in one sphere translates directly into the other.[71] "The material and cultural life of our state's [*guo*] masses of people has improved substantially in the last few years. But the lives of many families [*jiating*] are still not comfortable," the text reads. To raise the *jiating*'s level the masses must "industriously develop our state's industry and agriculture." The work of housewives (*jiating zhufu*) must mirror the work going on outside the *jiating*, in the *guojia*. "*Every housewife could be industrious and frugal in managing the family affairs, if she institutionalizes a rational planning schedule. . . . Industriousness and frugality in the family labor strengthens industriousness and frugality in the nation.*[72]

Women's Federation and *Funü* as a State Category

William Parish and Martin Whyte once commented that after socialist Liberation in 1949 the Chinese state took no clear measures to transform family structure, and that Fulian, the state's Women's Federation, was an "amorphous" government bureaucracy, the only mass organization that people belonged to by virtue of physiology.[73] This does not explain the very real powers of the Women's Federation. The importance of Fulian lay in its power to subordinate and dominate all inscriptions of womanhood in official discourse. It is not that Fulian actually represented the "interests" of women, but rather that one could not until recently be "represented" *as a woman* without the agency and mediation of Fulian. That fact is a measure of its success and its importance.[74]

In late 1948 the government commissioned its leading female officials, dignitaries, and luminaries in the Liberated Areas with the task of planning the All-China Democratic Women's Association's (later simply Women's Association) first meeting as soon as Beijing fell.[75] With formal gravity the Planning Committees and Standing Committee began directing the installation of new bureaucratic frameworks charged with deciding national policy and convening the association's first representative congress.[76]

In these initiating moments Fulian consolidated its power as a national, state organ for responsibly representing "new China's women." With mechanical deliberation the bylaws connect representation of "female masses" to the international socialist women's movement, through the accumulating processes of representation.[77] "What is most deserving of pride," one document read, "is that the representatives/*daibiao* from the liberated areas are all picked by election from the local area women's congresses. . . . We have been commissioned by the female masses. We must loyally represent their opinions."[78] And the proviso: "Representation/*daibiao* means representing the masses, [it does] not [mean] controlling/*guan* the masses."[79]

This bureaucratization and Fulian's transformation from active production of *funü* to formally representing them in Beijing relied on past struggle. But it emanated a new sort of definitional power. Representative bodies like congresses and the federation itself did "represent the masses" but they also consolidated and mediated internal differences/*tuanjiele gezhong butong de funü*, homogenizing, so to speak, through political democracy. The inception of Fulian initiated for "*funü*" unprecedented participation in the rituals of state formation and promised bureaucratic power: but only so long as it, Fulian, the government, retained the power to determine what, in fact, constituted a *funü*.[80]

Deng Yingchao, speaking to this issue, laid out the official view when she argued that Woman in the discourses of the state had achieved "political, economic, cultural, and social elevation and elevation of herself in the family."[81] Fulian's charge involved consolidating and expanding the political sphere carved out earlier under the fugitive state: a process, the document argued, that ensured achieved equal status for women by transforming them from consumers into producers.[82] By its third congress Fulian spoke in even broader, less autonomous terms, the gray, ponderous language of the state:

> The All-China Women's Federation is, under the leadership of the Chinese Communist party, an organization for the basic organization of every strata of laboring women. [It] has achieved enormous work success since the second National Congress. . . . [But now it] must improve and strengthen its mass viewpoint, and its mass-line work methods . . . be concerned with and reflect the real interests and demands of women, struggle energetically against discrimination and harming of women [etc.] . . . so that Fulian and the mass of women have an even more intimate relationship.[83]

The founding of the Fulian, however, was *not* specific to women.[84] The same ritual unfolded in the mass groups that "reflected and represented" youth, trade unions, and other politically delineated constituencies. The Fulian organization (and its replicants) took part in a reinscription of the nation itself, and thus, it represented at a subordinated level the processes of state-building commencing at levels superior to itself. The socialist state consolidated gender difference on the material grounds of scientific physiology. Part of this scientism, clearly reflected in Fulian documents, is the notion that people are in literal fact material because their organic reproductive capacity makes them like animals.[85] Thus gendering under Maoist inscription located itself as a process of reproductive differentiation within "scientific socialism." The fusion of peasant realism and socialist scientism gave rise to texts like "People and Wealth Flourish/*Ren yu cai wang*," which "encourage the people of the liberated areas not merely to work hard to get enough to wear and eat, but also to have more children, who, once they are born must be supported/*yanghuo*." Lyrically conflating "production" and "reproduction" the state vowed to train midwives, investigate infant mortality, propagandize for scientific sanitation, oppose feudal superstition, and publish popular chapbooks on infant care, all predicated on popularizing a modern understanding of reproductive physiology and sanitary childbirth practices.

Much work among women aimed at producing people who would collaborate in the biopolitical agenda of the state. Before the twentieth century, birth and death had possessed no direct link to the throne, or to state political economy. Life and death commenced in the spatial boundaries of *jia* or sect and took form as matters of pollution, rupture, reconsolidation.[86] Although late-imperial domestic and popular medical practices regarding menstruation, conception, parturition, suckling, and so on were sophisticated, they participated in the same neo-Confucian epistemic order as gendering—reference to the state through dyadic obligation to Father, Husband, and Monarch. The socialist state, on the other hand, made popular and clear the direct linkage of state's practice and modern obstetric medicine. *Study Guide for the New Woman* straightforwardly declaimed that "the 27 lessons in this book . . . are for the exclusive use of village women in their study/*xuexi*, literacy classes, and political lessons [which the CCP attempted to organize at the village level whenever possible]. It is appropriate as a refresher for teachers and active elements [representing the CCP's agenda at the village level] studying self-discipline."(1) The book concluded each of its lessons (see "The *lijiao*/ritual etiquette of the feudal society is the source of women's suffering," for instance) with an attached series of study questions like "How does the old power of feudalism in your village oppress women?"

Study/*xuexi*, or learning the correct "line," transmitted physiology as the foundation of gender difference. It inscribed this difference as scientific fact, and understood the base line of reproductive physiology as the basis for the production of male and female. Thus, as has been the case elsewhere, the CCP's statist discourse inserted anatomical difference into a discourse on life and death. It also assumed a binary base (the "physiology of the human female" versus the "physiology of the human male") for the reproductive biology that physiology took as its "scientific" foundation. But the inscription of gender difference at the level of reproductive physiology elided something very interesting. It required material (re)production as site of difference, but it did not reduce personality to physiological terms. In Fulian writing there is a tendency to inscribe difference at the level of physiology while still curtailing attribution of difference at the level of personality. This latter, the realm of feeling and identity, remained, until recently, bound to conventions identified under Maoism in terms of social class, not sex or "gender."

It is easier to see the statist construction of *funü* under Maoism in the wake of post-Mao critique. Particularly since 1985 in literary and social science theory, questions of sex and female subjectivity have become explosive.[87] The post-Mao state's efforts to reestablish mass organizations like Fulian brought on an overt conflict between the national subject *funü* and a defiantly sexualized, retheorized *nuxing*. The resurgence of subversive *nuxing* helps clarify the contradictory formation of *nuxing/funü* from a final angle.[88] Under the previous statist protocol, *funü* allowed for the social production of Woman in politics but disallowed any psychology of gender difference. The even older, initial May Fourth literary inscription of *nuxing* made Woman the "other" of Man, but proved insufficiently stable to resist statist inscriptions of *funü*. The recuperation of *nuxing*'s heterosexist male/female binary does enable difference as "femininity" and thus provides potential for resistance. Post-Mao *nuxing*, however, renders itself powerless in the face of clearly prejudicial "scientific" claims to female inferiority.

It is not surprising at all that the most intriguing new, post-Mao critique is not *nuxing* theory but women's studies/*funüxue*. Leading figures in this movement include Deng Weizhi, Li Min, Wang Fukang, and Li Xiaojiang. They and others work as women's advocates in the government, often within the Women's Federation. Contemporary women's studies scholarship is Marxist, historical, and seeks to resuscitate the Chinese women's movement in extrastatist terms, from a China-centered frame of proletarian revolution to an international frame of human liberation. The subject of women's studies discourse is neither *funü* nor *nuxing* but *nuren* (which I have glossed as woman in social science representation or, *nuren* as a category/*fanchou*).

Tracing a genealogy for the inscription of "modern Chinese woman" thus has allowed ways of thinking Mohanty's "historical specificity in the construction of women." I engaged Gayatri Spivak's question—what narratives produced signifiers for women in another tradition—and can now conclude with Judith Butler's insight that gender is not a relation but an apparatus of production that establishes the "sexes" as themselves.

Notes

1. Gayatri Spivak, "The Political Economy of Women," in Elizabeth Weed, ed., *Coming to Terms: Feminism, Theory, Politics* (New York: Routledge, 1989), 227. An earlier version of this paper appeared in *Genders* 10 (Spring 1991). Thanks to Mayfair Meihui Yang, Wendy Larson, Charlotte Furth, Renli Wang, Susan Porter Benson, Marilyn B. Young, Judith Farquhar, Inderpal Grewal, and Donald M. Lowe.

I am enormously grateful to the following pioneer scholars: Marilyn B. Young, Margery Wolf, Phyllis Andors, Kay Anne Johnson, Wolfgang Kubin, Charlotte Beahan, Roxanne Witke.

2. Judith Butler, *Gender Trouble: Feminism and the Subversion of Identity* (New York: Routledge, 1990), 7, 111.

3. One should, given requisite space, begin with a long discourse on the genealogy of Victorian Woman. (See Denise Riley, *"Am I That Name?": Feminism and the Category of "Women"* [Minneapolis: University of Minnesota Press, 1988]). But I will not do it here, to some degree for the reason Mary E. John has stated in her "Postcolonial Feminists in the Western Intellectual Field: Anthropolgists *and* Native Informants," *Inscriptions* 5, 1989.

4. I am indebted to Chandra Mohanty, "Under Western Eyes: Feminist Scholarship and Colonial Discourses," in *boundary 2*, 12:3/13:1 (Spring/Fall 1984), and her "Feminist Encounters: Locating the Politics of Experience," *Copyright* 1 (Fall 1987): 30–44. The quotation is, alas, from neither. The notion of differences without identity is from Donald M. Lowe, *History of Bourgeois Perception* (Chicago: University of Chicago Press, 1982).

5. See Mark Elvin, "Female Virtue and the State in China," *Past and Present* 104 (August 1984): 114–52.

6. The word translates as "state" or as "nation" depending on context and speaker.

7. Jean-François Billeter, "The System of Class Status," in S. R. Schram, *The System of State Power in China* (Hong Kong: Chinese University Press, 1985), 138.

8. Chen Hongmou, *Wuzhong yigui* [Five Posthumous Regulations], *"Jiaonu yigui"* [Posthumous regulation on educating women]. *Sibubeiyao* edition, vol. 3 (n.p., Zhonghua shujyu, n.d.). Henceforth cited as *ZNYG*.

9. Ibid., Introduction, 1b-2a.

10. Chen Hongmou did not have to provide his readers with charts of differential gendered positions since these constituted local common sense. For a discussion of the textual foundations of the cult of the gendered position and relation see Hsu Dao-lin, "The Myth of the 'Five Human Relations' of Confucius," *Monumenta Serica* 29 (1970–71).

11. Elizabeth Cowie, "Woman as Sign," *m/f* 1 (1978): 61–62.

12. Both Judith Butler and Teresa de Lauretis point out that gender for post-Cartesian Western subjects originates on the privileged site of heterosexuality. Indeed, the insight has become a commonplace of much feminist theory. Women become women within the compass of masculine, heterosexual desire. My point in focusing on the *jia* as the privileged site under Confucianism is to suggest: (1) heterosexuality, sexuality as an institution à la Foucault, and sexual identity as a European invention have no particular historicity here, and (2) the sexed body of "Western" gender processes does not serve as the place for gender inscription.

13. Many people have made the point that civilization/*wen* serves as the base of human existence in late dynastic episteme, but none so eloquently as Angela Zito, "Grand Sacrifice as Text/Performance in Eighteenth Century China" (unpublished Ph.D. dissertation, Chicago, 1989).

14. The statement is emended and reromanized from Charlotte Furth's "Androgynous Males and Deficient Females: Biology and Gender Boundaries in Sixteenth and Seventeenth Century China," in *Late Imperial China* 9 (December 1988): 1–31.

15. The instance cited could be joined by many more. Gendering proceeded in late-imperial China not at the level of one but in multiple discourses beyond my present scope, many, like *Yi* commentary, not directly addressing immediate persons at all, others placing "men" in "female" positions, yet others appropriating "female" for subversive purpose. Its processes changed under different social and discursive circumstances, and it produced bodily effects—the bound foot, for instance, forever after its infliction marking its possessor's body as feminine. But at no time was gender "a property of bodies or something originally existent in human beings"; it was always already "the set of effects produced in bodies, behaviors, and social relations" through deployment of "complex political technologies." The first part of the citation is Teresa de Lauretis, "The Technology of Gender," in *The Technology of Gender* (Bloomington: Indiana University Press, 1987), 3. The second part is Michel Foucault, as cited in de Lauretis, same page.

16. See Manfred Porkert, *The Theoretical Foundations of Chinese Medicine: Systems of Correspondence* (Cambridge, 1985), 22–23, to the effect that while *yang* initiates, *yin* constructs or completes action. The power of the weaker in the dyad "perfects" or shapes action.

17. Gender is accomplished not so much through female virtues per se as through the behaviors of persons in specific subject positions of kin relation. This sense is made explicit in Joseph Lau's discussion of *dayi*/public virtue but is not joined to a general discussion of *ren*/benevolence in "self." Tu Weiming provides an important discussion of *ren* in "The Creative Tension between *Jen* and *Li*," in Tu Weiming, *Humanity and Self-Cultivation in Confucian Thought* (New York: Asian Humanities Press, 1979). But Tu does not talk about women possessing *ren*/benevolence as Joseph Lau does. (For non-Sinologists: *ren* and *jen* are the same word in different systems of romanization.)

18. Chen, *ZNYG*, 15. Emphasis on learning how to act is commonly found in Confucian popular writing on personal behavior. The locus classicus is the *Lunyu* or Analects in which Confucius responded when asked about government, "There is government/*zheng* when the monarch is a monarch, and the minister is minister; when the father is father, and the son is son." One is not (only) born a son, one becomes a son; one is not born a wife, yet becomes one.

19. Ibid., 15.

20. Thanks to Jing Wang for reminding me of this fact. I am not unaware of the literary tradition that made "woman" the sign and cause of political instability. I simply think that the genealogy I draw here represents the naturalized base that supports the other, more pointedly misogynist tropes.

21. Chen, "Song Shanggong *Nulunyu*," in *ZNYG*, 6b.

22. In a larger sense, protocols are similar to what Spivak calls "regulative psychobiographies" ("The Political Economy of Women," 227). Having reached a similar conclusion independently, I agree with Spivak that the history of women must rely on the excavation of the narratives that have effected our construction, though I regret her choice of the term "psychobiography," which to me conjures up memories of the "psychohistory" movement of the 1970s.

23. For discussion of these politics see Roxanne Witke's venerable and still-unsurpassed dissertation, "The Transformation of Attitudes of Women During the May Fourth Era" (unpublished Ph.D. dissertation, University of California, Berkeley, 1970).

24. See my "*Zhishifenzi* [Chinese intellectuals] and Power," *Dialectical Anthropology* (Winter 1990). I argue that peripheralizing signs involved *zhishifenzi* in the appropriation and redeployment of "modernity" within a representational, nationalist, anti-imperialist economy of representation.

25. See Mary Backus Rankin, "The Emergence of Women at the End of the Ch'ing," in Margery Wolf and Roxanne Witke, eds., *Women in Chinese Society* (Stanford: Stanford University Press, 1975); Witke, "Transformation of Attitudes"; and Li Yuning and Zhang Yufa, *Jindai Zhungguo nuquan yundong shiliao* [Documents on the Feminist Movement in Modern China], vols. 1 & 2 (Taipei: Biographical Literature Publishing Company, 1975).

26. See Charlotte Beahan, "Feminism and Nationalism in the Chinese Women's Press, 1902–1911,"

in *Modern China* 1:4 (October 1975); and "Mothers of Citizens: Feminism and Nationalism in the late Ch'ing" (unpublished paper).

27. *Nuxuebao* [Women's Study Journal], cited in Beahan, "Feminism and Nationalism," 383.

28. Timothy Brennan, "The National Longing for Form," in Homi K. Bhabha, ed., *Nation and Narrative* (London: Routledge, 1990), 44.

29. Beahan, "Feminism and Nationalism," 384.

30. Zhen Ziyang, *Nuzi xin duben* [New Study Book for Women] (n.p.: 1907, 6th ed.).

31. Ibid., 2, chapter 10, "Lolan furen" [Madame Roland], 7b-9a.

32. Ibid., chapter 13, "Fulanzhisi," 10a-12a.

33. I am indebted to Theodore Huters for this phrase. The production of subjectivities in modern literary texts is developed very nicely in Wendy Larson, *Literary Authority and the Chinese Writer: A Study of Early Twentieth Century Chinese Writers* (Durham, N.C.: Duke University Press, 1991).

34. Tani E. Barlow, *Imagining Woman: Ding Ling and the Gendering of Chinese Modernity* (forthcoming, Duke University Press).

35. Talal Asad, "Are There Histories of People Without Europe: A Review Article," *Comparative Study of Society and History* 29 (July 1987): 606.

36. Mei Sheng, *Zhongguo funü wenti taolunji* [General discussion of the Chinese women's question] (Shanghai: Wenhua Books, 1929). The compendium of key articles allows the reader a marvelous overview of the debate on feminism.

37. Barlow, *Imagining*.

38. Ibid., chapter 2, "Chinese Feminism."

39. Ching-ku Stephen Chan, "The Language of Despair: Ideological Representations of the 'New Women' [*xin nuxing*] by May Fourth Writers," in Tani E. Barlow, ed., *Gender Politics in Modern China: Feminism and Literature* (Durham, N.C.: Duke University Press, forthcoming).

40. Tani E. Barlow, "Feminism and Literary Technique in Ding Ling's Early Work," in *Women Writers of Twentieth-Century China* (Eugene: Asian Studies Publications, University of Oregon, 1982).

41. Annette Kuhn, *The Power of the Image* (London: Routledge and Kegan Paul, 1985), 19, cited in Linda Hutcheon, *The Politics of Postmodernism* (London: Routledge, 1989), 22.

42. Carolyn T. Brown, "Woman as a Trope: Gender and Power in Lu Xun's 'Soap,'" in Barlow, ed., *Gender Politics in Modern China*.

43. See Suzanne Leith, "Chinese Women in the Early Communist Movement," who summarizes three articles: *Zhungguo zhishi funü di sanpai* [Three groups of educated women], *Zhungguo zuijin funü yundong* [The contemporary Chinese women's movement], and *Shanghai nuquan yundong zhihou ying zhudi sanjian* [Three things the Shanghai women's rights movement should concentrate on]. In Marilyn Young, ed., *Women in China* (Ann Arbor: Michigan Papers in Chinese Studies, 1973), 50–51, 61.

44. The references are in order of citation: Beibeier [Bebel], *Funü yu shehui* [Woman and society], Shen Ruixian, trans. (Shanghai: Kaiming Books, 1949); *Makesi, Liening, Engesi, Sidalin lun funü jiefang* [Marx, Lenin, Engels, and Stalin on Women's Liberation]; ed. Chinese Democratic Women's Association (Hong Kong: New People's Press, 1949), 1–38; *Makesi, Engesi, Liening, Sidalin lun Funü Jiefang* [Marx, Engels, Lenin, Stalin on Women's Liberation]; ed. Fulian (Beijing: Renmin Press, 1949). This collection has a slightly different composition. See page 39 for Stalin's "International Women's Day."

45. Du Zhunhui, *Funü wenti jianghua* [Lectures on the Woman Problem] (Hong Kong: New China Books, 1949). The argument is a straight Marxist narrative that classifies China as an interminably feudal country. Du's strength is her insistence that "*funü*" is a social category.

46. Jiangxi Women's Association, ed., *Jiangxi suchu funnu yundong shiliao xuanpian* [Selected materials for the Jiangxi Soviet women's movement], 1932.3.2/2, 53–54. It is absolutely true if you read the statement literally.

47. Ibid., 21.

48. Ibid., 1931.11, items #1–7, 38.

49. Ibid., 1931.12, 231. Considering the situation, this seems totally inappropriate.

50. Ibid., 1932.2.1, 46.

51. See ibid., 1932.2, 52, for the statement that "marriage is a relationship of two persons, male and female."

52. Ibid., 1932.2.1, 43.

53. Ibid., 1932.1.2, 44–45. This is a splendid document detailing instructions governing women's organizations. It clarifies how model organizers in the women's work movement establish proper form, possess preestablished work plans, fix topics for each meeting (for instance, "opposing feudal bonds," or "enlisting men, comforting troops, doing mass work, getting literate," etc.).

54. See ibid., 1932.3.2, 53, and many other subsequent documents. Women's Day and propaganda for the marriage law are the two major work areas for *ganbu* (cadres) undertaking women's work. 1933.2.7 uses it to demonstrate why Woman is connected to state and suggests that workers use magazines, newspapers, and storytellers to spread the word. The effort is also reflected in regional document 1933.2.10, 77.

55. The provisional nature of the laws and the multiplicity of voices are clear in 1932.6.20, 60–65, which talks about the resistance to certain laws, and the resistance to others. Its self-critical tone is significant.

56. Ibid., stipulation 5 in part 2.

57. Ibid., 1933.8.31, 104.

58. Ibid. "Provisional Central Government's Announcement Instructions to the People's Committees as regards Protecting Women's Rights and Establishing Women's Life Improvement Committees, Organizations, and Work."

59. Ibid., 1933.3.14, 87. The document gives instructions on the mechanics of representation. For example, set a time for a conference, locate the laboring women's Congress inside the system of other mass organizations, recruit according to certain forms, get 10 to 20 women, establish a representative, elect a presidium, etc., capped by a party member, and so on. See page 88 for a good discussion of how representation works.

60. 1933.6.25, 95, suggests that quite strongly.

61. Ibid., 90.

62. Ibid., 1933.3.28, 89.

63. See Patricia Stranahan, *Yan'an Women and the Chinese Communist Party* (Berkeley: Center for Chinese Studies Press, 1983) and "Labor Heroines of Yan'an," *Modern China* 7:1 (January 1981).

64. Lu Fu (pseud.), *Xinfunü duben* [New Woman's Study Book] (Hong Kong: Xinminshu Press, 1949), 60–61.

65. Zhou Enlai, "*Lun xianqi liang mu yu muzhi*" [On virtuous wife, good mother, and the mother's responsibility], *Jiefang Ribao* [Liberation Daily], November 20, 1942. Zhou argued that not just mothers but fathers, too, had a substantial political obligation to be the best parents possible. This was the founding statement from on high; ever after, kin-style protocols made their presence known within liberated constructs.

66. See Stranahan, *Yan'an Women and the Chinese Communist Party*, 63–86. This is the single best empirical documentary study available in English. Stranahan argues that, in fact, given the context, CCP post-1942 policy on women's affairs was remarkably fair and probably productive both in party terms and in the view of the women policy that was effected. See also Phyllis Andors, *The Unfinished Liberation of Chinese Women, 1949–1980* (Bloomington: Indiana University Press, 1983) and "Studying Chinese Women," *Bulletin of Concerned Asian Scholars* (October-December 1975).

67. See the case histories and subject biographies in the Fulian, ed., *Zhongguo jiefangchu nongcun funü fanshen yundong sumiao* [A rough sketch of the fanshen movement among rural women in the liberated regions of China] (n.p.: Xinhua Books, 1949).

68. Fulian, ed., *Zhongguo jiefangchu funnu canzhan yundong* [Political participation movement of the women of the Chinese liberated areas] (Hong Kong: New Peoples Press [date not available]), 7–11.

69. See Lu Fu, *Xinfunü duben* [New Woman's Study Book], 74–80, particularly the chapter "*Women yao yanjiu xin fajiesheng*" [We want to study new methods for assisting in childbirth], 78–80.

70. This at least is how I interpret the writing on love and family construction that appeared in

the 1950s. See, for example, Dan Fu, *Mantan liangxing guanxi zhong de daode wenti* [Conversation about moral questions concerning relations between the sexes] (Shanghai: Xuexi Shenghuo Press, 1956). Also see Li Di, *Zhufu shouji* [Handbook for housewives] (Beijing: Tongsu weni Press, 1955).

71. Fulian, ed., *Zhongguofunü disansi quanguo daibiao dahui zongyao wenxuan* [Selected key documents of the third national congress of Chinese women] (Beijing: Zhongguo Funü Zazhi Press, 1958), 27.

72. Ibid., 2.

73. William Parish and Martin Whyte, *Village and Family in Contemporary China* (Chicago: University of Chicago Press, 1978), 39.

74. For information on founding and early propaganda/literary outreach, see Elizabeth Croll, *Feminism and Socialism in China* (London: Routledge and Kegan Paul, 1978); E. Croll, *The Women's Movement in China: A Selection of Readings, 1949–1973* (London: Anglo-Chinese Educational Institute, Modern China Series #6 [1974]); Vibeke Hemmel and Pia Sindbjergh, *Women in Rural China: Policy Towards Women Before and After the Cultural Revolution* (Curzon: Scandanavian Institute of Asian Studies #7, [1984]).

75. These luminaries and dignitaries were, in descending order, Cai Chang, Deng Yingchao, Zhang Chinqiu, Li Dechuan, Chen Shaomei, Kang Keqing, Ding Ling, and Ho Xiangning. Fulian, ed., *Quanguo funü diyici quanguo daibiao dahui* [First Congress of the All-China Women's Association] (Hong Kong: Xinmin Press, 1949), 102–8. The only real surprise here is Ding Ling, who, it will be recalled, had been purged from her women's work following the publication of her "Thoughts on March 8" essay in 1942. To my knowledge there is no history of the Women's Association presently available.

76. Ibid., 5.

77. Ibid., "*Zhonghua quanguominzhu funü lianhohui zhangcheng*" [Regulations of the All-China Democratic Women's Association] and its various articles of incorporation, provisions, and systems, 94–100.

78. Ibid., 20–21.

79. Ibid., "*Linqiu funü daibiaohui jieshao*" [An Introduction to the Linqiu County Women's Association], 73.

80. Ibid., 73–74.

81. Ibid., 28.

82. Ibid., 31. I quote this slogan because it is so outrageous. How Chinese women became "consumers" in the rhetorics of state discourse before there was anything to consume is suggestive, to say the least.

83. Fulian, ed., *Selected key documents of the third national congress*, 3.

84. Nor, of course, was inscription as *funü* exclusionary, since a woman could at the same time be inscribed as "youth," as "worker," and as "daughter of a revolutionary martyr."

85. See David Kwok's underused and very keen book, *Scientism in Chinese Thought* (Berkeley: University of California Press, 1965).

86. See Emily Martin [Ahern], "The Power and Pollution of Chinese Women," in Wolf and Witke, eds., *Women*.

87. For instances of literary representations see Wang Zheng, "Three Interviews," *Modern Chinese Literature* 4:1 & 2 (1988 [1990]) for Dai Qing's and Wang Anyi's discussions about sexuality in their work. The concluding arguments are taken from my article "Politics and Protocols of *funü*: (un)Making the National Woman," forthcoming in Gail Hershatter et al., eds., *Engendering China* (Harvard University Press, 1993).

88. For a succinct formulation of this contradictory relation of feminism/Asian women, see Aihwa Ong, "Colonialism and Modernity: Feminist Re-Presentations of Women in Non-Western Societies," *Inscriptions* 3/4 (1988). Lydia Liu suggests that this disdain may have more to do with popular loathing of Fulian than real antagonism toward "feminism."

TEN

No Basta Teorizar: In-Difference to Solidarity in Contemporary Fiction, Theory, and Practice

Fred Pfeil

> *No — no — no basta teorizar*
> *Hacen falta muchas cosas*
> *para conseguir la paz*

(adapted from "No basta rezar," a song of the Salvadoran popular movements)

I come to this piece, and this anthology, aware of my own "situatedness" not only vis-à-vis non-Western women and feminism, but in relation to theory as such. I am a white male, a native of the United States, and, as a member of the professional-managerial class, a relatively privileged one at that, however much my life has been marked by a youth spent largely with women and within working-class culture. So I would expect whatever arguments I lay out here to be heard by feminists, nonwhite and non-Western feminists especially, against the background hum of a justifiable skepticism or even distrust. At the same time, however, I am also what I do inside that position; and what I do, and have been doing for some years, is not only write and teach, but act politically as well. That is to say, what Teresa de Lauretis calls the "double shift" (in an essay of hers we shall shortly be examining) — not, in the history of feminism she is constructing, the traditional "double day" of the woman who must move constantly between her paid labor in the realm of production and her unpaid work in the domestic sphere of reproduction, but the "double shift" once expected of the feminist intellectual — has been an accepted feature of my life for several years. So, while I have written for *Social Text*, *Socialist Review*, the *Nation*, and the *Village Voice*, and tried to keep up with feminist, Marxist, and "post-" or non-Marxist radical theory, I have also leafleted, phone-banked, held house parties, gone to demos, done civil disobedience, donated money, dashed off press releases, and gone to more meetings than I like to think about; and I have often, indeed almost always, done so either for various feminist causes or in working partnership with women, white and nonwhite, Western and not, who consider themselves staunchly, even militantly feminist.

198 / Fred Pfeil

I present the fact of these "double shifts" here, though, not as a set of credentials warranting the correctness of what I have to say, but as the context for the buzzing discomfort that pushes me to speak at all. For if I feel—and *should* feel—a doubt as to my fitness to speak to the question of feminist theory in relation to postcolonial or non-Western women, that doubt is mitigated by my sense of the increasingly large chasm that divides those who produce putatively radical theory and those who are "out there," as activists still say, organizing for social change.

I write this last sentence and remember, against the mutters and growls I can already hear in the distance, the painfully sincere testament of a middle-aged Marxist I heard speak at an academic conference, who quite ingenuously remarked that he once used to spend many hours every week leafleting workers at docks and factory gates in the town where he works (in a grindingly hard, low-paying, untenurable position, as I recall); only then he read Althusser, and found out that he no longer had to do that—he could wage class struggle at the level of theory instead. Although of special interest and appeal to socialist academics like my friend and myself, Althusser's dispensation to erstwhile theorists is hardly the only one around; nor are the other dispensations—whether in the form of the critique of the sign, the notion of discourse as material practice, or, for that matter, the less theoretically rigorous invitation issued by identity politics to work on simply finding and asserting the true self—for Marxists only. My aim, however, is not to take up those arguments directly, but rather to scrutinize a few examples of what are taken to be progressive representations of and discourses about non-Western women, and ask a few questions about them: whether and how such representations and discourses link up with or lend assistance to the struggles of such women against patriarchal and other (e.g., capitalist) forms of oppression; and, if they do not, why they do not, and what, regardless of the intentions of their authors, they are likely to be doing instead.

I have chosen as my examples either two or seven texts, depending on how you want to count them; Bharati Mukherjee's award-winning collection of short fiction, *The Middleman and Other Stories*, and four papers and two panel discussion transcripts published as the bulk of a recent issue of the journal *Inscriptions* on "Feminism and the Critique of Colonial Discourse," published by the Group for the Critical Study of Colonial Discourse in the History of Consciousness Program at the University of California at Santa Cruz. I do not claim that these texts display every form of Western, or Western-approved progressive and/or feminist discourse about postcolonial women.[1] But I do want to argue (1) that the discourses and representations contained in them exhibit a deep kinship in the invitations to pleasure they issue us as fellow observers of the social, and in their perplexed, or even negative, attitudes toward engaged dialogue or struggle, and (2) that this problematic of pleasure and reluctance is symptomatic of a blend of hesitation, seduction, and paralysis whose debilitating presence can be discerned throughout much of the feminist and left intelligentsia resident in North America today. To discover such invitations and baffled disinclinations in the texts, I will be looking at various critical moments in their formation and argumentation; but I will also be setting them alongside other similar and contrasting texts to give us a sense of what is, and is not, politically at stake in their valorization and further elaboration — and to see whether there might not be, for those who wish to enlist in the manifold and heterogeneous liberation struggles of non-Western women, some other, more enabling discourses and representations available than the ones examined here.

In-Difference 1: The Rush of Displacement

Within what Terry Eagleton has called the "literary mode of production," the review's function is not merely to give prospective readers an up-or-down normative evaluation of a given work but to nominate and advertise the officially approved pleasures of the text. Reviewing involves not just gatekeeping, but promotions. But this in turn means that we may always read the review or puff quote backwards — as the description of not only the text but of how the culturally dominant audience can have fun reading it as well. So it makes sense to start our investigation of Mukherjee's award-winning collection, *The Middleman*, by sampling some representative book-jacket "puffs" for what they can tell us about the recommended ways in which her fictions are to be consumed.

New York Times Book Review
A romance with America itself, its infinitely possible geography, its license, sexiness, and violence.

Los Angeles Times
Eleven stunning stories of strangers in a strange land . . . struggling to discover what they want to be in a world of bewildering possibility. Until you read these witty and subtle contemporary tales, you can't imagine how much adventure that process entails.

Washington Post Book World
Funny, intelligent, versatile, and unexpectedly profound.

Voice Literary Supplement
Mukherjee brings a feverishly clear voice to her fierce, on-the-mark fiction. These sexy tales are a must for immigrants and their descendants — and natives too.[2]

What are these puffs inviting us to get from Mukherjee's representations of the new, non-Western immigrants and their lives in a United States transformed by their presence? A bunch of laughs, for one thing ("funny," "witty"); plus the more insistently proffered pleasure of highly charged, even violent, "sexy" "adventure" in a land of "infinitely possible geography," "bewildering possibility." Above all, the reading experience promised us older and whiter immigrants, and children of immigrants, is a painless one; the world of these non-white newcomers, we are promised, is characterized by "license," not constraints or coercion, erotic comminglings rather than struggle or conflict, a world we too may imaginatively enter without any fear of being accused or getting depressed while we are there.

Puff quotes often exaggerate or even distort the actual properties of a given book; and it is only fair to Mukherjee to note that a good deal of her book (chiefly the last four of its eleven stories), fails to be as much of a romp as the reviews suggest. Yet most of *The Middleman* does deliver on these puff promises, does "depict the shaky ground where East meets West and the sound of cultures clashing could shatter glass"[3] (the *L.A. Times* again) in such a way as to render that shaky ground a carnival ride, the breaking glass a goofy acoustic treat; so it is worth a closer look at just what immigrant experiences are being offered us, and just how Mukherjee uses her talent to make them fun.

We might begin, though, by noting where the fun is *not* in most of these fictions—in their characterizations and plots. On characterization first: most of the stories in *The Middleman* are cast in first person, present tense, in the instantaneous mode of narration so popular in "quality lit" in the United States today. Yet nothing is more distinct about these first person voices than the effacement of any individual markings or inflections, any "character notes" in the speech itself. Here, for example, are two narrators, one an Indian, last name Patel, married to a factory owner in India but in this country studying for her Ph.D. in special ed, the other a younger, white Italian-American who clerks in a boutique. The Indian woman is talking about her Hungarian friend, Imre; the Italian-American about her last lover, Vic, and her new Afghani lover, Ro:

> "You make things tough on yourself," says Imre. He assumed Patel was a Jewish name or maybe Hispanic; everything makes equal sense to him. He found the play tasteless, he worried about the effect of vulgar language on my sensitive ears. "You have to let go a bit." And as though to show me how to let go, he breaks away from me, bounds ahead with his head ducked tight, then dances on amazingly jerky legs. He's a Magyar, he often tells me, and deep down, he's an Asian too. I catch glimpses of it, knife-blade Attila cheekbones, despite the blondish hair. In his jagged jeans and leather jacket, he's a rock video star. (*M*, "A Wife's Story," 26)

The first time Vic asked me out, he talked of feminism and holism and macrobiotics. Then he opened up on cinema and literature, and I was very impressed, as who wouldn't be? Ro, my current lover, is very different. He picked me up in an uptown singles bar that I and Cindi sometimes go to. He bought me a Cinzano and touched my breast in the dark. He was direct, and at the same time weirdly courtly. I took him home though usually I don't, at first. I learned in bed that night that the tall brown drink with the lemon twist he'd been drinking was Tab. (*M*, "Orbiting," 61–62)

And here, yet another narrator, this one an Iraqi Jew, the "middleman" of the title story, describing the unnamed, rebellion-plagued Central American country to which he has fled to escape arrest for financial dirty dealing in the United States:

There are only two seasons in this country, the dusty and the wet. I already know the dusty and I'll get to know the wet. I've seen worse. I've seen Baghdad, Bombay, Queens—and now this moldering spread deep in Mayan country. Aztecs, Toltecs, mestizos, even some bashful whites with German accents. All that and a lot of Texans. I'll learn the ropes. (*M*, "The Middleman," 1)

The tonal and stylistic equivalence of these voices is, paradoxically, their most salient feature. Despite the enormous diversity of these characters' backgrounds, itineraries, and histories, and for all the ostensive differences in gender and class, they all speak the same hip, jumped-up wordjazz.

Indeed, the voracious imperative of such a style, the demand it advances for ever more of the same, is so great as at times to override plausible motivation altogether. Take the following passage, in which a white, midwestern American responds to the pleas of the Amerasian child he conceived while in Vietnam and later adopted to snuggle into bed with him. The little girl, Eng, is running a fever; the lover who lies beside the narrator, Sharon, wants the kid to go back to her room; so this is what the narrator does, and thinks, in the present-tense moment:

I hold my arms out wide for Eng to run into. If I could, I'd suck the virus right out of her. In the jungle, VC mamas used to do that. Some nights we'd steal right up to a hootch—just a few of us intense sons of bitches on some special mission—and the women would at their mumbo jumbo. They'd be sticking coins and amulets into napalm burns. (*M*, "Fathering," 115–16)

If a student handed this story to me in one of the fiction workshops I teach, I would have an old-fashioned objection to this passage. I would say that at this particular moment in the story, I cannot believe that the drift of this narrator's thoughts slides over to "VC mamas"; nor that such thoughts would articulate themselves in such staccato rhythms and such witty, juicy jive.

To criticize Mukherjee's stories in this way, however, is to miss their point, which is precisely the *dis*-location of the narrative voice, its profligate dispersal of verbal energy across an unfixable range of languages and tones. When the narrator above thinks or says the phrase "intense sons of bitches," is he being ironically self-critical or sincerely emphatic? How does he feel about, what is his attitude toward those "napalm burns"? These and similar questions are, in the context of this fiction, not only irrelevant, but slightly gauche, as out of place as the Hungarian Imre who tells the narrator of "A Wife's Story" her sense of offense is at the racial slurs against Patels she has heard in the Mamet play they have just left.

"You have to let go a bit," he tells her, and, as the passage just quoted continues, does a little dance for her in which he momentarily takes on the look of a "video rock star." The advice, it seems, is not just for the character but for us readers as well; Imre's transformation reads as both sign and cue of the spectacular pyrotechnic pleasure we get when one cultural signifier—a turn of phrase, a bit of data—collides with the next, and both burst into sparks. The narrator of "The Middleman" in his Central American troublespot/hideaway knows "it's best not to ask how Dutch beer and refrigerators and '57 two-tone Plymouths with fins and chrome make their way to nowhere jungle clearings" (*M*, 14), and so should we; for if we do, we can experience the same decentered pleasure, simultaneously transgressive and inconsequential, that the narrator of "A Wife's Story" feels when she submits to Imre's advice and lets it all blur into one enormous, gorgeous, drifting, fading blur: "Memories of Indian destitutes mix with the hordes of New York street people," she tells us of her walk down the street, "and they float free, like astronauts, inside my head" (*M*, 27).

Such free-floating permits us, moreover, as readers, to lift off from these stories' plots as well, and dance around whatever moral and/or political reactions we might otherwise have had to their events and eventfulness. In the collection's title story, for example, Alfred Judah the middleman narrates a tale that, stripped of its dazzling semic trappings, plays out a depressingly familiar and pernicious formula for First World stories about Third World revolution and counterrevolution, in which all sides turn out mainly to be struggling over— guess what?—property rights to the lush body of Maria, "big-boned, dark-skinned," a "near-Miss World" with "thick dark hair and smooth dark skin," which disclose that "she has to be mostly Indian," a figure of rampant, volatile sexuality who "in her pink Lycra bikini . . . arouses new passion" (*M*, 5). Or there is the Vietnam vet/hired killer of "Loose Ends," who goes to hide out after a particularly nasty hit, but ends up raping the daughter of the Patel family who own the dingy motel where he stops. Surely, you will think from this plot summary, we must be invited to shock and outrage at this narrator's actions, however much we are to understand their source in his history, attitudes, and previous experiences. Yet although we do get some hint of our narrator's motivation, albeit in a typically tropic form—he calls his victim Alice, alluding to a previous riff in which he has been raging (or was it just goofing?) over the question "Where did America go?" and concluding "Down the rabbit hole . . . Alice knows, but she took it with her" (M, 47- 48)—Mukherjee's rendition of the rape offers us far more opportunity for "sexy," transgressive fun than perspective:

> I pounce on Alice before she can drop down below, and take America with her. The hardware comes in handy, especially the kris. Alice lays hot fingers on my eyes and nose, but it's no use and once she knows it, Alice submits. (M, "Loose Ends," 55)

So much for the rape; and if we can also forget outmoded questions concerning the character and psychology of the rapist (who, after all, is stylistically indistinguishable from the Patel woman narrating "A Wife's Story" or the Vietnam vet/father of "Fathering"), all that is left for us to take in are the quirky, nervy surprises of the prose: the sudden full deployment of the "Alice" trope, swiftly followed by the deadpan professionalism of "the hardware," the surprise of "the kris," the sensory burst of "hot fingers," and the abrupt, rhythmic clinch at the end of the final run-on sentence itself.

Such pleasures of the "semic" may recall in their turn that post-'68 French theorizing, which not so long ago sniffed its disapproval of the intrinsically repressive, sublimated gratifications of the emplotted ("proairetic") and interpretive ("hermeneutic") registers of narrative, calling instead for a protofeminist "Revolution of the Word," and for the text which, while furnishing us with one vertiginous instant of *jouissance* after another, "shows [its] behind to the Political Father."[4] And it is not just Mukherjee's text that should arouse our suspicion of such a "political" style choice today, but also the ubiquity and function of such semic pleasures in other nontextual discourses that we in the professional-managerial class hear around us all the time, and have learned to savor. Like the story I myself have trotted out at a slack moment, say around dessert, about the American acidhead I met in France a few years back, son of an Oklahoma farming family, who, before taking up his present job coordinating famine relief flights to Ethiopia, peddled lots of American bull sperm to the heads of postcolonial African countries, but who still retained, through all his ravings about drugs and debauchery in his home base in Morocco, a discernible Okie twang in his voice—a story that provides its listeners the same pleasures as, in Mukherjee's "Orbiting," the Italian-American narrator's discovery on her first night with her new Afghani lover Ro that back in the singles

bar where they met, "the tall brown drink with the lemon twist he'd been drinking was Tab" (*M*, 61). Or, for that matter, the same narrator's exposition of
her sister's lover's disjointed bio:

> Brent wasn't easy for me to take, not at first. He owns a discount camera and
> electronics story on Fifty-fourth in Manhattan. Cindi met him through Club
> Med. They sat on a gorgeous Caribbean beach and talked of hogs. His father is
> an Amish farmer in Kalona, Iowa. Brent, in spite of the obvious hairpiece and
> the gold chain, is a rebel. He was born Schwartzendruber, but changed his name
> to Schwartz. Now no one believes in the Brent, either. They call him Bernie on
> the street and it makes everyone more comfortable. His father's never taken their
> buggy out of the county. (*M*, 61–62)

With such stories, such jokes, we — both First World professional managerial
types and mobile Third World elites (as most of Mukherjee's non-Western
characters are, or have been) — invite each other into a new phantasmic freedom
and community: the freedom, that of "A Wife's Story's" narrator, who, across
from sleeping husband who has come from India to reclaim her, "stand[s] here
shameless, in ways he has never seen me," and proudly proclaims she is "free,
afloat, watching someone else" (*M*, 41); the community, a blissfully serialized
collective of the permanently alienated, a carnivalesque disownership of our
past and present lives.

In the wake of such poststructuralist manifestos and the bliss they legitimate,
we might want to ask who our companions are in such a collectivity, and who
gets left out. One answer to the first question is a species of Reaganite yuppie,
my best example of whom is the comic writer P. J. O'Rourke, a white guy in
his early forties who, as the man behind *Rolling Stone*'s "Foreign-Affairs Desk,"
appears about as often in that magazine as Mukherjee does in the putatively
progressive *Mother Jones*. Recently, a number of his pieces appeared in book
form under the title *Holidays in Hell* — for, as the title suggests, it is O'Rourke's
pleasure to journey the path taken by Mukherjee's characters in the opposite
direction, from First World to Third, to have a wacky first-hand look at Nicaragua, El Salvador, Beirut, and the like. And, to be sure, every piece that results
from his journeys has its reactionary moral-political moment when O'Rourke
flames on about the treachery of the Sandinistas, or wonders "what I'd think
if I were South African and looked at the rest of Africa and saw nothing but
oppression, murder, chaos, massacre, impoverishment, famine and corruption — whereas in South Africa there was just some oppression and murder."[5]
What O'Rourke and Mukherjee have in common, however, is not such openly
reactionary opinions, but the warrant for them which in O'Rourke's work
comes through the same decentering game of recognition and surprise, and the
same stand-up comic prose that we have seen as the main attraction of

Mukherjee's work. Here are a few typical quotes, from O'Rourke's piece on
El Salvador:

> I went to get some clothes at a new, upscale shopping center. It looked like a
> mall in Dayton. Because I'm obviously *norteamericano*, a half dozen people
> stopped and introduced themselves. What part of the States was I from? And
> how was the Ohio State football team doing? It was a handsome crowd. The
> conquistadors weren't as civilized as our own founding father; they fucked the
> Indians before they killed them. Now everybody in El Salvador is a slight mix, a
> sort of Mestizo Lite, Iberian of feature but prettier colored. The women are
> heartbreaking. (*H*, 129)

> A band at one of the cafes was playing "For What It's Worth," by Buffalo
> Springfield ("Paranoia strikes deep/Into your life it will creep . . . "). We ate at
> a restaurant called Ciao, which looked exactly like a restaurant called Ciao
> would look in Atlanta—pink and black art deco with neon highlights—but we
> sat well back from the windows in case of grenade attacks. (*H*, 139)

Chuckle away as these strings of braided firecrackers go off, join in the joke
of their juxtapositions of familiarity and difference, and you are softened up
for O'Rourke's Neanderthal conclusions, which are stated with an admirable
succinctness in the introduction to the book. If they're asking about Ohio State
in the Salvadoran mall, after all, if what the Syrians at the checkpoints in Beirut
are really "looking for in your trunk . . . is *Playboy* magazines" (*H*, 37), why
not push this politics of pleasure to the max, declare "people are all exactly
alike," and force the ones who keep on cutting up in dangerous ways to cut
it out? "The trouble in Lebanon, South Africa, Haiti and the occupied territories of Palestine," O'Rourke says, "should simply be stopped by the military interventions of civilized nations." Yet, postmodern sage that he is, he is wise
enough to draw the moral top, which Mukherjee's own "The Middleman"
might have led him without having to leave home:

> This won't stop trouble, of course. Trouble is fun. It will always be more fun to
> carry a gun around in the hills and sleep with ideology-addled college girls [or
> the lush "near-Miss World" Maria?] than to spend life behind a water buffalo or
> rotting in a slum. (*H*, 4)

Out beyond the accidents of class and culture, we are all incipient fun-seeking
yuppies under the skin. (We men, that is; O'Rourke's consumerist sexism is
casually consistent throughout the book.)

Admittedly, there are large differences between O'Rourke and Mukherjee
in terms of their explicit political statements and public press; all the more striking, then, that the invitation their texts issue to their privileged readerships is
virtually identical. Let specific conflicts dissolve into universal complicity, lift

off from the determinations of the social, float up to the mirrored dance floor in a heaven of in-difference in which otherness and identity have merged. Such is one form of what is nowadays called "postmodern geography"—a geography that in this case simultaneously herds and disperses its consumer subjects into a nonposition like that of Pascal's God, a circle of infinite circumference whose center is everywhere and nowhere at once, a form of cognition/consumption in which the similarities between the destitute of India and the homeless of New York merely, pleasantly, boggles the bedazzled mind.

Yet there are other postmodern geographers around as well, in comparison to which the similarity between *Rolling Stone* reactionary O'Rourke and *Mother Jones* progressive Mukherjee becomes more striking still. I might mention Maria Mies, for example, and her *Patriarchy and Accumulation on a World Scale*, or the recent work of A. Sivanandan in *Race and Class*, including and especially "New circuits of imperialism," a concise yet passionate charting of the patterns of exploitation that channel the flows and resistances of men and women, white and nonwhite, around the world.[6] Yet since these are hardly texts of pleasure, let me bring this section to a close by describing a little-known, recent piece of writing that, while offering us a map of a postmodern space, also delivers or invites us to share its own peculiar, tart pleasure of the text.

The piece I have in mind here is, of all things, a conference paper, entitled "Third-Worlding at Home: Transforming New Frontiers in the Urban U.S." I first heard it delivered by its author, cultural anthropologist Kristin Koptiuch, at a conference on "Marxism Now" in Amherst, Massachusetts. Yet for all the greyness of the title, with that familiar, dulling colon we academics seem unable to forgo, for all the lack of entertainment potential in the conference situation, those of us who heard Koptiuch that December afternoon had a good time. We smiled and laughed while she was talking; we clapped hard when she was done. And, in so doing, we were taking the pleasure that any story, or book of stories, promises to provide us: the pleasures of narrative, of participation in the imaginative experience of a story-shaped world. For telling stories was, after all, primarily what Koptiuch was doing that afternoon, and what her paper does; but there the resemblance between her work and Mukherjee's ends.

Except, I suppose, for the similarity of their subject matter; for both would seem to be offering us a look at an America radically transformed by the influx of new, nonwhite and/or non-Western immigrants. Yet the physical and discursive space of the Philadelphia Koptiuch describes and lives is scarcely recognizable as part of the same America Mukherjee evokes in her fiction. Koptiuch began with a description, drawn from newspaper reports, of the bold foray of a team of Christian missionaries into "the jungle where they could share hardship with 'the poor,'" and of their extensive preparations for this arduous task—only to reveal that the "jungle" in question lies within "the world's fifth largest (and growing) Spanish-speaking nation; but it is also an important African country, and its Asian and Caribbean diasporas are increasingly worth reckoning with as well."[7] The country is, of course, the United States; and the site of the "civilizing mission" "a dilapidated, drug-infested, trash-strewn, graffiti-riddled, Puerto Rican barrio in the *urban* jungle of North Philadelphia" (87). In swift succession, Koptiuch sketched out the ongoing war within the inner city between billboard ads and graffiti tags (including the side skirmishes waged by art dealers seeking to convert the latter into a new, hot commodity, and government authorities mounting a lame "antigraffiti" graffiti campaign); the massively overdetermined transfer of "commercial urban space" from the inner city to Philadelphia's new, postmodern commercial fortress, center city's Gallery Mall; the demonizing "panic-discourse" of the press, drumming its Othering tattoo behind the constant, and increasing, state repression of the new jungle's multinational, multiracial inhabitants as, simultaneously, they are either pressed out of the economy altogether or dragooned into hyperexploitation at the base of its service or sweatshop divisions; and, last but not least, the inevitable appearance of the academic rear guard, in the form of a squad of Ford Foundation-funded anthropologists deployed to determine whether the problems of the "urban jungle" are, finally, " 'differences in language or culture' " (97 — but quoted there from the *Philadelphia Inquirer*), and to "reinterpellate national subjects in a transnational frame via new deployments of gender, race, and ethnicity" (98).

Through such micronarratives, Koptiuch's paper thus traces out the contours of a hegemonizing grid whose authorized explanations and police actions aim not merely to map the new, volatile urban spaces and subjectivities, but to pin them down. Accordingly, and despite Koptiuch's own disinclination to join in the naming frenzy she describes, even her few references to specific groups—Chinese immigrant garment-factory workers, black and Puerto Rican graffiti "artists," Korean immigrants who "rent last week's news broadcasts by Korean networks in . . . Korean-run corner stores" (96)—emphasize the extent to which she and Mukherjee are talking not only in two different ways but about two different worlds. Mukherjee's world—the world of "The Middleman," "Orbiting" at "Loose Ends"—is centered around the figure of the privileged postcolonial emigré, for whom the pleasure of perpetual oscillation between dislocation and identification is as available as it is for her First World readership; whereas in the world Koptiuch describes, travel is less a form of dialectical exoticism than a practical economic or political necessity, and "floating free" less a pleasure than a catastrophic trauma—or even, for unemployed young black youths, for example, an imposed form of doom. In Mukherjee's fiction, as we have seen, the Third World's appearance within the First supplies the pretext for the loss of any sense of stable identity, and the yielding to a giddy placelessness; in Koptiuch's Philadelphia, it is the occasion for new mutations in old containment strategies, domestic and imperial, within a fresh round of race and class war.

We need not linger long over the question of which of these representations of the new immigration and the new America will be embraced as the cultural dominant—or, more precisely, as the fun postmodernist side of the coin whose "tails" is the discursive and physical policing action Koptiuch describes. But it is worth emphasizing once again that the choice will not be made simply on the basis of how much higher the Mukherjee version of America lifts the applause meter's needle of fun. Koptiuch's paper, after all, also got us laughing on that bleak December afternoon: but an angry laughter, a bitter risibility that can, and usually does, accompany an enabling rage. To invoke Gramsci's still-vital distinction, the pleasure of Koptiuch's text is that of an "impassioned sarcasm," which is the "appropriate stylistic element for historical-political action"; the pleasure of Mukherjee's stories lies in that exquisite "irony" that indicates "a distancing related to a more or less dilettantish scepticism belonging to disillusionment, weariness, and '*supernominismo*' "[8]—which latter takes the form, in her work, of the privileged ability, shared equally by characters, reader, and the writer herself, to "lift off."

And as our cultural gatekeepers know well, more and less consciously, such differences in pleasure and (dis)connection make all the difference in the world.

In-Difference 2: Difference and Politesse

Let us move now from narrative to theory, and the essays by Trinh Minh-ha, Aihwa Ong, Donna Haraway, and Teresa de Lauretis in the aforementioned issue of *Inscriptions*—essays whose unity is supplied by their admirable shared intent to avoid the pitfalls and limits of essentialism, and to clear a space in which previously silenced subaltern voices (particularly those of postcolonial women and women of color) may speak and be heard.

Filmmaker Trinh Minh-ha's "Not You/Like You: Post-Colonial Women and the Interlocking Questions of Identity and Difference" is not only the first in order of these pieces, but the shortest and most readily summarizable of them. Moreover, her essay begins with an explicit critique of essentialist notions of identity that echoes through the essays that follow—even when, as we shall see, some versions of essentialism are allowed to sneak in unquestioned through the side door. For Minh-ha the concept of identity as the (re)possession of an "essential, authentic core . . . that requires the elimination of all that is considered foreign or not true to the self, that is to say, non-I, other"[9] is disabling in two main ways: it leads to a quest for the "lost, pure, true, real, genuine, original," and "authentic" that is both false and doomed; and its strategy of identification reproduces that "simplicity of essences" and "leveling of differences" within subordinated groups that has historically been wielded by hegemonizing oppressors with such signal success (I, 72).

Against such oppositional Self-Other polarities, then, Minh-ha proposes a countervailing deconstructive slogan: "let difference replace conflict" (I, 72). "The concept of difference," she writes, can be used "as a tool of creativity to question multiple forms of repression and dominance" rather than "as a tool of segregation, to exert power on the basis of racial and sexual essences" (I, 73). To demonstrate how such a concept of "difference" rather than "conflict" might work, moreover, she cites four examples of cultural practice that have too often been seen from an "Othering" perspective that diminishes their real complexity: Islamic veiling "as reality and metaphor," "the use of silence," "the question of subjectivity," and "the question of outsider and insider in ethnographic [and cinematic] practices" (I, 73–74). In each of these cases, she argues, the traditional discourse of Self and Other has functioned to stigmatize and repress—to devalue, demonize, or efface the site-specific effectivity of silence, the so-called subjectivity of both female and non-Western subjects, the empowering potential, in various contexts, of either wearing or removing the veil, and the legitimacy and capacity of non-Westerners to investigate either one another's cultures or Western culture itself; whereas the recognition of all selfhood as inevitably nonunitary and heterogeneous, the affirmation of the self which says, to all others and every outside, both " 'I am like you' " *and* " 'I am different' " and, in so doing, "unsettl[es] every definition of otherness" (I, 76) clears the ground for a fully self-reflexive understanding, dialogue, and enablement.

Minh-ha's manifesto serves admirably as statement of first principles for the critique of "feminist re-presentations of women in non-Western societies" by Aihwa Ong that follows. Ong begins her essay "Colonialism and Modernity" with the claim that a good deal of feminist work on non-Western women and capitalist development is infected by a "tendency to treat gender and sexuality as categories that are measurable," to assess the "status of non-Western women . . . according to a set of legal, political and social benchmarks that Western feminists consider critical in achieving a power balance between men and women" (I, 82). The result, she argues, is either an overly hasty celebration of the new freedoms and powers the non-Western woman gains from her new-found place inside the expanding sphere of urban industrial life as capitalism continues to develop outside the First World metropole, or an unreflective nostalgia for the older freedoms and powers such women once held, and here and there still enjoy, within the vanishing space of preindustrial "traditional society"; in either case, the scholarship displays "little interest [in] indigenous constructions of gender and sexuality" and so "miss[es] the dense network of cultural politics that we demand of a study of women and men in Western cultures" (*I*, 87).[10]

Ong's call, therefore, is for Western feminists "to maintain a respectful distance" from "the ideas and values of Third World women," one that "leave[s] open the possibilities for an understanding not overly constructed by our own preoccupations" (*I*, 87). And she concludes by offering her own work on Malay factory women as an example of the fruit such careful listening and distancing procedures can bear. Her research discloses the full, contradictory range of discourses that seek to interpellate Malaysian women into a corresponding welter of subject positions: a "corporate discourse elaborated on the 'natural' accommodation of 'oriental female' fingers, eyes, and passivity to low-skilled assembly work" (*I*, 88–89); a religious discourse of "Islamic womanhood" that counsels "religious vigilance" against any increase in individualist assertiveness, and any accompanying erosion in "social boundaries" or sexual morality; and, beyond and alongside these official, institutional positions, a contradictory set of personal and political discourses around "modern forms of consumption," "sexual liberation," and "working class defiance" (*I*, 89). Such discoveries, or recoveries, of "conflicting sets of genders," and the "deep divisions, confusion, and unresolved tensions between tradition and modernity," remind us that the non-Western women Western feminists study "may not seek our secular goal of individual autonomy, nor renounce the bonds of family and community," and that we should "accept their living according to their own cultural interpretations of a changing world" (*I*, 89).

Such caution, in turn, is also at work in the scrupulous self-positioning and benign agnosticism of Donna Haraway's "Reading Buchi Emecheta: Contexts for Women's Experience in Women's Studies"—an essay that begins by endorsing Trinh Minh-ha's call to move beyond fixed, essentialist notions of the self out to "the ungraspable middle space" in which, "especially for the complex category and even more complex people called 'women,' *A* and *not-A* are likely simultaneously true." Accordingly, feminists must exhibit an ever-vigilant sensitivity to contradiction and a "wariness of . . . resolution" in "even the simplest matters in feminist analysis" (*I*, 108), even as they insist on the situatedness of all knowledge produced from this or that point on the endless web of differences in which we are enmeshed. To illustrate this situatedness, Haraway displays and glosses a diagram labeled the " 'Bush' or 'Map' of Women's Consciousness/Experience," in which "experience" is shown opening out into an antidialectic without fixed limits or ends into particular "situated knowledges" formed by the interplay of two pairs, the "local/global" and the "personal/polit-ical" (*I*, 108–9); the diagram thus serves as a reminder that "what counts as 'ex-perience' is never prior to the particular social occasions, the discourses, and other practices through which experience becomes *articulated* in itself and *ar-ticulable* with other accounts" (*I*, 110).

To demonstrate how to operate with such emphases and caveats in mind, Haraway gives the example of her own women's studies teaching, and in partic-ular her use of the work of the Nigerian novelist Buchi Emecheta. Or, more precisely still, her use of both that work and various readings of it by women in quite different situations from those of Haraway's students, and Haraway herself. For the fiction of Emecheta—whose complex itinerary Haraway re-hearses from colonial to postcolonial Nigeria, and from First to Third World and back, as, variously, "a mother [married and single], an immigrant, an Afri-can, an Ibo, an activist" (*I*, 113) and now a writer with a massively overdeter-mined, multiply determined, international audience—provides Haraway and her students a large canvas to map; all the more so, since the fiction itself refuses to fall into either of the traps Ong warns First World feminists against in their writings on non-Western women. "For Emecheta," writes Haraway, "there is no moment of innocence in Africa's history before the fall into the conflict be-tween 'tradition' and 'modernity' " (*I*, 114)—nor any unproblematic liberation after that fall.

For Haraway, though, the point is not to bring her students up against that refusal alone, and unreflexively, but to have them develop their responses to Emecheta's text alongside and against the pressure of other readings: one by African-American feminist critic Barbara Christian, one by Chikwenye Okonjo Ogunyemi, Nigerian "womanist" critic of African and diasporic-African literatures, and the last Haraway's own:

> I wanted my women's studies undergraduate students to read, mis-read, re-read, and so reflect on the field of possible readings of a particular complicated au-thor. . . . I wanted us to watch how those stakes locate readers in a map of feminist politics and women's self-consciously liberatory discourses, including con-structions, such as womanism, that place 'feminism' under erasure and propose a different normative genealogy for women's liberation. (*I*, 116–17)

It is this latter "construction" she describes for us first, in the work of Ogunyemi, for whom "womanism" is intended to designate both those women "committed to the survival and the wholeness of the 'entire people,' men and women, African and the people of its diaspora," and that project of recovery and empowerment. For Ogunyemi, then, in whose discourse both "*the married woman*" and the *socius* of " 'amicable co-wives with an invisible husband' " (*I*, 116) function as privileged utopian figurations, Emecheta's fiction must be simply rejected, since (to say the least) it does not "affirm marriage as the image of full maturity that could represent the unity of Black people internationally" (*I*, 117). For Barbara Christian, however, whose political allegiance is to the development "of a diverse culture of Black women engaged in finding selfhood and forming connections among women that promised to transcend race and class in a worldwide community patterned on the ties of mother and daughter," Emecheta's *Joys of Motherhood* is valuable insofar as it may be read together with Alice Walker's *Meridian* as marking a moment in a "narrative of maturation in the history of the writer of her literary foremothers" whose teleological end point and illumination is a "feminism that also carried with it an agenda of affirming lesbianism within Black feminism and within the model of the inheritance from Africa of the tie between mother and daughter" (*I*, 118). Finally, too, there is Haraway's own appropriation of Emecheta's work, whose dramatically staged contradictions she finds of use as warrant for her own search for "affinities that refused to resolve into identities or searches for a true self," but rather prefigure a "feminist image" of utopia centered on "not mothers and daughters, co-wives, sisters, or lesbian lovers, but adopted families and imperfect intentional communities" (*I*, 120). For us, however, as for Haraway's students, the point is not to choose among these competing readings, but to map them all as "part of contemporary struggle to articulate sensitively-specific and powerfully-collective women's liberatory discourses," and to locate one's own "specific, non-innocent" position on that map (*I*, 122–23).

Finally, in "Displacing Hegemonic Discourses: Reflections on Feminist Theory in the 1980's," Teresa de Lauretis constructs a personal, political, and theoretical genealogy of the concept of the nonessentialist feminist subject all four theorists hold in common: a subject that is "*not unified* or *simply divided* between positions of masculinity and femininity but *multiply organized* across positionalities along several axes and across mutually contradictory discourses and practices" (*I*, 136). The personal narrative she spins is, of course, that of de Lauretis herself, dis-placed from an Italy marked by its own internal and external displacements, as "colonial preserve or . . . vacation spot for other countries of Europe" (*I*, 127), and from its own internal colonial relations, mainland/island and North/South, to a United States from which all Europe was seen as an unproblematic unity, speaking its own single "Eurocentric" discourse. And this personal life history is overlapped by a tale of American feminism's move away from its starting point: an unproblematically unitary view of women's oppression, coupled with a hostile suspicion of theory as either male or foreign, and an insistence, in any case, on earning "one's credentials in movement politics," pulling the aforementioned "second shift" (*I*, 131).

In de Lauretis's view, that initial consensus has crumbled under both assaults from without and impasses within. The latter were reached through gradual recognition of the limits of voluntarism, the emerging perception that "one who lives in a sexist culture does not simply choose not to be sexist" but must "work through her own internalized sexism" (*I*, 131); and, likewise, through dissatisfaction with the divergent and inadequate strategic vectors derived from a monolithically conceived "opposition of female to male, Woman to Man" (*I*, 132): either an assimilationist politics of "equal status," which leaves untouched the classist, gendered, and racial implications embedded in the very notion of First World bourgeois rights, or a radical separatism in which a "polarized, oppositional stance to 'men' " accompanies the project of (re)constructing an authentic, uncontaminated " 'women's language' or 'women's culture' " (*I*, 132–33).

Finally, though, and most decisively, "the crucial shift in feminist consciousness . . . occurs with the intervention of women of color and lesbians in the contested terrain of feminist theory" (*I*, 135); for it is under the pressure of these women's "speaking out *within and against* feminism" (*I*, 133) that white, straight, First World feminists were forced to acknowledge "the presence of power relations that just could not be analyzed, altered, or even addressed by the concepts of gender and sexual difference" (*I*, 133–34). De Lauretis warns us that such forced recognitions should not result in a genial pluralism, in which the "various axes" of "race or color and ethnic or sexual identification" are simply, additively heaped together with those of gender. Against such an outcome, she cites African-American lesbian critic Barbara Smith's assertion that "Black male critics . . . are, of course, hampered by an inability to comprehend Black women's experience in sexual as well as racial terms" as an instance of her own more general point, that "The layers of oppression are not parallel but intersecting and mutually determining" (*I*, 135). Only through such understandings, de Lauretis suggests, does it become possible both to understand the anger "against white women, and feminists in particular" that drives Ogunyemi's "womanist" pan-Africanism, *and* to critique that anger by comparison to the more precise and properly political rage of Maxine Hong Kingston's woman warrior, in her book of that same name, which openly exhibits its utopian dis-placement from both male power and the feminine realm (*I*, 137–38). It is this dis-placement that de Lauretis also finds in the recent work of Monique Wittig, and in Biddy Martin and Chandra Mohanty's revision of Minnie Bruce Pratt's autobiographical essay, work her essay concludes by describing as exemplary instances of the practice she invites us to take up: an "operation of understanding reality" that begins with the knowledge that "the subject of feminism is multiply organized, unstable, and historically discontinuous" (*I*, 141).

I have felt the need to rehearse these four essays in some detail, with extensive quotation, to reassure myself and my readers of my fairness to the work I now want to critique—my fairness, and, indeed, to a great extent my sympathetic agreement as well. For what white First World male, after all, struggling from his position against oppressions racial, sexual, and economic, can the current assaults against essentialism come as anything less than a desperately welcome (if, inevitably, properly provisional) breathing space? I breathe and move in that space with gratitude—even while admitting the value of the exclusions to which I, and other putatively progressive white men, have been quite legitimately subject, not only for the empowerment those exclusions have provided others, but for the object lessons in marginalization and demonic Othering they have provided the otherwise socially dominant self. So it may seem perverse of me now to entertain reservations about a theoretical practice that offers me too the opportunity to offer an account (one that, moreover, quite readily comes to mind) of my own historical dis-placement from any ontologized binarism of gender, or color, or sexual preference—the equivalent, in effect, of the dislodging of Italy from Europe at the beginning of de Lauretis's piece.

Yet even as I read and learn from these pieces, there is something in their uniform emphasis on multideterminate specificity and multiple differences that unsettles the hum of agreement in my head with a nagging buzz—or, perhaps more accurately, with the noise of a certain silence, a sound that derives less from what this discourse says and does while in motion than in what it is silent about and where it stops. Or, to put it differently, it lies in the similarity of this shared discourse to another, *dis*abling discourse of difference, and the consequent ease with which it can be employed to buttress a far less progressive politics than its authors intend.

The example of Mukherjee's text here, of course, lies close to hand; and I mean to turn back to it again before I conclude. But first, let us take a less-textual example of the politics that can flow from an undialectical embrace of difference and situatedness: that of the "great kerchief quarrel" in France.[11] The incident began in October 1989, in the town of Creil, when a junior high school principal—himself, interestingly enough, an Afro-Frenchman from Martinique—ordered three Muslim students (two Moroccan sisters and a Tunisian friend) to remove the kerchiefs from their heads or leave the classroom. The students refused, the state stepped (uncertainly) in, and the French press moved in on the story; in the ensuing fracas, the French left, feminist, and antiracist communities and movements split both internally and against each other. Spokeswomen for feminism tended to align themselves with secular, liberalizing tradition, arguing that "a left attached to principles" must reject the wearing of the kerchief as "apartheid for women." Similarly, an open statement published in *Nouvel Observateur*, and signed by Elisabeth Badinter, Régis Debray, and four other authors, asserted that "The right to be different so dear to your heart is a liberty only if accompanied by the right to be different from one's difference. Otherwise it is a trap or a servitude."

Such views were opposed not only by the extreme right, whose intellectual spokespersons cheerfully endorsed the challenge the kerchiefs put to the "ideologies" of democracy, human rights, and secularism, but by the more upscale, technocratically minded sectors of the French left itself, including both the majority of those in Mitterrand's "Socialist" government and the media-driven antiracist movement SOS Racisme, whose generous funding sources include "some of the biggest and smartest money in France, including the pro-Mitterrand 'modernizing' billionaire Seydoux family (heirs to the vast Schlumberger fortune), and Pierre Berge, fashion designer Yves Saint Laurent's business manager." According to the voices of this newer "anti-authoritarian" left, denying Muslim female students the right to wear their kerchiefs would only deepen the antagonism and alienation felt by the Muslim community in France, while allowing them to do so would permit the students themselves to make their own choice, in their own good time, to discard them; after all, as SOS Racisme's leader Harlem Désir has said of such fundamentalist codes in general, eventually "blue jeans will win out over the chador" anyhow.

In the event, however, the incident drew to a close without a clear victory for any side except the extreme right, whose overtly racist National Front, cashing in on the controversy, managed to place its first candidate in the National Assembly with an absolute majority: one Marie-France Stirbois, who argued in her campaign appearances for a new policy of "preference for the French against the North African invasion." The students themselves, meanwhile, had dutifully returned to school without head coverings—thanks to the expression of royal displeasure sent by King Hassan II of Morocco to the fundamentalist father of the Moroccan sisters, to the effect that the whole affair was generating too much negative publicity. Thus the final irony of the whole affair: that an issue formulated as a clash between a laissez-faire, individualist politics of difference and a universalizing politics of secular equality was resolved in favor of the latter, but by a single, crude swipe of the Phallic/Patriarchal sword across the Gordian knot.

Against the backdrop of this example, then, with all its multiple positionalities, ironies, and sheer politico-discursive "thickness," we might return to the comments on veiling that appear in the essays we have been studying. You will recall that the subject first appears in Minh-ha's essay, as an example of how the political-theoretical perspective of difference ought to work on the "veil as reality and metaphor":

> If the act of unveiling has a liberating potential, so does the act of veiling. It all depends on the context in which such an act is carried out, or more precisely, on how and where women see dominance. Difference should neither be defined by the dominant sex nor by the dominant culture. So that when women decide to lift the veil one can say that they do so in defiance of their men's oppressive right to their bodies. But when they decide to keep or put on the veil they once took off they might do so to reappropriate their space or to claim a new difference in defiance of genderless, hegemonic, centered standardization. (*I*, 73)

Something, moreover, of the same hands-off perspective comes through in the transcript of Panel Discussion 3, when copanelist Mira Kamdar expresses her suspicion of Ogunyemi's Africanist "womanism," centered as it is around the "transcendental, phallocratic signifier" of the invisible African husband, and invites Haraway to weigh in with her judgment as well. Instead of judging, however, Haraway enacts the abstention Minh-ha calls for, directing her and our attention instead to the appreciation of the differences themselves, and of the sheer distance between Ogunyemi's entry point into the "bush of consciousness" and her own:

> One very practical dimension of it is that she [Ogunyemi] is very interested in affirming the revaluing of polygamy in Nigerian cities right now, and naming the sort of rural-city relationships around questions of forms of marriage. *I think it is bound to have some of the same complexity as the debates around veiling and unveiling.* The connection I make is that marriage has been used as a trope in feminist discourse coextensive with the field that Teresa and I are talking about to argue just about everything. And the particular way Ogunyemi enters that field immediately brings up the similarities as well as the differences. (*I*, 152 – italics mine)

All four writers, as we have seen, are concerned to affirm this emphasis on difference, distance, and determinate complexity, as opposed to any tendency – in these essays, one usually associated with the First World – toward essentialism or totalization. Yet this new consensus, for all its value, bends the theoretical stick in a direction that carries its own determinate risk. Perhaps that risk is already apparent in the contrast – or, perhaps more accurately, *gap* – between the principled forbearance from judgment that Haraway recommends, and the crowded, overheated politico-discursive terrain of the French "kerchief quarrel" we have sketched. Or it might be suggested by the partial parallel that could be drawn between the question of veiling in Islamic societies, which Minh-ha seems to assume will be a strategy of empowerment for Islamic women however it is decided, and the long-lived "doctrine of the two spheres" in American culture, according to which women are granted superior moral and affective capacities, and a degree of special legal and social protection, in exchange for their relegation to the domestic sphere and the margins of public life. Most American feminists, I think, have no problem recognizing the lure of such distinct, if subordinated, power and the fear of its loss as primary components of the explicitly antifeminist backlash of the seventies and eighties, in the work of Phyllis Schlafly, Marabel Morgan, and others; nor do they have any qualms about insisting that the eroded fragments of that doctrine, in discourse and in practice, must be renounced for the liberation of American women to succeed.[12] What, then, we must ask, is the point of forbearing to re-present this same political perspective in dialogue with women from Islamic societies as one possible liminal option, or asymptotic line—or, for that matter, in the French "kerchief quarrel" specifically, in which the available evidence strongly suggests that the "decisions" to wear and to remove the veil were both at least highly influenced by the patriarchal powers of Father and King? And what effect in either context, specific or general, is that forbearance likely to have?

I will return to these questions shortly; first let us take another look at where the proponents of this forbearance are willing to fall silent, and what they keep silent about, by returning to the place where Ong declares her analysis of Malay factory workers stops *on principle*: with the discovery of "conflicting sets of genders, and their embeddedness in political struggles over cultural identity and the transition to industrial modernization," and the perception of "how meanings attached to gender can generate deep divisions, confusion, and unresolved tensions between tradition and modernity" (*I*, 89). What is to be done, however, with the sense of conflict, ambivalence, tension, beyond appreciating it (as, certainly, exposure to high modernist culture and its normative aesthetic values of ambivalence, irony, and tension has taught us First World intellectuals to do quite well), is by no means clear. Ong concludes her essay with the assertion that "We begin a dialogue when we recognize other forms of gender- and culture-based subjectivities, and accept that others often choose to conduct their lives separate from our particular vision of the future" (*I*, 90). But this is, I think, a curious statement; is it not more true to say that having set recognition and acceptance as a precondition for dialogue, one enters into dialogue *both* by listening to the other's discourse *and* by offering one's own in comparison, affirmation, contestation, and contrast—that dialogue consists not only of careful listening, but of self-disclosing response as well?

What I am trying to express here is a doubt more than an accusation, a concern more than a critique. The concern, to put it plainly, is that a tonic admonition to Western feminists (and, of course, a fortiori, leftists) to "hold back while other people recover their own history" (*I*, 101) may become a warrant for dis-engagement from the struggles of nonwhite and/or non-Western others for their liberation from the multiple oppressions that afflict them – that the properly ethical concern for serious consideration for other determinate points of view may devolve into an apolitical aesthetic of postmodern delectation in masquerade costume as politics. Surely Aihwa Ong herself is not arguing for the adoption of such an apolitical perspective; yet some of her remarks follow-ing her paper, in Panel Discussion 2, nonetheless lend unwitting support to its construction. Ong is asked, by copanelist Roberto Rivera, to comment on the similarity of her work on women factory workers in Malaysia to that of Patricia Fernandez Kelly and Lourdes Arguelles on, and with, the Chicana and Mexicana workers employed in the *maquiladoras* on either side of the Mexico-U.S. border. Her response is, first, a denunciation of their work's tainted status as "political economy," itself perceived as part of a "tradition of an unfolding rationality," one of a number of "male-dominant discourses" feminists have too uncritically adopted for their work. Then, when Rivera presses his defense of these women's work, arguing that it is neither "essentializing" nor "reductionist" but rather exists as both a careful articulation of the links between the local and global contexts of their struggles and a principled intervention in them, and proposing that "we can redo our ideas of how political economists function and do things by looking at the practice of individual people," his rejoinder is more or less casually dismissed. "Well," Ong says, "I wasn't talking about all feminists, and in fact I was trained as a political economist. I'm trying to go beyond that" (*I*, 102).

Similarly, in Panel Discussion #3, when Jim Clifford raises the question of "the geopolitical ground" that provides "a historically specific context" for the emergence of these new discourses of difference and situated knowledge – not, he ever so tactfully insists, to posit "multinational capital" as "primary geopoliti-cal cause of it all" but merely as a context for location and self-reflection (*I*, 145) – the conversation simply moves straight on to another topic. It is, one feels, as though any reference to political economy, any evocation of the sys-tematicity of global capitalism is not so much simply wrong as . . . well, *un-seemly* somehow. Nor is linkage to the macroeconomic the only no-no for those seeking to "go beyond"; the flip side of the same etiquette would seem to forbid intervention in the political discourses of others, even when those dis-courses flaunt the essentialism our theorists are united in opposing. Minh-ha's slogan "let difference replace conflict," the banner slogan of this set of essays, has some funny contradictions in practice. We have already quoted Donna Haraway's decorous refusal to join Mira Kamdar in her critique of Ogun-yemi – a refusal framed, by the way, by the suspicion evinced by panelists

Kamala Visweswaran and Vivek Dhareshwar toward the privileged character of the "joking" pleasure Haraway takes in mapping her reading of Emecheta together with Christian's and Ogunyemi's, and "trying to see what our various stakes are" (*I*, 149–151), and matched, in Haraway's paper, by her equally respectful/joking "in-difference" to the totalizing and essentialist elements of Christian's project of constructing from the texts she reads a teleological "narrative of maturation" in which the protolesbian bond between mother and daughter figures as both originary African truth and utopian end point.

But Haraway's "joking" agnosticism is not the only attitude struck in the *Inscription* essays toward the essentialist discourses of nonwhite and/or non-Western others. In "Displacing Hegemonic Discourses," Teresa de Lauretis seems to sound a more consistent call for *all* feminists to leave the essentialist "place that is safe, that is 'home' . . . for another place that is unknown and risky, that is not only emotionally but conceptually other, a place of discourse from which speaking and thinking are at best tentative, uncertain, unguaranteed" (*I*, 139). From that perspective, de Lauretis is able and willing to judge Ogunyemi's "womanism" as an essentialism centered—as all essentialisms are—around "a place of non-contamination, of moral and ideological purity" (*I*, 137). Yet, oddly enough, de Lauretis's way to that perspective proceeds through its own essentialist moment, when, in the course of arguing against a merely "parallel or coequal" view of the various axes of oppression—racial, sexual, gendered, and classed—she quotes approvingly from Barbara Smith's "Toward a Black Feminist Criticism" the charge that "Black male critics . . . are, of course, hampered by an inability to comprehend Black women's experience *in sexual as well as racial terms*" (*I*, 134—italics added by de Lauretis). It must be said that de Lauretis deploys this quotation on behalf of a point important enough to be quoted again here: "The layers of oppression are not parallel but intersecting and mutually determining" (*I*, 135). Yet, by uncritically evoking Smith's argument, complete with the Othering swipe of that "of course," it would seem that she has admitted through the back door of her argument the same essentializing politics she is at pains to turn away from the front—or, even less charitably, that "letting difference replace conflict" is a must for women speaking to each other from different classes, races, cultures, sexualities, and so on, but is hardly required when dealing with essentially ineducable men, who, along with political economy, can only go into the permanent penalty box.

My point here, however, is not to whine about de Lauretis's treatment of men, but to note how even her comparatively aggressive antiessentialism turns a blind eye toward at least one manifestly essentialist argument, which, far from being criticized, is called to serve at a crucial moment as the unproblematic Voice of Truth. For de Lauretis is properly concerned to mark what she calls "the crucial shift in feminist consciousness that occurs with the intervention of women of color and lesbians in the contested terrain of feminist theory, an epistemological shift affecting the whole of feminism, theory and practice, *and* their relationship" (*I*, 135; italics in original). Yet in her paper as in Ong's, the level of practice—of practice narrowly understood as political organization, strategizing, and struggle, however enmeshed in discourse and informed by theory such activity must inevitably be—is never actually addressed. For de Lauretis as for Haraway, we reach the point at which "the feminist subject . . . becomes redefined" as "*not unified* or *simply divided* between positions of masculinity and femininity, but *multiply organized* across mutually contradictory discourses and practices" (*I*, 136), and everything aside from the (sitespecific, particularized, massively overdetermined) talking stops.

Or, perhaps, had already stopped for de Lauretis even before this shift occurred, judging from her story of North American feminism from the 1970s to the present. The first moment in that narrative, you will recall, was characterized by the "double shift" of obligatory political activism combined with a relatively naive and even antitheoretical "feminist critique" in "one's teaching and writing context" (*I*, 131); the second moment, the moment of the present, by "the end of the women's movement as such" and the recognition of "the relevance of theory to feminism," thanks to the critiques put forward "around issues of racism, homophobia, and moralism" by those women excluded from or marginalized by the feminist theory and practice of Moment #1. And this progression, at least as I read de Lauretis's history, is valorized precisely *as* progress: the "women's movement as such" has ended, but "feminist theory" has become "possible as such" (*I*, 131), and that is all to the good.

This is, I think, a weird history, in terms of both its attitudes and its assumptions of fact. For starters, I do not know what de Lauretis means by "the end of the women's movement as such." Is it not rather the case that far from ever positing a "women's movement" on the order of, say, the Second International or the Comintern, second-wave feminism has been from the outset decentralized and site-specific by definition, more or less consistently exhibiting a hardwired wariness toward any totalizing tendencies in theory or strategy, even those that have shown up (e.g., in the work of Andrea Dworkin or Mary Daly) on its own terrain—or, to put it another way, that within North American feminism by and large the Fanonian "national moment" of pure and positive unity against a monolithically conceived Man has tended to be, for better or worse, of short duration, and to play a relatively minor role? Yet conversely, when an issue of concern to the majority of women has arisen—as, most strikingly, around reproductive rights in the United States today—the turnout has been breathtakingly impressive: when 650,000 women and men turn out to demonstrate for choice as we did in Washington in spring 1989, what does it mean to speak of "the end of the women's movement as such"? Likewise, on a local level, many of the self-identified feminists I know — women working at the battered women's shelter in town, for the local chapter of the National Abortion Rights Action League (NARAL), with women's organizations in El Salvador, with other black women struggling for control over their home spaces in the murderous, drug-saturated projects of North Hartford — have no idea that the movement is over; most of them, I dare say, are under the delusion they are carrying it on.

De Lauretis's reports of the death or disappearance of the North American feminist movement thus seem greatly exaggerated; but so, for that matter, does her claim for the appearance of "feminist theory." For it is precisely "theory" in singular that, by her own admission, North American feminism lacks today, and precisely for the reason she herself cites: ever since "the writings of women of color, Jewish women, and lesbians constituted themselves as a feminist critique of feminism, and an intervention in a feminist discourse that was anchored to the single axis of gender as sexual (or, rather, heterosexual) difference" (*I*, 132), the fate of any bid to construct a unified field theory of women's oppression has largely been foreclosed — even as the opportunities to proliferate "the bush of consciousness" in theory have exploded, as elsewhere on the left, into a kind of free-trading speculative frenzy of exchange with psychoanalysis, deconstruction, Marxism, poststructuralism, semiotics, and so on.

But I have, obviously enough, been playing with words here, since, after all, for de Lauretis such proliferation is precisely what "theory" means: an aggregate of theories in particular, first a hundred, then a thousand heterogeneous (site-specific, overdetermined) flowers of discourse blooming in perpetual spring. And her essay, moreover, is no doubt correct in its account of the social factors and agents behind this burgeoning — correct, and yet perhaps both too uncritical in its characterizations and too unself-consciously confident in its valorization of such theorizing's effect. For it is possible to argue, as Jennie Bourne has, that for all the justice and necessity of the feminist critique of feminism by women of color, lesbians, and Jewish feminists, that critique too often sprang from an essentialist and "personalist" politics whose first move was to refuse *on principle* the possibility of political linkage or cross-cultural dialogue.[13] It was, in effect, but a short step from the famous formulation of the Combahee River Collective in its critique of mainstream feminism, that "The most profound and potentially the most radical politics come directly out of our own identity as opposed to working to end someone else's oppression"[14] to a politics "based," as Bourne says, "on rejecting not just the internalised oppression of

222 / Fred Pfeil

one's gender or sexuality . . . but all other oppressions including those of class or 'ethnicity' so as to find one's true identity"[15] – a step made all the more irresistible when fueled by the rage that was the natural by-product of the marginalization of lesbians and women of color within the feminist movement itself. Yet, however comprehensible this reaction may have been, for Bourne the result has been the creation of a "stunted, inward-looking and self-righteous 'politics' which sets its face against the politics out there in the real world."[16] Identity politics, as it is sometimes called, far from developing and sustaining "the most profound and potentially the most radical politics" in practice, is far more apt to freeze its subjects in the unreflectively valorized "particularity of their experience" and make "identity itself a substitute for liberation"[17] – particularly the liberation of those living in some other balkanized kingdom of value and victimage than one's own.

Once we lever this moment of identity politics up into full light from within de Lauretis's history, admitting both the value of its critique of feminism *and* the depoliticizing impasses of its literally self-righteous anger, the slogan "Let difference replace conflict" manifests itself in all its historically situated ambiguity or oscillation between two possible senses, one radical and the other liberal-pluralist at best. "Let difference replace conflict" may be read as a *universal* summons to each and all of us, to engage in what Gramsci calls an "inventory" of those historically produced discourses, practices, and institutions that have determined us, as a necessary preliminary to our engagement in a common liberation struggle against inequality and oppression;[18] or, it may be taken as a license for a kind of relativist liberal isolationism, in which the privileged (white/heterosexual/Western) subject's self-consciousness of her (or, a fortiori, his) own historic situatedness requires her to accept whatever the (nonwhite, nonheterosexual, non-Western) subject says or does, and keep her mouth shut: "to accept," as Ong says, "their living according to their own cultural interpretations of a changing world, and not simply acted upon by inherited traditions and modernization projects" (*I*, 89). And this crucial ambiguity, I want to say, is constituted by a political moment in which we – on the left and within feminism, in theory and practice – remain largely stuck: a moment in which the universalizing claims of mainstream feminism and left orthodoxy have been widely and justly assailed by the constituencies they have marginalized and excluded, yet in which the discourses and practices through which those challenges have taken place have been frequently marked, as we have seen, by a "nationalist" essentialism of their own.

For who among us, after all – white or nonwhite, Western or not – is *not* always caught precisely in the space between "inherited traditions" and "modernization projects"? And where else, how else, do "cultural interpretations" come from—"theirs" or "ours," local or global, resistant or complicit, as the case may be—other than from the spaces between the two, and with the ensemble of materials they provide (or, indeed, from the lack of space, the sometimes desperate need for new conceptual and material resources)? That, at any rate, is the lesson I take from the French "kerchief quarrel," in which a language and politics of secular equality, insisting on "the right to be different from one's difference," offered the only alternative to the choice between subordinated subservience to tradition and the consumerist free play of the market, the veil or blue jeans. And it is the lesson I take as well from Emecheta's fiction, with its bitter depictions of the ways in which African women's lives are ground to bits by the brutal interaction of the sexual subordination required by tribal tradition with the exploitative exactions of capitalist urban life—depictions that, as I read them, cry out for the construction of a discourse and politics of women's liberation from both the bad old days and the bad new ones; as, for that matter, does the nonfictional example of the struggles of Latin American women today, which Jean Franco describes in much the same way in "Killing Priests, Nuns, Women, Children."[19] Franco's essay, written in memory of a "disappeared" activist friend from Guatemala, brilliantly puts before us the space—or, more accurately, the nonspace—of the contemporary Latin American woman whose formerly sanctioned and utopian yet subordinated places in traditional patriarchal society are all under siege by the armed forces of a genocidally sterilizing modernization project. The church of the Madonna, the convent of the virginal nun or unmarried girl, the home of the Mother, the "house" of the whore—all these previously sacralized and/or delimited "felicitous spaces" of female power are being invaded and destroyed "not by the left but by the right-wing military" seeking to construct in their place a new dystopian regime of "commodity culture, a debt-ridden economy" and a postcolonial capitalism without limit or restraint.[20]

What, I want to ask, shall our response be to the workings of such "negative dialectics" around the world (including, as Koptiuch's analysis shows, within the United States)? What does it mean, in the face of such examples, such lives, and such deaths, "to accept their living according to their own cultural interpretations of a changing world," or "to hold on to that pleasure"—the words here are Haraway's—of "mapping these readings and re-readings . . . to see what our various stakes are and . . . to joke about them all very seriously"? (I, 150). What does it mean to celebrate the (supposed) passing of the day in which one was required to join one's theoretical work with political practice in a feminist movement that, "as such," is now said to be over, or to dismiss political economy as something we now ought to "go beyond"? It means—or can at least all too easily mean—that, pressed into silence on the one hand by the essentialist voices of those whom our politics and theories used to exclude, we are now released from the responsibility of joining in struggle with any others, of making our discourses and politics available to them for their use. It means—or can mean—abandoning those others to whatever discursive and political resources their own "inherited traditions" and "modernization projects" provide, regardless of however meager or mutually oppressive these may be; and it means—or can mean—that we retreat from Sabina Lovibond's call for feminists to

> continue to think of their efforts as directed not simply towards various local po-
> litical programmes, but ultimately towards a global one—the abolition of the sex
> class system, and of the forms of inner life that belong with it. This programme
> is 'global' not just in the sense that it addresses itself to every corner of the
> planet, but also in the sense that its aims eventually converge with those of all
> other egalitarian or liberationist movements. (It would be arbitrary to work for
> sexual equality unless one believed that human society was disfigured by inequal-
> ity *as such*.)[21]

It is not hard to imagine the objections that might be mounted against Lovibond's language here, from a vantage point near that from which the discourses we have been studying come: that its globalism or universalism effaces the cultural particularities of those it seeks to include, and is, moreover, irrevocably tainted by the Eurocentrism and/or male chauvinism of its origins. But Lovibond's anticipatory response to such charges deftly points to the contradiction that underlies their critique, insofar as such objections themselves are driven precisely by the utopian power of the universalist values they deride. Feminism, in other words, is (or ought to be) specifiable not for any potentially abusive and inevitably specious proposition of a unified subject position but on the basis of the liminal unity of its political *project*. If, for example, Lovibond says,

> European and/or North American feminism is alleged by black women to share
> in the racism of the surrounding culture, then their complaint rightly creates a
> new political agenda—a new set of pointers towards the goal of a genuinely 'het-
> erogeneous public life'; and this sort of development certainly makes the move-
> ment (empirically speaking) less unified than before. But it does not prejudice the
> *ideal* unity of feminism. Instead, it calls attention to a certain respect in which
> feminism has fallen short of its own idealized self-image as an occupant of the
> 'universal standpoint' (in contrast, say, to the traditional—male-dominated—
> Left).[22]

To the compelling internal logic of this rejoinder, moreover, I would add a strictly historical note of my own, to the effect that there is surely something wrong with summarily dismissing the language and politics of rights, equality, and collective solidarity with the poison-skull labels of Eurocentrism and masculinism, and leaving it (and them) with that. For insofar as they are also, and, indeed, preeminently concepts formed out of the long experience of *capitalism* – or, if you will, industrial culture – itself, precisely as the always contested, uncertain terrain of countercultural resistance to the exploitation and degradation intrinsic to that culture's workings and effects, then regardless of its geographical point of origin or initial exclusions, some transliterated version of them will become necessary in any place or situation in which capitalism is found at its deterritorializing/reterritorializing work – which is to say, very nearly everywhere on the planet, and not least in Central America or Emecheta's Nigeria.

To say that the language and politics of radical democracy is necessary, however, is not to say that they will be anywhere sufficient, nor that they should be everywhere hegemonic; no more than the universality of the values they assert requires that those values be everywhere uniformly incarnated or absolute. Rather, they must be always held in a global-local tension with the cultural particularities – discursive and institutional – they encounter in any specific situation: as, for example, with the discourses and institutions of Christianity in Central America today, or those of Islam in the Malaysia in which the women Ong writes of go blind and numb at their machines. But the construction and continuance of that tension do require something more than a disengaged appreciation of the other's sheer, nonnegotiable difference from one's own; it requires the active *engagement with others* over and through those differences as well. What is missing from the slogan "Let difference replace conflict," as that slogan is worked through the essays we have reviewed, is precisely that third term – dialogic, dialectical *tension* – which the slogan's opposition excludes, a tension that is worked, discursively and in political practice, through the fluttering gap between the potentially leveling universality of a discourse and politics opposed to *all* forms of exploitation, and the potentially centrifugalizing differences in the discursive and practical repertoires from which our separate yet multiple identities are drawn.[23]

Conclusion: In-Difference in Practice

Absent from the narrative practice of a Mukherjee, and lacking in the theoretical practice of the *Inscriptions* writers, is any sense of this crucial way *through* difference via a praxis whose goal is neither the totalitarian effacement of difference nor the delirious celebration of a limitless and ever-proliferating "in-difference," but the construction of flexible, practical relations of *solidarity*. Solidarity, that is, as a relation constructed through forms of dialogue and struggle that presuppose a common commitment to ending all forms of oppression and exploitation, however organized through the intertwinings of race, class, gender, sexual orientation, or cultural difference, and that work out, and work through, the differences from there.

Such a formulation, I hasten to add, does not mean that I know, or can ever know, in any lived existential way what it is like to be an African-American lesbian or a female Salvadoran union organizer. But it does mean that I *can* understand the oppressive and exploitative relations in which these women are enmeshed well enough to serve them in the struggle against those relations; to make available to them whatever discursive and material resources are available to me in that struggle; and, in working with them, simultaneously to work on those structures of privilege, internal and external, that have, disablingly and enablingly, produced me—working to disengage and defuse those structures, indeed, in no small part with the help of those discursive and material resources the others I work with make available to me.

I know I can do these things, moreover, because like many, and many different others, I have learned that I can from the experience of the practice I have described: from "double shifts" working as a white man against institutionalized racism at the college where I teach, as a straight man with gay and lesbian groups, as a man working with feminist women and groups against various forms of sexism, as a North American in the struggle for freedom and democracy in Central America. And in working those "double shifts" I have also learned the other side of this lesson: that, as Steve Burghardt says,

> a white person must understand that he or she can be deeply involved in fighting racism and still be viewed as a racist by blacks; indeed, you *will* be. . . . [A] white person can accept this and can understand this as a necessary perception for blacks to have about most whites (or, in varying degrees, women about men, gays about straights, etc.).[24]

And so-called Third World people about First World people too, of course; "their" acceptance of "us" is always, *must* always necessarily be provisional, and contingent on our actions and behavior far more than our mere words.

My experience here is hardly unique; it, and the lessons it teaches, are common knowledge to activists everywhere working "across the lines." Yet that experience and the lessons it offers are foreclosed in advance by any analysis or perspective that commits itself in principle to the fetish of difference as an unbridgeable distance between differently constituted individuals or groups. For once the "nationalist" critique of feminism (or, for that matter, of the left) is enfolded within a poststructuralist critique of the Self-Other relationship, the result is all too likely to be a pseudopolitics that mindlessly cheers on the endless balkanization of a "politics of subjectivity" (itself often herded under an in-

finitely expanding and undifferentiated congeries called the "new social movements"), while confining its own operations to "mapping" and "joking" – albeit
while remaining "full of hope" that somewhere off in an ever-receding future
"we will learn how to structure affinities" (*I*, 111).

Here again I am quoting Donna Haraway, from whom, along with Teresa
de Lauretis, I have learned a great deal. So it has been with the greatest respect
(and, I confess, no small amount of trepidation) that I have engaged in the critique these pages provide. But the practical stake in our theoretical differences
have seemed too crucial for me, or anyone else, to keep silent about them: because, to put it plainly, a theoretical perspective, feminist or otherwise, that
one-sidedly emphasizes "a wariness of . . . resolution" and defers the structuring of affinities to the future is likely to warrant or issue in a devolution of
political praxis itself into a mixture of aesthetics and politesse eminently com-
mensurable with and recuperable by late capitalism in the metropole, an exqui-
sitely mannered, politically correct life-style for all those cosmopolitan travel-
ing theorists, white or nonwhite, Western or not, who have the cultural and
literal capital to afford the passage into the new heaven of in-difference, who
can make the ticket price for the endless shuttle run, with Mukherjee's "Middleman," between dislocation and complicity, a flight that is itself the newest Club
Med vacation around.

Within feminism, then, white and nonwhite, in the "postindustrial" and "un-
derdeveloping" world alike, as throughout the field of progressive discourse and
praxis, the point made so eloquently by the late Allon White must ever be insisted upon:

> Though our current fashion is to prioritize difference, and rightly, in the struggle
> against the false universalism and essentialism which has so oppressed all those
> who do not conform to the European, white, male heterosexual shape which
> "Man" is evidently supposed to have, nevertheless, an ultimate political perspec-
> tive of humanity as a unity-in-difference, a complex of co-existing and mutually
> understanding cultures, is just as important to any radical politics.[25]

How do we, privileged intellectuals that we are, keep this importance always
before us? By being as wary in our theoretical work of irresolution as we have
learned to be of glib totalities; by remembering always the seductive dangers
of the postmodernism Nelly Richard describes in which "no sooner are . . .
differences – sexual, political, racial, cultural – posited and valued, than they become subsumed into the meta-category of the 'undifferentiated,' " with the result that "all singularity . . . become[s] indistinguishable and interchangeable
in a new, sophisticated economy of 'sameness' ";[26] and by trading in the oscillation between dislocation and identification, the different and the same, for the

long work, and deeper pleasure, of constructing "structures of affinity" now, in theory and practice. Or, to put it more sloganistically, by replacing "conflict" not with "difference," but with the construction of the always provisional solidarity I have just tried to describe.

And, I will add as final provocation to my intellectual/academic colleagues, if only by way of keeping us honest, of reminding us that the social field in which most people live is not just a polyvocal text—perhaps, just perhaps, by putting in a few more "double shifts"?

> Listen   listen with care   class and color and sex do not define   people do not define politics   a class society defines people by class   a racist society defines people by color   We   feminists   socialists   radicals   define people by their struggles against the racism   sexism   classism   that they harbor   that surrounds them[27]

The words here are Rosario Morales's; and they are probably all that I have been trying to say here all along.

Notes

Although I am responsible, of course, for my own argument here, this essay has nonetheless had many collaborators and interlocutors, some knowing and some not. It was first sparked in a conversation with Wahneema Lubiano and Barbara Harlow at the Marxist Literary Group's Summer Institute in Pittsburgh in the summer of 1989. Caren Kaplan and Inderpal Grewal then fanned the flame by inviting me to shape my inchoate thoughts into a contribution to their anthology; without their encouragement and support, it is safe to say that, for better or for worse, I would not have presumed to write this piece at all. I owe an additional debt of thanks to Inderpal Grewal for her insightful criticisms of my first draft, to Ted Swedenburg for his comments on the second, and to the anonymous readers of the manuscript for the University of Minnesota Press for their thoughtful responses.

Finally, I should like to note that this piece was written quite literally in memory of Sally Hacker and Febe Elizabeth Velasquez, North American and Salvadoran feminist activists both, and that it is dedicated to the example of their lives.

1. I want to specify in particular that they should not be conflated with, or seen as stand-ins for, the work of Gayatri Spivak, arguably the most prestigious feminist theorist of postcoloniality in the contemporary West. The relationship between Spivak's protean work and the problematic examined here is a rich and complicated one, rife with both affinity and contradiction (or so it seems to me), so much so that the question of that relationship, itself clearly too large a subject to be taken up in an already long essay, might nonetheless be said both to inspirit and to haunt what is here. See her *In Other Worlds* (New York: Methuen, 1987) and *The Postcolonial Critic*, ed. Sarah Harasym (New York: Routledge, 1990).

2. All quotes taken from the back dust jacket for the hardbound copy of Mukherjee's *Jasmine* (New York: Grove Weidenfeld, 1989)—quotes puffing the new novel on the basis of the praise for *The Middleman*, as is common practice nowadays.

3. Quoted from the back cover of the paperback edition of *The Middleman* (New York: Fawcett Crest, 1988), from which all subsequent quotations from this book will be drawn. Page numbers for those quotations will be given in the text itself, following an *M*, to designate this text.

4. Julia Kristeva, *Revolution in Poetic Language*, trans. Margaret Weller (New York: Columbia

University Press, 1984); Roland Barthes, *The Pleasure of the Text*, trans. Richard Miller (New York: Hill and Wang, 1975), 53.

5. P. J. O'Rourke, *Holidays in Hell* (New York: Vintage Books, 1989), 164; hereafter, page numbers will be given in the text, following an *H*, to designate this book.

6. Maria Mies, *Patriarchy and Accumulation on a World Scale: Women in the International Division of Labour* (London: Zed Books, 1986); A. Sivanandan, "New Circuits of Imperialism," *Race and Class* 30, 4 (1989), 1–19, since republished in his collection *Communities of Resistance* (New York: Verso, 1990).

7. Kristin Koptiuch, "Third-Worlding at Home," *Social Text* 28 (1991): 87–99. The quote given here occurs on page 87. Page numbers of all subsequent quotations will be given in the text.

8. Antonio Gramsci, *Note sul Macchiavelli, sulla politica e sullo stato moderno* (Turin: Einaudi, 1974), quoted in Tim Brennan's "Cosmopolitans and celebrities," *Race and Class* 31, 1 (1989): 16.

9. *Inscriptions* 3/4 (1988): 71. Page numbers of all subsequent quotations from this issue will be cited in the text itself, following an *I*.

10. It may be worth mentioning that Ong's critique of Western feminists' analyses of non-Western women largely echoes that put forward by Chandra Talpade Mohanty's "Under Western Eyes: Feminist Scholarship and Colonial Discourses," *boundary 2* 12 (Spring/Fall 1984): 333–58. Mohanty's essay may indeed be taken as one of the first and most influential indictments of Western feminism drawn up by postcolonial women for dissemination in the West, and thus as a paradigmatic signal or place marker of the context in which all four of our theorists find and seek to position themselves.

11. The account from which the following information and quotations are drawn is Diana Johnstone's "In 'great kerchief quarrel' French unite against 'Anglo-Saxon ghettos,' " in *In These Times*, January 24–30, 1990, 10–11.

12. The classic formulation of this analysis and argument is, of course, Barbara Ehrenreich and Deirdre English's *For Her Own Good: 150 Years of the Experts' Advice to Women* (Garden City, N.J.: Doubleday, 1978).

13. Jennie Bourne, "Homelands of the mind: Jewish feminism and Identity Politics," *Race and Class* 29, 1 (1987): 1–24.

14. The Combahee River Collective, "A Black Feminist Statement," in Zillah R. Eisenstein, ed., *Capitalist Patriarchy and the Case for Socialist-Feminism*; quoted in Bourne, "Homelands," 2.

15. Bourne, "Homelands," 2.

16. Ibid., 18–19.

17. Ibid., 20.

18. "The starting-point of critical elaboration is the consciousness of what one really is, and is 'knowing thyself' as a product of the historical process to date which has deposited in you an infinity of traces, without leaving an inventory." Quoted from *Selections from the Prison Notebooks*, trans. Quintin Hoare (London: Lawrence and Wishart, 1971), 324.

19. Jean Franco, "Killing Priests, Nuns, Women, Children," in Marshall Blonsky, ed., *On Signs* (Baltimore: Johns Hopkins University Press, 1985), 414–20.

20. Ibid., 417, 420.

21. Sabina Lovibond, "Feminism and Postmodernity," *New Left Review* 178 (November-December 1989): 28.

22. Ibid.

23. Lest the sentence to which this note is attached seem too blithely optimistic as to the outcome of such dialogic encounters, I would add that my most vexed choice in composing it was that between the words "dialectical" and "disjunctive." As Gayatri Spivak has taught us, after all, dialogue may be just as necessary and productive in an "interruptive" mode as in a negotiational or reconciliatory one. For a paradigmatic instance of such dialogue, in fact—one in which the gaps and exclusions between one political perspective and discursive practice and another (cultural nationalist, Marxist-feminist, liberal feminist, poststructuralist [Lacanian] feminist) are emphatically marked as tension-laden incompatibilities, not as "jokes"—see the one she conducts, in every sense of the word, around a story by Mahasweta

Devi, "A Literary Representation of the Subaltern: A Woman's Text from the Third World," in *In Other Worlds*, 241–68. Spivak's essay, in my reading of it at any rate, is, for all its chronic difficulty, exemplary of a political-theoretical practice that insists on positionality and discontinuity without foreclosing on the possibility of constructing provisional yet productive relations of practical solidarity such as those described in the following section.

24. Steve Burghardt, *The Other Side of Organizing* (Rochester, Vt.: Schenkman, 1982), 111.

25. Allon White, "The Struggle for Bakhtin: Fraternal Reply to Robert Young," *Cultural Critique* 8 (1987–88): 233.

26. Nelly Richard, "Postmodernism and Periphery," *Third Text* 2 (1987/88): 5.

27. Rosario Morales, "We Are All in This Together," in *This Bridge Called My Back: Writings by Radical Women of Color*, ed. Cherríe Moraga and Gloria Anzaldúa (New York: Kitchen Table: Women of Color Press, 1981), 92–93.

ELEVEN

Autobiographic Subjects and Diasporic Locations: *Meatless Days* and *Borderlands*

Inderpal Grewal

In her essay "Postmodernism and Periphery," Nelly Richard suggests that post-modernism "is adorned with ciphers of plurality, heterogeneity and dissidence," with emphasis on "specificity, regionalism, social minorities and political projects which are local in scope, on surviving traditions and suppressed forms of knowledge."[1] Although Richard reminds us that it is important to recognize the problematic "economy of sameness" that has also been a part of postmodernism, one impact has been a breakdown of the center-periphery formation that was an important aspect of colonial relations that structured the formation of the so-called First and Third Worlds.[2] Thus an important implication of this postmodern is the critique of those binary oppositions that have structured Western epistemology, and the consequent rejection of such structures including the notion of the unified self, of the well-defined center easily separable from and created out of a clear distinction from the periphery and the Other. The deconstruction of such binaries is an important element of postmodernism as an aesthetic/literary/cultural phenomenon that is distinct from postmodernity as a condition of life in the contemporary world.[3] Postmodernism's rejection of the center-periphery division is particularly apparent in the work of Third World writers, work whose importance is being acknowledged in the First World, though the distinction between the Self and its Other remains to be examined as a central element of modernist writing and ideology in its various forms and locations.

In the study of autobiography, or of autobiographical forms such as life histories, narratives, and testimonies, the question of margin-center and its homologue, Self-Other, has become crucial. Most critics agree that the "subject" has become a major issue of debate, though some are in favor of postmodern subjectivities and some believe these are problematic. For instance, Bella Brodzki and Celeste Schenck suggest in their introduction to *Life/Lines*, "the case of autobiography raises the essential problem in contemporary feminist theory and praxis: the imperative situating of the female subject in spite of the postmodernist campaign against the sovereign self."[4] Much contemporary criticism and writing seems to struggle with the embedded binary structures, while often challenging them as well.[5]

Many life narratives have recently been published in First World locations that are authored by those from the so-called margins. Recent publications in the United States include, for instance, writings by women of color, Asian immigrants telling their lives, memoirs, novels, short stories by minorities. Often such writing not only challenges the margin-center formation but also seeks to represent what are often taken as the unpresentable challenges resulting from the postmodern breakdown of modernist verities—those new subjectivities, those new identities that challenge the disciplinarity of the modernist discourses that remain hidden within the postmodern, insisting on a Self or a Center that needs an Other for its formation.

One problem is that socioeconomic relations in the United States have sustained the reference to what have been termed "minority" concerns, suggesting the continued utilization by many on the left as well as the right of the binaries that the advent of postmodernism supposedly brought into question. Such a usage suggests that although both modernism and modernity are under attack, many elements of modernism such as the Self-Other formation, and aspects of modernity such as progress and nationalism continue to be utilized in antiracist and anticolonial formations. In the 1980s and 1990s, the emergence of a politics of identity continued the utilization of margin-center, self-other formulations within recent leftist criticism. Such a politics often carries with it the promise of a recuperation of the subject, one that was hitherto only available to the white male of the dominant power structure.[6] Because it is the goal of certain forms of identity politics to provide this full subject position to those who were only seen as objects, postmodernism, taken as a critique of binaries, is seen as a threat to this subject.

Thus Nancy Hartsock critiques postmodernist theorists for denying the possibility of ever attaining this unified, full, subjectivity, even while she suggests paradoxically that "one of our first tasks is the construction of the subjectivities of the Other, subjectivities that will be both multiple and specific."[7] She asserts that by foreclosing the possibility of this subject, these theorists undercut the basis of nationalist politics. Thus, postmodernism is seen as a depoliticizing move that undercuts the advancements made in recent years by feminists and other minority groups. Hartsock calls for new subjectivities, in which "nationalism and separatism are important phases" for recognizing that our perspectives are "primary." Seeing postmodernism as the domain of Richard Rorty and Michel Foucault, she argues:

Why is it, exactly at the moment when so many of us who have been silenced begin to demand the right to name ourselves, to act as subjects rather than objects of history, that just then the concept of subjecthood becomes "problematic"?[8]

My concerns with this call to subjecthood are many, the first being the difficulty of reconciling Hartsock's "multiple and specific" subjectivities with the "us" referred to in the passage above. This "us" presumes that white, bourgeois women in the United States are as silenced as women in any other locations, and that issues of "silencing" and "naming" are urgent to all women that constitute this collectivity. Taking the binarism of Western modernism as a necessary construct, Hartsock maintains unchanged, hegemonic, exclusionary notions of history, the subject in history, and nationalism as the way to a new order. So, while the disenfranchised were earlier seen as the "Other," they must now become the "Self." Western models of imperial subjectivity, which structured the male subject from *Robinson Crusoe* to Indiana Jones, consequently remain the goal and the promise of those who had been Othered. It becomes difficult to understand what the new subjectivities are when what Hartsock seems to be calling for is the autonomous, full subject, the imperial subject that has structured both colonial power relations and Anglo-American feminism.

Yet, as ethnic and religious struggles in many postcolonial nation-states around the world reveal at the present time, such a subjectivity has historically been created through exclusions and Othering. Race and class power relations aside, many societies are being shaken at the present time by indigenous movements fighting the exclusionary and patriarchal nationalisms of neocolonial elites, those who took up where European colonialists left off and who modeled themselves after the colonialists. Often insurgency movements themselves are striving for similar and problematic forms of subjecthood and nationalism. It is thus with skepticism that one reads Hartsock's claim that "marginalized groups are far less likely to mistake themselves for the universal 'man,' " when alliances between neocolonial elites and global multinationals show us how this co-opting occurs. Further, even if they do not see themselves as the "universal man," the power they claim in search of this "man" does harm to subaltern subjects that cannot be underestimated or ignored. In both the so-called First and Third Worlds, class and gender positions do forge some oppressive alliances to accede to this "universal man." As "subjects" these postcolonial elites discriminated against those less powerful and powerless. It was business as usual.[9]

It is imperative for us to examine new forms of subjectivity that are radically different from this European imperialist and state-nationalist subject that is binarily constructed and essentialist. This new subject, following the critiques of individualism within feminism that have been powerfully argued by Gayatri Spivak and Norma Alarcón, does not share the position of the subject as individual (i.e., unitary and centered and created out of the binaries of Self-Other, Subject-Object) that has been part of the Western philosophical tradition.[10] Rather, this new subject, or "subject(s)," as Norma Alarcón calls them, is heterogeneous as well as political, destroys binarism, and is inclusive. This subject provides a constant critique of nationalist and even insurgent agendas, of power relations that structure global economic flows, and will never be complete. For such a nonessential subject, difference would not be an obstacle to political praxis, since differences usually are taken to mean essentialist differences that are insurmountable for the formations of coalitions or for solidarity with various struggles.

Such postmodern subjectivities are not as unattainable as they are believed to be, despite their problems and difficulties, nor are they the domain of white, male, European theorists, as many opposed to a postmodern politics would like to believe. There are many narratives by women of color around the world that propose and enact new forms of locating themselves within societies.[11] These forms are both oppositional and nonessentialist, and confront and fracture the self-other opposition in the name of inclusions, multiple identities, and diasporic subject positions. Contrary to those who would like to believe that all postmodern subjectivities are similar in their difference, they are varied according to the locations and conditions of their emergence. A nonessentialist position does not imply a nonbelonging to a group, nor does it imply loss of agency or of coalitions and solidarities. For some feminists of color, identity politics remains central, though the identity may be multiple.[12] One may position oneself or be positioned in many different groups for different reasons. One may belong to different groups by gender, sexuality, class, race, ethnicity, and so on. There can be syncretic, "immigrant," cross-cultural, and plural subjectivities, which can enable a politics through positions that are coalitions, intransigent, in process, and contradictory. Such identities are enabling because they provide a mobility in solidarity that leads to a transnational participation in understanding and opposing multiple and global oppressions operating upon them; that is, these subject positions enable oppositions in multiple locations.[13] Multiple locations also enable valuable interventions precisely because the agendas of one group are brought along to interrogate and empower those of another group.

Thus praxis is not prohibited by a politics of not belonging, as occurs with the insider-outsider opposition, even though, within coalition politics, there may be problems regarding what agendas are attended to or left out that vary over time and location. Furthermore, for many minorities, for immigrants, and for subaltern groups, it is important to disrupt the home/abroad and the margin/center constructs for more complex positionings that account for the formation of what Norma Alarcón calls "the multiple-voiced subjectivity."[14] As Chandra Mohanty and Biddy Martin have suggested, "home" is a category that, especially for women, is extremely problematic;[15] for diasporic communities, in particular, a multiply *placed* and a multiply *linked* subjectivity is also to be constructed.

Many of these narratives come from women writing about their specific positions, for it is not the micropolitical that is invisible but instead the essentialism of faceless, passive, exploited masses. Furthermore, in these narratives, the notion of a multiply placed/linked subject works to fracture the designation of margin and center, that dualism that means power and privilege on one side and exploitation on the other.

Sara Suleri's *Meatless Days* is one such narrative that addresses the issues of gender and diasporic subject positions within the area of autobiographical writing. Her memoir of events, nation, childhood, and family in Pakistan, reveals the continual "negotiations," as she calls them, that Pakistani women undertake, of how to be a wife, child, mother, and so on.[16] Her text delineates the specific diasporic locations from which these new subjectivities arise, but suggests also the modernist threat to these postmodern positions. Suleri's text reveals, in all its contradictions, the difficulties arising from the coexistence of postmodernist and modernist conceptions of the subject, and the power and impact of modernist discourses that still influence political practice within a diasporic, postmodern, position.

My focus in the rest of this essay is to reveal the colonial and postcolonial locations of diasporic subjects as they are delineated in Suleri's text. In contrast, I will also examine how a structurally similar but historically and locationally different subject position is described in Gloria Anzaldúa's *Borderlands/La Frontera*.[17] I suggest how political practice, albeit within the parameters of a nonessentialist and contingent identity politics, can become possible within so-called postmodernist discourses. By bringing together two texts by postcolonial writers, one from South Asia and one from the United States, I discuss the politics and problematics of feminist collaborations and affiliations within U.S. academic locations and the discourses within which these collaborations occur.

In examining the specific histories and postcolonial spaces from which these two books are written, what is most interesting is the difference in feminist positioning. While Suleri's narrative of women in Pakistan does not leave the reader with a strong feminist statement, Anzaldúa's exploration of the "borderland" consciousness powerfully asserts itself as feminist. Both *Meatless Days* and

Borderlands/La Frontera reveal different modes of multiple positioning and practices around issues of feminists and feminism. Although Suleri's work is a powerful critique of the Western unified subject and suggests that postmodern subjectivity is the only viable Self possible within a diasporic world, it does not enable any practices of feminist resistance. Presenting the contradictions resulting from the encounter between modernist and postmodernist subjectivities, Suleri's text reveals that the project of postmodernism is one that remains within a theoretical critique of writing and remembering. To the extent that such a critique intervenes in modernist discourses of the subject that form the basis of politics on both left and right, it is important. However, how such a critique enables new kinds of political practices is a question that is not answered by the text. In contrast, Anzaldúa, delineating the oppressions resulting from modernist discourses of unitary selfhood, goes on to create new political stances, seeing the decentering and the postmodern self as empowering an *identity* politics of multiplicity. It is a work that locates its political agenda outside some modernist aspects of oppositional discourse in the United States, while remaining within identity politics and thus within certain accepted modes of opposition for people of color in the United States.

Suleri's text suggests that women are heterogeneous, powerful agents, but it also implies that this postmodern, postcolonial, diasporic heterogeneity that grounds itself in poststructuralist thought may have little to do with feminist oppositional and transnational practices that resist patriarchal power. In fact, there is very little belief in feminism of any kind in Suleri's work apart from a strong concern with how women live with each other within families and outside them. On the other hand, what seems most powerful about Anzaldúa's text is its grounding in feminism; this is not Anglo-American feminism but a feminism of women of color working through differences based on multiple subjectivities and trying to find dissimilar but overlapping positions that enable specific coalitions and struggles on nonessentialist grounds.[18] Yet both texts can be read as oppositional to binaries such as home and exile, center and margin, power and passivity, dominant and dominated, personal and political, public and private histories.

What is visible in both these narratives is that there is no clear delineation or formation of the "subject of feminism" to be found in "micropolitical practices," as Teresa de Lauretis suggests.[19] Norma Alarcón has critiqued de Lauretis, arguing that in Anglo-American feminist theory, difference, when it concerns women of color, becomes untranslatable into theory and then reconfirmed as a "unified subjectivity through gender."[20] What is most useful about both Suleri's and Anzaldúa's narratives is that there is not one, agreed-upon "subject of feminism" that is to be forged. Their texts demonstrate that a politics of multiplicity reveals only that there are as many subjects of feminism as there are feminisms, even though there may be overlapping concerns and issues that need to be addressed regarding shared subordination and power differentials among women. Even positing the possibility of this unitary subject of feminism implies a homogeneity, some similarity that is to be the goal of any kind of feminist endeavor. Since feminist concerns and agendas vary geopolitically, an emphasis on "the subject of feminism" arouses the suspicion of a hegemonic discourse where a white, middle-class, North American, feminist agenda is to be the mark by which all feminist practice is to be judged.

What we see in Sara Suleri's autobiography *Meatless Days*, however, is a desire to be dissociated from Anglo-American analytic models of a feminist subject. This dissociation is apparent when Suleri says in the first chapter of her autobiography that "my reference is to a place (i.e., Pakistan) where the concept of woman was not really part of an available vocabulary"(1). Furthermore, in response to a question from her class at Yale as to why she does not include the work of Third World women in her class syllabus, she claims that "there are no women in the third world," and that there is no such place as "third world" except as a "discourse of convenience" (20). Consequently, Suleri argues that categories such as "third world women" do not approximate a reality that is specific, various and diverse, and escapes classification. Instead she prefers to approach her life and that of the other women she describes in terms of a diachronicity of social roles: as the delineation of the "precise negotiations with what is meant to be a sister or a child or a wife or a mother or a servant"(1). As negotiation, position, and identity become coalesced, experience is available only as a shifting sense of positioning within a context that incorporates West and non-West, Pakistan as well as England and the United States.

Suleri is aware that by denying that women in Pakistan live with the "concept of woman" she is opening herself up to attack, for her account may then be seen as antifeminist. Because of this concern she adds, "My audience is lost and angry to be lost" (2). Yet the desire to reach this audience is present when she quickly explains to the reader, "You did not know dadi" (i.e., you did not know this particular woman, my grandmother, whose life cannot be formulated in any terms available within Western feminist theory). A variety of lives is recorded in the text, showing the different ways in which women, though from the same class, negotiate their lives within families of women and men. Furthermore, Suleri's insistence on "negotiation," with its implication of the complex and varied agency of women in forming their roles and living within them, is important in showing Pakistani women as neither full subjects within society nor as mere objects of European imperial subject formation.

Suleri's concern is justified by any close reading of so-called Western writing on "non-Western" women. As Aihwa Ong has pointed out, quite often the status of women in the Third World is "analyzed and gauged according to a set of legal, political, and social benchmarks that Western feminists consider critical in achieving a power balance between men and women."[21] Particular social contexts are not taken into consideration, creating an anthropological totality in which all Third World women are considered passive, nonresistant, living in destructive, uniformly and similarly repressive, patriarchal families.[22] Quite often, the identity politics that was intended as a resistance movement for people of color is itself based on essential notions of identity that reify women from the Third World.

Given such scholarship, Suleri is presented with the problem of representing the experience of living in diasporic locations, with a specificity and variety that are elided when "third world women" are spoken of only in terms of oppression or subordination. A reductive scholarship cannot approximate the diasporic and immigrant positionality that exists in the Suleri family. With a Pakistani nationalist father and a Welsh mother, the family is both English and Pakistani and divides its time between England and Pakistan. This diasporic subject position is complicated during the period of Pakistani nationalism by the presence of an English mother who is a reminder of the colonizer. Suleri's subjectivity (as well as that of her family members) is therefore constructed within the complex nexus of gender/race relations between colonized/man and colonizing/woman. In addition, Suleri also describes her position in another location: academia in the United States, where the nexus of her location and her political positioning is quite different.

Such a complex construction of subjectivity enables a critique of autobiographical writing and criticism in European and U.S. academic contexts. With such diasporic and multiple identities, even the terms in which Western autobiographies have been analyzed do not seem to apply. In recent criticism these analyses have been rendered in terms of the opposition of male and female autobiographies. The canon of European and North American white, male, autobiographical criticism has utilized Georges Gusdorf's formulation that an autobiography is the record of an awareness of an individuality that is "the late product of a specific civilization," by which he means Western civilization.[23] Gusdorf sees an awareness of history and of the "singularity of each individual life" as well the self-knowledge of man as "a responsible agent" (31) as products of Western culture. He proclaims, therefore, that "autobiography is not possible in a cultural landscape where consciousness of self does not, properly speaking, exist" (30). Thus he claims that Gandhi, for instance, writes his autobiography by "using Western means to defend the East" (29).

In this formulation, it is only in the "West" where a person sees himself or herself as an individual, an entity separate and positioned against the society in which he or she lives. This separation allows autobiography to occur; otherwise, one presumes, there would be narratives of collectivities (i.e., anthropologies) or traditional histories rather than autobiographies. Using an old colonialist argument, Gusdorf implies that within non-Western cultures, individuals live without consciousness that they are separate from society. Yet, unlike the European subject of the Enlightenment, women and men in various contexts are well aware of their uniqueness within their culture; they possess an agency that allows them to act against, within, and outside of norms in many ways.

The opposite of the Gusdorf position is suggested by Susan Friedman when she proposes a collective identity as the impetus for women's autobiography. Friedman draws on Sheila Rowbotham's view that women's sense of self emerges from a collective identity as women rather than as the male individualized sense of self. This collective, gendered identity, it is suggested, can also be used to create group solidarity.[24] Friedman asserts that group consciousness exists within autobiographies of minorities, and that a collective identity is forged in the writing of autobiography. There seem, however, to be a number of problems with this formulation, not the least of which is its denial of unique and varied forms of agency that women deploy. What is not described in analyses such as Friedman's is the definition of terms such as "group" or "collective"; are these "groups" "cultural" ones, as Bernice Johnson Reagon sees them?[25] What are the boundaries of the group or culture? If there are conflicting group identities, which one is to be privileged, and when? Are these transhistorical or shifting? What is the place of a patriarchal family or kinship structure within this community or group? Is this model applicable only to minority women, as Friedman suggests? What about men who are part of oppressed minority groups? Can we talk about collective group identity that includes both white women and women of color? Can we even speak of a collectivity such as "Third World Women"? How can we speak of the testimonial as a collaboration between Third World women and First World editors and translators without an analysis of the power differences between them, or of differences between the narrator and the reader?[26]

If this notion of "collective identity" is applied to those who are termed "minorities" in the United States, specificities and differences are elided. Asian women from various cultures and locations, for instance, are seen within such scholarship by Eurocentric feminist analyses as an oppressed, monolithic category. Thus if there is not the anomalous Indira Gandhi or Benazir Bhutto, there remains "the Indian or Pakistani woman." Yet such a "collective identity" is untenable, for women in Pakistan or India or any place around the world see themselves within historically changing contexts of community, caste, class, religious, and regional differences. Even the categories themselves are changing and contingent. Women certainly do not see themselves as a collectivity, even if they may see some element in common with other women. For instance, the shifts in India and Pakistan between national and "communal" identity since independence disallow any simplistic formulations.

Although Suleri's focus is the upper-class women of her family, her text, in raising the specific context of postindependence Pakistan, reveals many such differences of color, caste, and class. Recalling the women who affected her life, the narrator thinks of "unequal images (that) battle in my mind for precedence—there's Imperial Ifat, there's Mamma in the garden and Halima the cleaning woman in there too, there's uncanny Dadi with her goat" (20). The mention of the cleaning woman is important here because even though we are not told much about her, her very mention and presence, for those readers who are familiar with the class/gender relations between domestic servants and their employers in postindependence South Asia, is a reminder of her separation from Suleri, suggesting that women's lives are lived with such interaction of classes. This mention of classes is important in that it reveals Suleri's own class, the educated upper class, where women live within patriarchal, and modern, families while having certain class-specific spaces within which they operate. Thus, despite the patriarchal domination of her family, during this period of modernization in Pakistan, the narrator can refuse a suitor and a marriage being arranged for her, and she even goes touring with a theater company, although under an assumed name. Moreover, class position, in addition to having an English mother, is an important factor in her being able to go to college, to the university in Pakistan, and in her becoming an academic in the United States. Such choices and advantages make her life and the way she negotiates it very different from that of Halima and Munni, the women who live and work in the Suleri house.[27]

Suleri's text reveals a concern for the specific histories of gender positionality for it examines—in the process of writing the memoir and probing and contextualizing her own shifting notion of herself in relation to others—the lives of her friends and relatives as well. The text shows how patriarchal power exerts its influence differentially upon the varying trajectories of women's lives among the upper classes in Pakistan. For instance, we see the difference between the life of Ifat, married to an upper-class Pakistani, and the narrator, who chooses not to marry like her sisters and becomes an academic in the United States.

These historicized and specific subject positions problematize any analyses of the "collective" subject. Yet without being "collective," subjectivity here is neither singular nor separate. In being specific but also heterogeneous, it is a complex subjectivity that is multiple and varied but with shared overlappings.

That is, having a multiple subjectivity does not mean that all women in Pakistan share the same multiplicities, since these are specific according to historicized locations in various social categories that are not limited to race, class, and gender. Such a heterogeneous and shared subjectivity is suggested when Suleri says that she feels that her sister Ifat is her twin, that she is herself "the sleepy side of Ifat," and that Ifat herself is multiple. We are told that Ifat has "several voices in her throat" (131–32), that there were "always several Ifats with us in the room" with multiple "successions of her face" (139). These multiple selves reflect the conflicting and various locations in which Ifat places herself, not only in her different roles but also in the different groups with which she aligns herself. She is not only daughter, wife, sister, mother but also chooses to be within different "companies of women": her sisters and her friends at Kinnaird College. These change with time, according to the conflicts and directions Ifat chooses to take or feels compelled to take (the range of choices varies with class, although this is unsaid in the text). By changing, these selves become part of other multiple contexts. Thus, for Ifat to marry a Pakistani is part of becoming an intrinsic part of the body of Pakistan, the nation, in an attempt, which is ultimately tragic, to resolve the contradictions within which she lives. Pregnancy, eating, motherhood, and injury (Suleri's brother's and her grandmother's) become metaphors for the elasticity of the boundaries of this subject made up of unstable parts. The prevalence of the metaphor of food all through the narrative emphasizes the notion of incorporation and multiplicity, rather than a complete whole.

Such an entity made up of discrete and contingent parts does not seem to become stable even in the retrospective writing of the autobiography. Although many critics and writers make the claim for a stable collective identity, Suleri's text reveals that instability is an intrinsic aspect of autobiographic representations, for neither memory nor history can claim stability. The metaphor of the sweetbreads reveals this point. We are told that in her childhood, Suleri thought that the word "kapura" meant sweetbreads, whereas her sister tells her, in a visit to New Haven, that "kapura" actually meant testicles. She thought she had eaten sweetbreads, but she had instead been ingesting testicles (27). Such revisioning implies the modifiability of the writing and remembering self and makes history a problem of semantic instability. Furthermore, the interjection of incidents from Suleri's present life in New Haven suggests that even in the writing of the autobiography—that act often taken to be the consolidation of a self—identity remains uncollected, nonunified. Whereas she used to think, she tells us, that memory was "a matter of a catalogue, some list I could draw with loving neatness" (171), she discovers that there is so much "availability of significance" (175) that she cannot write as though she were disclosing secrets that she had only come to understand in retrospect and that she could record. Thus we are told that significance must be constantly "baled out" (177); like the alphabet written on the board during her childhood that was erased every night only to be written over again, remembering implies a continual erasure without any closure.

Suleri's text, therefore, intervenes in life narratives as it critiques both the construction of the imperial full subject and the female collective one that is based on the notion of the full subject. In *Meatless Days*, the writing of history via the memoir can be done from the margins, from an "author" whose location in the United States as a Pakistani woman and an academic prevents her from seeking or attaining a dominant or oppositional subject position.

Meatless Days, therefore, may seem an exemplary text of postmodernism in its rejection of the unitary subject and its delineation of a diasporic, multiple, incomplete subjectivity. Yet it disquiets feminist readers, especially those who seek to make postmodern subjectivities empowering for women. Such readers are disturbed by a text that seems to reject all feminist practices, including those by women of color in the United States, and that suggests, therefore, that only a single, modernizing, and hegemonizing feminism exists. While ignoring the oppositional valence of terms such as "Third World" in histories of decolonization in various locations, Suleri's text does not address the complicated nature of feminist practices that are demanded by the positionings of postcolonial female subjects in various locations.

The first textual example of this refusal to engage with complex, transnational, feminist, historical practices is brought up around the problem of the category "woman." When her students at Yale ask why there are no texts by Third World women in her syllabus, the narrator replies that it is because "there are no women in the third world" (20). Here she raises the issue of how women see themselves or how they are interpellated as subjects in various parts of the world; are they within a commonality such as the category of "woman" or women, or do they, as Suleri suggests, see themselves as "negotiating" roles within a family?[28] Yet crucially, in saying that "there are no women in the third world," instead of saying "there is no Third World Woman," Suleri suggests that it is not the monolithic "Third World woman" she critiques, but rather the existence of a category of persons termed "women," even while she also suggests that these female persons live among "companies of women." In critiquing the category of woman, however, she elides colonial history in attempting to escape Western essentialism. Even if the term "woman" is not indigenous to Pakistan, colonial intervention forced some notion of commonality among female persons into the representational practices of the Subcontinent. The Reform movement in the nineteenth century, involving reformers who were both

English and Indian (Pakistan was part of British India at that time), utilized repeatedly the notion and the term "woman," as did nationalism within its modernizing discourses. It thus necessarily brought about an ideology of commonality among female persons, suggesting a category of people who could be seen and came to see themselves as gendered in similar ways.

Such a notion of "woman" can be seen in the literature by women at the beginning of the twentieth century. When, in 1905, a Muslim writer, Rokeya Hossain, could begin her famous short story on feminist utopias, "Sultana's Dream," with the sentence "One evening I was lounging in an easy chair in my bedroom and thinking lazily of the condition of Indian womanhood," it is clear that what she has in mind is the essence of being a woman, that being a woman is seen as an ontological state common to female persons across class, caste, and religion, but also in a political sense, as a position within society that is structurally open to oppression.[29] The onset of modernity necessarily changed the earlier notion of women as defined by the roles they played within families—a notion suggested in Suleri's text when she suggests that women in contemporary Pakistan see themselves within such roles.[30] It is not easy to dismiss Rokeya Hossain's concept as one that emerges from her upper-class access to Western feminism, for by that time notions of "woman" and "womanhood" had been around for almost half a century and continued to be deployed within Gandhian and nationalist philosophy throughout the nationalist period.[31]

As Tani Barlow suggests in regard to China, the term "woman," not part of a Chinese terminology prior to Western influences, came into existence and power partly because it could be utilized as a category by the state to discipline female persons.[32] Similarly, in Pakistan as in many other countries, the "woman question," which materialized during the nineteenth-century colonial period, continues to be a category that the state uses, as do bodies such as the World Bank and the IMF. All these institutions contribute to the interpellation of female subjects in varied ways in most parts of the world. Thus while the term "woman," as a political category, cannot be dismissed so easily, what needs to be remembered is not only Simone de Beauvoir's notion that "woman" is a social construct, but that first, women are constructed differently within different social categories such as class, caste, and so on, and second, they are constructed variously as women in addition to being constructed variously within social roles as wives, mothers, and so on, in relation to other social categories.

The danger of rejecting the term "women," besides that of eliding the effects of modernity, is that of foreclosing feminist struggles that are increasingly transnational in this interconnected world of diasporic populations and multinational corporations. Such social and material conditions require coalitions among women of different cultures and races and classes. On the other hand, there is also the danger of taking the category as a monolithic one, or even of not seeing it as a disciplinary category that is often utilized by the state, as Barlow suggests.[33] Yet the challenge is to work across differences among women; in the Pakistani context discussed by Suleri, the difference lies in the various ways that family roles in different social categories function in the construction of women. If "woman" has been a part of the colonial and nationalist discourse of modernity, it is difficult but necessary to dismantle this construct without recuperating the also problematic discourse of "role" within the patriarchal family (of wife, mother, sister) and consequently of "tradition." Furthermore, the latter is not a radical dismantling of modernity because it is simply the very necessary Other of modernity. Thus, even while it is important to critique an ahistorical category of "woman," it is just as problematic to seek authentic versions of women's locations within societies. The reaction against the modernist discourse of "woman" is not to revert to its Other "traditional roles," but to delineate the problematics of both these forms of female gender construction and the complex ways in which they intersect. In staying within the poles of tradition and modernity, Suleri's text reaffirms the power of modernist discourses.

A second problem with *Meatless Days* is that it does not go beyond a critique of modernist binaries to create a politically empowering self. In Suleri's text, postmodern selves seem sometimes to be disquietingly marginalized, unsure, silenced, and sometimes even seeking for some surer grounding for identity that seems not to be available to them. New antiessentialist, nonexclusionary, postmodern subjects seem to be available here as syncretic, diasporic, immigrant selves, but we do not find ways in which to make these positions politically powerful. Although it is an important critique, this dissatisfaction with the multiple and decentered subject reveals a nostalgia for the full subject as the basis of praxis. Many anti-postmodernist feminists such as Hartsock are taking this position, one that is comfortingly "self-making and self-determining," as Norma Alarcón terms it, but unavailable.[34] Such nostalgia suggests the threat and power of discourses of modernity that assert themselves in easy reaction to the uncertainties of their deconstruction, especially for those who wish to oppose dominant power structures.

Two characters in the text reveal this problem of a postmodern self that cannot see itself as oppositional: the narrator's friend, Mustakori, and her mother, Mairi. For these characters, identity is often theater, dependent upon the audience's gaze, and therefore contingent. Here the loss of a centered self becomes a problematic of women's lives. Multiplicity for women becomes uncertainty, loss of agency, even loss of difference, because it implies that sameness can be imposed by others in a world where modernist discourses are still powerful. A postmodern, multiple subject position is shown to be an extremely difficult path to take, unlike the ease of taking on a group identity through an essentialist belonging. Mustakori's multiple self is a result of her race and her national multiplicity; yet, she is seen in Pakistan as a "brown European." Therefore, coming from East Africa, the daughter of parents from Indian Punjab, Kashmir, and Hong Kong, having lived in Dublin, England, and Kenya, she becomes the receptor of a "deep historical dislike" in Lahore (49). She counters suspicion by creating a self that is theater; it is all performance, so that a student at Kinnaird calls her "an actress." Because Mustakori is so many races and countries and selves, she has to accept slights and rebuffs on many counts. So fragmented is she that Suleri describes her body as suggesting "deep allegiance to the principle of radical separation, so that mind and body, existence and performance, would never be allowed to occupy the same space of time" (49). Not possessing a stable self, or even a centered self, Mustakori is compared to postindependence Lahore, which is described as structured by a central lack that can only be reached by a road full of monuments that build up anticipation.

Not only are race and colonialism an issue in Mustakori's identity, or in what Suleri describes as her "ventriloquist's" trick of loss of centered self, they are also central to the representation of Suleri's Welsh mother. Her mother teaches at the university in Lahore, which, replicating her racial transgression, lies between British Lahore and Mughal Lahore (153). As the second wife, Suleri's mother symbolizes not only her husband's rejection of his first wife (who was his cousin and therefore from his family), but also of his race. To marry a woman of British origin, one of those who had colonized England, indicates Z. A. Suleri's complex colonial relationship with those he fought against in order to free his country. When Suleri's mother comes to live in Pakistan directly after its independence, she is placed in a position in which she has to distance herself from what she is or what she stands for, so that she is compelled, according to Suleri, to "walk through her new context in the shape of a memory erased" (164). The consequence of this immigration becomes the fashioning of a self that is "more invisible, more difficult to discern" than even a "Mrs. Ramsey" (153–54). In the text, Mairi is compared to Jane Austen, to Virginia Woolf's Mrs. Ramsey, suggesting that she acquires an Englishness that is "disembodied" (156). We are told she was "particularly absentminded," with a "dispersed aura" (156). She developed, therefore, "the distracted manner of someone who did not wish to be breaking rules of which she was ignorant" (163).

Although Suleri's mother is shown to be occupying a difficult position, the text tries not to show her as completely peripheralized by these racial, geographical, and gender conflicts. She is represented as being active, actively changing herself according to the multiplicity of the desires of others but not losing her difference. It is suggested that she refines and improves her sense of self so that she loses interest in possession or belonging, no longer living according to the gaze of others, thus freeing herself from expectations, and therefore wishing no longer to "bother to differentiate between what the world imagines you must be, and what you are." In not belonging to Pakistan or to England, but in loving differences in race and color, she "intended to become herself in every available manner" through the process of her "successive transformation" (168). This move does not emerge as being unique to her mother, but as a possible mode of living as a woman, a teacher, and an immigrant. *Meatless Days* reveals a longing to adopt and valorize Suleri's mother's mode of disinterested love, and the negotiation of a life formed by an oblique connection to the society in which she lives.

Such a position of unbelonging is not, according to this text, a peripheral or oppositional position; it is an oblique one, unlike the contingent theatricality of Mustakori caught between the reifying discourses of modernity. Just as Mairi's position in Pakistani society is tangential, so is that of the memoir's narrator to struggles in the United States. Instead of being in coalition with various feminisms, this narrator sees herself as attached marginally to feminist agendas by an edge, with a disinterested concern with their goals and politics. Whereas a "multiple-voiced" identity would enable one to be in solidarity with feminisms, this text shows that multiplicity allows only a tangential relationship, since nowhere can one belong, nor can any diasporic location be "home." Instead of a politics that enables one to participate in different struggles according to multiple and transnational needs and to be involved with them, this subject seems quietly removed, with only a glancing interest in such struggles. Unlike Mustakori's "performances" of multiple participation, this self, also decentered, stands obliquely to practice.

What contributes to the oblique stance of this narrator is not only the complex situation of postmodern subjectivity in a nationalist Pakistan in which the master narrative is that of modernity, but also the situation of the postcolonial writer in the United States. In her essay on "Postcolonial Feminists in the Western Intellectual Field," Mary John suggests that histories of postcolonials need to be examined. Thus not only does the issue of the colonial education of postcolonial subjects need to be attended to, but also their "very site of enunciation, their location and audience."[35] Here I wish to add to John's excellent analysis by suggesting that postcolonial feminists are also as varied as their affiliations and their locations; Suleri's text may be coming from a positioning that is very different from other South Asian intellectuals in U.S. academic locations, as well as from other women of color who are situated there. One issue that needs to be looked at in the case of Suleri's text is that of affiliations with U.S. feminists of color. There is little in Suleri's text that suggests such collaborations, and that, importantly, would lead her to a contemplation of feminisms that concern or emerge from women of color, or of transnational feminist practices that are based on differences. These would also prevent her from being as aloof from feminist concerns in the United States as is her mother in Pakistan, for her location is very different. She, unlike her mother, does not occupy the position of a gendered colonizing subject in a postcolonial state.

The difficulties of collaborations between postcolonial intellectuals who grew up in Asia or Africa or Latin America—and thus, as Mary John points out, did not, for various colonial reasons, read Harriet Jacobs or *This Bridge Called My Back*—and those who grew up in the United States, are many. It is not the differences that are unfortunate, for these are necessary and various, but the ways in which these differences are being utilized in academia and elsewhere to pit "minorities" from the United States and elsewhere against each other while keeping academic curricula and the power status quo unchanged. Such pervasive practices bear looking into more thoroughly than I intend to here. What I am pointing out is that these practices are part of the "sites of enunciation" that, in addition to Suleri's positioning in postindependence Pakistan, influence her choices of her nonfeminist stance and her oblique positionality, especially in the elite academic institution in which she is located.

As Gloria Anzaldúa points out in "Speaking in Tongues: A Letter to 3rd World Women Writers," communities of women of color from various locations do not happen everywhere.[36] Yet where they do, there is a tremendous sense of feminist affirmation for those who are involved. Perhaps this is one reason why Anzaldúa's practice is so different from Suleri's, why in her work there is no "oblique" stance but a full assault on modernist and white, bourgeois practices of subject formation.

For a text that is unequivocal about its commitment to feminisms and postmodern identities and its assault on modernist ones, one must turn to Gloria Anzaldúa's *Borderlands/La Frontera*. This is a narrative of self that refuses closure. It remains open, complex, and contradictory. It mixes genres, languages, and nationalities. It fractures the idea of a margin as a border between the dominant or the dominated. As opposed to a border, which constructs national differences, Anzaldúa's borderland is described as "a vague and undetermined place created by the emotional residue of an unnatural boundary. It is in a constant state of transition" (3). This is the "borderland" in which people who had seen themselves as Mexican found themselves, sometimes without moving, to be in the United States. Yet they were never acknowledged as belonging to a nation that defined its nationalism in terms of whiteness, conquest, and colonization of nonwhite peoples. This is the specific location from which Anzaldúa speaks, one that is quite different from Suleri's diasporic positionality. For the "borderland" cannot be analyzed through theories of Asian diasporas such as those suggested by Homi Bhabha;[37] British colonial methods in India were quite different from those used in the Spanish conquest as well as in the U.S.-Mexican wars, and contemporary U.S.-Latin America relations suggest yet another and different imperial project. The term "borderlands" has become specific to Chicano culture, thus designating the specific locations of Mexican-Americans.[38]

Furthermore, Anzaldúa's postcolonial marginality in the United States is quite different from Suleri's, since Anzaldúa describes her location as one where she can remain in her homeland and yet be seen as marginal because she is not white, male, or straight. The narrative itself suggests identity as transitional, recorded in a state of flux. This feminist subject is in process, though not necessarily with the fixity of one feminist agenda in view. Anzaldúa's identity is as mixed as her narrative form, for she is a mestiza, a woman, a lesbian, a Mexican, an indigenous inhabitant within a Catholic, North American culture. Living in the "borderlands," that is, where the term border has little meaning, she finds her life a "path that continually slips in and out of the white, the Catholic, the Mexican" (19). She describes the experience of having entry into two worlds at the same time, as being "two in one body, both male and female . . . the coming together of opposites" (19). The opposites also suggest the power differentials between Anglo and Chicana culture—a clash that leads Anzaldúa to the dismantling of modernist discourses of Self/Other, Subject/Object. Just as Suleri's narrative contradicted the easy duality of colonizer and colonized in the figures of her mother and her own immigrant self, Anzaldúa's speaks against such dualities: "What we are suffering from is an absolute despot duality that says we are able to be only one or the other" (19). For Anzaldúa, to accept these dualities is to accept the ideology of the border and to deny the existence of the borderlands.

The impetus for Anzaldúa's text seems to lie in the consciousness of cultural multiplicity, one that is very different from Suleri's. Anzaldúa sees the structure of her book as a metaphor for the new consciousness she represents. The duality of form and content becomes as inseparable as bone and flesh, with the boundaries of chapters spilling into one another. The languages, voices (her mother's, her aunt's, her grandmother's), genres, and disciplines (autobiography, anthropology, history) all merge. As she writes in her penultimate chapter, "This almost finished product seems an assemblage, a montage, a beaded work with several leitmotifs and with a central core, now appearing now disappearing in a crazy dance" (66). The text is described variously as her consciousness, her child, a puzzle, a "mosaic pattern," but one that is also female, "a dove, horse, serpent, cactus . . . a clumsy, complex, groping blind thing . . . alive, infused with spirit" (66–67). Anzaldúa fractures the Western duality of a dead "artifact" and a live action, for she sees her stories as performances, not, she tells us as "inert and dead objects" in a museum.

From her specific, Chicana borderland location she argues that the concept of the marginal needs also to be shattered. Oppression emerges out of imposition of such dualities, for instance, between white North America as center, and Chicano culture as periphery. While she describes her oppositional positioning as a "counterstance" that is defiant in its refutation of the beliefs of the culture in power, she sees it only as "a step towards liberation from cultural domination" rather than a way of life, for no new paths are forged in this combat locked within action and reaction. Like Suleri, whose text articulates the history of colonialism in order to subvert the duality of colonizer and colonized, Anzaldúa's text reveals the racism and oppression of Anglo-American society, but refuses to remain circumscribed by these repressive structures.

Although Anzaldúa's and Suleri's texts contain some overlappings, Anzaldúa's "counterstance" is the politicized and feminist version of Suleri's "oblique" stance. Anzaldúa has no place other than the United States that can be called "home," and her borderland is a powerful illustration of a politicized, multiple subjectivity forged by people who speak many languages. Anzaldúa suggests that those who live in the borderlands are "complex, heterogeneous people" who speak a "patois, a forked tongue" that is neither standard Spanish or standard English. Anzaldúa lists eight languages she speaks, from standard English to Tex-Mex and Chicano Spanish. She speaks these according to her location and to whom she is speaking. The various languages in her book become an example of her heterogeneity. Moreover, she does not translate, for that implies acknowledging the domination of one language over another. Anzaldúa struggles against the hegemonic "West" as a site of enunciation more than does Suleri, who speaks its language more smoothly because of a different colonial legacy and education, and a different contemporary, diasporic location. For Anzaldúa, the politics of language becomes the politics of inhabiting different locations without suggesting which is her "true" language. To do so would be to suggest a center, that fixity of an essential identity that her work so clearly repudiates.

Anzaldúa's examination of multiplicities, contradictions, and specificities lead her to create a feminist agenda that is particular to Chicanas but is also an example to other women of color who can connect with its oppositional positions. The figures of the Virgin of Guadalupe and the serpent women symbolize the fusion of opposites, the goddess-whore and the feared and oppressed woman, the unconscious and the conscious, the divine and the human. This fusion and ambiguity take shape in "the new mestiza," the new woman who lives in the borderlands, one who cannot "hold concepts or ideas in rigid boundaries" (79). This "mestiza consciousness," as Anzaldúa terms it, involves "a tolerance for contradictions," and suggests one who

> learns to be an Indian in Mexican culture, to be Mexican from an Anglo point of view. She learns to juggle cultures. She has a plural personality, she operates in a pluralistic mode—nothing is thrust out, the good, the bad and the ugly, nothing rejected, nothing abandoned. (79)

Out of this inclusiveness—which is not so much syncretic or merging as plural in its bringing of one consciousness with its interventions and agendas into another—emerges the new mestiza consciousness, which is not unitary or concrete, for it is always in the process of becoming. Anzaldúa does not offer a subject of feminism as an end product, for we are told that the creative energy of this process comes out of continual change: "its energy comes from continual creative motion that keeps breaking down the unitary aspect of each new paradigm" (80).

Anzaldúa's location in the borderland leads her to deny that there is any place that can be called home:

> As a mestiza I have no country, my homeland cast me out; yet all countries are mine because I am every woman's sister or potential lover. . . . I am cultureless because, as a feminist, I challenge the collective cultural/religious male-derived beliefs of Indo-Hispanics and Anglos; yet I am cultured because I am participating in the creation of yet another culture. (81)

This stance reveals Anzaldúa's difference from Suleri, and from other diasporic subjects who do have a country that is designated for them as "home," and therefore are seen as marginal in ways different from those suggested by Anzaldúa. Suleri's location is described most often as "postcolonial," while Anzaldúa's is not, even though it is postcolonial in a different way.[39] Nor can a postcolonial such as Suleri ignore the politics, agendas, and struggles of what is termed "home" for her. Yet Suleri's narrative also suggests that for a woman there is no "home." Her sister Ifat is quoted as saying that a woman cannot come home, that the only space for a woman to live is her body (147). Indeed, given a patriarchal nationalism, a country cannot be home for a woman. Nor can an immigrant call a country of adoption home, especially if the immigrant is a woman of color in a white, patriarchal society.

As the two very different narratives I have examined reveal, the locations of multiple, heterogeneous subjectivities are varied and specific. Yet differences can be accommodated without jeopardizing feminist agendas precisely because there is no one feminist subject to be forged. Suleri's and Anzaldúa's narratives share a concern with the breakdown of ethnocentric dualities, which they both see as sources of oppression, but the dualities that each writer shatters are different, as are their strategies and the components of immigrant, multiple selves. Yet what is common to both these narratives is a rejection of the modernist binaries that construct the "Western" subject. Instead of a female collective identity, there is a heterogeneous consciousness; instead of an identity consolidated in the practice of autobiographical writing, there is a self that is always revised, always in the process of becoming. Even the term "autobiography" does not work for such texts; *Meatless Days* is not a linear, chronological narrative, nor is it simply about Suleri.

Both *Meatless Days* and *Borderlands/La Frontera* address questions of location, diasporas, nation, family, and communities. Both are explorations of identity, politics, and the subject. Yet what these texts convey are the contradictions of positionalities that enable oppositional subjects to emerge, and that allow immigrants and minorities to live, work, and write within a hegemonic, racist, and sexist culture. Postmodern subjects are the sites of such conflicts and contradictions, and reveal their continuities and discontinuities with modernist discourses. Because postmodern subjects deconstruct modernist subjects while being connected to them, the encounter can be often useful but also fraught with difficulties, as *Meatless Days* reveals. Yet the power of *Borderlands* comes from the new forms of subject positioning that emerge out of such encounters and contestations.

In closing this examination of postmodern subjectivities and their varied specificities, I would suggest that, for those termed minorities, it is not the resolution of identity that is necessary for political action, but oppositional mobilization and coalitional, transnational, feminist practices. For, after all, many immigrants or diasporic subjects, even those multiply located or with multiple voices, are not automatically oppositional; it is the consciousness of the linkages between the specific and multiple hegemonies under which these minorities live that makes them so.

Notes

This essay could not have been written without discussions with and careful readings and comments from Caren Kaplan, Houston Baker, Jr., Kamala Visweswaran, Fred Pfeil, Denise Albanese, Eric Smoodin, and Margit Stange.

1. Nelly Richard, "Postmodernism and Periphery," *Third Text* 2 (Winter 1987–88).

2. For an extended discussion of postmodernism and the way that I use the term in this essay, see the Introduction to this volume.

3. See the Introduction to this volume for the distinction between postmodernism and postmodernity.

4. Bella Brodzki and Celeste Schenck, eds., *Life/Lines: Theorizing Women's Autobiography* (Ithaca: Cornell University Press, 1988), 14.

5. The essays in *Life/Lines* are a good example of such criticism, struggling with some form of identity as a necessary part of women's writing. While some of the essays reject feminist heterogeneity, others, such as Biddy Martin's, use Teresa de Lauretis's theories to argue for "provisional or partial identities." For more on this problematic and critiques of postmodernism see essays by Seyla Benhabib, Susan Bordo, and Christine Di Stefano in *Feminism/Postmodernism*, ed. Linda Nicholson (New York and London: Routledge, 1990).

6. For an excellent discussion that maps the issue of the "subject" that includes Spivak's use of "subject position," see Tani Barlow's "Concrete Women and Feminist China Studies," forthcoming.

7. Nancy Hartsock, "Rethinking Modernism: Minority vs. Majority Theories," *Cultural Critique* 7 (Fall 1987): 187–206. All Hartsock quotes are from this essay.

8. Ibid., 196.

9. *Feminist Review*, special issue no. 39 (1991), addresses the issue of feminism in the aftermath of the breakdown of the socialist governments in Eastern Europe. In her essay, "Postmodernism and its Discontents," Kate Soper, while using poststructuralist theory and allowing the necessity of much postmodern discourse to negate the opposition between postmodernism and socialism, still ends up maintaining this binary by saying that we should call ourselves socialists after all. Her argument suggests that logically argued, postmodern theories and their use of difference and fragmentation cannot take us to equality and justice. It is interesting that this argument can stand because her primary and only category of analysis is gender; further, that she expects a position to logically hold all the way through; finally, that she does not address the issues of power and elites, especially the issue of power differentials among women under both capitalism and socialism.

10. At this point I should mention that while much U.S. feminist discourse on the subject concerns itself with either French feminism or Anglo-American feminism, the theorists who have been most productive for this essay have been women of color feminists, whose work in this area has been groundbreaking and exciting. The essays I mention in the text have been seminal for me (Tani Barlow discusses their importance in her "Concrete Women and Feminist China Studies"): Gayatri Spivak, "French Feminism in an International Frame," in *In Other Worlds* (New York and London: Routledge, 1988), 134–53; and "Three Women's Texts and a Critique of Imperialism," in *"Race," Writing and Difference*, ed. Henry Louis Gates, Jr. (Chicago and London: University of Chicago Press, 1985), 262–80; Norma Alarcón, "The Theoretical Subject(s) of *This Bridge Called My Back*," in *Making Face, Making Soul*, ed. Gloria Anzaldúa (San Francisco: Aunt Lute, 1990), 356–69.

11. In the United States, there is much scholarship, started by women of color (*This Bridge Called My Back* was one of the first), that theorized forms of identity that were multiple, arguing that gender could not be the only or primary mode of analysis. Other examples include bell hooks's *Ain't I a Woman* (Boston: South End Press, 1981), *From Margin to Center* (Boston: South End Press, 1984); Combahee River Collective, "A Black Feminist Statement, April 1977," in Z. Eisenstein, ed., *Capitalist Patriarchy and the Case for Socialist Feminism* (New York: Monthly Review Press, 1979); Patricia Hill Collins, *Black Feminist Thought* (Boston: Unwin Hyman, 1990); Valerie Amos and Pratibha Parmar, "Challenging Imperial Feminism," *Feminist Review* 17 (Autumn 1984); Andree Nicola McLaughlin, "Black Women, Identity and the Quest for Humanhood and Wholeness," in J. Braxton, ed., *Wild Woman in the Whirlwind* (New Brunswick, N.J.: Rutgers University Press, 1989). White feminists have also theorized multiple identities, some through critiques of essentialism. Examples include Elizabeth Spelman, *Inessential Woman* (Boston: Beacon Press, 1988), and the collection edited by Teresa de Lauretis, *Feminist Studies/Critical Studies* (Bloomington: Indiana University Press, 1986).

12. *This Bridge Called My Back: Writings by Radical Women of Color* (New York: Kitchen Table: Women of Color Press, 1981) is a good example of such a position.

13. For more on the politics of location and multiple contexts, see Lata Mani, "Multiple Mediations: Feminist Scholarship in the Age of Multinational Reception," *Inscriptions* 5 (1989): 1–23.

14. Alarcón, "Theoretical Subject(s)," 365–66.

15. Biddy Martin and Chandra Talpade Mohanty, "Feminist Politics: What's Home Got to Do With It?" in *Feminist Studies/Critical Studies*, ed. Teresa de Lauretis (Bloomington: Indiana University Press, 1986), 191–212; also see Caren Kaplan, "Deterritorializations: The Rewriting of Home and Exile in Western Feminist Discourse," *Cultural Critique* 6(Spring 1987): 187–98.

16. Sara Suleri, *Meatless Days* (Chicago: University of Chicago Press, 1989), 1. Furthur references to this work appear in the text.

17. Gloria Anzaldúa, *Borderlands/La Frontera: The New Mestiza* (San Francisco: Aunt Lute, 1987). All further references to this work will appear in the text.

18. This "borderland" identity seems to continue the project begun by Anzaldúa and Cherríe Moraga in *This Bridge Called My Back*, in which, as Biddy Martin suggests, the "forms of solidarity forged . . . are based on shared but not identical histories, shared but not identical structural positions, shared but not identical interests." Biddy Martin, "Lesbian Identity and Autobiographical Difference(s)," in *Life/Lines*, 77–103.

19. Teresa de Lauretis, *Technologies of Gender: Feminism, Film, and Fiction* (Bloomington: Indiana University Press, 1987), 9–10.

20. Alarcón, "Theoretical Subject(s)."

21. Aihwa Ong, "Colonialism and Modernity: Feminist Re-presentations of Women in Non-Western Societies," *Inscriptions* 3/4 (1988): 79–93.

22. Chandra Talpade Mohanty, "Under Western Eyes: Feminist Scholarship and Colonial Discourses," in *Third World Women and the Politics of Feminism*, ed. Chandra Mohanty et al. (Bloomington and Indianapolis: Indiana University Press, 1991), 51–80.

23. Georges Gusdorf, "Conditions and Limits of Autobiography," in *Autobiography: Essays Theoretical and Critical*, ed. James Olney (Princeton, N.J.: Princeton University Press, 1980), 28–48. This collection, judging by the numbers of references to it, has been quite influential in defining the genre of autobiography. Citations that follow appear in the text.

24. Sheila Rowbotham, *Woman's Consciousness, Man's World* (London: Penguin, 1973). Quoted in Susan Stanford Friedman, "Women's Autobiographical Selves," in *The Private Self*, ed. Shari Benstock (Chapel Hill: University of North Carolina Press, 1988), 34–62.

25. Bernice Johnson Reagon, "My Black Mothers and Sisters or On Beginning a Cultural Autobiography," *Feminist Studies* 8 (Spring 1982): 81–95.

26. Caren Kaplan, "Resisting Autobiography: Out-Law Genres and Transnational Feminist Subjects," in *De/Colonizing the Subject: Politics and Gender in Women's Autobiographical Practice*, ed. Julia Watson and Sidonie Smith (Minneapolis: University of Minnesota Press, 1992), 115–38.

27. Nor do we know of their relationships with the Suleri family; for instance, while we know Sara plays tricks on Munni, the cook's daughter, and this is connected to her telling on Sara, the power difference is not Suleri's concern, whereas the gender difference among the upper class is the focus of the text.

28. Mohanty, "Under Western Eyes," 51–80. In this essay, Chandra Mohanty makes clear the difference between "woman" and "women" (the former suggests a monolithic "Third World woman," for instance, and the latter incorporates difference). I am collapsing them in my discussion here because Suleri's point is that in Pakistan female persons do not live as women/woman, but within roles such as daughter, mother, sister, and so on.

29. Rokeya Sakhawat Hossain, "Sultana's Dream," in *Women Writing in India*, ed. Susie Tharu and K. Lalitha (New York: Feminist Press, 1991), 342–52.

30. Meenakshi Mukherjee, *Realism and Reality* (Delhi: Oxford University Press, 1985), discusses the encounter between role and individual within the novel in India.

31. Sujata Patel, "The Construction and Reconstruction of Woman in Gandhi," *Economic and Political Weekly* (February 20, 1988): 377–87.

32. Tani E. Barlow, "Theorizing Woman: *Funü, Guojia, Jiating* (Chinese Women, Chinese State, Chinese Family)," in this volume.

33. Ibid.

34. Alarcón, "Theoretical Subject(s)," 357.

35. Mary John, "Postcolonial Feminists in the Western Intellectual Field: Anthropologists and Native Informants," *Inscriptions* 5 (1989): 49–73.

36. Gloria Anzaldúa, "Speaking in Tongues: A Letter to 3rd World Women Writers," in *This Bridge Called My Back*, 165–73.

37. The Bhabha essays cited most often on any kind of colonial issue are "Of Mimicry and Man: The Ambivalence of Colonial Discourse," *October* 28 (Spring 1984), and "Signs Taken for Wonders: Questions of Ambivalence of Authority under a Tree Outside Delhi, May 1817," in Gates, *"Race," Writing and Difference*, 163–84.

38. For instance, see the collection, *Criticism in the Borderlands*, ed. Héctor Calderón and José David Saldívar (Durham and London: Duke University Press, 1991).

39. For more on this topic of postcolonials see Ruth Frankenberg and Lata Mani, "Crosscurrents, Crosstalk: Race, 'Postcoloniality' and the Politics of Location," *Cultural Studies* (Spring 1993): 292–310.

Contributors

Norma Alarcón is an associate professor of ethnic/Chicano/women's studies at the University of California, Berkeley. She is the author of a book on the Mexican writer Rosario Castellanos, *Ninfomanía: El discurso de la diferencia en la obra poética de Rosario Castellanos*, numerous essays on Chicana writers, and editor/publisher of Third Woman Press.

Tani E. Barlow is an associate professor of history at San Franciso State University and is an associate at the Berkeley Center for Chinese Studies, where she is presently completing a manuscript tentatively entitled *Imagining Woman: Ding Ling and the Category Woman in Chinese Modernity*. Barlow is editor of the new journal *POSITIONS: east asia cultures critique*.

Robert Carr is an assistant professor of English at George Mason University. Born in Trinidad and raised in Jamaica, he writes and teaches on cross-cultural and interdisciplinary issues in African-American and Caribbean letters. He is completing a book-length manuscript on nineteenth- and twentieth-century black nationalism against the backdrop of new world orders.

Inderpal Grewal is an associate professor of women studies at San Francisco State University, where she teaches classes on feminist theory and topics concerning Asian-American and Asian women. She is completing a book, *Home and Harem: Feminism, Imperialism, Nationalism and the Culture of Travel*. She also works with Bay Area groups that organize resistance to violence against Asian women.

Caren Kaplan is an assistant professor of women's studies at the University of California at Berkeley where she teaches classes on cultural representations of gender, travel, and imperialism. Her publications include essays in *Discourse, Cultural Critique*, and *Public Culture*. She is completing a book, *Questions of Travel: Postmodern Discourses of Displacement*.

Mary N. Layoun is an associate professor of comparative literature at the University of Wisconsin at Madison, author of *Travels of a Genre: Ideology and the Modern Novel*, editor of *Modernism in Greece? Critical and Literary Texts on the Margins of a Movement*, and has written essays on colonial and "post"-colonial cultures, nationalism and gender, refugee stories, anthropology, and literary theory. The essay included here is part of a book-length study of cultural responses to nationalism in crisis, *Boundary Fixation? The Rhetoric of National Culture*.

Lydia H. Liu is assistant professor of Chinese and comparative literature at the University of California at Berkeley. She received her Ph.D. in comparative literature at Harvard University in 1990. She has written on the subjects of narrative theory, feminism, and nationalism and has published in China, Taiwan, Hong Kong, and the United States. She is currently writing a book on modernity and translingual practice between East and West.

Nalini Natarajan was educated in New Delhi and Bombay, India, and obtained her Ph.D. from the University of Aberdeen, U.K. She has taught at Jawaharlal Nehru University and Miranda House, University of Delhi, and is now associate professor of English at the University of Puerto Rico. She teaches courses on women's writing and postcolonial narratives. She has published articles on nineteenth-century fiction, women's studies, and Caribbean fiction. She is currently editing a book project on regional Indian literatures, scheduled for publication with Greenwood Press.

Fred Pfeil is a writer, teacher, and activist, currently working on a book-length project tentatively titled *White Guys: Studies in Postmodern Domination and Difference*, and some new fiction. He is also associate professor of English at Trinity College in Hartford, Connecticut.

Kamala Visweswaran is an assistant professor in the Department of Anthropology at the Graduate Faculty, New School for Social Research (New York). She is completing a collection of essays, *Fictions of Feminist Ethnography*, and is working on another manuscript, "Family Subjects: An Ethnography of the 'Woman Question' in Indian Nationalism."

Index

Compiled by Robin Jackson